Social Prisms

Social Prisms

*Reflections on Everyday
Myths and Paradoxes*

Jodi O'Brien

PINE FORGE PRESS
Thousand Oaks • London • New Delhi

For information:

 Pine Forge Press
A SAGE Publications Company
2455 Teller Road
Thousand Oaks, California 91320
E-mail: sales@pfp.sagepub.com

SAGE Publications Ltd.
6 Bonhill Street
London EC2A 4PU
United Kingdom

SAGE Publications India Pvt. Ltd.
M-32 Market
Greater Kailash I
New Delhi 110 048 India

Acquiring Editor:	Steve Rutter
Production Coordinator:	Windy Just
Production Editor:	Wendy Westgate
Editorial Assistant:	Stephanie Allen
Designer/Typesetter:	Janelle LeMaster
Cover Designer:	Tracy E. Miller

Printed in the United States of America

99 00 01 02 03 04 10 9 8 7 6 5 4 3 2 1

Library of Congress Cataloging-in-Publication Data

O'Brien, Jodi.
    Social prisms: Reflections on everyday myths and paradoxes /
Jodi O'Brien.
        p. cm.
    Includes bibliographical references and index.
    ISBN 0-8039-9031-6 (pbk.: acid-free paper)
    1. Social values. 2. Social role. 3. Social action. I. Title.
HM73 .O27 1999
303.3'72—ddc21   98-40123

To my students—for the courage of your questions.

About the Author

Jodi O'Brien is Associate Professor of Sociology at Seattle University. She is the author of *Production of Reality: Essays and Readings on Social Interaction, Second Edition* (Pine Forge Press) and the coeditor of *Everyday Inequalities: Critical Inquiries* (Basil Blackwell).

About the Publisher

Pine Forge Press is an educational publisher, dedicated to publishing innovative books and software throughout the social sciences. On this and any other of our publications, we welcome your comments, ideas, and suggestions. Please call or write to:

Pine Forge Press
A Sage Publications Company
2455 Teller Road
Thousand Oaks, CA 91320
805-499-4224
E-mail: sales@pfp.sagepub.com

Visit our World Wide Web site. Your direct link to a multitude of online resources:

www.pineforge.com

Contents

Paradoxes are the only truths.

—George Bernard Shaw

Acknowledgments

I acknowledge gratefully several colleagues who have read various drafts of this man-
uscript; they include Don Chambliss, Robert Christie, Jonathan Church, Alex Durig,
Raymond Eve, Peter Freitag, Thomas Gershick, Kate Hausbeck, Melissa Herbert, Henryk
Hiller, Michael Keen, Chuck Lawrence, Brad Lyman, Stephen Lyng, Alfredo Montalvo,
Kelly Moore, David Newman, Myron Orleans, Caroline Percell, Judith Richlin-Klonsky,
Robert E. L. Roberts, Winnie Sperry, Mitchell Stephens, Judith Stull, Debra Swanson,
Dana Vannoy, Janelle Wilson, and David Yamane. Thank you for your generous insights
and your focused criticism. You have stimulated my thinking. I have also benefited from
the keen and challenging editorial work provided by Alan Venable. Thank you for your
clarity of voice where mine was fuzzy. Thanks also to Kristin Bergstad for your sharp and
helpful copyediting.

This book would not be possible without Steve Rutter, President of Pine Forge Press.
Thank you for your vision and drive. Several of the essays in this book were originally
conceived for public lectures. I wish to acknowledge The Northwest Women's Center for
Research on Women, The Honors Program at Seattle University, and the President's Focus
Series on Civility and Conflict Resolution at Hamilton College. My views and my voice
have taken shape through countless conversations with friends and colleagues who have
pushed me to be more articulate, indulged me when I pontificated, and pushed me over
the edge where necessary. Thank you Earl Babbie, Kate Bornstein, Wendy Chapkis,
Gitana Garofalo, Jennifer Eichstedt, brenda hanson, Lori Homer, Kari Lerum, Julien
Murphy, Ron Obvious, Mary Romero, Arlene Stein, France Winddance Twine, Linda Van
Leuven. A high-five of shared accomplishment to Deb Wenneman who was tearing down
and rebuilding walls in my house while I was trying to rebuild the final pages of this book.
Thanks for the rhythm. Finally, a single perfect rose to you, Judy Howard.

Prologue

Recently I appeared on a television show called *Town Meeting*. This program, produced by the local PBS affiliate, features debates on contemporary controversies and social issues. The topic of the broadcast on which I appeared was "Citizenship and Civic Responsibility." Along with academics like me, the guests included local politicians and a city planner. The audience consisted of persons selected from various local organizations, community centers and political action committees. There were also students from area colleges and universities. The producer tried to initiate a debate pitting "big government" against "citizens." She instructed the host to pursue questions regarding excesses and unresponsiveness of government representatives versus the general apathy of citizens.

For a while this angle worked. Citizens accused politicians of making it unnecessarily difficult to pursue actions in the interests of the community; politicians defended themselves on the grounds that most people didn't pay any attention to civic affairs and that they, the representatives of the people, spent long, hard hours trying to run the city. This debate of who was more at fault (for an assumed erosion of civic responsibility?) continued for a while and then took a noteworthy turn. A young man from the local state university stood and expressed his frustration with the "older" generation who persisted in these debates of (ir)responsibility, but never seemed to have anything to say about what, specifically, the problems are and what should be done.

Immediately the tone of the program shifted. Both sides, politicians and community organizers, joined forces in a vociferous attack on contemporary youth. Phrases such as "apathetic," "selfish," "slackers," "lacking in ambition" were tossed about recklessly. The gist of the rant seemed to be that contemporary youth are both the cause and the consequence of an erosion of "community values." The speakers conveyed the unquestioned impression that the youth of the '90s are generally irresponsible, selfish and unconcerned with social life. When it was my turn to speak I mentioned that I taught at a local university and that it was my impression that students were very concerned with social and civic issues, but that they were being given very few tools with which to make sense of the complex world that they had inherited. It's difficult to commit to a course of social action when you can't map the issues and problems reliably.

In response, one particularly articulate young woman rose and suggested that what her elders perceived as apathy was, perhaps, paralysis. Paralysis about what to think and what to do about problems and issues that seemed, to her generation, much more complicated than they were being taught. She noted, by way of example, that she volunteered service at a shelter for battered and/or unemployed women with children. "I read in the newspapers that these women are abusing the welfare system and that the best way to help them in the long run is to limit welfare so that they will be forced to find jobs or return to their husbands. Excuse me," she continued in an exaggerated drawl that drew laughter from the audience, "but you don't need to be a college graduate to figure out that the problem is bigger than whether these women want to work or not." The audience quieted as she delivered her own analysis. "Most of these women make a fraction of what men make for working much harder, and at the same time they're supposed to pay for child care and other expenses? Do the math! They are not the problem!" The host cut her off as she launched into a description of the idiocy of those who figure that the problem would be solved if the women returned to the men (who beat them). But she had made her point.

The event was on my mind as I went to class the following day. "Thanks for sticking up for us on TV," remarked one of the students who had seen the program. I contemplated my class. The 40 or so assembled students struck me as fairly typical of college students in the contemporary United States. Their economic diversity was reflected in a spectrum that included students whose parents could afford a private university tuition as well as students who are recipients of the university's progressive outreach scholarship and financial aid programs. Most of them work at least part-time to supplement their education. Some of them are single parents, several have inter-racial backgrounds, some are the first in their families to attend university, others hail from a long line of professionally educated family. The majority are involved in voluntary service projects that take them into homeless shelters, community action programs and nonprofit agencies. The thing that unites this class of mostly junior sociology majors is their willingness, indeed their eagerness, to grapple with complex subjects of study and discussion. Many of these students suffer a "time bind" of overcommitments, but I am certain that they are not apathetic.

In recent years I've given much thought to comments among my colleagues, other sociology professors, who echo similar proclamations of student apathy and an overemphasis on grades. My impression is that students are not apathetic and grade-obsessed when they first come to college. I think students may become this way over the course of being fed a diet of material that is understimulating, lacking in challenge and largely irrelevant to everyday life. I see a conundrum here. In the past three years there has been a significant rise in the number of students who are choosing sociology as a major. As students, you seem to be saying that you want a course of study that will help you understand a complex social world and enable you to make a difference through your own actions. At the same time, I hear many college professors, including some of my own respected colleagues, express doubt about your abilities and inclinations. These teachers are deeply committed to teaching useful and meaningful material, yet at the same time, they seem to have cultivated an impression that students don't want, or are incapable of dealing with, complicated course material.

I was struck with the comments made by colleagues who have read advance chapters of this book. Many of them suggested that they were enthusiastic about the essays in the book because they deal with timely, meaningful topics. Yet they also expressed concerns that students would find the material too complicated. I was particularly startled by a remark made by one reviewer in response to my descriptions of student conversations (such as the one I have noted regarding the young people talking on the television program). "I like the references to student dialogues," the reviewer wrote, "but I find it hard to believe that these comments were really made by students. They seem made up. Students just don't talk that way." This remark made me angry. In thinking about it further I realized that I was angry at what seemed to be a lack of respect for and underestimation of student potential. My experience has been that students, like all individuals, are extremely articulate when they have something meaningful to discuss and have been given the opportunity to think about it in challenging ways.

This book is for you, the student/citizen who recognizes the complicated, shifting, contradictory social landscape that you inhabit and who wants useful tools for making sense of it. I was educated in accordance with an admonition from the philosopher Kropotkin who said, "Figure out what you need to know to make a difference in the world and then demand that your teachers teach you this." It's good advice regarding a student's entitlement to relevant course material, but it can be difficult to know what to demand if you're not sure what tools you need to begin with. The proffered sociological tools may have seemed simpler to identify and to teach in earlier decades when social life seemed simpler. Social roles seemed less complicated and mutually understood. Those who wouldn't or couldn't occupy their assigned roles in the social order were placed in the box marked "deviant" or "other."

Sociologists have led the way among scholars in pointing out that the world is not as simple as this; that there is not a single general perspective according to which some can be labeled "normal" and others "deviant." Nor is there is single best way to determine whose perspective is "right" and whose is "wrong." Einstein, in his theory of relativity, noted that the measurement of the distance between planets and other matter in the universe depended on the position from which the measurement was taken. In hindsight, this seems obvious, but at the time it required extensive mental stretching to wrap one's head around the notion that seemingly fixed things such as "time" or "distance" actually shifted depending on where one was located in the universe when "time" and "distance" were measured. This leap in consciousness required that we learn to think beyond our position on the planet Earth as the only site from which these measurements could be made. We had to learn to imagine ourselves in other positions in space and to make calculations accordingly.

Similarly, social research is enabling us to learn that there is no single perspective from which to describe and analyze social issues accurately. Our perspectives are shaped by social positions such as class, gender, race, sexuality, religiosity, political interests and so forth. Contemporary sociology has taken on the complex task of trying to describe some of the differences in these positions as well as the implications for analyzing social issues and problems.

For example, a sociologist who specializes in gender studies, Michael Messner, has studied ways in which boys learn "masculinity" through playing organized sports.

"Masculinity" is a social perspective. One feature of the "masculine" perspective as Messner describes it is the way in which boys learn to expect rewards based on performance ("We won because we played well"). Another feature is that boys learn to see their positions in terms of a larger game plan, rather than as an integral aspect of self ("I'm the pitcher in this particular game, and perhaps the outfielder tomorrow"). Compare this socialization with that of girls who, until recently, were not allowed to play organized sports and who are frequently subjected to evaluatory comments such as, "You have pretty hair" or "My, what chubby cheeks." These differences in socialization may lead to positional differences whereby girls are more likely to expect rewards/punishments based on who they *are* (particularly bodily image) and to assume a more fixed nature to these statuses than boys, who may be likely to see their particular circumstances as part of a temporary position (rather than a fundamental attribute of self). These differences in socialization might explain the observation that adult women in employment settings appear to "take things too personally" while men treat everything as "part of the game."

Describing these differences does not lead to an obvious answer about which perspective is "right" or more desirable. In the case of this example, it is assumed that the "masculine" trait of not taking things too personally is more desirable in an employment setting, but some sociologists point out that this perspective is not necessarily desirable; it is only presumed to be so because men carry it with them from the playing field into employment settings in which they have long held the upper hand. Determining the relative worth of various perspectives and positions requires an awareness of the differences and also an awareness of some of the taken-for-granted assumptions about which positions are more or less desirable. This is a complex agenda.

The enterprise is further complicated in that there are no single (univocal) answers. Contemporary sociology emphasizes the process of the discussion about different positions and the activities between those who hold different perspectives. Who is included? What degree of respect is accorded to different positions? Are we really trying to hear and learn from others in terms of their own positions or do we evaluate others in terms of their willingness and ability to move to our position? In writing these essays I have been fortunate to be able to incorporate the perspectives of the many students whom I have taught in the past decade. These students represent many different positions. One thing that they hold in common for me is the demand that I find ways to make my sociological knowledge relevant for them so that, together, we can figure out how to live meaningfully in this complicated social landscape.

"Prisms" as a Metaphor for Contemporary Sociology

In thinking and teaching about how to describe and analyze multiple perspectives, I have found the metaphor of a prism useful. Prisms are transparent and are used for "dispersing light into a spectrum." The prism reflects and magnifies the spectrum. Features within the spectrum appear differently depending on which panel of the prism they are viewed through. So it is with social awareness. I have found that social patterns look very different depending on which panel of the prism I look through. This does not mean that the patterns do not exist, but rather that comprehension of the social spectrum requires various viewing panels and multiple angles of awareness. A prismatic perspective is highly varied and multifaceted.

A decade ago Donald Levine wrote a book called *Flight From Ambiguity*. In this book he treats both the rise of modernity and the practice of social science as topics of inquiry. His thesis is that our attempts to render the world stable and predictable have resulted in a flight from much of what is noteworthy and unique to human experience—multivocalities, complexities and contradictions. Modern human cultures, including communities of would-be scientists, have pushed aside ambiguities in favor of the univocal. The contest has been to determine how to forge a singular voice in an otherwise complex world. Many voices and much of the richness of the human experience have been neglected in the process.

Recently I was discussing with a friend the differences between the quest for simple, univocal, uniform perspectives and complex, multivocal, multiple perspectives. In the former, truth and understanding are presumed to be absolute, value is transcendent and universal. In the latter, truths shift and value is located in the expression of particulars. Many people find this second view discomfiting. My friend, who is Jewish, reminded me that there are many traditions, Judaism being one, in which value is in multiple interpretations of a single concept. The Talmud is prized because it contains multiple readings of the Old Testament. It is the process of expressing and engaging varied perspectives that counts in Jewish scholarship. There are no answers, only more questions.

I pondered this as I contrasted it with Christianity, in which the endeavor, by and large, has been to "uncover" the single, absolute biblical interpretation—a quest for the ultimate answer. Prisms do not provide ultimate answers and single truths. A prism produces contrasting beams of light that illuminate various angles while casting others in shadow. A prismatic perspective results in continual questions: What happens if I tilt it this way or turn it upside down or peer from another side?

Prisms Reveal Myths and Paradoxes

Continual questioning leads to paradox. Paradoxes, like the prismatic perspectives that catch them in cross-beams, reveal tensions, fissures and cracks. Viewed through the prism of paradox, the social spectrum is a web of tensions and contradictions. The only thing that is revealed as certain is the complexity of it all. I enhance my social awareness when I grapple with these paradoxes. In the process I become mindful, more sociologically aware.

This book is a compilation of essays that have taken shape through a course I teach called "Myths and Paradoxes in Contemporary U.S. Society." In the course I use the prism of paradox to illuminate tensions and contradictions in everyday practices and ideologies. I believe that we cannot make informed assessments of the current political and cultural landscape until we are able to view it through a highly varied, multifaceted lens. Such a gaze inevitably leads to more questioning and new paradoxes. I am not convinced that paradoxes exist to be solved. However, much of what I view through the particular paradoxes that shape these essays leaves me outraged.

My goal in this book of essays is to reintroduce some of the complexities and ambiguities from which standard sociological topics and concepts have been abstracted. My reasons for wanting to do this are driven by my belief that much of what is interesting and relevant about human experience and about sociology is the result of attempts to grapple with paradoxes and contradictions. I'm less interested in how these paradoxes and contradictions have been solved, or in how complexities are simplified—I'm actually not even sure that they really ever are. Instead, I want to explore the process of grappling, the attempts at management and the consequences of these strategies. Cultural strategies for minimizing or managing complex issues often take the form of cultural myths. These myths, many of which are expressed as cherished cultural values and traditions, often work as blinders that keep us from seeing the implications and consequences of our own actions.

These essays reflect my own idiosyncratic prisms. It is my hope that others may be challenged by this prismatic perspective to shift some of the angles of their own gaze, to take up the process of questioning and set aside the quest for answers. My perspective is only one among many. These essays are not intended as a definitive treatment of the topics explored. Rather I hope to simulate additional interest in each topic by providing one possible angle of analysis. My goal is to invite further reading and discussion.

1

The Paradox of Reduction

Some Observations on Sociology as Science

PARADOX

How do we answer significant questions about ourselves and our environment? The scientific method is a dominant mode of inquiry in contemporary society. This method was conceived as a response to the philosophical paradox of subjectivity. The paradox of subjectivity arises from the fact that everyone sees things from their own point of view. If this is so, then how do we determine which points of view are more or less real or accurate? The scientific method reduces subjectivity by narrowing the focus of inquiry to very specific snapshots and statements; the scientist seeks to state a point of view as precisely and narrowly as possible. In this way, others can share the same perspective and debate and evaluate its merits. Thus, in science, truth is a matter of consensus about what to look at and how to look at it. This method is especially useful in the natural sciences where, for instance, scientists can identify certain phenomena, such as planets in the sky, make careful observations, cross-check these observations with other observers, and arrive at some probable truths about how the planets move through the universe. This method has some problems when used to study human behavior and societies. Most of what people do, think and feel is not something that can be seen and observed directly. In order to observe behavior scientifically, it is necessary first to define what it is that we think people are doing. For instance, in order to study love and attraction, we have to define what "love" and "attraction" are. This process of definition limits the focus to a narrow perspective so that all the observers can agree that they are observing the same thing. The paradox is that human behavior is not necessarily reducible to these basic definitions. In reducing human activity to observable definitions for purposes of scientific observation, the meaning and significance of the behavior is frequently lost or overlooked. Thus, paradoxically, the scientific method may provide some precise observations about human activity, but the relevance and significance of these observations is questionable.

This life is a test, it's only a test. If this had been a real life you would have been given instructions about what to do and who to be.

—Bathroom graffiti in Seattle Coffeehouse

The mind that has conceived a plan of living must never forget the chaos out of which it was conceived.

—Ralph Ellison, *The Invisible Man*

Consider some questions. Are you smart? Are you healthy? Are you a good person? How good is the quality of your education? Are we better off today than we used to be? Is Affirmative Action a good thing? Does democracy work? What is the distance between Earth and Venus? How do we detect whether someone has cancer? Can we detect whether someone will be a good parent? How do you know when you're in love? What is your purpose in life? How much money are you likely to make in the next 10 years?

How would you answer these questions? Would you use the same approach to answer each one? Are they all answerable? Which questions would be easiest to answer? To answer the question of the distance between Earth and Venus, I looked up a chart of the planets in the Webster's dictionary. According to the chart, the distance between these two planets is 41.4 million kilometers, or 25.8 million miles. Do these both mean the same thing? Yes. Although the answers are expressed differently, in terms of calculating the actual time and distance that I would have to travel to make it between the two planets, the answers mean the same thing. I am reasonably confident that most sources would give me the same answer.

What about detecting cancer? Like many people in this society, I have been taught to be on the lookout for certain signs that might indicate cancer. If I notice such a sign, for example, a change in the color and size of a mole, I can go to an "expert" who has learned ways of seeing cancer. The expert will take some tests and these tests will show whether I have cancerous cells in my body. I am somewhat confident that the expert's answer will be correct. If I want to be more certain, I can ask two or three experts. If they agree, then I will be reasonably certain about the answer.

Are there experts who can tell me if I'm a good person? For the most part, I think that I am a good person, but I know that this is an opinion that I have developed about myself over the years. If I wanted to check out this opinion I could ask several people who know me, but if they gave me different answers I would be faced with a new question: Which answer was the right answer?

The list of questions above, and the hundreds of others that could be asked, suggests that there are different ways of getting answers and different degrees of certainty about the answers. Some answers can be gotten by simply looking, or knowing what to look for. If you know how to look and have the right equipment, you can measure the distance between places or things, such as planets. If you know what signs to look for, you can tell the difference between healthy tissue and cancerous tissue. Most people will agree that there are specific ways to measure distance, and specific signs or symptoms that indicate cancer. These ways of getting answers are considered both reliable and valid. They are *reliable* because the same method is likely to give the same answer every time. They are *valid* because we think the answers are accurate. Another thing that you might notice about the list of questions is that some of the questions seem more *significant* than others. I may be able to measure the distance between Venus and Earth consistently (reliably) and certainly, but how important is this information for me? I may be much more concerned about whether Affirmative Action is a good policy than about the distance between planets. Yet the first question isn't so easily answered. I can't just go out and look. What would I be looking at? I can ask people what their opinions are, but I'm likely to get many different responses. How do I determine which responses are valid and useful?

Knowledge Systems

All societies have ways of gathering knowledge and finding answers to questions. Within societies there are different ways of finding answers and some ways are considered better than others. Different methods apply to different questions. For instance, most of us rely on our feelings and conversations with our friends to help us determine whether we are in love, or what our purpose in life might be. The process involves a lot of guesswork and uncertainty. We may have to sort through several different opinions and contradictory experiences, but we don't expect that there is any single, simple way to just look and find the answer. In contrast, we would scoff at someone who relied on his feelings to determine the distance between places. Just measure it, we might say. We might also be concerned for someone who relied on her feelings or conversations with friends to determine whether she had cancer. See a doctor, we might plead.

Some ways of finding answers to questions include looking (observation), speculation (guessing), relying on tradition (everyone else in this family is a shoemaker, that will be your purpose in life as well), and authority (the queen thinks that we are all better off, so we are better off). All societies have a mix of these ways of answering questions and rules or ideas about which methods are best for which sorts of questions. From this mix, societies also have *dominant* ways of gathering knowledge and answering questions. The *dominant* way is considered to be the best way to gain knowledge. Dominant knowledge forms are distinct from everyday common sense. Common sense is what most of us use most of the time to make sense of everyday questions and concerns. Common sense is a mixture of experience and opinion. A dominant knowledge system, on the other hand, is a way of gathering information to address questions thought to be beyond the realm of common sense.

Science as a Dominant System of Knowledge

The dominant system of knowledge in our society is science. This does not mean that science provides the best answer to all questions. There is common agreement that some questions, such as one's purpose in life, are outside the realm of science. There is also common agreement that scientific methods provide very useful answers for certain questions, such as how to calculate the distance between places and how to detect cancer. What we are a bit fuzzy about is the usefulness of scientific methods to address social questions. Do scientific methods provide useful answers to questions about the quality of education, or whether someone is likely to be a good parent, or the merits of Affirmative Action? Sociologists, whose purpose is to explore questions about society and social issues, have several concerns about using scientific methods. The main concern takes the form of a paradox, which is this: *Scientific methods provide accurate (reliable) descriptions of observable objects, but social phenomena are not observable objects. In order to make social phenomena observable through scientific methods, the complexity of the phenomenon has to be reduced to something observable. This process can render the results meaningless.*

In this chapter I describe the scientific method and provide a brief history of its rise to dominance. The historical conundrum about the rise of science is that scientific methods are best suited to describing objective phenomena, but science achieved dominance because philosophers and industrialists believed that science was also the best way to find answers to difficult social questions. It is not certain that science is very well suited for answering some social questions. Yet, because science is considered dominant, we sometimes believe that it yields the best answers. The *uncritical* use of scientific methods in social domains is referred to as *scientism*. There is also a tendency to take scientific concepts out of context and to use them as if they had real social meaning. This is called *reification*. When you read scientific studies intended to provide answers to social questions and issues, you need to think about reduction and reification, and whether or not science provides the best form of answer for the question. I will address each of these points in detail.

The Problem of Multiple Perspectives: A Philosophical Paradox

Scientific methods emerged in response to a philosophical paradox about truth and multiple perspectives. Let's begin the story with a discussion of this paradox. I'll use a personal example to illustrate. When I was a child my father took me to minor league baseball games. We never sat in the same seat for the entire game. Instead, we would move around and watch the game from different spots. Depending on where we were, different activities and plays would attract our attention. The experience of the game was different depending on which players I was closest to and what direction I was facing. Where we stood didn't influence the outcome of the game, but it influenced how we saw the game being played. As I child I marveled at this idea of multiple perspectives, of seeing differently from different positions. Later, as I began to hike, I came to realize how completely different a landscape looks depending on where you are standing. A friend of mine calls this the "peak perspective." Things look different, depending on which peak you are standing on.

Empirical Observation

One of the earliest philosophical questions was about the relationship between *truth* and multiple perspectives. The question became known as the *paradox of subjectivity and the possibility of certain knowledge.* Different people have different points of view depending on their position (which is subjective, or personal). If everyone's perspective is subjective, how are we to know what the *objective, or certain* picture is? If things are different depending on your perspective, how do you figure out what something really looks like? What is the *true* perspective? Is the earth really flat just because it looks that way to people who are earthbound and can't see beyond the horizon? One philosophical answer to this paradox was that we need to gather as many different perspectives as possible and put them all together to see what sort of picture or pattern emerges. This method is called *empiricism.* Empirical methods are based on the assumption that there is a real, objective phenomenon to be observed, but that getting the full picture involves looking at it from several different perspectives and seeing how these match up.

Philosophers and scholars in the sixteenth and seventeenth centuries worked at perfecting methods of empirical observation. The idea was to gather as many perspectives as possible and to be as systematic as possible. This idea can be illustrated with the old parable of the three blind men and the elephant. Recall that each had hold of a different part of the elephant and by feeling that part (an empirical method) tried to determine what the thing was. One guessed a snake, one a tree and one a wall. The logic of systematic empiricism is that by putting these individual observations together, a pattern closer to the real thing might become evident.

There were those who disagreed with empirical methods as a basis for finding *true* answers. The disagreement was based on the idea that no matter how systematically we observe something, our perspective will still be limited by (1) preexisting beliefs about *what* it is that we are seeing, and (2) the limits of our ability physically to take up alternative perspectives. The second concern seems obvious. Without the technology to gain new perspectives, it is difficult to know beyond what we can see. What's under the skin or over the horizon? Without ships that could travel great distances, it was impossible to see beyond the limits of the physical horizon. Given this, observers were limited to speculating about what might be on the other side. The first concern is a bit more complicated. You and I may go to the baseball field and see things differently depending on where we are sitting. Yet we are both likely to be in agreement that we are at a baseball game, that there are players who have certain positions, a single ball, and so forth. We share presuppositions about the general phenomenon that we are observing. When we are trying to make sense of the mysteries of the universe and the many unknown features of nature, however, we may not only be looking at different aspects of the object in question, but may have false preconceived notions about what the general nature of the object is.

An example from astronomy is instructive. Prior to the development of the telescope in the 1600s, no one had a close enough view of "those orbs in the sky" to confirm that they might be planets. Instead, the popular view of the day was that the orbs were celestial beings that revolved around the earth. Even the sun was thought to revolve around the earth. This belief about a system of orbs all revolving around the earth was based on a theological system of knowledge that the earth was the center of all things. Observations made by early astronomers took this belief for granted—they "saw" the orbs revolving around the earth because this is what they expected to see. The fact that we often see what we expect to see led some philosophers to decide that true knowledge can only be found by *transcending* the limits of the human senses and clearing our minds of preconceived assumptions. The idea was that we can't get a "God's eye view" through our own senses, which are limited to certain vantage points and shadowed by preexisting superstitious beliefs. Therefore, we have to learn higher forms of thought—a way of speculating that transcends common superstitions and individual opinions. The form of thought that was developed to address this concern was called *formal logic*.

Formal Logic as a Basis for Theoretical Speculation

Seventeenth-century philosophers were intrigued with the ideas of numerical logic developed by Pythagoras of Samos in the sixth century B.C. Pythagoras, who is credited with the rise of mathematics, developed the idea of the mathematical proof. Mathematics is an abstract way of posing questions and puzzles in a manner that is intended to apply across all conditions. Numbers transcend subjective beliefs and opinions. No matter what your opinion of the equation is, we are certain that $2 + 2 = 4$. You may recall learning the theorem that all right-angled triangles can be expressed in terms of the equation:

$$x^2 + y^2 = z^2$$

Which translates as:

in a right-angled triangle, the square of the hypotenuse is equal to the sum of the squares of the other two sides.

This theorem, known as Pythagoras's theorem, is true for every right-angled triangle that you can imagine. No matter where it is located, what its size or which direction you look at it from, this way of describing it describes *every* right-angled triangle. How did Pythagoras know this for sure? Through his development of the "proof." Using numerical logic and a process of logical elimination, the mathematical proof is a way of demonstrating conclusively the certainty of the theorem. Mathematical proofs were a form of religion for Pythagoras. He founded a Brotherhood devoted to establishing truth through mathematics. The Brotherhood, and many of its mathematical theorems, were eventually burned out as heretics, but the certainty of the theorems that had been passed along remained.

Seventeenth-century philosophers such as René Descartes proposed to construct systems of philosophical thought based on mathematical logic. This system would involve constructing definitive statements (theorems) that could be subjected to rigorous proof. The result is formal logic.

Those in favor of formal logic argued with the empiricists over who had the better way of finding knowledge and determining truth. The empiricists claimed to be able to gather more information about the physical world, the formal theorists claimed to be able to make more *certain* statements about how the world was organized. For a long time, knowledge generated through mathematical reasoning was considered superior. Different astronomers, for instance, used mathematical logic to propose alternative theories about what "those orbs in the sky" were doing. Copernicus was a Polish astronomer who lived at the end of the fifteenth century. He used mathematical reasoning to develop a theory that the earth revolved around the sun, rather than the other way around—but he kept this theory to himself, knowing that it would get him into trouble with Church authorities. A century later, an Italian astronomer, Galileo, refined this theory. He shared it with fellow scholars, who accepted it as the best theory on the grounds that it was the most "simple and elegant" theory. This was the rule for which mathematical theory was the best—the one that was stated in the simplest terms. Although Galileo's theory was accepted by scholars, the Church was not happy about the possibility of an alternative truth regarding the relationship between the sun and the earth. Galileo was made to recant his theory, which he did in order to not lose his head.

The telescope wasn't invented until later in Galileo's life. There was no way to look to see which theory was correct, the Church's theory or the mathematical theory. Which theory you believed depended on which knowledge system you thought best for the question—theology or mathematical astronomy. Observations made by astronomers who had been tracking the movements of the "orbs" by watching and making note of their positions in the sky (systematic observation) suggested that the mathematical theory might be the correct theory—the earth, and other orbs, seemed to be moving around the sun. The telescope later provided empirical evidence that confirmed this theory and observation. Still, it would be another century before most people would be willing to believe that this way of speculating (mathematical logic) and finding evidence (systematic observation) was a better way of finding answers to important questions than the answers generated by theologians who studied the word of God.

The *scientific method* that emerged from these calculations and observations in astronomy is a combination of the two ways of answering questions. It is a two part sequence:

1. *Logical Deduction (theory)*

2. *Systematic Observation (evidence)*

This system has come to be presumed superior to superstitious or traditional ways of seeking answers because it begins with a process of making a statement as precisely as possible (as in a mathematical theorem), and then seeks to confirm or refute the statement through observation. A key feature of the scientific method is to develop theoretical propositions and corresponding statements (called hypotheses) that are as unambiguous as possible. The more precise the hypothesis, the more certain it is that everyone will be looking at the same thing when they seek evidence. Precise theories *reduce subjectivity* by presenting the question in the least ambiguous way. Students of science may remember this illustration. Suppose I pose a question: What color are swans? I am likely to get a wide set of answers ranging from snowy ivory, to mottled gray, to midnight black. I'll get a set of answers based on the subjective impressions of multiple observers. Thus, all I will be able to say for certain is that swans are multicolored. But suppose I propose this hypothetical statement: All swans are white. This is a very precise statement. All that has to be done to disprove it is to find a single swan that is *not* white. Then we can say with certainty that "all swans are not white."

Stating something in terms of numbers is a way of putting it precisely and unambiguously. The question, "What does cancer look like?" is imprecise and ambiguous. If that were our starting point, we'd be tossing up answers as diverse as the color of swans. The hypothetical statement is more precise and unambiguous: Cancer cells reproduce at a more rapid rate than healthy cells. Having made this statement, we can now look for evidence that either supports or refutes the claim. Regardless of what we find, we will know something precisely. Science doesn't cover a lot of territory quickly. It is a slow, painstaking process of crafting statements that are precise and simple to test. The answers that this method yields are small in scope, but likely to be more certain.

Science inches forward through this process of generating very precise statements based on existing theories, and then looking for confirming or disputing evidence. If no disputing evidence is found, the theoretical statement is presumed to be *tentatively* certain. For the most part, the scientific method is a way of reducing the uncertainties about the world—we know that all swans are not white. Scientists, however, are very cautious about making claims of certainty because there is always the possibility of another perspective out there that may provide new evidence. The good scientist never forgets this.

Again, the point worth repeating is that what certainty there is in science comes from establishing starting points that are extremely precise. If the question is precise, then we can be assured that everyone is standing in the same spot looking for evidence. Precise questions and sources of evidence reduce the problem of multiple perspectives.

For some questions, science is an excellent method of inquiry. It is particularly useful for making descriptions of the physical world. But how useful is this method for other sorts of questions? Can scientific thinking be usefully and meaningfully applied to questions about social life? The short answer is that the scientific method is one of the most respected methods for studying human and social life today, but the story is more complicated than this. Many scholars are critical of the use of scientific methods for social studies. They consider the practice to be a misapplication of science and a misleading way to study social life. One question that is worth some consideration here is *why* science was adopted for the study of social life in the first place. The answer comes in two related historical trends. One was the philosophical idea that scientific thinking was a superior way of thinking, overall. Another was the success of the natural sciences. I will discuss each briefly.

Using Scientific Thinking for Social Questions

The scientific method emerged as a dominant form of seeking answers in the seventeenth century. The reason for this dominance is connected to another philosophical question, one that has very little to do with taking measurements and making numerical estimates. A central concern for the philosophers of this time was the question of who had the right to govern? The prevailing authority was the royal monarch who ruled by the authority of tradition, force and Christian interpretation that the monarch's authority was a "divine extension of God's will." According to this form of rule, the monarch, in conjunction with the Catholic Church, was the source of answers to significant social and political questions. There was a growing discontent with this form of authority and rule. Philosophers of what has since come to be called the Age of Enlightenment proposed that all people (meaning men with social status and property) had the right to govern themselves.

They could exercise authority and judgment over their own lives. Significant social and political questions should be addressed by "all the people," not just monarchs and priests.

The philosophical question that plagued these new thinkers was how to determine whose perspectives and interests and opinions were the best answers to pressing social questions. If everyone has different points of view and different interests, then how can any single way of governing be determined? The answer that these philosophers hit upon was "reasoned logic." People who learned to think logically could be depended upon to transcend their personal perspectives and to see from a "higher plane." From this plane of logic and reason, they would be able to see the "big picture" and thus come up with fair and just answers to difficult social questions. In short, the people most fit to rule and govern in the new age would be those who thought like the scientist. This period in history, the seventeenth and eighteenth centuries, is sometimes referred to as the "dawn of the age of reason." Reason—thinking logically and withholding judgment until systematic evidence can be gathered—was heralded as the dawn of a new age, an age that would triumph over the tyranny of "traditional" rule. Reason, or the possibility of reason, is something that is within the grasp of all people. This philosophy was a popular alternative to the traditional ideas that knowledge and truth were available to only a few who had been "divinely appointed." The "enlightened" answer to the philosophical question of how to determine which perspective is right in a world of multiple perspectives was: The "voice of reason" is right.

Scientific Reason as a Basis of Social Authority

Three centuries later, we take "reason" for granted as a basis for determining truth and justice. At the time, it was a fledgling way of thought that most people had difficulty comprehending. I show a clip from the film *Monty Python and the Holy Grail* to illustrate the rise of scientific reasoning as a basis for addressing social questions. Much of the humor in Monty Python is derived from a very nuanced understanding of medieval and classical history. As you read through this illustration, note that in order to qualify as scientific thinking, there must be (1) a standard, logically derived definition of what is to be observed, and (2) evidence for the observation.

As the scene opens, the camera focuses on a shot of a line of monks walking single file and chanting in unison. Throughout the chanting the monks rhythmically whack boards against their foreheads. As the head-thumping monks pass through the scene the camera pulls back to reveal a somewhat disheveled knight standing atop a platform attempting to tie a coconut to the leg of a swallow. He is jolted out of his concentration by a large crowd rushing noisily to the platform pushing a woman roughly ahead of them and shouting, "We've found a witch! May we burn her?"

Why are they asking permission from the knight, the viewer may wonder? The knight, who seems to recognize that he is in a position of authority, scrutinizes the crowd and asks, "How do you know she is a witch?" "She looks like one!" The crowd shrieks in response. The knight turns his attention to the woman, who is wearing a pointed black cap and has what appears to be a carrot tied to her face, resembling a long nose. "They dressed me like this," she appeals to him quietly. He frowns at the crowd. "Well, we did do the nose," they admit. "But she turned me into a newt," one crowd member bellows in the attempt to provide additional testimony. Silence follows this admission as he is obviously not a newt. "I got better," he mumbles in defense. At this point several other members of the crowd mutter similar accusations. It's clear that they're making this "evidence" up as they go. The knight frowns once again, holds up his hand for silence and then, with grave majesty, says confidently, "There are ways of telling if she is a witch. Ways of science." The crowd falls into a respectful hush and waits in awe for him to reveal these mysteries.

The knight then leads them through an exercise in deductive logic according to the syllogism that witches are made of wood, wood floats, so if the woman in question floats, then she must be a witch. The first rule of science is to construct a very specific, testable theory according to mathematical rules—logic. This method is considered more rigorous and less biased than simply asserting an opinion. The second phase of science is to put the theory to an empirical test. Having concocted a general theory of "witchness," how does one test it? In this case, the most direct test of determining whether the accused witch will float or not is to throw her into the nearby lake. Unfortunately, if she happens not to be a witch, this test will result in her drowning.

Keeping this in mind, the knight suggests an alternative test; logically speaking, if she were to float, in theory, then she must weigh the same as other things that float. Ergo, "What else floats?" he asks the crowd. They let loose with a range of responses that illustrate just how illogical such an exercise can be, "A bridge! Very small rocks! Wood!" The utterance of this last one reminds the crowd of their initial purpose and they return to their chant of "Burn Her!" Then, from the margins of the group, a single voice cries out, "A duck." "Right!" exclaims the knight. And thus the crowd proceeds to a large scale where a duck is placed on one side and the woman on the other. The outcome: They both weigh the same. Therefore, she must be a witch. In an ironic final moment of the scene, the camera focuses on the woman who is mumbling to herself, "'Twas a fair test."

The head-thumping monks shown on their way out of the village at the beginning of the scene are representations of the demise of religion as the basis for finding truth. The crowd represents the potential horrors of decision making by the process of superstition— we don't like your ways, you must be a witch, we'll burn you just because we think you are a witch. The knight's fiddling with the swallow and coconut marks him as a man of science. (This is based on a running Monty Python gag in which someone wonders how coconuts got to England. The theory is proposed that swallows flying at a certain velocity might have carried them from the South Seas and dropped them on the northern isle. Thus, as a man of science, the knight is conducting an experiment to test the feasibility of this theory.)

Definition and Evidence. The parody of the scene turns on the point that the twin pillars of the scientific method—logical deduction and systematic observation—are not especially easy to put into practice. The construction of logically precise theories is a real brainteaser; and the most straightforward means of testing a theory is frequently not advisable. The way a scientist goes about finding evidence in a systematic manner is largely determined by theoretical logic, which, in turn, is an exercise in *coming to a consensus about what constitutes the properties of the subject in question.* In detecting witches, scientific reasoning involves constructing a general definition of what a witch is (someone made of wood who floats) and then applying this definition to the case in question—the particular woman—to see if she possesses these qualities and can therefore be presumed to be a witch. *The entire process centers around conceptualization and classification. It's a matter of definition.*

As Monty Python portrays, the potential for logical fallacy is great in the process of concocting definitions and attempting to classify persons and objects. What is equally noteworthy, however, is the final comment in which the woman, despite the unfortunate outcome for her, believes the process to have been fair. Why does the crowd accept the knight's methods for determining the fate of the woman? Because scientific reasoning was gaining legitimacy as the central method for answering social questions. The scientific method arose as a corrective to superstitious thinking and decisions based on tradition. Scientific reasoning, because it is rooted in standard definitions and precise theories, was deemed a less arbitrary way of making sense then the rules passed on through custom, religion or magic.

Legal process in this country is organized according to the same rules by which science is conducted: a systematic search for and presentation of evidence that will either support or refute a hypothetical claim. Underlying this process are two somewhat paradoxical assumptions: There is a truth out there (something of real material consequence occurred in the moment designated as the crime and its causes are consistently real and potentially knowable), but we can never know with certainty what happened in that moment. The reality of the event can be reconstructed only through the filtered experience of possible observers and/or through bits of information pieced together by those who arrive later on the scene.

By agreement, we accept that the best form of evidence is a witness—someone who was also at the scene. Neither the law nor science accepts the observations of another outright. Many a courtroom drama turns on the moment when the defense is able to discredit a witness by demonstrating that her or his perspective on the scene is somehow obscured, biased or both. In retrospect, observations are not always what they seem to be. To be considered reliable, observations must pass the scrutiny of others who share a consensus about standards of acceptability. Note that when a witness's testimony is accepted it is not necessarily a statement that the witness possesses the truth, but rather a consensus that the witness is a credible storyteller. We are willing to accept her or his perspective as a premise from which to consider the evidence further.

Similarly, all evidence is not equally acceptable. Some forms of evidence are considered more factual than others. Information gathered by experts and analyzed through the use of technology is generally considered more reliable. Nonetheless, what counts as evidence remains a subject of intense debate in legal process. The issue of the admissibility of DNA tests as evidence in the Simpson trial is a case in point. The underlying question is to what extent do we trust scientific technology as a basis for establishing truth?

When each side has presented its corpus of evidence, truth is still not apparent. The evidence must be weighed and debated by the judge or jurors. The definitive criterion for the selection of these "evaluators of evidence" is that they be as unbiased as possible. The rule of the deliberation is to determine whether or not the person can be considered guilty *beyond reasonable doubt*. In other words, our legal code reflects an agreement that since we cannot know with certainty what really took place at the scene of a crime, we prefer to be as cautious as possible in arriving at tentative conclusions.

Science proceeds with similar caution. The methods of science have been carefully crafted as a response to two basic concerns: one is that the nature of things is not self-evident (it doesn't bite us on the nose), and the second is that in our endeavors to determine the nature of things we are inclined to impose preconceived expectations or biases on what we see. This is called subjectivity. For instance, it is not self-evident whether someone is a witch, nor if there even is such a thing as a witch. Furthermore, in the attempt to ascertain whether or not someone is a witch we must be cautious about making hasty assessments and imposing preconceived notions. The point of scientific methods has been to standardize this subjectivity so that any two persons making independent observations are likely to see the same thing.

In summary to this point, the scientific method was developed as a corrective for human subjectivity—the problem of multiple, idiosyncratic perspectives. The assumption that we are *all* subjective observers is the bedrock of science. The purpose of science as it was developed is to *reduce subjectivity*. Philosophers advocate a two-part process that, if followed rigorously, will encourage the scientist to be continually reflective about her or his own subjective biases and lead to "truths" that reflect common agreement among a group of similarly trained observers. The parts of this methodology are (1) theories arrived at through logical formulations and (2) observations made through systematic rules. The reasoning behind this method is that if scientific thinkers train themselves in the rules of logic and are required to state their premises in precise, unambiguous terms, then they are less likely to inflect taken-for-granted subjective biases into their observations. *Thus, theories must be as specific and unambiguous as possible.* Accordingly, observations should be made in the spirit of doubt, and evidence should be gathered systematically in a manner that can be easily replicated by someone else. If someone else following the same system makes a similar observation, then it can be concluded that there is agreement. Thus "truth" in science is a matter of consensus among those who have disciplined themselves to "see" in accordance with very precise rules of thought and observation.

Science consists of a community of persons who strive to establish standard rules for making observations and for drawing conclusions based on those observations. Practitioners of science are taught to suspend their initial reactions, to doubt their impressions and to proceed with open expectations into the field of inquiry. Ultimately science is a matter of consensus. Whenever scientists arrive at a "verdict" upon which they agree, it is not because they have uncovered an absolute truth (by our very nature as subjective creatures we can never know such "truths"), rather they have reached a consensus about what the properties of something are and how to test for its presence empirically. A witch is made of wood and floats; one can determine whether or not someone is a witch by weighing her against a duck. This conception of witchness reduces the ambiguities of a complex phenomenon to a single, shared definition arrived at through the use of consensual rules. The benefit of such a method is that it renders the basis for judgment standard and consistent, rather than whimsical and arbitrary.

Let's turn now to consider further ways in which science came to be considered the most appropriate method for answering questions. The idea that science could answer social questions took hold by proposing that social behavior can be reduced to natural, observable phenomena. This idea continues to be a subject of controversy.

Science Discovers Nature: Something to Be Catalogued, Predicted and Controlled

In the opening scene of her play *The Grace of Mary Traverse,* Timberlake Wertenbaker depicts a young woman of upper-class society practicing a conversation in anticipation of the evening's dinner guest, an explorer. The play is set in the eighteenth century and Nature has become a popular topic among those who consider themselves up to date on current events.

> Nature, my lord. It was here all the time and we've only just discovered it. What is nature?
> . . . Perhaps we will not exhaust nature as easily as we have other pleasures for it is difficult
> to imagine with what to replace it. And there's so much of it! How admirable of you to have
> shown us the way, my lord, to have made the grand tour of such natural places as Wales. Ah,
> crags, precipices, what awe they must strike in one's spirit. Yes. And I hear Wales even has
> peasants. How you must have admired their lives, their human nature a complement to the
> land's starkness. Peasants too I believe are a new discovery. How delightful of our civilisation
> to shed light on its own dark and savage recesses. You were telling me how we are to know
> nature. Do we dare look at it directly, or do we trust an artist's imitation, a poet. (1985:7)

This brief scene tells us a lot about the century from which and the people from whom we inherited the modern manifestations of the scientific tradition. The empirical strand of the scientific method—systematic observation—developed in the course of attempts to comprehend "nature." Nature, as the young woman reminds us, had only recently been discovered. Not that the natural world hadn't been there all along, but our interest in it as self-aware, thinking creatures who were inclined to define it as something apart from ourselves marked a new trend. This trend was a source of amusement, "delight" and "admiration" among the wealthy classes. Ambitious young men, and occasionally women, without fortunes or vocations of their own, could secure funds from the wealthy to outfit explorations and go off in search of natural wonders. These explorers brought back exotic specimens (butterfly collecting was hugely popular), stories of strange and different peoples, and drawings and maps of new territories. In an age without movies, explorers who had tales to tell and artists and writers who could paint and describe the natural world were sought-after dinner guests and favored members of high society. They were a source of entertainment as well as new information.

Different explorers told their stories in different ways, each with particular implications about the nature of Nature—what it was and how we should respond to it. Nature became a thing, an object endowed with subjectivity similar to "the king," "the church," or special persons. It was rendered as something definite and tangible. One theme related to the rendering of nature as a subject (Nature) is that Nature is somehow "purer" and more romantic than human existence. Another theme is that, through the study of Nature, we might gain hints about how best to organize and govern human societies. The idea of Nature as a site of purity and perfection can be traced to the Old Testament depiction of the Garden of Eden. In being cast out of the garden, humans were separated not only from God, but from Nature. Interestingly, having now rejected God as a source of knowledge and understanding, Enlightenment philosophers look to Nature as a source of knowledge in the quest to define human experience.

Young Mary's romantic musings about the "peasant" reflect the ideas of French philosopher Jean-Jacques Rousseau. Rousseau popularized the idea of a "noble savage" as a being who existed in a "natural state"—a state that had not been corrupted by the worldly institutions of selfish men and women. In a sort of Enlightenment precursor to modern hippiedom, Rousseau and his fellows suggested that the best societies were those in which persons endeavored to return to their "natural state"—however that might be defined. It is an interesting historical footnote that Marie-Antoinette, the Queen of France at the time that Rousseau's writing was popular, did her part for Nature by becoming an advocate of breast-feeding. She also had a "peasant's garden" built outside the palace at Versailles and lived in it for a time. A bit like modern-day camping.

As romantic as the peasant might be in its pure state, there was still the question of society—what it was, what it could be. Philosophers were inclined to adopt analogs from Nature and use these as a way of deriving definitions of human society. For instance, are we collectively most like a colony of ants, a school of fish, or a herd of elephants? What clues to our own nature and destination might we gain from studying these creatures in their natural habitat? Similarly, what understanding might we arrive at through observing different peoples, especially those who seem "primitive"? The natural sciences and anthropological exploration made great strides during the late eighteenth and early nineteenth centuries. Wealthy patrons financed expeditions and provided places of study for scholars seeking to describe and catalogue Nature.

Can Social Life Be "Seen" With Scientific Methods?

The question of how useful and meaningful the scientific method is for addressing social questions hinges on whether social phenomena are observable. What does social life consist of? Can we see it and measure it in the same ways as we can the physical universe? Many researchers think that the answer is yes. Scientific methods can be applied to social behavior if the focus is on observable human action. We can see people—we have an objective quality that makes our bodies and our actions observable. In some of the first theories developed for observing human behavior through science, human behavior is equated with other natural phenomena. Seeing humans as natural animals and studying them as objects of nature was a development that coincided with the rise of the natural sciences. Up to that point, inquiries about humans and society were considered the domain of philosophy and theology.

Two ideas in particular emerged as a matter of consensus among scholars, financiers and the literati during the ascendancy of Natural Science: the idea that human social life *can* be defined similarly to a natural organism; and the notion that organisms *evolve* into increasingly advanced states. This agreement resulted in a more refined consensus about what questions to ask. The questions of import among social philosophers became: What sort of natural organism is the human being, and what rules of conduct and organization will best ensure evolution? Thus, Mary is perfectly in tune with the times when she expresses delight at the possibilities of gaining a deeper understanding of ourselves and the potential of "civilized" society by comparison with the darker recesses of savagery. As an educated woman of her day, she can likely tell us what the definitional criteria are for establishing an evolutionary hierarchy among various species, including humans. She is probably also familiar with the derivative logic for these scientific definitions and the categories they suggest. For instance, there are logical reasons for cataloging hundreds of thousands of fossils discovered in various expeditions as either vertebrate or invertebrate (having a spine or not). The scientific advantage of such categorization is that it enables interested observers to agree upon what properties the fossils share in common and, from that agreement, derive theories about the nature, purpose and potential of each class. Very scientific.

Using a similar method, Mary's father, a nobleman, is able to make a case for the superiority of the British over the rebellious American colonies. As he puts it, "I demonstrated logically that God gave us the colonies for the sole purpose of advantageous trade. We are interested in their raw materials but not their ideas" (Wertenbaker 1985:9). His distaste for the ideas of the colonists is substantiated and given the weight of consensual authority because he has used the rules of science to classify the differences between and derive conclusions about the relative worth of people. When Mary's father chides her for talking too much about Nature and Reason, she protests, "But it's what people are talking about." He counters, "Yes, but a woman talking about reason is like a merchant talking about nobility. It smacks of ambition." And so she too is put in her place. Despite her obvious talent for the discourse of Reason and Nature, people are reasonable; women, by nature, are not. It's a matter of definition.

By the nineteenth century the idea of Science as the most useful and accepted means of seeking knowledge was cemented. Using the methods of science, observers learned to classify and catalogue the physical world. Like the foreign lands exoticized and colonized by the western Europeans, Nature was a source of mystery and intrigue and was ultimately there to be discovered and conquered for the materials and amusements of those who could afford to do so. The European world had a voracious appetite for knowing, and ultimately taming, the unseen world. It is quite reasonable to interpret the resulting fascination with and exploitation of Nature as a replacement for God as the ultimate source of wisdom and mystery and abundance. These early scientists were as eager to master the secrets of nature as they were awestruck in their quest to understand it. Through the process of cataloging and experimenting, nature was harnessed and new technologies were developed. The success of science is in large part due to a consensus that through the combined methods of categorization, empirical observation and logical deduction, scientists had rendered comprehensible the wild, erratic beast of nature. Predictability and control over this beast has been widely interpreted as progress. Thus science ascended to the throne.

Scientism: The Misapplication
of Scientific Methods to Social Life

The scientific method was conceived in a particular historical context for the specific purpose of introducing a rigorous system for observing and describing nature. Is human social life similar enough to nature to warrant the use of the same method for addressing social questions? It is not immediately apparent that a science developed for observing and describing the natural world is the best method for exploring human social life. Rocks and plants, and perhaps even some forms of animal life, may remain consistent enough in form that the definitions we have for classifying their properties and explaining their actions are valid. One problem with applying scientific methods to social behavior is that social behavior is not necessarily observable in the same way that rocks and plants and animals are. How do you *see* whether someone is a good person? How do you *see* quality of education? How do you observe emotions systematically? If we could reduce "goodness" or "quality education" or "emotion" to standard categories of definition that could be catalogued and counted, would we want to?

A well-known, prolific economist, Friedrich Hayek, has written a book on the topic. The title itself, *The Counter-Revolution of Science: Studies in the Abuse of Reason,* is indicative of his position on the question. Hayek suggests that the "persistent effort of modern Science has been to get down to 'objective facts' " (1952/1979:29). He traces the history of the development of modern natural science as an enterprise that gained a foothold only through overcoming several obstacles of "subjectivity," including the preferred method prior to the scientific age of taking as "fact" whatever prestigious philosophers and theologians had written about the nature of the world. The tendency to want to explain Nature "after man's own image" was another impediment to objective inquiry. These obstacles of "tradition" eventually gave way to a scientific method in which "the main task became to revise and reconstruct the concepts formed of ordinary experience on the basis of systematic testing" (1952/1979:29).

Hayek is quick to point out in his introduction that "nothing we shall have to say is aimed against the methods of Science in their proper sphere or is intended to throw the slightest doubt on their value" (1952/1979:23). His very sharp-tongued critique is leveled at those who have *uncritically* adopted the methods of science for the study of society. This transportation of the scientific method into social studies is, he claims, primarily the result of an "extraordinary fascination" among those working in other fields regarding the success in the biological and physical sciences in observing and cataloging nature. Fascination is a decidedly unscientific basis for the

> slavish imitation of the method and language of Science, [which we shall] speak of as *scientism* or the *scientistic* prejudice . . . a mechanical and uncritical application of habits of thought different from those in which they have been formed. The scientistic as distinguished from the scientific view is not an unprejudiced approach but a very prejudiced approach which, before it has considered its subject, claims to know what is the most appropriate way of investigating it. (1952/1979:24)

The scientific method, which was conceived as an attempt to overcome speculative and traditional methods of describing the natural world, relies on careful observation with the intent of reducing an object or species of nature—a rock, a plant, a bird—to its component factors. These factors can be precisely defined for the purpose of comparing, contrasting, and eventually cataloging and classifying different objects into meaningful categories, such as "species," "genus," and so forth. As Hayek reminds us, any good scientist knows that these categories are mere constructs of the human mind. These constructs must remain open to revision in order to objectively consider new and anomalous data.

Conceptual Ambiguities

Human feelings and expressions and social behavior may not be easy to "see" in an objective form. What about human bodies, how easy are they to classify? An example from Renaissance research on the "nature of the sexes" illustrates the openness of early scientists to revise categories and classification schemes in accordance with new data and ideas. The first scientific or medical studies of the human body, including differences between the sexes, indicate that the biological distinctions that we now take for granted were not at all self-evident to these scholars. Certainly some persons performed traditionally different roles in social life, but what made them different? Was there any natural basis for these expressed social differences? Medical discourses in medieval and Renaissance France suggest that "hermaphroditism" (sexually ambiguous genitalia) was probably the norm. The only described difference in genitalia between men and women is based on heat—a heat that causes the female vagina to "pop out" into the physical equivalent of a penis. We might wonder how they classified other seemingly evident differences such as female menstruation? It is possible that in a culture in which men were encouraged to undergo routine "blood-letting," this was not a recognized difference.

It is especially interesting that as eighteenth-century observers began to detail more specific physiological distinctions between the sexes, the classification that we now take for granted—the idea that there are only two sexes and that one's sex is immutable—was often revised depending on the specific features of the individual case. The records from this period include cases in which persons raised as girls later determined to marry women. In such cases, doctors would examine the persons and declare them male by redefining the "clitoris" as a "small penis." Given that the idea of a gender binary was still evolving, the idea of homosexuality was not even considered (Epstein and Straub 1991).

What I find intriguing about this historical account is the willingness of practitioners of science to revise scientific categories based not only on "evidence" that seemed not to fit the definitional properties of female/male; but the idea that a reexamination of the classification (girl or boy) was warranted when an expressed *social* behavior did not fit the definition. In other words, in almost complete reversal of contemporary practice, if someone behaved in a way that was inconsistent with the natural category to which they had been assigned, then the category was reconsidered. Social behavior was not necessarily reducible to natural categories because it was not assumed that these categories were fixed, real and absolute. They were merely tools of science.

Empirical Observation Versus
Interpretation in Social Research

Suppose you are interested in the question of the quality of your education. Is this a question that can be stated in such a way as to get a uniform answer? How do you answer that question? We could pose the question this way: How many graduates from your college are eventually employed in Fortune 500 companies? This is a precise question to which we can get a precise answer. But would you accept the answer as *useful and meaningful evidence* about the quality of your education? What about the cost of your education? Is this a good way to measure quality?

There is a great deal of discontent regarding the use of scientific methods for social questions. The discontent comes from the dilemma of precision. The scientific method can only be used with precise questions and observable phenomenon—something that can be seen and, one hopes, counted. Although it is possible to observe and classify human behavior in terms of natural science, many scholars have been critical of the practice of doing so. The primary argument against using natural science as a basis for studying human behavior is that the method eclipses, or reduces the complexity of, social life. When human behavior is reduced to observable individual actions that can be classified and catalogued, the *social* is taken out of the picture. Many scholars believe that humans are mostly social creatures. To study humans outside a context of social meaning makes no sense to these scholars. As an alternative to science, they suggest and use methods designed to *interpret* social life. The aim is make sense of the meaning of life rather than to catalogue it.

Nonetheless, the social "sciences" have achieved recognition primarily through studies conducted in accordance with scientific methods. Most research funding is awarded to proposals that follow scientific methods. Graduate students and young scholars who wish to have their work widely recognized are advised to follow these methods. Is the wide use of scientific methods justified in sociological research? Or is it a "slavish imitation" of the natural sciences? Sociology has been criticized for introducing and relying on concepts that have no solid meaning in real life. To some extent, this critique is justified. But does it mean that we should throw out the proverbial baby with the bathwater? When is sociological science, in its classical formulation, justified?

Demographic Research: Useful Science in Sociology

One domain that sociologists excel in is gathering information about observable features of human groups and large populations. Suppose you want to know how many people live in a particular area, how much electricity they use, how many automobiles they drive, what the average price of a house is, and so forth. This sort of information is called *demographic information,* and it can be useful in providing an overall picture, a sort of bird's-eye view, as it were, of masses of people. Most of our everyday encounters with other individuals take place in small gatherings. We may have an idea of what the "big picture" looks like, but this is often just opinion or loose speculation. For instance, do you know the racial composition of students in your college? Do you know how many of the people on your faculty are women? This is not the sort of information that most people have at their fingertips. How would you get this information, assuming that it wasn't available for you to look up? How would you do this sort of counting?

It turns out that getting a bird's-eye view of population dynamics is difficult (kind of like trying to measure the distance between planets before spacecraft were invented). Consider, for instance, how you would count the number of homeless people in a city. Social scientists have developed some very sophisticated and useful methods for gathering this kind of information. Population demographics are observations about humans as a group. The information tells us something about possible patterns and directs us to important questions. For example, we can observe that 51 percent of the adults in the United States are women. We can also observe that only 4 percent of the CEOs of major companies in the United States are women. Sixty percent of the students who get a Ph.D. in sociology are women, but less than 30 percent of the faculty who have tenure in sociology departments are women. This objective information may attract our attention, just as a fault line might in the side of a mountain. Something out of the ordinary appears to be going on. The demographic information is extremely useful in providing a big-picture view of observable social patterns, but the same information can't tell us anything about *why* these patterns occur. For this we need different methods of inquiry.

Reduction and Reification

I find it useful to maintain a distinction between methods of social science that provide information about observable social patterns and the methods that are necessary for making sense of these patterns. It is in this second area that the use of scientific methods is a problem. Consider again the question of "quality" education. You could gather a lot of objective, numerical information about differences between colleges. Cost of tuition, number of students, number of faculty per students, average number of years to degree, and so forth. You could use this information to make comparisons among schools, but can you use it to classify and rank order schools in terms of "quality"? If you wanted to do so, you would have to select one or more of these "countable factors" and use it as a *definition* of quality. Suppose you picked cost of tuition. You could say: Let cost of tuition equal quality of education. Then you would compare colleges in terms of cost of tuition and come up with a rank-ordered list. This procedure meets the qualifications of science. You have provided a precise definition that can be used to classify all schools, and it is a definition that allows you to gather unambiguous evidence. You can be certain that your classification of "quality" schools is accurate. But is it meaningful? Would you decide what school to attend based on your list?

The conundrum in this case is that if you want a scientific list, it is necessary to *reduce* large and significant questions, such as the quality of education, to fragmented elements that can be defined and classified unambiguously and observed in a way that can be counted. It can be done, but the results seem dubious. Much of the criticism of the social sciences concerns concepts and definitions that reduce the meaning and significance of the intended subject. It is true that sociologists have generated many concepts, such as "socioeconomic status," that seem like euphemistic and obscure ways of dealing with volatile social questions. I'm reminded of a character in a novel who was so frustrated with all the meaningless concepts in his sociology textbooks that he began using pages from the texts as toilet paper. This sort of image doesn't give sociology a very good name.

I do think that there is a considerable amount of slavish imitation of science within sociology. This imitation occurs mostly in the use of concepts and definitions that are easy to observe and count, but something about the essence of the subject matter is lost in the process. If asked to do so, a sociologist *can* reduce "quality of education" to an unambiguous, precise, observable definition. "Quality of life" can be measured in terms of "whether you make more money than your parents did" and other such observable, numerical concepts. "Good parenting" can be defined and measured in terms of "number of hours spent with children." Or, my personal favorite, "quality of scholarship" can be defined in terms of "number of publications in top journals." We can create and use these sorts of definitions. We have to if we want to practice sociology as a science, but it's not at all clear that these scientific definitions are meaningful. One of the paradoxes for sociology as a science is that the more we try to render social life in scientific terms, the less significant it becomes. We can pose and answer a lot of questions using scientific criteria. We can generate accurate answers to these questions. But in the process, we may reduce or squeeze out all the meaning.

Sociologists are somewhat guilty as charged on this count, but I don't think that we are entirely to blame for the perpetuation of a slavish imitation of science that detracts from meaningful questions. Much of the problem is the cultural value placed on science as a superior form of knowledge. People trust science. Governments and funding agencies are willing to pay scholars to do scientific research but are suspicious of alternative methods. There is a larger paradox here. We want knowledge and information, and we want it to be simple and unambiguous. The dilemma is that social life is complex, contradictory and ambiguous. To make it simple, we have to reduce the complexity, which means reducing a lot of meaning into simple definitions. The simplest and most precise information is expressed in numerical form. Many people want a numerical answer to a complex question. These numerical answers can be generated, but what happens to the overall meaning and complexity of the subject in the process?

One of the most problematic aspects of an overreliance on the scientific method as a basis for asking and answering social questions is the tendency to take definitions out of the context for which they were intended. Simple definitions intended for a specific scientific question are often adopted into general discussion as if the definition were something of real consequence. This process is called *reification*. Reification is treating as real something that is only a conceptual tool. Your GPA is a concept that consists of the numerical average of all your grades. To what extent do you think of your GPA as a real and significant aspect of who you are? To what extent do others, such as friends, parents, potential employers, treat your GPA as if it means something significant about you? The GPA can be one useful piece of information in *some* contexts, especially in situations where people have additional information, such as the sorts of classes that you took, your study habits, your interests, the abilities and interests of your teachers, and so forth. Taken out of context, the GPA doesn't mean much, scientifically. Yet, people put a great deal of personal emphasis on GPA as the single answer to the very complex question: Are you a good student? More shocking still is the emphasis given to GPA as a single answer to the extremely complex question: Are you a good person, or an intelligent person? This is reification.

As a final consideration of some of the uses and abuses of the scientific method, I turn to a discussion of recent work done by widely respected and well-funded social scientists. As you read this example, look for problems of reduction and reification. Consider whether this is a case of useful science or a case of *scientism*. In pondering the problem of scientism, you might want to think about the relationship between science as an authority versus science as one way of pursuing *some* questions. What's the difference?

Reducing Behavior to Single Factors

Despite the many limitations, the practice of reducing social phenomena to standard, quantifiable categories continues unbroken in social studies. The research that receives the greatest amount of attention and funding and holds the greatest weight of authority in the public mind is that which draws upon natural metaphors, seeks explanations for human behavior in natural causes, and reduces behavior to single, numerical definitions. Questions such as whether or not one is genetically authoritarian, homosexual, or creative, and inquiries into the "natural" distinctions between the sexes, between the rich and the poor, and between races is the sort of stuff that many people, both scientists and lay-persons, consider to be "legitimate" social research.

One such corpus of research that has recently gained national attention is reported in the 1994 book *The Bell Curve*. In their book, two widely published, nationally acclaimed scientists, Richard Herrnstein and Charles Murray, explore the question: Is the consistent difference in reported IQ scores between blacks and whites indicative of genetic differences? In other words, do blacks score lower because they are, on average, genetically less intelligent than whites? Herrnstein and Murray conclude that this is a plausible reading of their evidence. Several researchers, including those who use the methods of science for social research and those who do not, have written responses arguing that Herrnstein and Murray's conclusions are faulty for one reason or another. A frequently cited counterargument is that IQ tests used to measure general intelligence are culturally biased in such a way that the questions are worded to give an advantage to those familiar with middle-class (usually white) experiences. This is a critique that makes sense to an average reader and seems to retain the authority of science. There are several other critiques of the research, but in many cases one has to be well schooled in the logic of statistical methods in order to comprehend the alternative interpretations of the evidence. Several additional dissenting opinions written by well-respected scholars offer a subjective critique; they simply disagree with the political implications of the book. As well-informed and erudite as these critiques might be, they are accorded less general weight because they are not "science."

Paleontologist Stephen Jay Gould has written his own rejoinder to *The Bell Curve*. Gould is a tireless and witty critic who has written several books on the misuses and misapplication of science. According to Gould, the problem underlying the arguments in

The Bell Curve is not science, per se, but the attempt to reduce very complex aspects of human experience, in this case general intelligence, into single factors that meet the scientific criterion of precise and consistent definition. Gould has written an entire book, *The Mismeasure of Man* (1981), in which he attempts to demonstrate, using the language of natural science, that the complexity of human experience is not reducible to single numbers such as IQ. The conundrum for those engaged in social inquiry is that many aspects of social life and human behavior are not easily observable. Like the concept of "witchness," we can only speculate on whether or not something like "general intelligence" actually exists. If we are willing to assume that it does, then the exercise of defining its properties is the next step. But again, there is nothing self-evident in nature that tells us: (1) whether the conceptual feature does exist, and (2) how to define it, if and when we do agree that it exists.

Gould chronicles the invention of IQ. "Intelligence Quotient" was an *idea* constructed by Alfred Binet in 1904 for the very specific purpose of determining whether some school children might be in need of special attention. Binet used a hodgepodge of measures, in part because he was suspicious of any one test or task as a means of determining cognitive ability. His own reticence about the project is noteworthy. As Gould tells it, Binet was worried that people might make too much of this testing and try to use it as an indelible measure by which to judge whether certain children were worthy of education. Binet specifically declined to label IQ as a mark of inborn intelligence, and he refused to see it as a general device for ranking all students. He even refused to speculate about the reasons why some children performed poorly. For Binet, doing so would be the gravest act of nonscience, or projecting his own subjectivity onto the tests. The fact that we have subsequently rendered a scientific tool, IQ, "real" and proceeded to use it as a general measure of ability according to which we rank order people would startle poor Binet out of his grave.

Given that IQ is merely a conceptual reduction of an extremely vast and complex phenomenon known generally as human ability, Gould's rejoinder to Herrnstein and Murray is that it really makes no sense even to speculate about the differences in "general intelligence" between blacks and whites because the actuality of "general intelligence" is highly questionable. L. L. Thurstone, another critic of IQ testing, puts it this way: "different people are talented at different things." The only thing that makes one talent "better" than another, or that renders intelligence as something that can be measured in amounts of "more of or less than" is an agreement among persons that it exists and can be thus defined.

Gould makes a convincing case that among the very scientists who study intelligence, there is no such agreement. The most widely accepted contemporary theories of intelligence suggest that ability and creativity may be expressed in several distinct forms. In making the assumption that real people have real IQs, then attempting to demonstrate that these IQs can be linked to genes, Herrnstein and Murray are barking at a ghost. The question Gould leaves us with is why, given how simple it is to point out that IQ cannot possibly represent the complexity of human intelligence, the general public persists in supporting such conceptual sleight of hand? How many of us have not had an IQ test, or know people who have, and consider that we know something "very real" about ourselves or them as a result? Like Herrnstein and Murray, we may be susceptible to seduction by single, unambiguous concepts that promise to make sense of our complex abilities. But just as a coat thrown over a ghost provides only the illusion of tangible shape, IQ may be nothing more than a fancy gown that pretends to give shape to an otherwise nearly unfathomable human capacity.

The mystery that seduces people, Gould asserts, lies in the math. The logic of IQ as a conceptual category is predicated on a sophisticated method called factor analysis in which hundreds of different items that appear to be related to "intelligence" are reduced to a single definitional dimension by statistical association (even saying that is a mouthful). I was fortunate enough to receive my own training in social research methodology from a man considered to be one of the preeminent social researchers of our day, the only social scientist to be inducted into the American Academy of Science. This man, Hubert (Tad) Blalock, was fond of admonishing us that, "There is nothing to keep us from performing mathematical operations on things that are theoretically meaninglessness." These words of irony from a man who considered himself a scientist are a reminder that just because it can be rendered mathematically—consistent, reliable, predictable as it may be as an exercise in itself—doesn't make something an indicator of reality or even a useful concept.

Consider "love meters" by way of analogy. I'm thinking about those items sitting conveniently on checkout counters or for sale in novelty stores. The device usually consists of some liquid in a small, vertical vial. Below the vial is a place to rest your thumb. When you press your thumb on the spot and leave it there a few seconds the vial changes colors—different colors for different people. By comparing your color with a chart on the side of the vial, you can find out what sort of lover you are: very red = red hot; yellow = unfaithful; clear = shy; blue = melancholy; and so forth. As much fun as it is to do this, most of us agree that the "love meter" does not yield a measure of one's essential qualities as a lover. I'm not even sure there is such a thing as "general lover quality," but science offers me a way to find out.

One thing that I might do to ascertain the qualities of a "general lover" scale is to ask hundreds, even thousands of people to write down the top five qualities that they see in a lover. I might even ask them to rank order these qualities. When I had all these responses in front of me I could study them to see if I noticed any similarities or patterns. For instance, if nearly everyone noted "attentiveness" as a quality, then I could conclude that there was consensus among the people I asked that this was a quality they associated with "lover." (Of course, this emergent definitional property would reflect the particular points of view of the specific group of people that I asked, but it's a start.) If nearly everyone ranked "attentiveness" at the top of their lists, then I might further conclude that this was a very significant feature of "lover."

Having ascertained this quality, my next task would be to figure out how to determine whether or not specific persons are more or less "attentive" and therefore likely to rate highly on my scale of "general lover." What sorts of tests might I construct to measure "attentiveness"? Perhaps I could observe and calculate the amount of time that persons listen to others in conversations. This has the advantage of being something that I can see and also count, thereby giving me a numerical measure—for example, subject X appeared to listen to her grandmother for 30 minutes; subject Y listened to his father for 5 minutes; and subject Z only talks. Based on these observations can I conclude that X is likely to have higher "lover" potential than Y or Z?

If you are savvy in the nuances of scientific observation, you may be arguing with me that it is not possible to tell if someone is really listening just by watching them, or you may be arguing that I need to observe them all listening to the same person, or you may even argue that "listening" is not a very good indicator of whether or not someone is "attentive." All of these arguments would be valid objections in a conversation between scientists who were concerned with the methods for reliably and accurately measuring "attentiveness." But what do you think about my initial attempt to construct a "general lover" scale? How satisfied are you with this method for reducing one of the most ubiquitous, complicated and absorbing experiences of modern human experience into a single factor, one that we might eventually measure as a single number? Why would we even attempt such a thing?

Putting Social Issues Into Boxes

I use the somewhat absurd example of putting social issues into boxes to highlight the question of whether the methods derived for the very particular purposes of conducting natural science are appropriate to the study of human social life. Just as it is possible to state that the factors of 18 are 3 and 6, or 2 and 9, it is possible to claim that certain factors measured as IQ combine to form a concept called "general intelligence" or that "attentiveness" is a factor of "good lover." In order to employ the methods of science rigorously in the study of social life, complex, often ephemeral aspects of human experience *must be reduced to precisely defined concepts*. We may all "know" and agree that the expression of love is something much more vast and complex than "attentiveness," but if we want to study it scientifically, we have to be willing to accept, at least for the moment, that the complexities of the experience can be reduced to a few precisely defined factors. There are many occasions when this may be useful and appropriate, but the question remains, is this process of reduction the singularly best, most informative method for conducting social research? Consider a couple of final examples.

Putting Social Experiences Into Boxes

Which box do you check when you are filling out a form or questionnaire that asks your ethnicity? If you are responding to a form that has been constructed in accordance with the categories of the U.S. Census Bureau, your choices are African American, Asian American, Caucasian, Nonwhite Hispanic, and Native American. Five choices. Can you find your own place easily in this list of selections? When I ask students in my classes to write down their ethnicity as they describe themselves to others, we generally end up with a list of about 20 categories. When faced with a standard form asking them to check a box for ethnicity, many of these students end up checking the residual category, "Other." What does a real "other" look like?

If you are from a multiracial family, you are faced with a choice of leaving out one parent or the other. This not a minor matter in a country in which it is estimated that anywhere from 10 to 30 percent of the population may be racially mixed (it's hard to know how extensive multiracial identification is, given that the boxes allow only one choice). If your father is Chicano and your mother is Japanese American, for instance, which box do you check? Which parts of you do you choose to ignore when you reduce your ethnicity to a single box? I have a friend whose father is a member of the Muskogee tribe and whose mother is black. Whenever my friend, a college professor, is asked to fill in the box on race/ethnicity at the university at which she works, she checks both "African American" and "Native American." The university offices return the form to her and ask her to select one box or the other. If she tells them that she cannot make such a choice, they select one box for her—usually in accordance with whatever minority classification they want to improve the numbers for. The somewhat Monty-Pythonesque consequence of this is that her recorded ethnicity is different from one office to another across campus. Does this mean that she has more than one ethnicity? Does it mean her ethnic identity is constantly changing? I take it to mean that the human experience of ethnicity cannot be reduced to a single box.

For purposes such as looking for patterns in the way that resources are unevenly distributed to some ethnic groups over others, it may make sense to try to count ethnicity. In such cases, reducing ethnicity to single boxes may have some specific utility, but when we engage in this sort of reduction it is important never to lose sight of the fact that we are doing so for a particular purpose. The actuality is that the situation is much more complex than we have rendered it through our single, mutually exclusive, categorical boxes. There are many incidents in which such reduction is not warranted. Yet because it has been the practice for many decades of social research to "count" ethnicity this way, it is often assumed, unthinkingly, that real people actually do fit these boxes. The cost of this exercise in reduction is that we overlook, and sometimes forget altogether, the richly complex, in-depth experiences that constitute "ethnicity" as an aspect of social life. This neglect can also result in the fallacy of reification; we begin to think the categories themselves are real and assume that persons thus defined are no more than the sum total of the categorical definition.

Another example that may resonate for you is the use of standard scores such as GPA and GRE (Graduate Record Exam) test results to represent your entire educational experience. This is another incident of a reduction of complexity that comes at a cost. The purpose of transforming your educational experience into single, standard, easily calcu- lable scores is first and foremost a means of enabling comparison among large numbers of people. Students in any given class, or any specific pool of applicants for graduate or professional schools, are as diverse as a large bowl of fruit, but it's difficult to make "fair" evaluative comparisons between apples and oranges—any preference for one over the other is usually a matter of taste. By reducing educational experiences to single factors on a numerical scale, all the fruit in the bowl can be transformed into the same item and statements such as this apple is larger than that apple can be made. It is the case that this method of standardization yields a less biased basis for comparative decisions than taste. You probably don't want to be evaluated for admission to graduate or professional schools based on whether or not the evaluators like the sound of your name, the school you attended, or similar matters of taste.

The dilemma for the social researcher is whether or not constructs such as GPA and "ethnicity" provide a useful and relevant basis for conducting studies of significant aspects of social experience such as educational opportunity or racism? Ultimately it's a conundrum. A very complex one. Without constructs such as GPA and ethnic boxes we cannot count up and look for patterns in possible differences in whether or not some people tend to get more "educational privileges" than others based on ethnicity. As a social researcher I find this a worthwhile question. In order to arrive at a tentative picture of whether or not this might be the case, I may be willing to give up a complex understanding of the experiences of education and ethnicity. In other words, I may have to reduce these experiences to precise definitional constructs that enable me to count what is going on in large populations. Such an activity has its purpose. The slippery slope into "scientism" and reification begins when I attempt to *explain* any differences that I might observe using these same simple boxes.

Determining whether someone really fits a box can be like trying to determine if someone is a witch. Why do this at all? The reasons for reducing social experiences to simple categories and for cramming people into definitional boxes are usually cultural and political rather than scientific. A careful social observer who uses these conceptual boxes must remain critical of these nonscientific agendas and implications. We must continually ask ourselves what we gain and lose in these processes of reduction.

Conclusions

The cost of the scientific method in social studies is complexity. In order to construct precise definitional concepts we must put aside most of the richness of human experience. In reality, most of us experience social life as something that is shifting, dynamic, ambiguous, and frequently contradictory. This does not mean that there are not observable patterns in social life, but the patterns themselves are likely to be manifest as our *subjective* understanding of our experiences. For instance, most of us who have experienced the process of "higher education" could write volumes about *why* we have the particular GPA that we do—major, types of courses, specific faculty with whom we may or may not be simpatico, the rhythms of our specific bodies (are you just not a morning person?), various family and employment obligations . . . the list is endless. What is interesting to me as a sociologist is the observation that despite these complex explanations, most of us still consider GPA as something "real," something about which we feel pride or shame. How do you explain that? How should we go about the business of making sense of creatures who can simultaneously invent boxes for the purpose of one activity—doing science, and simultaneously "forget" that these boxes are constructs and instead internalize them as reflections of real, personal experiences? I do think that this rather amazing feature of human experience can be described, but probably not using the methods of science as conceived for observing the natural world.

Science expands knowledge and simultaneously limits understanding. In the attempt to reduce ambiguity and to provide single-perspective definitions, the richness and diversity of human experience must be distilled to single common denominators. This process of transmuting differences into calculable uniformities obscures human experience. The meaning gets lost. A goal of science has been to reduce complexity, to find uniformity, to discover the general laws that govern the universe (and thereby perhaps tell us something about who we are and what we're supposed to be doing). In the chapters that follow I have tried to reintroduce some of the meaning and complexity that underlie these topics. Each topic is the basis of ongoing social discussions and debates about very significant social questions. These questions cannot be reduced to simple, precise definitions for which we can gather unambiguous evidence. Be suspicious of claims to the contrary.

Sociology, perhaps more than any other social science, has attempted to grapple with the ambiguities and complexities of human social life. Sociology came into being as a discipline in conversation with nineteenth-century philosophers and scientists intent on reducing this ambiguity into simple patterns. The history of the discipline itself reflects an uneasy teetering between the attempt to simplify the social world into a sort of general social physics and the recognition that social life everywhere is complex, shifting and contradictory. The best sociologists, like the best scientists, proceed with doubt about their theories; we highlight our own confusion and questions and make this ambiguity the subject of inquiry. It makes the way a bit of a thicket, but the outcomes are likely to be more representative of reality as we experience it—shifting, complex and contradictory.

Sociologist Avery Gordon, in a reflection on sociology and ethics, cites the Latin American writer Eduardo Galeano, who has suggested that we conjure social life in terms of "one half reason, one half passion and one half mystery." About this smiling expression of ambiguity, Gordon writes:

> In its most general terms, Galeano's story is about the power to re-narrativize society, to tell social stories in which the world as it is—with its global systems and its local particularities, with its stubborn regularities and its intriguing anomalies, with its overwhelming obviousness and its haunting silences, with its causalities and its hopes—comes out looking differently than it is usually represented by scholars. . . . Classifying, categorizing, or draining the blood out of all that we are trying to describe and explain won't do it. Acting like we're not part of the story won't do it either . . . [the act] is inextricably bound up with the power of the imagination to conjure something out of nothing but reason, passion and mystery. (1997:6)

2

The Case of the Designer Genes

Reconsidering the Nature/Nurture Binary

PARADOX

Why are we the way we are? Why do you think, feel, and act as you do? These are some of the most basic questions in the history of social studies. There are two major ways of answering these questions. One way is "nature," another is "nurture." According to the "nature" perspective, much of what people think, feel, and do is an expression of inborn physiological and biological traits; your behavior is an expression of your basic "nature." Proponents of the "nurture" perspective emphasize the ways in which people learn patterns of thought, feeling, and behavior from their social and material environment. From this perspective, behavior is considered to be shaped by external conditions. These perspectives are not necessarily in opposition, but contemporary discourse tends to pit one against the other in what is frequently referred to as the nature/nurture debate. In fact, there is actually very little disagreement among most biologists and geneticists who study the way in which the human body works. These scientists tend to agree that environment is a major factor in determining how people express their biological and physiological impulses. From a scientific perspective, the idea that nature causes us to behave certain ways is largely a myth. Why do we continue to believe in the myth of naturally determined behavior? One answer is that in this culture there is a tendency to assume that behavior is more real if it is assumed to be caused by natural forces rather than social forces. Also, it is assumed that nature transcends human authority. Defining a behavior as "natural" or "unnatural" is a way of saying that it is right or wrong without having to assume social responsibility for the judgment. As a culture we are also illiterate about the power and prevalence of social forces. We are resistant to the idea that human behavior is shaped in the context of significant groups, especially the definitional value systems of these groups. It is a paradox that people who want to think of themselves as having "free will" prefer to think of their most basic behaviors as being caused by nature. Discussions of gender or race or sexual differences in terms of nature distract us from a critical and responsible understanding of the social history of sorting people into these boxes.

In the most intelligent of races, as among the Parisians, there are a large number of women whose brains are closer in size to those of gorillas than to the most developed male brains. This inferiority is so obvious that no one can contest it for a moment: only its degree is worth discussion.

—Gustave Le Bon (1879)

One is not born, but rather becomes a woman . . . it is civilization as a whole that produces this creature which is described as feminine.

—Simone de Beauvoir (1949)

"There are three kinds of people in the world. Those who know how to count and those who don't." My father watches his grandsons wrinkle their brows trying to figure out this riddle. "That's only two kinds," blurts out the eight-year-old. His older brother, world-wise at age 11, laughs at him. "Grandpa tricked you!" he giggles. The youngest of the three brothers, a five-year-old, takes his cue from his oldest brother and laughs too, but he looks confused. Later I overhear him say to his younger cousin, "You wanna hear a joke? Some people can count and some people can't." He doubles over with laughter while his cousin looks on in bewilderment. My sister shakes her head at her youngest son and announces, "Something's definitely wrong with his funny bone."

Earlier in the week this same five-year-old, my nephew, asked me if I was a boy or a girl. We were driving at the time, returning home from a boating trip. I am the oldest in a family of six girls and one boy. My family likes sports and outdoor activities. I am accustomed to handling boats, hauling heavy equipment and getting wet and dirty. Prior to our departure, my nephew had been helping me load the pickup truck. Now, I glance at him sitting next to me in the cab and see that he is surveying my torn cut-offs, ripped T-shirt and tousled short hair. He is a middle child; two older brothers and a younger sister. He's good at t-ball and other sports. He also likes to play with his sister's barrettes, hair ribbons and clothes. His brothers snicker at this behavior. My sister, his mother, tries to ignore it. Curious about the impetus for the question about what I am, I decide to probe a bit and don't answer directly. Instead I say, "It depends on what I'm doing, sometimes I'm a girl and sometimes I'm a boy." A lightbulb seems to go off in his head as he exclaims, "Like grandpa! He's both too."

I laugh out loud. "Grandpa told you about kissing his elbow, eh?"

My father is a master of ambiguities. When my sisters and I were young he would often attempt to cajole us to do something or other by beginning with the phrase, "When I was a little girl . . ." We would inevitably interrupt, shrieking that he had been a little boy, not a little girl. Not so, he would counter. "I was a little girl until I accidently kissed my elbow one day and turned into a boy." "Was Mom ever a boy?" we would ask delightedly as we contorted ourselves trying to kiss our own elbows. "Mom could be anything she wanted to be," he would reply. Indeed, in his eyes it seemed this was so.

He loved to watch my mother apply her makeup and often complimented her looks. He also insisted that she was the smartest person (not woman) he knew, and he glowed with pride every time she hit a home run (which was frequent) in our family softball games.

My parents held traditional roles in our household economy: My mother was a homemaker and my father a breadwinner. They did not look androgynous, but my dad didn't mind if we "fixed" his hair with our barrettes and bows, and I recall that he did a lot of housework in his three-piece suits. My mother often mowed the lawn, a task that she later passed on to me. She also coached the basketball team for the young women in our church. Girls couldn't play Little League when I was young, but my dad coached a team and let me work as his assistant. I warmed up the players, ran practice and kept the books. The boys respected me because I was the best player and I also owned the best equipment. No one seemed to know what to make of the fact that I wasn't allowed to play officially. No one in my family seemed disturbed, either, when my father let me shave alongside him using a table knife and taught me three different ways to knot a tie.

Is my family confused about gender? Did we fail to realize that there are two kinds in this world, each with a set of related, presumably immutable characteristics? Or did we succeed in providing some opportunity to play out variations on the traditional theme? Despite a comparatively androgynous youth in the realms of sports, academic activity and household chores, my sisters and brother now enact relatively traditional gender roles through traditional marriages. I no longer shave my face, but I do take pride in my abilities to tie a tie and I can still handle any kind of a ball. I can also cook and sew as well as or better than my sisters. But for some reason, they seem to forget this. I've "become" the tomboy. Was I always a tomboy? Can someone be a tomboy in a family in which there is so much play on the traditional gender behavior? Is my markedly different behavior as an adult—for example, my unmarried status, my pursuit of a career, my sexual preference for women—a result of this gender ambiguity? If so, why didn't my six siblings turn out similarly? Am I who I am because of a genetic aberration? Or because, as the oldest child and grandchild, my relatives nurtured me in a way traditionally reserved for the firstborn male child? *What* am I anyway? Which *kind* am I?

The recent family photograph hanging in my parent's living room is a portrait in gender types. The men in their dark suits stand behind the women in dresses, who sit holding children in their laps. The little boys wear ties and the little girls have ribbons in their hair. Has their true gendered nature finally been revealed? Or is the picture indicative of everyday social expectations that write on us, layer upon layer, until, despite myriad differences and complexities, we become frozen in a simple, single, sharply contrasted binary? There is nothing in this photo to suggest my mother and sisters' athleticism or my father and brother's nurturing capacities. Even my lesbian mate and I seem to blend into this composition. Am I looking at an exposure of pure, natural gender or a social institution?

Nature/Nurture: A Problematic Dichotomy

Do you wonder why you are the way you are? How have you come to have certain special talents? What's the source of your particular tastes and desires? Do people remark that you seem more or less like one parent or another? What does this sort of remark mean? That you have inherited the talents, temperaments and tastes of a family member, or that you have picked up similar characteristics and behaviors over a lifetime of similar experiences and exposure? Do people attribute certain skills and behaviors to your ethnicity, such as getting good grades and being of Asian lineage? Or excelling at sports and being of African or Native lineage? Do you see yourself as a compilation of bones, blood and tissue that have formed in unique ways because of your particular DNA structure? Or do you consider yourself an expression of the sum total of experiences (known and unknown) that constitute your unique existence? Or some combination of both?

One of the most enduring questions in the study of human behavior is why people are the way they are. In response to this riddle, science offers two kinds of answers: nature or nurture. The biological sciences focus on organic and physiological characteristics, the social sciences emphasize factors such as language, and material and cultural environment. Both branches of science are interested in the relationship between nature and nurture and human development and behavior. A curious development in the study of human behavior has been a tendency to insist that certain behaviors are shaped entirely by nature. For instance, it is commonly assumed that race and ethnicity are primarily physiological characteristics of difference, or that intelligence and athleticism are inborn traits. The related assumption is that inborn (natural) traits are immutable—nature makes someone a certain way and this can't be changed over time regardless of social and environmental conditions.

The reasons for the overemphasis on nature and the underemphasis on nurture as determinants of human behavior are ideological rather than scientific. Most scholars of biology, psychology and sociology agree that behavior is a complex combination of genetic codes and environmental factors. An interesting question, one that I will take up in this chapter, is why, if scientists agree more than they disagree, has the debate about the influences of nature and nurture become so convoluted? I suggest two main reasons. One is the tendency to convert concepts of biological nature into ideological statements of Natural Law. This is a practice called "naturalism." Another reason is a basic cultural illiteracy about forces of socialization. A common assumption is that "nurture" means free choice—a choice to be whatever you want, to behave however you wish. This kind of thinking reflects a lack of understanding about the web of social forces in which behavior is shaped and expressed. I will explore both these factors in detail. Following a discussion of some of the differences that comprise the nature/nurture debate, I explore "gender" as an example.

Classifying Nature

The biological, or natural, sciences emerged as an endeavor to catalogue and classify various species of plant and animal life (see Chapter 1). A driving interest in these pursuits was the classification of humans as a species: How are we similar and dissimilar to other species? Early natural scientists would identify a feature that seemed integral to the human being and then compare the presence or absence of this feature in other species. Thus, one of the first classification systems was based on the simple distinction between animals that have a spine and those that don't (vertebrate/invertebrate). Once species were sorted according to this distinction, naturalists would then look for additional features that seemed to be present in one group and not the other. In this way, scientists used empirical observation to isolate and identify features that are unique to humans. You probably recall learning that upright posture and an opposable thumb are descriptive characteristics of humans; that our closest "relatives" in the animal kingdom are apes. Apes share many physical features with humans; the lack of an opposable thumb is an observable difference.

In this century natural scientists, including some anthropologists and psychologists, have extended this type of analysis to an interest in forms of social organization: Which species live in groups, keep their offspring close to them for a number of years, select mates, engage in acts of dominance/submission and so forth? Again, this form of cataloguing proceeds from assumptions about human social organization—humans live in groups and provide early nurturance for their offspring—and then focuses on similarities and differences across species.

Nurture

There is another basis for making sense of human behavior, for addressing questions of why we behave as we do and the moral implications of this behavior. This basis of explanation is referred to as the "nurture" theory. The social sciences developed alongside the natural sciences—indeed, there was little initial differentiation; both were considered branches of philosophy. Anthropologists pursued an interest in characteristics that seemed uniquely human—specifically language and cultural organization. The human capacity for language enables us to transcend the immediate physical environment. You may be sitting in a chair reading this page right now, but because you can think conceptually (a language-based skill), you can imagine that you are doing something else. In this way you literally talk to yourself about being elsewhere. Because of this capacity we can tell one another things about the physical environment, such as, "stay away from that fire, it will burn you." We do not have to experience the burn of the fire directly in order to learn to avoid it. Culture can be defined as a shared body of knowledge, expectations and practices that members of a group pass on to one another. Passing on cultural knowledge through language means that individuals do not have to experience things directly in order to learn about them. For instance, even though you have never encountered one directly, you have probably been taught to be afraid of bears. If you are hiking in the woods and suspect that bears might be present, your behavior—wearing bells, talking loudly, keeping food wrapped up—is based on the fact that you have been told to avoid bears and what to do to avoid them. This is cultural knowledge.

This focus on human culture led one philosopher, Ernst Cassirer, to conclude that "physical reality recedes in direct proportion to symbolic activity." Symbolic activity refers to language and culture. What Cassirer means is that even though humans are biological creatures who live in a natural world, the capacity for language and culture shapes how we behave and respond to the world. We do not respond directly to a physical stimulus, but rather indirectly through how we have learned to think about the stimulus. In the presence of a bear in the woods a person is likely to experience an increased heart rate, shortness of breath and other symptoms that we associate with fear. If we took a blood sample, we would find increased levels of adrenaline present in the person. This leads us to conclude that the body has a physical reaction (fear) to the bear, but we would think it silly to conclude that the body—our biology—caused us to be afraid of the bear. In fact, we also know that we can cause the same physical reaction in people by showing them scary movies about bears. In this case, it is the symbolic idea of a bear, not nature itself, that produces the biological response of fear. We have learned to be afraid of the idea of a bear.

It is a long leap from cataloguing physical differences to making claims that biology causes social behavior. Yet one of the most enduring debates in contemporary society revolves around the question of whether what we do and who we are is determined primarily by our nature—our specific physiological characteristics—or by the material and social circumstances of our upbringing, our nurture. Contemporary arguments about nature versus nurture are further complicated in that several additional issues are conflated into the concepts of "nature" and "nurture." Yet the fact is that for many social and biological scientists there is very little debate. Human behavior is seen as a combination of both physiological properties and material and cultural factors.

Early natural scientists were interested in cataloguing nature. For the most part they were not interested in using classification schemes to make pronouncements about morality. And they certainly made no claims that biology determined behavior. For example, it would have been ludicrous to claim that having an opposable thumb caused humans to write. Rather, the presence of an opposable thumb facilitates writing; what we write and how we write it is a cultural accomplishment. Consider further that a person born without thumbs can still learn to read written text. She may have a limited physical capacity to engage in the act of writing, but she can still participate fully in a culture in which the primary form of communication is based on written language.

"Nature Hints, It Doesn't Determine"

When I was an undergraduate studying biology we were required to learn the dictum, "Nature hints, it doesn't determine" and to recite it often as a sort of pledge against committing the fallacy of confusing social forms of organization with biological structures. As I noted in the first chapter, early scientific study was fettered by a tendency to attribute anthropomorphic intentions to natural phenomena. Explaining a storm as an expression of an angry god is an example of anthropomorphism. Explaining the spread of HIV viruses as God's vengeance against homosexuals is a similar form of scientific fallacy. The inverse of the fallacy, which is equally unscientific, is to attribute a social phenomenon to natural causes. This is the fallacy that the dictum warns against. It would be silly, for instance, to say that "nature" causes us to play football. It is possible, however, that a natural event, such as snow, may provide us with a hint that we won't be playing football on a particular day. It is also possible that a child who is robust in build might make a good linebacker. Does this mean that nature *intends* the child to be a linebacker? Is a child's girth the best indicator of whether he will excel at football? Physical size may play a role, but it is only one of many interconnected factors such as diet, training and opportunity that will determine whether a child becomes a professional football player. One thing that is certain, at least at this moment in history, is that a girl child is not likely to become a professional football player. Is this because nature has determined that girls cannot play football or is this the result of social tradition?

Biologists are among the first to suggest that most physiological characteristics in humans are triggered by environmental factors. Environmental factors include external physical variables such as the quality and type of food eaten, and social variables, such as living conditions and learning conditions. Even when a genetic basis for a particular illness can be isolated, biologists are quick to point out that living conditions are what trigger the manifestation of the illness. The relationships among genetic structure, material conditions and social structure are highly complex. What does appear certain, at least to the leading geneticists working to study the human genome structure, is that "the harder we work to demonstrate the power of heredity, the harder it is to escape the potency of experience." Many characteristics that have long been associated with genetics are now being shown to be shaped by environment. For example, several studies conducted by biologists and psychologists have demonstrated that an environment full of toys and complex play structures increases synaptic response levels in the brains of infants. This means that the complexity of the learning environment appears to shape intelligence. The point, according to these scientists, is that the more we look, the more things like talent and intelligence appear to be extraordinarily malleable through social conditioning. In the words of one genetic psychologist, William Greenough, "To ask what's more important, nature or nurture, is like asking what's more important to a rectangle, its width or its length."

The Authority of Values

If scholars of biology, psychology and sociology agree more than they disagree about the influence of "nurture" in shaping the development and expression of natural characteristics, then why the debate? In order to understand the complexities of the nature/nurture debate, it is useful to consider the relationship between theories of behavior and ideals of behavior. Theories of behavior attempt to describe *how* people are and *what* they do. Ideals are statements of value that suggest the ways in which people *should* behave. Historically, theories of behavior have been closely associated with ideals for behavior. Ideals prescribe which behaviors are "good" and "bad" according to a society's accepted cultural practices. Theories of behavior often provide support or authority for these ideals.

Some theories may serve as an underlying story or rationale that grants authority to value systems that proclaim certain behaviors and ways of being as expected and acceptable and others as deviant and unacceptable.

For instance, a central theoretical proposition of the nineteenth and twentieth centuries is that humans are "rational beings" who are self-aware, who can take note of their own actions and understand the consequences and who can exercise restraint over their own desires and impulses. This theory of "rational behavior" is the basis for a moral-political system whereby the ideal is that each person retain as much liberty as possible, so long as he or she does not trespass against the liberties of another. Morally and politically we are held accountable for our own actions based on the theory and observation that we are beings who are capable of taking responsibility for our own actions.

Those who cannot manage themselves—who, for example, kill and maim others without remorse, or those who have behavioral conditions that lead them to violate laws unwillingly, such as those with certain forms of schizophrenia—are deemed mentally incompetent. The moral authority of the ideals of "social competence" are rooted in theories that we *are* capable of exercising self-control in the interest of others. The legal verdict of "incompetence" is rooted in this same authority. The "incompetent" is not subject to the same legal and moral expectations, because he or she is deemed incapable of comprehending and acting on those expectations. The person's behavior is seen as "abnormal" and this abnormality is the basis for explaining deviant actions. Such persons are not subject to the same punishments as those who "willfully" violate moral and legal expectations (the former "can't help themselves"), but they are also not granted full personage—they do not have full rights and freedoms within the moral system precisely because they are deemed behaviorally (fundamentally) incapable of following the rules of social membership.

The moral-political system of ancient master-slave societies provides another example of a theory of behavior that justifies cultural practices. In this case, claims of natural limitations were made to support cultural hierarchies. According to the accepted theories of human behavior at the time, entire groups of people were assumed to be animal-like and others were assumed to be of a "higher mind"—a mind capable of reasoned social behavior. Depending on the group into which one was born, one was either a "slave" or a "master." Masters, it was theorized, had more developed intellects and a propensity toward being "virtuous." Slaves, like pets, were deemed incapable of behaving in a civilized and virtuous manner. These societies held masters responsible for their slaves in much the same way as one would be responsible for a pet. The theories of behavior that divide people into "higher" or "lesser" minds justify a social system whereby certain people have full rights of citizenship and personal freedom and others have no rights.

In both cases, personal rights are granted to those who are deemed capable of acting in accordance with prevailing moral codes. Those who can distinguish between "good" and "evil" and who are able/willing to act accordingly, are considered to be appropriate models of behavior. Thus, an age-old philosophical question has been the distinction between "good" and "evil." In some systems of belief, "good" and "evil" are values that are unchanging—the same rules apply to everyone, everywhere, all the time. In other systems, "good" and "evil" are not constants, but are "functional values" that reflect particular historical circumstances. In both cases, the prevailing question is the authority of the values: Who or what determines these values? This is perhaps one of the most enduring and challenging questions of history. Two primary authorities in modern history are "God" and "nature." The dictum, "Have faith in God's word," suggests that God, a transcendent being, will reveal what is right and good. The contention, throughout modern history, has been how to know God's word. Who has the authority and the right to interpret and speak for God?

In the first chapter I discussed the replacement of God with Science as the prevailing authority for describing the nature of the universe and the human place in it. Recall, for example, that when Galileo used mathematics as an alternative system for explaining the nature of the universe, he concluded that the earth revolved around the sun. This statement was at odds with the belief that the sun, and everything else, revolved around the earth. This was a central belief in the moral system of the day. To state otherwise, regardless of the supposed accuracy of his mathematics, was willy-nilly to imply that the entire cultural system was in doubt. This was unacceptable (or perhaps inconceivable), and Galileo was made to choose between taking back his "scientific" assertion or losing his head. Galileo publicly renounced his science and kept his head. This example shows how prevailing systems of belief grant authority to certain claims about what "is" and what "isn't." Science was a heretical upstart at the time of Galileo, and although, as I discussed in the first chapter, it later ascended the throne to become the basis for contemporary moral authority, the hegemony of Science continues to be infused with ideals of God as an ultimate authority for what we are and how we should behave.

Science achieved its position as philosophers (including theologians) looked for new ways to discern God's word. Recall that during the Renaissance there was a growing dissatisfaction with the prevailing statements of God's word as revealed to priests. These priests were seen to be in the service of the nobility, and God's word, as they interpreted it, seemed to serve the same interests. The rising middle class sought to equalize the moral foundations of society, to usher in a liberal democracy, by claiming that God's word was available to "any man of reason." These scholars looked to nature as a potential source for discovering God's intentions. Nature was seen as a larger force, something transcendent and less changing than human behavior. If patterns could be discovered in nature, they might reveal God's wishes and secrets—His plan for the universe and our place in it. Thus Nature took on a special significance, and the search for patterns in Nature (i.e., early science) was done in the name of discerning God's will more directly than through the revelations of an elite priestly caste. Science, in its initial conception, was the handmaiden of God.

Vestiges of this tradition have carried over into the late twentieth century wherein there is an intriguing, and not always happy, marriage between Science (i.e., the study of Nature) and God. These are a couple of the twists in the recent history of Science/Nature as the basis for understanding, and subsequently legitimizing, certain behaviors.

Nature as Value-Neutral. Nature was appealing as a place to look for answers to big questions, such as how the world works and what our place in it is, because it was assumed to be free of preexisting values and interests. Nature was not subject to human preconceptions. Thus, to the extent that we can free our minds of existing notions, and look, without culturally colored glasses, upon Nature, we will find universal and unchanging "truths." In the first chapter I discussed the difficulties in this endeavor—attempts to describe the way things are, including natural patterns, always reflect preexisting assumptions—but it is the legacy of this practice that concerns us here. This legacy includes a quest to establish certain patterns as being "natural"—the idea that there are certain natural propensities and that these propensities, once "discovered," are indicative of a universal natural order. The second outcome of this legacy is the notion that the "functional values" of our society can and should be ascertained in terms of these "natural laws." Who we are and what we should do and be can be sorted out in accordance with patterns observed in Nature. Nature will reveal "good" and "evil." If Nature stands outside human judgment and biases, then it is assumed that Nature offers a potentially "fair" basis for establishing moral laws. In this way, behaviors once described as good or wicked come to be considered as "natural" (normal) or "unnatural" (abnormal).

Nature as an Expression of God. Another twist is the notion that Nature is God's way of telling us how things should be. Natural events, such as weather and animal behaviors that we cannot control through human will, are deemed larger than life and therefore indicative of the will of a higher being. Many persons refer to natural events as testimonies of God's will. These statements are not necessarily based in the methods of scientific observation, but they mimic the authority of science by making claims based on nature. Natural events such as plagues, earthquakes, floods and the like are sometimes used as "evidence" that God is upset with people. For instance, Evangelist Pat Robertson recently preached that the occurrence of fires and other natural disasters was evidence of God's dislike of homosexuals. The mere utterance may strike many as foolish, but it's worth wondering why so many people do believe these seemingly ridiculous claims. It is still common for people to believe that the HIV virus is God's punishment of gay men, just as there are those who continue to believe that dark skin pigment is the "curse of Cain."

It is easy to say that such claims are a misappropriation of natural science, but this doesn't help to explain the fact that many similar claims have long held sway in contemporary Western culture based on the authority of natural science. For instance, it took a couple of centuries before practitioners of science were willing to question the claim that women were "naturally" incapable of reason (and therefore unworthy of voting and holding property).

Currently, there is an uneasy union between the scientific study of nature as a basis for understanding human behavior and interpretations of God's will as a basis of moral authority. Some of the intricacies of this tradition are revealed in a scene from the movie *Contact.* In this film, Jodie Foster stars as an earnest and energetic scientist who has managed to make contact with an alien world. The aliens have sent instructions for building a device that will enable someone from Earth to travel to the alien realm. This discovery has stirred considerable interest among everyone on Earth. Defense personnel worry about the threat to Earth's security. Scientists are riveted on the possibilities for expanding knowledge of the galaxy. The president is concerned with public relations. A tension in the film revolves around the selection of the person who will make the trip in the alien device. Jodie Foster, as the scientist who made the discovery, would seem to be the rightful choice. However, there is a concern expressed by religious leaders around the world that her agnostic stance toward God and religion will render her incapable of knowing the "truths" revealed when she encounters the aliens.

Foster represents the supposedly "value-neutral" science of the modern age. Her claims to the rights of further exploration are founded on the presumed universality of science to discover and represent truths that apply to everyone. When questioned by a hearing committee about her suitability for the mission, she refuses to state a belief in God. Her contender for the position, another scientist, slickly tells the panel that of course he believes in God and that he believes in science as a path toward revealing the mysteries of God. On the basis of this statement, he is chosen for the mission. He represents the science-cum-religion tradition that undergirds the political, moral system of our time. This union has resulted in a sort of mishmash of ideologies masquerading as science. Such a tradition doesn't yield "objective" answers to the questions of who and what we are. Rather it reflects existing cultural beliefs and ideological prescriptions about who we should be and what we should believe, but dresses them up in the authority of science and calls them "good." This tradition is manifest in various cultural practices that are based in what has come to be called Natural Law, or "naturalism."

Naturalism equates normality with morality and presumes that the basis of authority for this moral order is natural. Nature, in this sense, is seen as a manifestation of God's will. Thus, the moral equation becomes:

normal = natural = moral
abnormal = unnatural = immoral

The Legacy of Natural Law

The ideology of Natural Law is usually promoted by those who seek a justification for the perpetuation of social hierarchies—a means of justifying the status quo without taking any responsibility for it. Social Darwinism is one example. In nineteenth-century England rapid social changes and industrialization had resulted in mass poverty. People were, quite literally, dying in the streets for want of the price of a piece of bread. Social Darwinism was a philosophy that proposed that those at the bottom of the social heap were there because they were naturally inferior. This philosophy appealed to the upper classes because it absolved them of any responsibility for the poor. Rather than see extreme poverty as a result of social-economic practices wherein employers had to exploit laborers in order to make a profit, the newly emerging business classes turned to a philosophy of Natural Law to justify the expanding inequities in industrial society. The poor couldn't be helped because they were, by nature, not "fit" for industrial society.

This philosophy did not emerge from scientific evidence. It did, however, prompt some scientists to seek evidence in its support. Studies of head size and body type became popular during this time. The assumption was that persons of higher intelligence and ability had certain physical characteristics that were markers of their higher breeding and potential. These studies have since been thoroughly debunked, but this did not stop the study of several related, equally ludicrous explorations into "natural differences."

Tendencies. Another feature of Naturalism is a focus on the individual biological entity rather than the social entity. Behaviors that are defined as social expressions in many other cultures have, in our scientific culture, become defined as manifestations of individual biological *tendencies.* Someone who does not have enough to eat relative to others in a culture may steal food. Stealing can be explained as a behavior that reflects social position and circumstances (a social expression), or as an expression of individual tendencies. The nature/nurture debate is predicated on a shift that emphasizes individual tendencies as a basis for explaining behavior. This shift was accompanied by developments in medical and psychological sciences that seek explanations for behavior at the individual level. One consequence of this shift is that a person's behavior, no matter what the context, is assumed to be a revelation of personal tendencies. These "tendencies" in turn are used to make attributions about personality and identity. Someone who steals may have a biological tendency to steal and probably has a "thief" personality. The hungry person who stole food becomes a "criminal identity." When the emphasis is on tendencies and personality traits, explanations for behavior are sought at the level of the individual—outside of social and environmental context. Thus we find ourselves debating what it is that "makes someone a criminal" (genetic disposition? bad mothering?) rather than asking under what conditions might crime be likely to occur?

Historically, this line of reasoning has been used to explain the behavior of those who do not fit prescribed social norms. Scholars attempted to measure the physical differences between criminals and law-abiding citizens. Criminals, it was hypothesized, would be more ape-like in appearance. Breaking the law was considered an expression of an "atavistic" or underdeveloped human physiology. People stole, for instance, because they were animal-like, not because there was mass poverty and unemployment.

One nineteenth-century criminologist made quite a name for himself and for criminological studies as a science by positing a thesis that related body types to a propensity to engage in criminal behavior. Lombroso reported correlations that indicated a relationship between a mesomorphic body type (compact, muscular) and violent crimes. Much ado was made of these correlations, and persons were held to be more or less likely offenders depending on their body type. (The esteemed, presumably noncriminal body type was the endomorphic, or long, lean body frequently observed among white Anglo-Saxon aristocratic people.) The theories fell by the wayside when it was demonstrated that the correlations were largely spurious—the presumed pattern disappeared when other factors, such as living conditions and the way in which the measurements were made, were taken into account.

A similar theory put forth at the time but since dismissed as ridiculous was the *atavistic* theory of prostitution (certain persons are more primitive or "atavistic"). Prostitutes, like other socially defined criminals of the day, were generally believed to be less advanced in their civil development. This presumed lack of a civilized temperament was attributed to primitive development. In support of this theory, researchers looked for physical signs that the person was less developed as a human being. The popular method of the day was to measure the distance between the big toe and the second toe on the feet of prostitutes. These measurements were intended to indicate that prostitutes had feet more like those of apes than humans.

Early arguments against women's rights were based in similar philosophies of "natural differences." Women, it was popularly assumed, were biologically incapable of rational thought and were therefore undeserving of the rights of full personage. One of the legacies of Western colonization has been the perpetuation of the idea that colonized peoples (i.e., anyone who was not of Saxon or Anglo descent) were "savages" and, as such, also physiologically incapable of higher thought and civilization.

In hindsight, these theories may seem silly. The political and cultural legacies prompted by these ideas have had a profound influence on contemporary society, however. The idea that certain people are less than human and are therefore not entitled to full rights and protections of citizenship is a direct implication of the philosophy of Natural Law. This ideology has been commonly used to justify the domination of one group over another throughout history in terms of class, race, gender. Persons are assigned roles and this is justified by claims that these roles represent the "natural order of things." In accordance with Natural Law, if people refute these role assignments, they are acting in disharmony with nature. Women or slaves seeking emancipation, for instance, were frequently denounced as an "affront against nature."

We cringe at the idea of Hitler experimenting on certain groups of people and exterminating others in accordance with the belief that they were a natural threat to the "master race." Yet the ideals of White Supremacy and other forms of natural superiority continue to creep into contemporary politics and cultural agendas. Whenever we seek to establish "natural differences" as a basis for explaining intellectual and social abilities, we fall prey to the ideology of Natural Law. Current manifestations of Natural Law ideologies include ongoing studies that endeavor to establish "natural differences" in abilities between racial groups and between men and women. In a contemporary liberal society it is tempting to assume that such studies of "difference" simply reveal the distinct natures of certain groups and individuals, but the legacy of Natural Law continues to rear its ugly head every time these presumed "natural differences" are used as justification to limit social resources for particular persons who are deemed not just different, but "naturally inferior." Natural Law language is used to justify limiting social programs intended to level the playing field for groups that have been historically disadvantaged, and is used to argue against behavioral/cultural practices that violate existing norms.

The insidious reality of Natural Law ideologies is that they provide a handy excuse for some groups of people to insist that they have more privileges than others because "nature intended it this way." The master is entitled to the slave, a man may dominate his wife, one ethnic group may suppress another, governments may refuse assistance to some people on the grounds that "we are acting in accordance with natural law." This sort of thinking props up the status quo and justifies inequities without requiring any responsibility among those who benefit from the inequities. It cuts off discussion and debate by claiming authority vested in a "higher power," Nature, a "nature" presumed to reflect the will of God or some similarly transcendent system of values. Naturalism is the trump card of social politics.

Biological Versus Social Patterns
of Difference: An Example of Gender

In the following section I explore gender as an example of behavioral practices that are largely social, but that we tend to think of as "natural." The evidence that gender is a social behavior—a series of expressions and practices molded and shaped by cultural expectations—is quite compelling. Yet, this evidence is frequently ignored or altered to fit arguments to the contrary. These counterarguments are more ideological than scientific. One observation that is increasingly clear but also highly contentious is that gender is probably not a binary in the way that we have learned to think of it (boy/girl), but rather a spectrum of expressions variously linked to social and biological roles. There is also ample evidence to make the case that gender is not a fixed physiological feature, but rather a malleable, changing state of being. These observations prompt discussion about the rationale for the continued study of "natural differences" between males and females. They also raise questions about the presumed connection between biological reproduction, gender behavior and sexuality. Are these all manifestations of the same physical characteristics and propensities, or do they reveal cultural systems for sorting people and regulating behavior? If the evidence points toward a cultural basis for these behaviors, then how much sense does it make to treat culturally deviant behaviors, such as homosexual or transgendered practices, as "unnatural" and to seek natural causes as explanations? I will explore each of these themes.

Contemporary gender theories are similar to theories regarding the earth's position in relationship to the sun during the time of Copernicus and Galileo. Just as Earth-centered philosophies were pivotal during the sixteenth century, "gender" is a foundational cultural pillar in current society. Almost everything that we understand about who we can be and how we can behave in contemporary society is linked to systems of gender—gender behavior, gender identity, gender roles. Studies that examine the basis of gender (nature or nurture) tend to be rooted in unquestioned existing cultural beliefs that assume gender reflects a natural binary and, in many cases, a natural hierarchy. Truly "scientific" studies of gender behavior would scrutinize these assumptions. One thing that gets in the way of this scrutiny is the continued belief in the natural reality of a gender binary.

The good scientist questions the most basic of assumptions in order to formulate alternative perspectives on a subject. In this chapter I intend to question some of the taken-for-granted assumptions that form the basis of our belief that gender is an expression of nature. I have picked the case of gender because of its current relevance and also because gender is arguably one of the human expressions that we are most convinced is natural. If you are like many thoughtful people, as you read this chapter you will be inclined to quibble with observations that gender behavior is a social expression. When you find yourself in this state of mind, remember the first dictum of science, which is to proceed in doubt. In presenting this case, I overstate the evidence for "nurture" in order to raise doubt and foster questioning about the extent to which we have assumed, unquestioningly, that gender is a natural phenomenon. This lack of questioning and underemphasis on evidence for the social construction of gender is a decidedly unscientific approach.

Gendering Nature

Imagine that you had to fit everyone in the world into either a square box or a round box. After you had done this, you were told to do research on the differences between the "squares" and the "circles." Suppose, for example, you noticed that the squares seemed to perform better on certain math tests than the circles. Would you conclude that being a square caused one to perform better? Or would you conclude that it was something about being in the square box that caused persons in that box to perform better? What's the difference? In the first case, you are saying that there is something essentially different about being a square. To make this argument, you have to make a case for why you put people into the square box to begin with. What was the essential difference? In the second conclusion, the reasoning is that there is something about the box itself that may shape the experiences and behavior of those placed in it. For instance, perhaps only persons in the square box had been allowed to go to school. In either case, you have to be able to give a plausible answer to the question, What criterion did you use to sort people into the boxes?, before you can go about making arguments for differences between them. It would not be acceptable to say, "Nature grouped them that way."

Ironically, most studies that report evidence of "natural differences between the sexes" assume that gender itself is a real and fixed binary in nature. In other words, it is taken for granted that there are only two boxes and that nature does the "sorting." Given this assumption, many researchers often don't bother to define what they mean by "the sexes." They simply assume that the binary gender box is natural. This is one problem in the scientific assessment of gender differences. Another problem is a logical error committed by those who try to present evidence for the "naturalness" of the gender binary. The evidence in these arguments is based on ad hoc, or tautological, reasoning. In other words, the researchers study people who are already in the boxes and then try to make the case that because people are in these boxes, the boxes are an expression of nature.

Within the social sciences, the nature/nurture debate on gender is an argument about whether or not certain gendered abilities and characteristics are a result of biological coding or social learning. For instance, do boys excel at sports relative to girls because they are boys, or because in our culture boys are encouraged to play sports and girls are discouraged from sports? Are women naturally more nurturant of and attendant to children because of their female biology or because these skills are repeatedly stressed as a desirable activity for women? In making a case for nature, the researcher would have to show that people in the boy box do better at sports even when people in the girl box are given the same opportunities to do sports. Similarly, a researcher would have to show that women turned out to be better nurturers even when men were given the same training and held to the same expectations as women regarding playing with dolls, tending children and so forth. It turns out that it is very difficult to provide this sort of proof. In a culture that is saturated with gendered expectations, it is difficult to sort out nature from nurture. The proof that does exist seems to support the side of nurture, especially in domains such as sport, mathematical ability, management skills and other domains traditionally attributed to men. To the extent that women receive equal training and opportunity, gender differences fade away in these arenas.

Some might be inclined to quibble that there are real physical differences in body height, size, weight and agility. Indeed, this is so; but these differences are not necessarily differences of gender so much as they are differences in physical features among all persons. Whether or not these differences mark natural differences that separate men from women, in the same way as say, adults can be physically differentiated from children, remains uncertain. Height and weight are a function of diet and life activities as much as they are a function of genetics. It is a fallacy to assume, for instance, that a group of people who have been, for decades, smaller in stature than another group who eat a better diet, are skinny because nature intends them to be. Observable differences between women *as a group* and men *as a group* do not imply that these differences reflect an intended natural (biological) pattern.

Another significant observation, one that is often overlooked, is that many individual men and many individual women engage in similar physical activities. Many women, for example, excel at sports. Many men do not. The social expectation that men play sports and women don't confounds this observation. In fact, what is noteworthy from a "nature" perspective is that many people seem to act in discordance with the expectations for their assigned gender. And we have names for this; boys who don't like physical activities are sissies, girls who do are tomboys. Is this nature talking or nurture? If athleticism is about body type, in part, then we might more accurately group people as "sporty/nonsporty" rather than assign an expectation of "sportiness" based on presumed natural differences in gendered bodies.

Despite the evidence and the increasing awareness that the expression of biological traits, including gendered characteristics, is intricately tied up with material and social conditions, researchers continue to fish for evidence that supports "natural differences." As with the case of race, these research agendas are often politically motivated rather than scientifically based. The theme that I emphasize here is that the whole debate about "natural differences" is misguided and unscientific. My logic is based on the assertion that the boxes by which we sort people are social constructions, not natural phenomena. The claim that gender is a social construction does not make the experience of gender any less real. It does imply that the differences imputed to gender reflect cultural patterns rather than natural forces.

Biological Reproductivity as the Basis of Difference

Imagine that your entire social existence was shaped according to the city of your birth. Your main identity might consist of being a San Franciscan or an Atlantan or a Muscovite or Berliner or São Paulan. You would have other social statuses, but this would be your primary one. Everything else would follow from this. In your early years you might be expected to socialize only among "your own." In your adolescence you might be expected to travel a bit and eventually to find someone from another city to settle with. Your life aim would be to reproduce the cultural traditions of your city. Would you be punished if you wanted to make a home with someone from your own city or if you chose to practice the cultural traditions of another city? You might be taught that it is "natural" to want to protect, pass on and nurture the city of your birth. Most animals don't wander too far from their initial habitat. Would this be considered acceptable evidence in favor of the ideology that sorted you primarily by city of origin and entreated you to organize your life accordingly?

Gender differences as a primary means of sorting persons are rooted in the cultural assumption that our primary interests and activities revolve around reproduction of our physical bodies. Attempts to "biologize" human behavior (to construct biological explanations for human organizations) are rooted in two unquestioned assumptions that have been derived from evolutionary theories of natural selection. The first assumption is that the primary natural drive of all individuals (animal or human) is physical reproduction. The second assumption is that biological sex is the primary distinction within a species. The conclusion is that nature intended us, first and foremost, to be breeders. Given this, our primary understanding of who we are and our role in social organizations is based on our role in the breeding process. Anything else that we might do or hold as a personal identity —citizen, leader, artist, lover, preacher, teacher and more—is secondary. Sociobiology proceeds from this premise to explain various forms of social organization in terms of how they are connected to the breeding process and the (presumed) attempt to maximize individual reproduction.

For instance, a common sociobiological argument for the (presumed) observation that males are promiscuous and females are selective is that males enhance their "reproductive fitness" by planting sperm in as many women as possible, whereas women benefit by making sure that they allow their eggs to be fertilized by only the most fit males. This argument about promiscuity and selectivity is problematic on several counts:

1. There is no evidence that men are *naturally* promiscuous or that women are *naturally* selective. Sociobiologists seek a biological (reproductive) explanation for an observation that can easily be attributed to social arrangements in which men help themselves to as many women as possible while actively restricting women from nonmonogamous sexual contact. In cultures in which they are not restricted, there is some evidence that women are equally "promiscuous."

2. Evolutionary theorists emphasize survival of entire species, not individuals. Accordingly, it is not necessary, or even desirable, that all members of a species engage in biological reproduction as a primary activity. The assumption that biological reproduction is the primary human drive is just that, an assumption. Survival, especially of the cultural systems that support human life, may require that some members of the species prioritize activities that promote cultural, rather than biological, reproduction.

3. By positing reproductivity as the basic drive, sociobiologists must treat as anomalous all the many aspects of human behavior that seem disconnected from, or even antithetical to, reproduction. A couple of these "aberrations" are noteworthy here:

   a. Reproductive capacity is a relatively short occurrence in the span of human life (and an even shorter occurrence among many animals).
   b. Many individual members of species never have reproductive capacity (but do seem to perform other functions for the species).
   c. Many individual members of species who have reproductive capacity do not act on it.

Even if we grant biological reproduction as one basic activity of human behavior, are you willing to accept it as the *exclusive and primary basis* for determining who you are and for explaining your inclinations, tastes and desires?

Gender Classification and Biological Reproduction

Early naturalists classified species according to type of biological reproduction. The classification scheme was based on a binary: sexual reproduction or asexual reproduction. Species that reproduce based on a division of labor in which one organism supplies the egg and another fertilizes it are grouped in the sexual reproduction category. All other forms of reproduction are classified as asexual. Within a species that reproduces sexually, organisms can be classified according to whether they possess eggs or sperm. Categorization by sex is the result. Sex in this case is defined as possessing one set or another of complementary reproductive organs (uterus or testes).

The prevalence of a reproductive scheme of classification that divides humans into males and females as defined by their sex organs can be traced to social customs in Western Europe during the Middle Ages. According to popular belief, men not only provided sperm in the reproductive process, but each sperm was a fully developed human being (hence the caution against spilling even a single drop on barren soil). Once planted in a woman, this being would grow to a regular size. According to this line of reasoning, men are the carriers of the species and women are merely the vessels for incubating new members of the species. This once-scientific logic now seems ludicrous, but at the time it made sense because it supported an additional binary assumed to be "natural," the binary that posits that men are the embodiment of natural reason in the image of God and women are essentially of the earth—soil in which seeds grow.

There are several scientific questions about this classification that must be addressed in order to proceed with the argument that nature intends these distinctions as a primary classification scheme. Is this classification mutually exclusive and reliable? In other words, in all species classified as reproducing sexually, do all organisms have only one set of reproductive organs? It turns out that we're not certain. Some species appear to reproduce sexually, if sexual reproduction is defined as the fertilization of an egg, but do it within a single organism. Some bivalves (clams), for instance, reproduce themselves sexually, but not with a partner. It might be said that their reproduction is sexual but not sexual-social. What about species that do require a partner? Again, if we look at the physical evidence, it is unclear what nature is hinting at. Some species appear to have both forms of reproductive organs, but only one set functions at a given time. Oysters, for example, are the equivalent of males in one reproductive cycle and females in another.

It is often assumed that the reproductive functions are completely distinct and unproblematic in humans. If this were so, it might be evidence that nature intends us to classify ourselves by reproductive functions. But again, there is counterevidence. Some people are born with elements of both reproductive organs (testes and a uterus)—biologically, they are both male and female. Others have nonfunctioning reproductive organs. Does this make them neither male nor female? It is not clear how prevalent this phenomenon is because reproductive organs are not visible at birth and no one thinks to look unless the child's secondary sex characteristics (penis or vagina) appear ambiguous. The point is that nature is not giving us clear, unambiguous messages. Certainly, a large majority of the human population can be classified according to whether they have testes (male) or a uterus (female), but this does not prove the assumption that our predominant nature is rooted in our biological reproductive organs. It also fails to acknowledge the regular occurrence of "anomalies." This regularity is suggestive of the idea that the classification may be useful, but neither mutually exhaustive nor an exclusive determinant of human behavior.

There are many additional questions that the skeptical scientist could pose regarding whether sexual reproduction is the most natural basis for sorting and classifying humans. I have suggested that it is at least worthwhile, from a scientific perspective, to question whether our primary function is indeed sexual reproduction and our primary form, following from this, a manifestation of our reproductive organs. There is enough evidence to the contrary for any good scientist to proceed with at least some doubt. Even if sexual reproduction is one basic function necessary to the perpetuation of species, it is not at all certain that is the primary distinguishing feature. Many animal species remain reproductively dormant for long periods of time. What is their nature when they are not engaged in reproduction? Evolutionary biologists who assume reproductive primacy have the burden of proving that everything else a species does is somehow connected to reproduction. Clearly this is a significant feature of human life, but is it an adequate and accurate basis for ascertaining our motives, drives? Is it the basis of all social institutions? Are other animal species an appropriate comparison group? Biological reproduction seems to be one of the only features that we share in common with many species. Is this commonality our best basis for understanding the essence of human nature?

What Is It?

When used in reference to an expected child, the phrase, "What is it?" is commonly understood to mean: "Is it a boy or a girl?" This bit of information is considered basic to understanding a child's identity. Regardless of whether they express a preference for one or the other, new parents are especially keen on knowing the gender of their child. Well-meaning strangers who coo over a baby but mistake its gender cause distress and embarrassment for parents. How is gender assignment made at birth? Is the infant classified in accordance with an examination of reproductive organs?

At birth, in response to the question, "What is it?" a child's genitals are examined. Biologically, genitalia are secondary sex characteristics, which are presumed to indicate the presence of one set or another of reproductive organs. Fully functioning reproductive organs are not yet developed. Instead, secondary features are used to classify the child's gender. A penis signals testes and implies eventual production of sperm, in which case the child is classified "male." A vagina signifies ovaries and a uterus and leads to a classification of "female." If it all lines up according to the biological definition, then the child will eventually have the capacity to fulfill the related reproductive function. Is this what being a boy or a girl means? Does this assignment make everything else fall into place?

In the case of ambiguity, how should the child be typed? The procedure in such cases is to obtain further information about the presence of reproductive organs. If the child has what appear to be both a penis and a vagina and also has signs of a developing uterus, then the physician may recommend castration so that the child will conform more to the "girl" category. In the case of ambiguity in secondary characteristics, unambiguous reproductive organs may clear up the matter. At least upon initial assignment.

What are some additional ways to classify gender biologically? In addition to secondary sex characteristics and reproductive organs, gender classification can be based on hormonal levels (estrogen, progesterone and testosterone) and chromosomal structure (XX or XY). Hormones were initially studied (and continue to be studied) in relationship to the functioning of reproductive cycles. All humans have all three hormones, but in varying levels. Shifts in hormonal balances have been shown to be related to reproductive activity. Hormone levels presumably line up with reproductivity to suggest gender category. Similarly, the presence/absence of a Y chromosome determines the embryo's sex-chromosomal structure. Presumably, these features line up to tell us who is really a boy and who is really a girl. If gender is biologically based, then, in accordance with the theoretical classification, all the features should fall neatly into one box or another—girl: vagina, uterus/ovaries, lower testosterone/higher estrogen, XX; boy: penis, testes, high testosterone/low estrogen, XY. Note that, according to the definition of biologically based gender, this is necessary but not sufficient to prove the case.

Interestingly, evidence is controversial even in this arena. Things just don't line up so neatly. When a baby is typed at birth, it is assumed that all the additional definitional factors fall into line. But do they? Are you aware of your relative reproductive capacity? If you are a woman, do both ovaries work or just one? If you are a man, what is your sperm count? Do you know what your hormonal balance is? Is it the same over time? What about your chromosomal structure?

It turns out that there are several variations on this classification theme. Geneticists have isolated at least five chromosomal types (rather than the assumed two); hormone levels seem to vary much more than research based on reproductivity has led us to believe. In fact, in terms of hormones, occupation may provide a better classification of levels than gender. Science writer Deborah Blum points out research that suggests that levels of testosterone in both men and women vary with environmental factors such as profession and intensity in intimate relationships. For example, people in high-stress professions such as police work or corporate law have been shown to have higher testosterone than people who work in the ministry or child care (1998:48). Perhaps most interesting in sleuthing the case for a biologically determined gender binary is the observation that chromosomal structure and reproductive organs do not line up the same way in all species. Birds, for instance, have a structure whereby the bird that lays the egg has an XY and the bird that fertilizes it has an XX. According to our scheme, which is the female and which the male? The distinction can be made on either reproductive function or chromosome, but it has to be specified because it doesn't match the gender boxes as they are currently defined. In short, there is evidence to suggest that, *biologically,* many species, including humans, don't fit neatly into a gender *binary* as defined by the existing criteria.

Forcing a Fit. The more we learn about biology, the more we see just how complicated, intricate and non-box-like nature is. Ironically, at the same time that we are learning about this complexity, we are striving harder than ever to force a fit into categories—categories that, according to available evidence, are not representative of the spectrum that may exist in nature. Anne Fausto-Sterling provides a compelling review of literature on the "intersexed" body. This literature reveals that, "biologically speaking, there are many gradations running from male to female; and depending on how one calls the shots, one can argue that along the spectrum lie at least five sexes—perhaps even more" (1993:20). She cites medical specialists who study congenital variation in sexual organs. These experts observe that as many as 4 percent of all infants may be intersexed at birth—meaning that they appear to possess aspects of both male and female secondary sex characteristics. Fausto-Sterling's conclusion is that there is enough evidence to argue that "sex is a vast, infinitely malleable continuum that defies the constraints of even five categories." Despite the fact that the natural existence of intersexuality is old news, Fausto-Sterling notes that the attempt in the medical community in the latter part of this century has been to use technology and surgery

> [toward the] complete erasure of any form of embodied sex that does not conform to a male-female, heterosexual pattern. Ironically, a more sophisticated knowledge of the complexity of sexual systems has led to the repression of such intricacy . . . [these] medical accomplishments can be read not as progress but as a mode of discipline. Hermaphrodites have unruly bodies. They do not fall naturally into a binary classification; only a surgical shoehorn can put them there. (1993:70-1)

Those who wish to argue the case for the naturalness of gender binary classification make the argument that the number of individuals who don't conform to the gender binary is small. Again, the evidence is ambiguous. The actual number of people who don't fit the biological classification scheme is difficult to assess, precisely because of cultural practices that operate to "shoehorn" persons into one box or the other despite strong evidence that they don't fit. Children whose genitalia are ambiguous are surgically altered to fit one box or another. Adults whose biological reproductive capacity does not match the expectations that everyone should reproduce, receive medical treatment to "correct" the situation. Persons whose hormonal levels produce secondary features that are inconsistent with gender stereotypes (presence of facial hair on women, enlarged breast on men) also receive medical treatments. These "treatments" are social interventions that have the effect of reducing the natural spectrum of physical features manifest by human bodies into an expression that fits a stereotypical binary.

Also, we don't know the chromosomal structure of most people. From the standpoint of the scientific method, it is difficult to assess the number of persons who fall outside a biologically based binary because the tendency is to "fix" anything that doesn't fit rather than count the cases so that we might see just how robust the categories really are. Given this lack of empirical evidence, we can hardly conclude that "gender is natural" or that gender assignments based on presumed biological reproductive functions are representative of a natural pattern of *primary* difference. Yet the lack of evidence in support of the thesis does not rule it out entirely. However, when combined with evidence that may suggest a wider range of biological types than our current classification scheme allows for, it is sensible to be skeptical about the natural reality of a gender binary based on biological reproduction. In fact, much of the evidence seems to suggest that we engage in a great deal of social engineering designed to fit people into one of two boxes. This activity reveals an investment in a gender binary as a primary *social* institution.

Gender as a Social Institution

Sociologist Judith Lorber (1994) defines gender as a social institution. By this she means that gender is a primary cultural means by which we are taught who we are, how to behave and what our appropriate roles in society will be. From the moment of birth (or even sooner, now that ultrasound tests reveal sex characteristics) gender performance is shaped through clothing and other props used to signal gender identity. Layers of skills and appropriate behaviors are added on to this early socialization to produce the appropriately "gendered" person. We come to know our place in the social order by taking on the identity of girl or boy.

Lorber is not necessarily disputing the realities of biological reproduction as an aspect of human behavior. She is emphasizing that our most significant cultural behavior is based on a gender system and that this system is socially engineered, not a reflection of nature. The equation of gender with biological reproduction is one aspect of this cultural scheme. Accordingly, persons are assigned cultural tasks and roles that are deemed to be a manifestation of these biological roles (nurturing for women, earning a living for men). Variations in the expressions of these roles, and the ways in which they are manifest by individual males and females, indicate, to Lorber, that gender is not fixed and unchanging. For instance, many men are excellent nurturers and many women are excellent earners. The cultural investment in gender as a social institution is manifest in the ways that we respond to these variations. A woman who chooses not to have children is frequently subjected to questions about what is "wrong" with her. Persons who engage in cross-dressing and other nonstereotypical gender behaviors are subjected to cultural scrutiny and, frequently, derision and outrage.

For Lorber, the noteworthy observation is that there is a considerable amount of nonconformity and also strenuous attempts either to get the nonconformers to comply with expected gender roles or to denounce them as "abnormal." The practice of nontraditional gender behavior is an indicator that gender behavior is not necessarily equated with physiological features, such as a penis or lack thereof. Attempts to make people conform are indicators of a very strong cultural investment in maintaining gender as a social formula for determining who can be and do what.

According to Lorber, we are constantly "doing gender." Gender, precisely because it is a cultural performance and not necessarily a manifestation of natural differences, must be enacted continuously. We are so accustomed to performing gender that we rarely notice that we are doing so. Rather we tend to notice disruptions to this performance—those whose gender we cannot readily identify or whose behavior is inconsistent with the expectations for their gender. One way in which we can see that gender is a social institution is the way in which persons are punished, sometimes severely, for deviating from expected gender behavior. If gender were a "natural" expression, then we might be less concerned socially with whether or not people actually conformed to gender expectations. Individual manifestations of gender, regardless of how "deviant," would be taken as mere expressions of a wide spectrum of possibilities of who and what we could be. Lorber's main thesis, however, is that gender is the primary way by which we are sorted into social roles, including who can and should do which tasks.

The Social Construction of Gender Classification

Consider Adam and Eve. The Bible refers to them as "man" and "woman" respectively. But what sort of distinction does this refer to? A physiological distinction or a social one? In this culture we make gender assignments at birth by examining the infant for evidence of secondary sex characteristics—a penis or a vagina. The Bible makes no mention of these physical characteristics, yet we tend to assume that Adam has a penis and Eve a vagina. We make this assumption automatically, even though they are usually depicted with leaves covering their genitalia. Well, it's obvious, you might argue. Eve has long hair, she's smaller than Adam, she is shown with breasts (another presumed secondary sex characteristic). He has facial hair and larger muscles. Are these reliable features by which to determine gender? The Bible is silent on the matter. Artists' renderings reflect their own assumptions about what gender is and what it looks like. Given this, would you conclude that biblical portrayals of a gender binary (man/woman) are based on physiology or culture?

Two social psychologists, Suzanne Kessler and Wendy McKenna, published a book in 1978 on the social construction of gender. They cite numerous cross-cultural illustrations of cases in which a family may cultivate a cultural gender identity for their child that is different from the child's biological sex characteristics. In a society in which only men hunt, a family who has several daughters but no sons may decide to make one of their children a son so that the child can train in the ways of the hunter. In still other families, a son may shun male tasks and show an interest in female tasks, so the tribe might test the child by placing it in a small tent with a bow and arrow in one corner and basket-weaving material in another corner. They then watch to see which items the child grabs and plays with. If it selects the basket-weaving materials, they raise the child as a daughter (1978:21).

Through cross-cultural examples such as these, Kessler and McKenna, and many scholars before and after them, ask us to rethink the taken-for-granted relationship between biological sex characteristics and gender behavior. Gender, according to their schema, is a cultural attribute. People are not born with a gender, they develop one over a lifetime of participating in cultural expectations about what it is to be a boy or a girl. As evidence for this thesis, scholars point to myriad disjunctions between biological sex and gender performance. Research suggests that all cultures examine the genitals of their newborn to ascertain biological sex; but, unlike in our culture, in many cultures it is the child's *behavior* that determines gender assignment. In some cultures, if there is a disjuncture between biology and behavior, the genitalia are simply ignored and the child is treated as the gender most consistent with its behavior. In other cultures, such as some Native American groups, this disjuncture is accorded a special status. Termed *berdache,* these children take on special roles in society based on their third-gender assignment. These examples suggest that the link between biology and cultural conceptions of gender is not necessarily a natural phenomenon. In other words, nature is not necessarily the blueprint for gender *classification*; gender may be assigned on the basis of behavior rather than physical attributes, and these are not necessarily the same thing.

Kessler and McKenna make useful distinctions among biological sex characteristics, gender assignment, gender identity, gender roles and gender attributions. Biological sex characteristics are the physiological features that are used to catalogue human sex. In our culture the features used for sex typing include reproductive organs, chromosomes, hormones and genitalia. These features are used to make a gender assignment—at birth the baby is typed as a particular gender. There are only two choices in our culture, boy or girl. Gender identity refers to the way in which persons think of themselves. In our culture it is presumed that normal, healthy persons will have a gender identity that matches their biologically based gender assignment. Gender roles are the behaviors associated with gender assignment (e.g., women gather, men hunt; women keep house, men earn money). Gender attribution refers to the gender that someone is assumed to be by others in their everyday interaction.

In cultures with a biologically based gender dichotomy it is assumed that each of these aspects of gender will fit neatly together. Babies with penises will be assigned a male gender, they will grow up to think of themselves as boys, do boy things, and other people will recognize them as boys. Similarly, babies with vaginas will behave and be seen in accordance with the category of "girl." It is an indisputable fact, however, that these lines of classification do not always match up. Some children have ambiguous genitalia—they don't fit the binary classification. What did nature intend them to be? Some children grow up thinking of themselves as the opposite gender than the category to which they have been assigned. Which is the dominant criterion, physiology or identity? Some people identify with their gender assignment but resist the associated roles. For instance, some boys want to take care of dolls and some women don't want to have babies. Does this mean there is a problem with the categories or with the individuals who don't fit them? There are also many people who seem to be one gender in their social appearance and behavior but are biologically another. Which are they *really?* One important sociological question is how different cultures deal with deviations from the gender scheme. This is difficult to ascertain because Western observers, no matter how objective they intend to be, tend to see everything through a biologically based binary—meaning that in our culture, we think that people's *real* gender is revealed through their biology. For instance, Kessler and McKenna quote an anthropologist writing in 1907 who states: "the person was dressed like a woman but had a stubby black beard; there could be no misunderstanding about the sex to which he really belonged" (1978:33). In this case the researcher is giving precedence to secondary physical characteristics, facial hair, over the person's apparent cultural assignment, role enactment and attribution as a woman. The tribe referred to the individual as "she." The person engaged in women's tasks and was seen as a woman by tribe members, but in making his own gender assessment, the anthropologist ignores this cultural evidence in favor of presumed biology.

Some scholars study the terms used in tribes where there seems to be a third group of persons whose gender assignments, and subsequent roles, are not based on biology. They note that unlike the term *transsexual,* these people are often referred to by names that denote a cultural rather than biological classification scheme. The term *transsexual,* which is often used in conjunction with *transsexual male* or *transsexual female,* underscores a cultural insistence on a biological gender binary—the term for the deviation connotes the cultural idea that gender attribution must be qualified if it doesn't match up with physiology. The linguistic terms used to describe some *berdache* suggest that the cultural attribution of gender is accepted as the *real* attribution of gender. We can draw two conclusions from these cross-cultural examples: (a) all cultures do not place similar emphasis on biology as a basis for cultural knowledge, and (b) in some cultures the determination of what is *real* is based on behavior.

Western industrial cultures practice the belief that the physical, tangible properties of nature are the basis of reality. We treat something as "real" to the extent that we can isolate and classify its physical properties, which are assumed to be less malleable than cultural practices. Thus, for the Western anthropologist quoted above, the person is really a man because the presence of facial hair suggests levels of hormones that are used to classify males. This is a basic physical fact about the person. Without physical intervention, it's not likely to change. This is what the Western anthropologist sees. He does not give equal weight to the observation that the individual behaves and is treated as a cultural woman, because in Western cultures we doubt the primacy of our own cultural institutions.

Gender as a Social Role

Prior to the rise of science there had long been an established cultural distinction in gender assignment and gender roles. Genitalia were used as a basis for making gender assignments, but the basis for ascribing and enforcing differences between men and women ranged from nebulous ideas about distinct "spirits" to a loose association with different bodily humors—different balances of blood, phlegm and bile were thought to give men and women distinct temperaments (sort of an early precursor to hormonal research). Although there were attempts to make connections between the cultural distinction of gender and the inner workings of the body, it was not widely believed that the body actually determined gender. Rather the body was taken to be aligned with cultural expectations regarding gender, but not always perfectly so.

The de-coupling of gender assignment and gender roles is illustrated in several documented cases in Renaissance Europe whereby women who had been living as men—either by fighting in armies, marrying other women or similar male roles—were officially declared to be men. In these cases it was not deemed necessary to establish a physical basis for this deviation, rather it was presumed that in a culture in which the gender roles were not only different, but often accorded more privilege to men than women, it made sense for some women to want to live as men. The official decree meant that the woman-living-as-man now had the right to engage in male activities and to be accorded male privilege. What's interesting about these cases is that the women did not necessarily have an altered gender identity, and even after they were officially given status as men they were not necessarily assumed to be men in the full cultural sense of the time; rather, the decree underscores the tight connection between gender role and privilege.

The recent death of a well-known jazz musician, Billy Tipton, revealed the little-known fact that Billy was a biological female. In addition to his music, Billy had a reputation for his philandering ways with women. He had been a husband to five women, raised children and was considered a "real dandy." Billy, who was born Dorothy, discovered early in his musical career that clubs were not inclined to hire female musicians, regardless of their talent. Passing as a man enabled him to make a career for himself and, evidently, to lead a full and interesting life as the sexual partner and companion to several women. Regarding his wives, readers of Billy's story are inclined to wonder, "How they could not know?!" This statement reflects the cultural assumption that gender identity, gender attributions and gender assignment are one and the same.

In the case of Billy, it is clear that the gender attributed him by others (male) was not the same as the gender that had been assigned to Dorothy (female) at birth. What gives people pause is the apparent fact that Billy engaged in sexual relations with other women. Alone with these women, Billy may have assumed a female gender identity. This gender identity, which would have been at odds with the gender publicly attributed to Billy the musician, may have been the couple's "secret." In such a case, it might be said that Billy cultivated a gender attribution that enabled him to enjoy a particular cultural status not available to Dorothy. It might also be the case that Billy maintained his gender identity as a male with even his lovers. The specifics of how this might be accomplished are less significant here than the point that it is possible to do so. Billy's male gender behavior, a social expression, may have completely eclipsed his female physiology such that, even with his lovers, the male gender identity was the evident expression.

This and similar stories raise several questions (as well as eyebrows) about the presumed relationship between gender and sexuality, and about the basis for and the likelihood of possessing a "true" (i.e., fixed) gender. There are those who will insist that Billy was "really" a woman, that the entirety of Billy's lived experiences as a male were insignificant in comparison with the fact that he possessed a vagina. Furthermore, they will conclude that he must have "tricked" his lovers into believing that he functioned sexually as a male. This sort of thinking is indicative of a cultural institution whereby "true" gender is defined as existing only in the body, as a fixed, unchanging aspect of person and personality and as the only real basis for sexual behavior.

Misfits or Cultural Pioneers? Was Billy a liar and a scam? One of "nature's mistakes"? Or someone who exercised his own will to transcend the cultural boxes that obstructed his choices of who he could be and what he could do? What happens to individuals whose gender is ambiguous at birth and who are surgically and hormonally "shoehorned" into one of two gender boxes? Recent research reports that many of these persons become unsatisfied with their gender assignment as they grow older. In several cases, these individuals later undergo gender reassignment surgery to reverse the initial gender assignment. Proponents of the "gender is natural" thesis interpret this behavior as evidence of a natural gender binary. Their logic is that if we do have a single, true gender, then a misassignment based on ambiguous features at birth will be manifest in the person's growing dis-ease with her or his assigned gender. This discomfort is taken to be a sign of the "true" gender calling out for expression.

I have a different interpretation. My logic is based on my skepticism about the existence of a natural gender binary. It seems to me that the simplest explanation regarding what nature might be hinting is that these persons don't fit either box. Nature's marks were ambiguous at birth. Having had a forced assignment into one box, despite contradictory characteristics, such a person is very likely to experience discomfort in her or his assignment. In a system with only two choices, we are likely to believe that if we are uncomfortable in one box, we must belong in the other. Such a person doesn't necessarily imagine other possibilities and may assume that by changing the root of the "problem"—by altering physiological sex characteristics—he or she will find a more comfortable place in society. In a documentary film on female-to-male transsexuals titled *You Don't Know Dick,* one person who has had surgery to transform from a female to a male states: "It's not that I really needed the surgery to make me a man. I've always felt more comfortable as a man. But I live in a society where people won't let me express myself as a man unless I look like a man."

There are many more individuals whose gender assignment at birth seemed routine but who, as they grow up, experience gender "dysphoria" (the sense of not being the "right" gender). Are these people aberrations—nature's abnormalities—or are they the normal manifestations of a wider range of biological and social possibilities than the current classification scheme allows for? It's not clear what nature intends. What is clear is that these people are subjected to intensive and invasive procedures (including involuntary psychiatric hospitalization) designed to get them to conform to their initial gender assignment. These attempts frequently include hormonal injections and other forms of medical intervention. If and when the person receives permission for "gender reassignment treatment" (note that we don't allow persons to ascertain this for themselves), the case is made that they were assigned to the wrong category initially. Is this nature taking its course or is it social manipulation to make persons fit categories?

Are these individuals misfits or cultural pioneers? The expectation that one can have only one gender, that this gender is a manifestation of biological reproductive features, and that it is fixed, is an expectation that seems to make all of us feel out of place at some time or another. It is noteworthy that we choose to ignore the many signs in each of us of gender nonconformity, rather than to acknowledge these and use them to question the general relevance of a reproductively based binary as a foundation upon which to formulate an entire self-image. Nature may be hinting very strongly. The hint may be that we don't fall neatly into a binary classification scheme that is based on biological reproductive organs. To the extent that we do, it needn't be a primary form of self-awareness, certainly not an immutable one. The question that interests me is why we don't take this hint.

Social (Il)literacy

My interest at this juncture is why we, as a culture, are so ill-equipped to pose and argue the alternatives to Naturalism? At the very least, scientific skepticism implores us to be aware of and to be able to respond to counterarguments. The most enduring and scientifically valid explanations of behavior posit environmental forces (social and material) as the primary determinants of who we are and how we behave. Yet, there is a tendency in Anglo American cultural history, which emphasizes individualism, to be suspicious of "social forces." The result is a curious and problematic dichotomy wherein behavior is seen to be either an expression of nature or an expression of individual will. Individualism is the sort of empty explanation of behavior that would have us believe that we are who we are simply because "we are." Culturally, we are suspicious of sociological explanations because they imply "brainwashing by social forces." As a culture we suffer a sort of *social illiteracy*—an inability to recognize social patterns and to comprehend the ways in which these shape and channel our inclinations and behavior. The inability to speak and read a language of social forces leaves us unaware of the many factors that influence us. Like tourists in a foreign country who can't read the signposts, we travel along blindly following the flow of traffic through various boxes and mazes that make only vague sense. It's difficult to know where you're going, let alone map a purposeful journey, if you can't read the signs. It's all the more tragic when we begin to attribute the reasons for the routes that we take to natural causes.

One sign of this illiteracy is a studied indifference to social forces in the history of North American philosophy. Our belief in the sanctity of the individual leads us to reject out of hand the fact that we are social creatures—creatures who take on self-meaning through interaction with others; creatures who organize our actions (including rebellion) through an awareness of culturally shared expectations and obligations. This inattention to the social forces that shape us does not make them any less real, it simply makes us unaware. A related misunderstanding is the notion that social forces can be easily manipulated. We seem to have adopted the notion that if something is socially formed it is less real, less enduring and more malleable than nature. The fact that humans make their own cultures and self-consciously construct their own habitats, both physical and ideological, does not make these manifestations any less real. Human constructions, although not based in a state of nature, are certainly real in their consequences.

Emile Durkheim, a nineteenth-century sociologist, urged that society was a thing in and of itself: a set of forces according to which we organize our own behavior, gain self-awareness and evaluate our conduct. We contribute to the maintenance of these forces through our participation in them, and at the same time they exist independently of any given individual. Baseball, as a game with a particular set of rules and cultural history, exists whether you are playing it right now or not. It exists in your conscious awareness of it. A shared awareness of baseball, a collective consciousness, enables you and others to enact the form of baseball when you play a game. The shared awareness of the game and the act of playing it are both real. Durkheim referred to social forces as "social facts." A social fact is a socially recognized rule that we become aware of whenever we bump into it—usually through minor transgressions. If a player stayed at bat after three strikes, others would boo and make comments until the player realized that a rule had been violated. In this instance the player can choose to try to remain at bat, she may even privately believe that the three-strike rule is unfair, but chances are that the collective pressure of others in the game will prevail and she will be "forced" to leave the batter's box.

The rules of baseball are so well established that we can say that it is a social institution. Social literacy involves being able to identify the various social institutions in which we take part and that shape our behaviors. Many of these institutions (and the corresponding social facts) are difficult to recognize because we take them for granted. The study of social norms (normative behavior) is a study in recognizing well-entrenched social patterns that shape our actions. Many entry-level sociology students are asked to perform "breaching" or "norm-violating" activities. These activities can range from something as simple as facing the wrong way in the elevator to refusing to acknowledge the role of the professor by sitting in her chair at the front of the room. A favorite among some of my students is "shopping from someone else's grocery cart." There is an unwritten rule in grocery store shopping that once you have selected an item and placed it in your cart it belongs to you. Technically, it is still the property of the store, but the collective understanding is that the item is now in your possession. What do you suppose happens if you help yourself to items that are in the carts of other people rather than selecting items from the shelf? In the experiences of my students, reactions range from stunned disbelief to feisty attempts to snatch the item back. In all cases there is a sense from the "victim" of the breach that a social rule has been violated. He or she may not have been aware of the rule prior to the breach, but the occasion triggers an awareness that an unwritten but shared boundary has been violated.

It turns out that these activities are extremely difficult for students to perform. Contemplating and planning the activity causes a rush of enthusiasm and laughter, but actually doing it can be as difficult as trying to knock over a physical wall. It is this difficulty that enables students to see the realness of social forces. The expectations and rules of conduct that constitute a particular social institution exert a pressure on us to act accordingly. We feel this pressure as a real boundary, a real presence that entreats us to engage in some behaviors and to avoid others. *Obviously these rules and the social institutions that they constitute are not "natural," but they do shape behavior in ways that can be described and predicted. And they are real in their consequences.*

Karl Marx noted that persons make their own circumstances, but they do not make them just as they please. Rather we are born into preexisting circumstances that shape our opportunities and mold forms of expression and awareness. We gain consciousness through participation in cultural routines with others. We are born into cultures with preexisting rules and institutions. The logic of the "nurture" argument is that these cultural institutions are the primary forces that determine how we express ourselves and how we will act.

Gender is a social institution (not a biological expression of nature). Consider this circumstance. You are in a restaurant and you go to the bathroom. There are two doors, one marked "men" and one marked "women." You proceed to the one that matches your gender and find that there is someone else already in line. The person says to you, "No one is in the other one, why don't you take that?" What do you do? The person prods further and says, "It's okay, I'll watch for you." What are they watching for? The bathroom gender police? Why is it that a simple sign distinguishing "boy" or "girl" can elicit feelings of transgression when you do something practical such as use whichever bathroom is available? If there is no sign, that is, if the bathroom is designated gender-neutral, such as in our homes or in certain public spaces, we rarely hesitate to use the same space that someone of the opposite gender may have occupied moments earlier.

When I use bathroom facilities that are publicly marked as the opposite of my assigned gender, I feel the presence of the "gender wall" and experience some discomfort in knowing that I might be subjected to disapproval if I remove a brick or two. When gender lines are blurred, interaction often grinds to a confused halt. Like baseball, gender-as-institution has a set of rules for which positions can be played, who can play them and how. The gender institution in which we find ourselves offers only two positions. A position is established at birth and is considered fixed for life. Gender is also one of the *primary* institutions in our culture. Almost every other institution that makes up this culture is connected to gender. In other words, gender roles shape which paths you are more or less likely to take throughout your life and the various ways in which you will express and understand yourself as a result.

Forces of social conditioning, like natural forces, are malleable with the right understanding of how the forces work and the right tools. If gender is not a natural endowment, and if the social institution is particularly narrow (only two boxes and you can never deviate), then it makes sense that many people would fall outside the lines of the box. Physically, as I have noted, many people's bodies don't match the cultural expectations for gender. Imagine living a life in which you are constantly bumping up against social "facts" in the form of other people's stares, giggles and rejections, facts that remind you that you do not quite fit the expected cultural box. It strikes me as quite plausible that under these conditions one might want to try a different box.

Or suppose you fit the physical prescriptions for the gender box to which you have been assigned but you find yourself resistant to follow through on some of the rules, like heterosexual marriage and compulsory biological reproduction. What do you do in this case? Some people feel the exertion of social forces quite keenly and can't see any other route for themselves. They may follow the recipe on the box but live a life of quiet desperation. There could be a large number of persons living such lives, but we wouldn't necessarily be able to tell this from their behavior alone. Imagine on the other hand that you learn that there are possibilities outside the box. If you are in the girl box you may discover that there are other girls who want to play sports (such as football, ice hockey or boxing) and do things that are not part of the girl box. You may begin spending more time with this group until, after a while, their behavior, which has its own set of rules, comes to seem normal to you. You may find that you prefer the company of these woman even though you keep bumping into cultural messages that you should be dating men. You may even find that as you become increasingly sexually active, the box that equates gender and sexuality no longer holds you either. Does this mean that you are a lesbian?

The answer will depend on what additional boxes your culture gives you. One does not simply wake up one day and decide to become a lesbian. Sexual identity, like gender identity, is an ongoing, constantly changing process in which culture and experience forge the individual. The advantage of this form of explanation is that it gives us a realistic account of the variations in individual deviance from the norm. According to this account, it is reasonable to assume that many people will not fit the prescribed norms. Furthermore, how they express their deviance will be shaped by the alternatives available to them. A young person who only knows that he doesn't fit in with the boys who tease him and beat up on him and call him a sissy, may believe that he is a gender misfit and, perhaps, even an immoral person, if that is the only cultural story available to him. Are we to understand his subsequent attempt at suicide as an act of nature or an act of desperation that reveals the limitations of a particularly restrictive cultural binary? How do we explain the biological male who has himself surgically altered to become a biological female but still prefers sex with women, and not just any women, only self-described lesbians? Is this nature trying to find its box or a person who is capable of constructing a life for herself entirely outside of cultural boxes?

Stories shared among lesbians, gays, bisexuals and transgendered persons indicate that a life outside the prescribed cultural boxes is not easy. Cultural prejudices weigh heavy and can be a constant social battering ram aimed at keeping the deviant on the prescribed cultural path. These experiences indicate the realness of gender as an institution and point simultaneously to the fact that this institution may not be the best form through which to live out the variety of possibilities indicated by the spectrum of deviance. "Queer" as a category of self-expression has expanded in recent years to include just about anyone who is uncomfortable with traditional gender roles and the associated expectations of sexuality. This could be the heterosexual couple who doesn't want to have children or who likes to reverse gender roles in their sexual play, or it could be the female-to-male transgendered gay husband living with his male-to-female transgendered lesbian wife.

Do these myriad and colorful variations reveal a wider range of natural possibilities than the original categories allow for, or are they indicative of the vast potential of humans, once they recognize the limits of preexisting boxes, to stake out new frontiers? Either way, an informed assessment of "nature versus nurture" requires a full comprehension of the ways in which social institutions imprint on individuals. There is a great deal of evidence that supports the nurture thesis that early socialization is a form of cultural imprinting in which the child is slotted into a sort of master template. The child's subsequent life can be seen either as a realization of the template or an attempt to alter it. Either way, the portrait of the individual, whenever we look, will reflect a process whereby cultural expectations and experiences, experiences that include resisting as well as incorporating these expectations, are literally etched into the physical, emotional, psychological and social fabric of the being. This is a social definition of expressed character. The realness of social forces, whether one accepts them uncritically or wrestles them continually, can be seen written across the body.

The Search for the Gay Gene and
Other Misapplications of "Bio Rhetoric"

If they find a gay gene, what will it be a gene for? The ability to pick out designer suits and fabulous draperies?

—Kate Bornstein
(personal communication, 1997)

The political philosopher Michel Foucault refers to one basis of contemporary political power as "bio power." Knowledge in biochemistry, endocrinology and embryology coupled with advances in surgical techniques enables us to manipulate nature so that it matches our expectations of what we think it should be. It is a cultural paradox that we are misled into thinking that our bio power—our ability to manipulate nature—is a reflection of a natural morality. It would seem that the very ability to manipulate nature to fit social categories would reveal the social construction of these categories. We seek causes in nature because it is nature that we think we can manipulate. The absurdity is in thinking that nature implies moral authority as well.

One contemporary arena that reveals the complexities and contradictions of "biologizing," bio power, and an investment in natural authority is the current research that seeks natural causes for homosexuality. In recent years some scientists have launched a full-scale exploration in search of natural causes for homosexuality. Purported findings range from observed differences in portions of the brains of gay men (the thalamus) to differences in the inner ear membrane of lesbians. The method of these inquiries is based on the logic of correlation. Recall that the logic in support of a pattern in nature that reveals a gender binary holds that if you put all the individuals with a penis into the box marked "boy" and those without a penis into the box marked "girl," then all the persons in one box should have matching characteristics that those in the other box don't have. For instance, it can be said that those who don't have a penis, those in the "girl" box, also all have wombs, whereas those who do have a penis don't appear to have wombs. Thus, having a womb correlates with not having a penis. In building up a lexicon of correlations we move toward a definitional classification of what a "girl" is and what a "boy" is. This sort of logic has led some researchers to wonder if there is a pattern of physical distinction among homosexuals. Are there physical features that reliably distinguish homosexuals from heterosexuals?

To assess the answer to this empirical question it is necessary to have boxes of people who are indisputably heterosexual and indisputably homosexual so that their characteristics can be compared. This turns out to be a tricky issue. How do you determine who fits each box? Is someone a homosexual because he or she has sex with others of the same gender? Because he or she does not have sex with members of the opposite gender? Because he or she does not have sex at all? Because he or she does not conform to gender expectations? Because he or she makes a domestic life with a member of the same gender? Homosexuality, like heterosexuality, is a social construct that differs in definition from culture to culture and across historical periods. The problem with trying to determine a reliable natural basis for a social construct is that there is no initial natural basis for grouping people into the different boxes.

For the sake of convenience, as a sort of starting point, researchers seek individuals who claim to be exclusively homosexual in their sexual activity. Once a group of such individuals has been assembled it is possible to attempt to find some feature that seems to distinguish them from those in the other (heterosexual) box. This sort of exercise is not unlike the ways in which young children learn classification. Think for instance how they learn the differences between a cow and a horse. They have to make increasingly intricate distinctions in order to develop an awareness that these are more than the same big animal. Similarly, once we have grouped homosexuals into one box and heterosexuals into another, it is possible to isolate some differences. For instance, we may note that those in the heterosexual box are more likely to have had a formal wedding ceremony than those in the homosexual box. Obviously it would be absurd to conclude, based on this, that having a wedding ceremony is the definition of heterosexuality. It would be even more absurd to conclude that having a wedding ceremony *causes* someone to be heterosexual. Clearly having a wedding ceremony is a reflection of a social practice regarding marriage and gender.

This example may seem trite but the point is not. Once persons have been sorted into comparative boxes it is also possible to find corresponding distinctions. Whether or not these distinctions are meaningful is another matter. And the idea that such distinctions, if they can be reliably ascertained, actually *cause* a state of being, is an entirely different matter. A first-order rule of science is that correlation does not imply causation. Cows have four stomachs. Horses do not. This is a reliable physical difference, but we would not be so silly as to say that having four stomachs causes something called "cowness." What is cowness anyway? Being a cow?

Whether or not the inner ear membrane of lesbians is reliably more like that of men's than women's is a debatable point because the definition of who goes into the lesbian box is based on a social rather than physical construct. Even if we were to accept the observation as reliable, what does it tell us? That the ears of some women look more like the ears of some men. Even then, what would we know? That some women with some types of ear membranes have, at some time in their lives, an expressed preference for sexual relations with other women?

The logic is problematic on several counts. One is the assumption that lesbianism is an *essential* characteristic, something that, like the four stomachs in a cow, is a defining feature of one's being. The corollary assumption is that if we could catalogue such features we would understand what lesbianism is and what *causes* it. There is nothing to stop those so intended from going on correlational fishing expeditions, from attempting to establish a catalogue of physical differences. If the group is large enough it is the case, mathematically, that anyone can find significant correlations. So what?

If we look, we will probably find a preponderance of lesbians who do have very short hair cuts and who do wear "manlike" clothing compared with women who define themselves as heterosexual. These observed differences may reveal a social pattern, but they do not reveal anything about nature. Obviously women make choices about what length to wear their hair and what social costumes express them best. These choices also shift with time and cultural influence. The interesting thing is that we realize that these choices probably reveal more about the significance of lesbianism than ear membrane does. Yet, precisely because these expressed characteristics are based on choice, we do not consider them "real." Would we really rather search for this "realness" in physiological distinctions such as the shape of the ear membrane?

Perhaps the most troubling (or comic, depending on how you look at it) aspect of attempts to isolate physical correlates of a social behavior (sexuality) is the uncritical acceptance of a biologically based gender binary. To date, the scientific logic underlying research that seeks evidence of a "gay gene" and other physical correlates assumes that homosexuality is an aberration of gender. Recall that the definitional basis for grouping people according to sex-based characteristics is reproductivity as a driving force. If we assume that reproductivity is the driving force, then we can posit that the basic essential (and immutable?) distinction among human beings is gender as defined by reproductive organs. If this is nature's intent, then individuals who manifest a disinterest in reproductive sexual activity can be seen as anomalous. Hence the question, What features cause them to not fit into the gender boxes? makes sense, but only if we assume that the gender binary boxes are natural manifestations.

The search for a "gay gene" is predicated on the unquestioned assumption that there is a natural gender binary and that the natural basis of this binary is biological reproduction. If one accepts these assumptions, then it follows that homosexual behavior *may be* aberrant in nature. Note that it makes no sense to look for a "gay gene" unless it can be established that homosexual behavior is an expression that is aberrant. If this can be established, then it is possible to ask if there is a physical basis for this aberration. From a social perspective, it is a very long leap from the observation that homosexuality is not a normative social institution to the assumption that nature intends everyone to have a single gender that corresponds to a drive for reproductive sexual contact. The biological evidence does not support these claims. Even if the claim of a biologically based gender binary is supported (and this is a very dubious claim), it still must be proven that sexuality is driven *only* by the intent to reproduce. Biologically, we cannot know this with any certainty. There is considerable evidence among animals and humans that sexuality is an expression of play and pleasure, even spirituality, and sometimes aggression. It is a form of engagement that is neither driven by nor experienced solely as reproductive sex.

I do not think that a breakdown of our entire gender binary is coming around the cultural corner anytime soon. However, the variation in both sexual and gendered behavior is indicative of the claim that both sexuality and gender are social expressions that are shaped and channeled through corresponding cultural institutions. Gender and sexuality, like most of what we do and who we think we are, are based on social forces. The fact that both gender and sexuality are primary social institutions can be seen in the way in which we organize our very sense of who we are accordingly. Whether we identify as a heterosexual, a bisexual, as transgender, or as lesbian or gay, we are saying that we recognize that in this culture one has to have a gender and the gender is supposed to correspond with sexuality in a patterned way, even if it is a pattern of deviance.

The contemporary use of the term *queer* as a self-referent is meant as a denial of the cultural boxes themselves, particularly the gender binary box. "Queer" is an expression that can mean: I am a biological male who likes to pass as a social female and have sex as such but only with biological females who interact socially as males. Or it can mean: I am a biological and cultural male who enjoys sex with both men and women. Or it can mean: I am aware of my biological sex assignment but realize social gender is a spectrum and I can play it any way I want. The idea of "queerness" indicates an awareness of cultural institutions and reflects choices about the positions one wants to claim for oneself in terms of various cultural boundaries. Is there a gene for this? If so, what would we call it? The nonbigot gene? The queer gene? The boundary maverick gene?

Regarding the search for a "gay gene," Donna Haraway, whose writings on the development and implications of cybergenetics have been widely cited, remarks, "[T]his emphasis on the gene as the core of identity takes us away from asking questions about where we are in our history and what are our responsibilities." Another interesting statement comes from Simon LeVay, the biologist who originated (but later doubted) the hypothesis of a "gay brain." In a conversation about cloning, LeVay notes: "diversity has nothing to do with sexual reproduction and everything to do with rearing, cultural differences and education. People are going to realize the genes are not the whole story."

I have attempted to make the case that there is no particularly compelling scientific reason, either theoretically or empirically, to accept the assertion that gender is a manifestation of nature. The evidence suggests that gender is a social construct. Given this, it simply makes no sense, scientifically, to search for natural causes for what appear to be deviations from socially prescribed behaviors. Another first-order rule in science is that, all else being equal, the simplest explanation is the best explanation. This rule is referred to as Occam's Razor. The simplest explanation for both homosexuality and transgendered behavior is that our cultural boxes are too narrow. This explanation does not provide us with an immediate answer to the question of why particular individuals deviate from expected patterns of gender and sexual behavior. Rather, it turns the question on its head, prompting us to inquire, instead, why certain people *do* follow the proscribed behaviors. What is defined as deviant behavior—bisexuality as well as homosexuality, nonreproductive sexual practices, practices of gender nonconformity—can be more readily understood if we begin with the assumption that rules for both gender and sexuality are social (not natural) constructs. Our culture has particularly narrow constructs, which means that it is not only possible, but highly probable, that many persons will not fit the boxes. From this perspective, so-called deviant behaviors require a social rather than a natural explanation. Scientifically this is the more robust assumption because it can account for a variety of social behaviors that do not fit the boxes. It also accounts for the fact that many individuals are "shoehorned" into the boxes through coercive social and legal processes and through the use of medical technology (i.e., cultural practices).

"There Are Three Kinds of People in the World"

All cultures have stories for how to make sense of practices that fall outside taken-for-granted normative behaviors. These stories are consistent extensions of the accepted discourse for how to make sense of behavior in general. In cultures in which behavior is understood in connection to a pantheon of spirits and demons that populate the everyday environment, "deviant" behaviors may be attributed to possession by these spirits. In cultures in which behavior is religiously prescribed, deviations from normative expectations may be considered an expression of sin caused by a sick soul. Depending on the behavior and the individual doing it, deviance may also be considered a form of prophecy. These cultural stories are a basis upon which behaviors are sorted into boxes of normal and not normal. Behaviors deemed not normal are then variously understood as either problematic or as a source of good for the community. Thus we have both the sociopath and the pioneer.

Western culture has looked increasingly to nature as a force by which to explain human behavior. I have attempted to demonstrate throughout this chapter that there is very little actual evidence for natural explanations of human behavior. Natural science has developed an impressive and useful catalogue of descriptions of the human body and its functions, but these descriptions are not necessarily accurate or sufficient as a basis for explaining *why* we think, feel and act as we do. Most natural explanations of behavior are based on cultural assumptions rather than evidence.

The study of the natural world is not a problem in itself. My critical emphasis has been the misapplication of natural science toward an understanding of social behaviors. I have suggested that the prevailing trend for natural explanations is rooted in a general (largely uncritical) acceptance of natural science as a basis of cultural authority. This path has led us to individualize social behaviors and to look for corresponding causes in the biology of the individual. Advances in medical technology have made it possible to manipulate individual biology, most recently in the form of genetic engineering. Ironically, this manipulation, which is a social accomplishment, is sometimes taken as proof that behavior is biologically determined according to some particular natural design.

I have suggested that this overemphasis on nature theories and the neglect of nurture theories is due in part to our illiteracy regarding the social forces. We are not well versed in the ways of social forces—how to identify them and how to ascertain intricate ways in which they shape behavior. In addition, theories that attribute behavior to individual biology are more consistent with a cultural legacy that places emphasis on individual action over social process and grants medical science legitimacy for identifying and managing behavior. Natural theories may seem especially satisfying as explanations of behaviors that fall outside social boundaries and make us culturally uncomfortable. To the extent that the deviance can be linked to natural causes we don't have to look too hard at the counter-idea, which is that our cultural boxes may be insufficient to contain the variety that exists in human expressions.

It is a paradox that in spite of our tremendous "bio power" we continue to participate in rhetorical practices that "biologize" differences and then conclude some categories of difference are inferior (defined as "not natural"). How far have we come since times when women were not allowed to participate in active games because it was believed that their delicate constitutions prevented them from doing so, or were denied education on the belief that it would damage their reproductive organs?

Biologizing social behaviors has enabled us to render certain social categories as "natural" and then vest them with the authority of legitimacy. From this perspective, those who don't fit the categories can be labeled freaks of nature and then, depending on the cultural mood, determined to be persons in need of special therapy and benevolent tolerance, or persons who do not deserve equal rights and protection under the law. Our cultural political rhetoric posits the transgendered person, for instance, as unnatural. This claim of "unnaturalness" is used to uphold cultural practices that deny the person a right to safe passage. It is acceptable in our particular culture to attack, even to murder, a person who is transgendered and then to enter a plea of self-defense on the grounds that one was misled into an "unnatural arousal." Naturalism is a cultural story rather than an accomplishment of natural science.

The logic of social forces, the "nurture" side of the debate, has the theoretical advantage of being able to explain our cultural fixation with biological explanations, and simultaneously to account for both patterns of social behavior and deviation from these patterns. Social forces shape us. They do so in complex and intricate ways. Understanding these forces gives us a more comprehensive social literacy with which to make sense of who we are and what we do. It also implies that we have to assume responsibility for the cultural institutions that shape us and which we, in turn, through our own participation, reproduce. Deviance is a form of resistance that has consequences. How well versed are we in ways of considering these consequences? Passing the buck to nature as a source of authority is not only indicative of bad scientific practice, but strikes me as a shortsighted vantage point from which to consider fundamental questions such as whether those who deviate from the status quo are social misfits or cultural pioneers. It is both illogical and irresponsible to assume that nature will render moral judgment.

3

To Belong or Not to Belong?

Paradoxes of Community

PARADOX

Humans are social creatures. We gain an encyclopedia of knowledge about who to be and how to behave through participation in significant social groups. We derive our sense of self from the values and customs of these groups. Many social and political issues can be usefully understood in terms of some of the paradoxes of social groups. One paradox is that groups must have well defined rules and regulations in order to be distinctive from other groups and to attract members. This has led many philosophers and sociologists to wonder why some people would voluntarily agree to abide by some very strict group rules. An answer is that people derive a sense of meaning and purpose from these groups. Which leads to another paradox, the tension between individual desires and group expectations. Without significant social groups, we would have no sense of self and no forum through which to express ourselves. However, group expectations place a limit on how we can express ourselves. Much of who we become can be analyzed in terms of the struggle between individual expression and group expectations. There is another paradox that arises in group politics. This is the paradox of exclusion. In order to maintain its distinctive value system, groups exclude those who do not conform or whose ideas threaten the status quo. These exclusionary practices can become a source of tension and strain within the group. The ways in which groups resolve these tensions are likely to result in social changes. External forces may also exert pressure on certain groups to be less exclusionary or to alter some of their practices. The struggle to maintain group distinctions amidst these tensions is a useful basis for understanding social conflict and social change.

Consider the following three vignettes:

* * *

Early in the spring of 1983 the temperatures in Northern Utah changed suddenly from the '40s to the '80s. Several consecutive days of abnormally high temperatures immediately melted the enormous snowpack in the mountains that surround the Salt Lake Valley. Flood disaster experts warned that homes and city buildings would have to be evacuated. One engineer posed an alternative. The risky plan called for a dike to be constructed along main streets adjacent to the creeks that carried the usually slow-paced run-off. The dike would form a river channel capable of containing massive volumes of water as it gushed downward through the city en route to the Great Salt Lake. The problem with the plan was that it would require the efforts of thousands of volunteers to pile sandbags around the clock for several days, perhaps weeks. Despite the willingness of people to volunteer in times of crisis, the magnitude of organizing such an effort seemed impossible to the engineers.

Not to worry, responded city officials when they were presented with the plan. A couple of phone calls will take care of it. Within hours a brigade more than ten thousand strong had assembled in orderly fashion at designated points to begin the assembly-line process of filling, hauling and piling sandbags along a 20-mile route. With the efficiency of ants, the brigade continued its activity for the next two weeks, maintaining a dike that contained a river running from the hillside neighborhoods down through Main Street and out onto the salt flats—a river so high that some locals attempted rafting excursions. National observers touted the event as one of the most amazing feats of spontaneous collective organization in the history of the country. Over 200,000 volunteers worked for two weeks to build the dike. Twenty thousand people continued the efforts of maintaining the flood over the following weeks. How was such a massive effort launched and sustained with such minor fuss?

* * *

In the 1985 film *Witness*, a young, recently widowed Amish woman, Rachel, wrestles with her romantic feelings for an outsider, John Book. Book is a cop who has taken refuge with the Amish while awaiting the opportunity to expose a police conspiracy that involves the murder of another cop. Rachel's young son, Samuel, was witness to this murder. In a sentimental scene that is familiar to Western audiences for its romantic overtones, John and Rachel are moved to dance together to a popular song that comes over the radio in the car that John is attempting to repair in the barn. When Rachel's father-in-law discovers the pair he sends Rachel back to the house with the admonition that if she doesn't watch herself she will be shunned by the Amish community. "I'll be the judge of my own actions," she protests. "No," he whispers sternly in reply, "*they'll* be the judge. And they can shun you, You know they can. And you know what shunning means. I can't talk with you, can't attend services with you, can't even take food from your hand."

My classes of college juniors who watch the film are dismayed when in the end Rachel chooses to stay with the Amish rather than follow John Book on his return to the contemporary world. "How could she stay?" they invariably exclaim. "She cares about him so much and the Amish are so repressive, they won't even let her dance or listen to the radio!" The following day I ask the students to write essays in response to the questions: What are your values? What groups/sets of people have been influential in shaping these values? In the essays the majority of the students claim that no group has shaped their values, their ideals are their own. Listening to them I am reminded of the stark individualism expressed by Thomas Jefferson when, in response to an increasing number of religious and secular organizations populating the new west, he announced, "I am my own sect!"

* * *

The tone is celebratory when a respected Free Methodist university announces that it has successfully courted and hired an eminent poet to join the faculty of the English Department. The poet's work has been published in the best journals and the faculty are impressed by his reputation as a teacher, his commitment to Christian ethics, which is a requirement for employment at the university, and his general collegiality. They consider his hire a boon for the university. Several weeks later turmoil breaks out when it is announced by the President of the University that the poet's offer has been rescinded. Cries of dismay echo through the campus community. What could have gone wrong? Rumors circulate. The local secular press accuse the university of unconstitutional hiring practices. Eventually the university issues an official statement in which it is explained that it has been discovered that the poet's work includes the publication of erotic material. This work makes him an unsuitable candidate for membership in the Christian campus community. The startled poet responds that the work in question, a poem published in the prestigious *Paris Review,* is part of an intended trilogy in which he explores the relationship among the body, sexuality and spirituality. His aim, he states, is to reclaim the body as a worthwhile subject within the boundaries of Christianity. He reiterates his own commitment to Christianity. His supporters within the university draw attention to his reputation as a *Christian* poet and his untarnished record as a practitioner of the faith. Yet university officials remain firm in their decision to deny the poet entrance to their ranks. The incident wreaks havoc in the campus community. The Chair of the English Department quits his post in protest. Schisms form. The erstwhile peaceful Commons becomes the site of loud, angry deliberations on the subject. This is a community in turmoil.

What Is Community?

What is community? The concept is ubiquitous in social studies but definitions of *community* remain elusive. Anthropologists and ethnographers often assume the meaning and presence of community in their studies. We read about various ethnic communities, religious communities, neighborhood communities, the gay community, the women's community and so forth. Conversely, many of the persons who consider themselves representative of such groups question whether or not a publicly recognized collective, such as women, or Christians, or gays, actually constitutes a "community." Journalists, clergy and laypersons speculate a great deal on the demise or absence of community without really defining what they mean by the idea of community.

Nineteenth-century sociologists Emile Durkheim and Ferdinand Toennies asked the question: What bonds persons to one another? They compared the connections among members of primitive tribal groups with people in newly industrialized, bureaucratized societies. They concluded that in primitive circumstances in which persons are forced together through geography and a lack of alternatives, there is a sort of automatic interconnection. Durkheim called this *mechanical solidarity*. Under such circumstances, which characterize primitive, nonindustrial groups, people had no social knowledge other than that of the group into which they are born. The group is organized by a division of labor that sorts its members into interdependent roles. Rituals and beliefs reflect and reinforce these roles. The lack of alternative groups ensures membership. The appearance of everyone having a place and working cooperatively toward shared goals is suggestive of what we tend to think of as a community. In such cases the bonds of community can be said to be mechanical. They occur automatically.

Alternately, when persons move from agrarian groups to industrialized societies the scene they encounter is very different. Work groups are separated from domestic groups. The commodification of work separates it from the realm of sacred or meaningful rituals that might otherwise be associated with the cultivation and production of life-giving substances. In short, the basis for mechanical domestic, religious and creative connections between persons does not exist in urban spaces. Early sociologists were wary of the consequences of industrialization and the rise of urban life because they feared that these would erode the basis of mechanical connections between people; they feared the demise of automatic community.

Toennies predicted a drift from community (small villages and extended families), which he termed *Gemeinschaft,* to a more individualistic, purposive form of social organization based on society or the nation-state. He called this latter form *Gesellschaft.* In this stage, he suggested, people would be loosely connected through their material and civic needs. Civic needs would necessitate allegiance to a particular government in return for protection of civil rights and the expectation of basic services. Material needs would require persons to transact with one another in market exchanges of goods, but such alliances were likely to be anonymous, or at least without strong feelings of connection.

The contemporary relationship between bankers and farmers is an illustration. Farmers rely on banks to front the cash necessary to purchase seed and basic supplies while awaiting the harvest. For decades American farmers worked in concert with local banks. The bankers themselves were likely to have grown up in the farming community and to know the farmers. Credit was extended and renewed based on long-term relationships. People knew one another and trusted one another. Business transactions were based on honor and familiarity. In recent years, as large corporate businesses have absorbed local banks, the criterion for credit has shifted to a standard numerical rating system. A farmer is extended credit based on a "risk calculation" and a resulting point scale. There is no place for a relationship history in these assessments. Numbers are impersonal. One result of impersonal corporate assessment of risk is the demise of family farms whose financial viability was dependent on a community relationship with the bank. As local banks disappear, so too do family farms.

In chronicling the excesses and abuses of the industrial and economic revolutions, historical observers have probably romanticized the presumed communality of the previous agrarian era. The concept of mechanical solidarity makes sense in its depiction of persons as interconnected in all of their affairs—subsistence production, family, politics and religion. Obviously, if all these enterprises are conducted simultaneously among the same persons there will be a form of connection that is similar to that which occurs among members of biological families who have only each other to rely on and to interact with.

However, despite the bucolic renderings of such "communities" there is nothing romantic about being in a group because there is no other choice. The modern conception of community implies a self-conscious awareness among members of the group—an awareness that they are part of the group and willingly connected to it. Self-aware community members are motivated by a sense of being *for* the group. This is something altogether different than simply being *of* the group. Durkheim called this form of connection *organic solidarity*. He posed a question that has occupied sociologists ever since: What bonds people together when social conditions don't force them to cooperate with one another mechanically? Given the thesis that urban industrial life would erode mechanical solidarity, Durkheim noted that people still formed meaningful connections with one another and grouped themselves into self-defined communities. If it wasn't a matter of necessity, what *was* the basis of connection among these groups, he wondered. How did community emerge organically?

The question is profound. I find it useful to think about it this way. In modern urban life we encounter countless individuals every day and engage in numerous collective activities. We encounter some people repeatedly and perform the same transactions over and over. Consider the activities of buying gas or groceries. You may purchase gas once a week from the same station attendant and pick up groceries in the same store every few days. Do you consider the gas attendant or the grocery cashier to be important persons in your life? Would you expect to exchange birthday gifts with them or to celebrate meaningful occasions together? Unless you are related to these people in some other way, you probably find the idea preposterous. Yet it is noteworthy that we spend more time with many such persons than we do with our so-called loved ones or in the presence of groups we consider to be our "communities."

Proximity and the Stranger

Premodern (i.e., preindustrial, prebureaucratic) morality and community emerged from *proximity.* Persons considered themselves to be bound to those in close proximity, not just physical proximity, but metaphorical proximity. The degree of bondedness was considered a degree of social distance between Ego and Other. Edmund Leach, an anthropologist, noted the overlap among kinship, animal and geographical categories of relations. Consider the relations "self-sister-cousin-neighbor-stranger." This social measurement of degree of expected bond paralleled the agrarian relation of "self-pet-live-stock-game-wild animal." This matches the geographical chain "self-house-farm-field-far away." In this arrangement, if someone comes from "far away," she is a stranger.

The possibilities for relating to the stranger include either absorption—she will remain and hence become a neighbor; or expulsion, should she appear to be "wild" or an enemy. Thus, community is a mechanical state of being that includes those within close proximity and excludes those who are "far away." "Far away" and "stranger" are one and the same. Strangers are out of sight, and therefore out of mind. Those in close proximity are "community." Whether one wants to or not, one must be "engaged" with them. Several social and philosophical observers have suggested that this face-to-face proximity *demands engagement* and it is this engagement that is the basis of community and morality. The nature of communal relations *emerges* from the demands of engagement.

In modern, industrial society all this changes. The urban metropolis is a space in which one encounters "strangers" all around. Strangers are not "far away" and therefore beyond engagement. They occupy proximal space. Sociologist Georg Simmel, who wrote in the mid-1800s, was intrigued with the combination of the Stranger and the Metropolis. According to Simmel, in order to live in the midst of strangers, people must cultivate a posture of *indifference.* You and I are able to occupy the same physical space, even to transact certain business dealings, without being required actually to *engage* one another—as long as we remain indifferent or blasé. In an urban setting in which strangers are forced together indiscriminately, indifference is a civil response. The well-mannered person of the modern age knows just how much social and psychological distance to grant strangers. Too much engagement entreats a response from the Other, and this would be considered a violation of "their space" and poor conduct. This cultivated indifference is what Miss Manners might call the "cuticle" that guards against the friction of the proximity of strangers. It is indeed a civil response for modern society, but the effect of this indifference is a *loss of face.* We soon learn not to see the Other at all.

Within this context, Durkheim's question of the basis for community in the modern age is extremely compelling and paradoxical. In premodern times, civility *is* community. In the modern age, civility *erodes* community. If frequency of contact and proximity do not connect us to one another in what we consider *meaningful* ways, what does? Consider this scenario: Your local basketball team has made it to the national play-offs. Many persons who never pay attention to sports suddenly find themselves swept up in the heat of game fever along with those who consider themselves sports fanatics. Strangers in checkout lines, bars and other public venues strike a conversational connection in spontaneous discussions of the big game. What is this about? Why do otherwise mildly interested individuals suddenly feel so worked up over a team to which their only connection is geographical?

This sort of experience can be described as *episodic* engagement. For a brief moment, through some shared passion, we become engaged with the strangers around us. In the place of indifference, we show a bit of face and look for similar responses in others. Whether we are cheering for the same team or fighting for opposite teams, we are engaged. The experience is episodic because it is fleeting and finite. Once the moment has passed, we will be on our way, tucked comfortably into our respective cloaks of indifference.

Somewhere between these episodic encounters of arousal and everyday, sustained indifference is something that people experience as community. *In a world where we are free to remain anonymous and indifferent to one another, what are the experiences and connections that bring us together in sustained engagement?* How do we identify these experiences and the groups that emerge from them? What is the basis of the bonds that entreat us to remain engaged with a collective of Others in a spirit of investment and passionate arousal? This is the heart of Durkheim's query.

Normative Routines Versus Habits of the Heart

Durkheim never really provided a definition of community. The profundity of his question is in the recognition that we humans seek out meaningful connections and form committed attachments to one another and to ideas even when we are not forced to do so by circumstance. Rather than ask why we do this he observed simply that we do, and turned his attention to the question of *how* we do this. How, under circumstances that are not necessarily conducive to community formation, do people form meaningful attachments? Attachments that capture the heart and prompt engagement? In this regard he turned on its head the issue that preoccupied the Utilitarian theorists of his day. A major puzzle for these theorists was "the social contract." Why did people voluntarily follow the rules of society? Utilitarian philosophers answered that we do so because the rules serve our interests in transacting with another to meet our needs. For instance, I don't cheat you by stealing from your store when you are not looking and, in turn, you provide me with quality goods that will keep me returning to do business with you. Abiding by the rules makes for orderly and less risky business transactions. These actions are "routines" that enable us to conduct good business. We are only attached to them to the extent that we expect to be rewarded if we follow them and punished if we do not.

In contrast, Durkheim (who was quite vehement in his opposition to the Utilitarians), proposed that the social contract is a *consequence* of social commitment, or "community." Persons don't follow the rules because they expect to get something out of doing so. They follow them because they value the rules as meaningful in themselves. They are meaningful codes of conduct that reflect a commitment to a particular group. When people value a group, they will voluntarily abide by its rules of conduct and organize their lives accordingly. They are also willing to make sacrifices and to fight for their "community." Thus, an operative definition of community, one that has since been picked up by some social psychologists (e.g., Tajfel, Turner), is that a community consists of members who are self-aware of their connection to the group and who, when faced with choices, choose in accordance with group expectations. This latter clause, as we shall see, is pivotal in ascertaining "commitment." Furthermore, member commitment is a key factor in assessing the dynamics of communities.

The remainder of this chapter is about some of the remarkable features of community. It is also about the paradoxes that shape community dynamics and, in turn, individual self-awareness and commitments. The thesis throughout this chapter is that both individual behavior and social processes can be understood by focusing on how individuals and communities grapple with these paradoxes.

Group Propositions and Paradoxes

One of the remarkable features about communities is that because they consist of persons who are devoted to the group, these persons can be counted on to give their time and energy willingly to community endeavors. This can be stated in the following sets of related propositions:

1a. The more committed the members, the more highly they will value the community.
1b. The more they value the community, the more likely they will voluntarily follow community standards.
2a. When voluntary commitment is high, group solidarity will be high (a strong community).
2b. The stronger the community, the more likely it can respond effectively to collective problems and chart its own history.
3. Those groups that are able to solve collective problems efficiently and to chart their own course are most likely to influence socioeconomic conditions (to make a mark on history).

Two central paradoxes are revealed in these dynamics. One is the paradox between the individual and the community, another is the paradox of group boundaries. The expression of individuality is in constant tension with collective expectations. The paradox of individual and community is that individuals derive self-meaning from involvement in communities. Community commitments are the basis of individual desires and ideas. At the same time, the community also places limits on how we can express these desires and ideas. This leads to a subparadox, the paradox of "free choice." The paradox of group boundaries involves the need for groups simultaneously to retain a distinctive collective identity—this is done by sustaining a particular definition of the group's goals and exclusive membership practices—while being flexible enough to accommodate new membership and to shift with external social pressures, such as changing politics. I will explore each of these paradoxes in detail.

Individual and collective commitments can be usefully studied by focusing on the friction that comes from wrestling with these paradoxes. In studying this we also begin to understand why some groups are better able to capture the hearts of their members than other groups. Despite the lack of a general definition of community, one thing that we seem to agree on is that habit, circumstance and convenience are not sufficient to explain what we mean by the experience of community. Community is a matter of the heart.

The Paradox of Individual and Community:
Who Would I Be Without This Group?

Consider the first vignette, about the flooding in Salt Lake City. How was this feat of collective action accomplished so swiftly and efficiently? In order to pull this off the city needed to mobilize individuals who were willing to serve immediately, willing to follow instructions, willing to take direction from others and willing to continue this action for an unspecified amount of time. As anyone who has tried to convene a committee meeting and keep members on task for a couple of hours knows, this is a nearly impossible achievement in a society in which individuals are accustomed to doing things their way, and to engaging in long drawn-out deliberations about who gets to be in charge, and asking continuously: What's in it for me. Even a severe threat such as having one's house washed away is not sufficient to guarantee that someone will adhere to a collective plan for saving the entire city. The more likely scenario is of individual neighbors pitching in to help one another in a sort of random fashion.

Salt Lake City was able to accomplish this amazing feat because of the Mormons. Utah is Mormon territory. The descendants of the Mormon pioneers who made their home in the Utah valley in the mid-1800s constitute more than half of the state's population. The Mormon community is illustrative of each of the propositions listed above. One particular aspect of Mormon communities is a top-down hierarchical structure that enables efficient communication and mobilization of thousands within a matter of hours. In the case of the 1983 floods, city officials called Mormon Church leaders. These leaders then instituted a chain of command that mobilized what was literally a small army and kept it operating with adequate reserves for many days. A pertinent question is what compels the members to adhere to such authority? Adherence to this chain of command is one of the definitive obligations for membership in the Mormon church. Why would someone voluntarily agree to these obligations?

I made this question the subject of my own dissertation research several years ago. I had been schooled in the Utilitarian theories and research. I was looking for a case in which groups were able to solve collective problems effectively, including the issue of how to retain members. This dilemma is solved most effectively when members value the group itself. Theoretically, when people place a high value on membership in a group, they will voluntarily adhere to its rules and obligations—the group will not have to police them, which, as I have discussed, eats up additional group resources. Thus, high voluntary cooperation strengthens the group's resources. I had grown up among the Mormons and knew that they fit this criterion. In my dissertation field research I asked why Mormons value their membership so much? Why are they so committed that they are willing to sacrifice some of their individual authority in order to be in this community?

This inquiry regarding the tension between individual autonomy and collective obligations is a classic American theme. An archetype of American culture is the lone hero breaking the bonds of society in order to forge new paths. This hero is rendered as the maverick, the cowboy. We celebrate individual athletes above the accomplishments of the team; we recognize individual artists and musicians and neglect the collective talents that are required to make the final product. When was the last time you saw a film that featured a community as the "star"? Americans are suspicious of societies that place the group before the individual. We assume that someone has been brainwashed if he or she shows allegiance to a group. These cultural beliefs are reflected in our constitutional history whereby legal decisions generally follow a pattern of protecting individual rights over collective concerns—if a choice must be made. Thus, the question made sense to me—why are you willing to give up so much in order to belong to this group? It did not make sense to most Mormons.

"Who would I be without my membership in the Church?" Mormon members would invariably reply when I probed into their rationale for belonging to the community. Mormons require a stricter code of conduct than other Protestant religions. In addition to abstinence from premarital sex and from drugs, rules of membership include abstinence from caffeine, alcohol, tobacco. Members are also asked to pay a tithe (10 percent) on their pretax income and to follow all guidelines established by church leaders. A question that haunts the outsider is why people would agree to these rules when they could belong to another religion that isn't so strict. The Mormons just don't see it this way, however. For them, these rules mark the boundaries of membership. Adherence to these regulations sets them apart from others and gives them a sense of belonging together in a significant community.

Consider these words from Durkheim:

> Irrespective of any external regulatory force, our capacity for feeling is in itself an insatiable and bottomless abyss. . . . [I]f nothing external can restrain this capacity, it can only be a source of torment to itself. Unlimited desires are insatiable by definition . . . inextinguishable thirst is constantly renewed torture. . . . To achieve any other result, the passions must first be limited. But since the individual has no way of limiting them, this must be done by some force exterior to him [sic]. A regulative force. (quoted in Farganis 1996: 81-2)

Durkheim is suggesting that persons want and need regulations on their appetites and desires. A completely unrestrained individual will is intolerable. In such a state we would all run amok with an overabundance of behavioral choices. Social groups act as a regulative force. They provide persons with guidelines for behavior. Over time these social expectations may even become automatic, or what sociologists refer to as *normative*. We follow social rules and expectations because we expect to be rewarded for doing so and punished for not doing so. Or, we simply haven't thought about possible alternatives—we're following the expectations mindlessly. The majority of our actions are normative. The logic of normative behavior does explain how social expectations help to curb individual excess, to socialize us into harmony with collective expectations. But we still haven't explained why persons follow the rules of a particular group or community and not others, especially when choices are available.

Durkheim provides an answer for this as well. He suggested that, more than anything, persons want to value something beyond themselves:

> Life is said to be intolerable unless some reason for existing is involved, some purpose justifying life's trials. The individual alone is not a sufficient end for this activity. . . . The influence of society is what has aroused in us sentiments of sympathy and solidarity drawing us toward others. . . . The wise being limits himself [sic] to a few well-chosen attachments which are not in constant need of replacement and serve as an anchor, a touchstone in the hour of difficulty. (quoted in Farganis 1996: 77-8).

And where are these "attachments" to be found? According to Durkheim:

> [T]he clan, by the manner in which it acts upon its members, awakens within them an idea of external forces which dominate and exalt them.

The community takes on a life of its own in the eyes of its members, it becomes a touchstone, a reference point from which individual members derive personal meaning and motivation. In the words of sociologist Randall Collins, the group creates a sort of "cocoon around the individual" (1995:128). Thus, significant groups are not only a source of regulation, but of meaning and transcendence for the individual. The group becomes a source of guidance and aspiration; a raison d'être.

The next question is: How are some groups able to elicit this devotion from members? In a word, through *sacrifice*. Durkheim proposed that those persons who are required to give something of themselves to the group will find the group more meaningful. They will feel a sense of investment in and involvement with the community. The group must also be successful in order for individuals to retain a sense of attachment and willing investment. This is a paradox in that the very success of the group depends on investments from individual members. Group success is a function of high individual-level commitment. Paradoxically, individual commitment is likely when the group is successful. Participation in organized sports is a good example. For the team to be successful, individuals players must be willing to work hard, to sacrifice, for the team. This often means a willingness to adhere to strict routines regarding practices and care of one's body. As the team begins to win, players (as well as fans) become deeply committed and are likely to give even more to the team. They are also likely to identify strongly as team members.

In addition to sacrifice through adherence to strong regulations, strong groups also have special *symbols and rituals*. Symbols establish the group as a distinctive entity; they serve a totemic function around which members gather and manifest their connection. Symbols also mark certain objects and practices as sacred. Through sacred symbols and practices, members are able to rise above the mundane and to look toward certain things as especially meaningful. Symbols are complemented by rituals. Regarding rituals, Durkheim suggested that participation in sacred ceremonies "awaken[s] within members that idea that outside of them there exist forces which dominate them and at the same time sustain them." Rituals give the individual a "larger than life" sense of meaning and bring the group together in shared focus. And when they:

> once come together, a sort of electricity is formed by their collecting which quickly transports them to an extraordinary degree of exaltation. . . . One can readily conceive how, when arrived at this state of exaltation, a man [sic] does not recognize himself any longer. Feeling himself carried away by some sort of external power it seems to him that he has become a new being: the decorations that he puts on and the masks that cover his face and figure materially aid this interior transformation. And at the same time his companions feel themselves transformed in the same way and express this sentiment by their cries, their gestures and their general attitude, everything is just as though he really were transported into a special world. (Durkheim 1915:241-42)

Rituals, according to Durkheim, enable members to throw off the yoke of reason and to come together in emotionally charged moments that capture the deepest sentiments. He concludes: "Groups without rituals will not hold their members' hearts nor gain their cooperation." Durkheim has in mind the sort of rituals that we usually associate with religious experiences, but there are similarities with contemporary secular practices; singular occasions and ceremonial events that can be likened to his description of ritual and that call to mind the "exaltation" of such shared moments, no matter how fleeting. For example, I am always amazed at the enthusiasm with which people who have no other connection to one another come together to participate in sports events. Eager fans purchase clothing and accessories that signal which team they are rooting for. Rituals such as tailgate parties, waves and gleeful adornment with team costumes signal the significance of the moment and mark it as something extraordinary. Seen this way, sports can be analyzed as a sort of modern-day religious experience.

A sociologist, Rosabeth Moss Kanter, studied several nineteenth-century American communes that sprang up in the new west (upper New York State, Ohio, Kansas and Iowa). Besides the Mormons, only a few of these communities were able to sustain themselves longer than five years, or one generation. Originally numbering in the hundreds, the only communities that are now household names include the Amish, the Shakers, Oneida, Amana and a handful of others. Why did these communities fare so well while others did not? Using Durkheim's theory, Kanter points out that the successful communities met three criteria: They had strong regulatory boundaries, they required members to make sacrifices and they practiced rituals. The groups that fared the least well were those that espoused the philosophy of "do your own thing." It turns out that people who are bonded together for no other reason than to do their own thing have very little to connect them to one another. Not surprisingly, the most successful of the communes had a religious basis. Established religious groups usually have firmly entrenched rules and regulations that include sacrifices and participation in ceremonies that separate everyday affairs from sacred moments.

As a community, the Mormons meet each of these criteria. According to Durkheim, this should make them a strong group that has captured the hearts of its members. Indeed, most active Mormons consider their religious affiliation to be a "total way of life." As many members put it: "It's not just about going to church once or twice a week, or obeying the rules. It's who I am." The implication sociologists draw from this is that community is manifest when persons are self-aware of membership in a group and when they derive meaning from and organize their lives around the group. Mormons not only follow strict rules of membership, they embrace these rules as a basis of who they are and what they stand for. It is through their sacrifices and participation in the group that they develop a sense of themselves as individuals. This is community of the heart.

Following the propositions, if members willingly commit to these regulations, the community will prosper and will achieve its own distinctive identity. Currently the Mormons are one of the fastest growing churches in the world and their reputation as a distinctive cultural group is so widespread that some observers have begun to refer to Mormonism as a form of pseudo-ethnicity. As a case study, the Mormons seem to bear out the propositional equations of group solidarity.

Consider some of the rules that you use to guide your own activities. What are some of your values? With whom do you share these rules and values? Think of 10 responses to the question: Who am I? Do these responses indicate particular types of connections to others? For instance, if you mentioned "student," you have referenced a college group from which you derive your position as a student. Most persons respond to this question in terms of social identities such as "brother, mother, teacher, minister, etc." These are *roles* that take on significance through the social relations in which they are enacted. This question is the basis for determining the significant reference groups in your life—the collectivities that give you a sense of meaning and purpose and serve as guidelines by which you organize your behavior. Do any of these groups fit the criteria for community that we have been discussing? Think about some of the difficult decisions that you make in your life; decisions about how to allocate your time and energy, when to change your plans for someone else and so forth. What are some of the most wrenching conflicts you have experienced? What do these choices and conflicts reveal about your own commitments to particular groups and ideals?

The Paradox of "Free Choice"

Mormonism is a strong community that has made a significant social impact because there is a critical mass of members who organize their lives around the church. Belonging to this group is a primary value for them. They also have a shared sense of themselves as a community. Does this imply that all Mormons are always content with the ways of their community? Are all of them equally willing to submit to the obligations of membership? One dilemma of community is that in order for it to thrive, individuals must willingly sacrifice some of their free will to the collective good. Conversely, one of the cherished beliefs in Western cultures is that the truly free individual is the one who is able to differentiate herself from the common mind. Robert Bellah, coauthor of a widely read book on the topic, discusses "mythic individualism": "A deep and continuing theme in American literature is the hero who must leave society in order to realize the moral good" (Bellah et al., 1985, p. 284). The consequence is the community/individual paradox: If individuals are not willing to regulate their tastes and drives within group boundaries, then there will be no group to speak of. This means that the individual will no longer have the community as a basis from which to derive personal meaning. On the other hand, the individual who is completely driven by the expectations of the community is considered to be a sort of social robot, an automaton with no will of its own.

Are Mormons automatons? Is the price of strong community a loss of individual drive and initiative? How do we make sense of groups such as those consisting of the hundreds at Jonestown who died after knowingly drinking cyanide-laced Kool-Aid in response to a directive from their leader, or the members of Heaven's Gate who took their lives in order to follow a comet? Have these people given their individual minds completely over to the group? Can we consider them in the same terms as the Mormons or other seemingly productive communities that have a high degree of member commitment? Is it simply a matter of degree?

These are the questions posed to me by students when discussing the film *Witness.* One of the most compelling scenes in the film depicts a barn raising. In a single, joy-filled day the Amish come together to build a barn for a newlywed couple. The collective coordination and harmony elicits hushed oohs and ahs from the class as they watch the film. As the film portrays it, through their strength of community the Amish are able to build something magnificent, enjoy one another's company and experience the pride of accomplishment all in a single activity. In spite of their wonderment at this concerted effort, the students are worked up over questions of what one has to give up to belong to this community. They are not particularly disturbed by the lack of amenities that is a result of an agrarian, minimal technology mode of production. The Amish philosophy of nonviolence is even agreeable to many outside observers. What rankles so many of the students is the apparent absence of individual will. For instance, several students note the rigidity of gender roles, particularly at the barn raising where the men and boys climb, hammer and build, while the women cook, visit and quilt. Like the Mormons, the Amish are a patriarchal community in which men are the voice of authority in their homes and a group of male elders is the supreme authority for the collective. For the most part, members of the community do what the elders tell them to do. The students are particularly distraught that Rachel and John do not pursue their mutual attraction. This, it seems, is a supreme sacrifice: giving up true love in order to remain a member of the community. "How could she do it!?" several students exclaim in dismay. "What a sad ending."

Why is this considered a sad ending? The community will continue to thrive because its members give up forbidden attractions and intrigues, such as romance with an outsider. Is this such a terrible outcome? Modern romance is perhaps one of the cumulative indicators of a culture of individualism. The deeply held ideal that one should be able to mate with the person of one's choice marks a succession of cultural arrangements whereby the desires of individuals supersede the needs of the group. Such choices include decisions to move away from the family home, seek a vocation or employment beyond family subsistence production and venture out into the larger society. These individual choices were facilitated in the nineteenth century by the forms of transportation and the rise of urban centers that ushered in new lines of work related to industrial growth. Shifts in laws during this period, often labeled legal "reforms," reflect a new interest in protecting the individual's right to choose over the collective needs of family, community or work group.

Patterns of courtship and marriage shifted concurrently. Marriage has always been a political and economic arrangement in most societies. In many societies the marriage of two individuals symbolizes an alliance between different groups. In such cases marriage is not the culmination of attraction, but a political gesture that has explicit consequences for the community. Marriage continues to be an economic arrangement in many societies in which the family is the basic unit of production. Whether the group practices monogamy, polygyny or polyandry, marriage partners constitute units who share the tasks of providing food and nurturance for offspring. Sex for the purposes of reproduction is not necessarily associated with "love" in these arrangements. Contemporary ideals of "romantic love" imply an Other who is the object of the individual's infatuation or some "deep" form of individual emotional arousal. The emphasis on an *individual* love interest—a subject that is pleasing to the individual—reflects a culture in which individual mate selection does not have immediate consequences for the community. Even when marriage became a matter of individual choice, it was generally assumed that people would select a partner from within the group, thereby ensuring that the group's culture is passed on to the next generation.

Although choice of mates is certainly encouraged among the Amish, members of the community are also aware that they have a primary responsibility to form a self-sufficient household with a mate with whom they will share the tasks of raising children, providing their own subsistence and contributing to the community. If such marriages are the result of "true love," so much the better, but the first obligation is to perpetuate and strengthen the community through the formation of families as economic and cultural units. Rachel is aware of this and is pleased when John shows a talent for carpentry—a skill that is valued among the Amish (unlike police work). Even so, as an outsider he represents a threat to the community; his ways, particularly his association with violence, stain the practices considered sacred to the group. Thus, members are displeased with Rachel's apparent affection for John. If she pursues this affection, she will be considered selfish. Her individual desires put the group at risk. The group may feel compelled to ostracize her if she chooses John—a course of action that places individual desire above community. This is not acceptable in a group that places community first.

Alternately, contemporary Americans who value individualism consider it one of the grossest violations of human rights to prevent someone from choosing her or his own mate. Mate selection is considered a matter of personal choice because we do not see this act as having any consequences for community, and even if it did, ours is a culture that values the rights of the individual over the group. We cherish individual choice so much that we have made it a foundational pillar of the United States Constitution. Nonetheless, cultural debates over the acceptability of particular forms of mate selection continue to this day. Inter-racial marriage was illegal until 1967, families still struggle when members select a mate from a different economic or religious background, and many political and religious groups continue to seek legislation to ban same-sex unions. These attempts to restrict individual choice are usually explained as being in the best interests of the "community." In the case of inter-racial marriage, for instance, it was argued that such unions would dilute "racial purity." To this day, one can read letters to Dear Abby and Ann Landers in which couples from different religions seek advice about which set of religious community beliefs to pass on to their children. Despite cultural insistence that it is a personal choice, mate selection continues to be scrutinized in terms of community consequences, real or imagined.

The makers of the film *Witness* have set up a wrenching paradox that pushes our deepest buttons as individualists—from such a perspective Rachel is making the "ultimate" sacrifice. As John Book observes, however, one of them would have to change themselves fundamentally in order for the two of them to be together. Both of them derive significant personal meaning from their group; they would not be the same persons if they removed themselves from their respective groups in order to be with each other. Sociologists who study marriage and attraction have observed that even in our culture of "choice," persons tend to select mates who are similar to themselves in terms of ethnicity, education, socioeconomic background, religion and other factors that designate a person's sense of group membership. It's not that we don't develop attractions for persons who have very different group alliances. Rather, in cases where someone is attracted to someone who is not representative of Ego's significant group's values, the struggle to maintain a connection with this group while developing significant ties to someone of whom the collective disapproves eventually leads to a choice in which the person may feel compelled to select either the group or the mate.

Forging Self Through Choice

Let's return to the question of whether individuals who submit to the regulations of their groups are "brainwashed." Recall Durkheim's assertion that persons derive meaning from their membership in groups. We can interpret this to mean that we forge a sense of who we are through the choices we make regarding group boundaries. Rachel *is* free to choose. Her choice is a difficult one, but we can imagine that in the process of wrestling this difficult choice she becomes more aware of her own values; she may reconsider some of the benefits of her membership among the Amish that she has taken for granted before she was faced with a choice. In the end, her decision will reflect a process of self-awareness through which she articulates her rationale for belonging to the group, and in so doing, becomes more committed. Having made a sacrifice for the group, Rachel may feel more attached to it. At the same time, she may also expect more from her community and become more vocal in saying so. Thus, she may become a more active participant. So long as one has a choice, it is possible to conclude that self-aware commitment is the basis of strong, responsible community participation.

Utilitarian philosophers, such as Jeremy Bentham, have suggested that a person's true commitments are revealed only when a difficult choice must be made. Until such choices are thrust upon us, we are often unaware of our commitments. Once we have made such choices, especially those that involve sacrifice, it can be said that we hold a heartfelt commitment. Durkheim's thesis leads to the conclusion that the strongest communities will be those whose members are consciously aware of their obligations and heartfelt in their commitments. The communities will thrive because the members are voluntary participants who are actively engaged both *in* and *for* the group. Observations made by Bellah and colleagues, Kanter, and other scholars of community support this thesis. Thus, one set of criteria for assessing the potential endurance and impact of the community is whether or not members make self-aware, voluntary choices that require sacrifice. According to this criterion, we would not expect to find a high level of commitment in groups with "unreasonable rules" and no choice. In such cases, compliance with the rules would be considered a result of coercion and/or lack of alternatives.

This is a useful framework for assessing a variety of commitments and the subsequent erosion or development of various social institutions. For instance, observers who attribute the "decline of the family" to a loss of moral commitment to marriage often refer to earlier times as a sort of golden era in which spouses were deeply and irrevocably committed to one another. Consider, however, the circumstances of a woman who is living on an early twentieth-century farm with no close neighbors and no cash resources. She has several children to feed and no means of support other than her husband's labor. We could say that she is dependent on her husband, so dependent that she may "put up with" abuse and infidelity. Is this dependency the same thing as commitment? Does the fact that these women did not leave their husbands, just as many women in similar circumstances do not today, indicate a strong moral commitment to the institution of marriage? Or is it indicative of a lack of choice?

In contrast, as women have become more educated and have found other sources of social and economic support many of them have chosen not to remain in "loveless" marriages. In a culture that prioritizes the "authentic love experience" as a basis for marriage, a "loveless" marriage is neither desirable or acceptable. As a result of this expression of individual freedom of choice, the rate of divorce has indeed increased, but can we interpret this increase as a lack of commitment to the *idea* of marriage? Choice-based marriage, like any individual-level institution that requires struggle and sacrifice, works best when it is nested in a larger community that provides individuals with support and ritualistic reminders of the significance of the institution of marriage— collective celebrations of anniversaries, conversations among community members about how to treat spouses, and so forth. In this way the practice of marriage retains a degree of specialness. It becomes something from which individuals derive personal meaning.

Groups such as the Amish and the Mormons report a high rate of successful marriages. Marriage is an obligation of membership in both groups; it is highly valued. The community also supports individuals, economically and socially, as they struggle with the sacrifices that are necessary to make marriages work. Are these people brainwashed? To the extent that they feel that their choices are their own it is possible to conclude that their actions reflect heartfelt commitment, a commitment forged of making difficult decisions within a cultural framework that supports and values these sacrifices. Coming full circle, a consequence of this commitment is strong community, which in turn, enriches the individual lives of members who value the group. This model makes a hero of community members such as Rachel and individuals who make sacrifices for the good of the group. This a far cry from the popular image of the lone maverick as hero.

One conclusion that can be made at this point is that commitment and community solidarity can be understood through an analysis of the paradox of choice. Another conclusion is that who we are as individuals can be understood as an expression of the frictions that arise in the struggle between individual desires and collective obligations. *Who we are, how we think of ourselves and express ourselves, is a reflection of how we wrestle with these choices.*

Durkheim made another noteworthy observation. He noted that moral philosophies are a significant aspect of communities. The ideals and values of the group take root in the hearts of individual members, who then share a collective morality—a sort of collective moral conscience. Community members *trust* one another to hold the same expectations and values. These values, which are often referred to as group boundaries, mark the community as distinctive from the rest of society and constitute the basis for self-meaning among members. In this regard, group boundaries, rules and regulations constitute a sort of community identity. This leads us to a second set of paradoxes.

Two Paradoxes of Group Boundaries

All groups face the question: What makes us unique? Why would persons voluntarily give their time, energy and money to belong? Recall Durkheim's postulate that persons want to belong to something larger than themselves. Not only do we want community, we want to participate in collective moral orders that provide us with ideals, goals and aspirations beyond ourselves. We want something to believe in. Groups provide this for us by establishing and enforcing shared ideals and goals. Once we have made a commitment to a particular group, we can harness our passions in the service of group causes (sometimes it is the case that persons become committed to the group through participation in a shared cause). This mission gives us a sense of meaningful purpose to which we willingly contribute personal resources.

As anyone who has helped to write a mission statement for a new group knows, group boundaries are not set in stone. Members hash them out through ongoing discussions of what the group's purpose is and how this purpose should be achieved. These mission statements usually include rules and regulations of membership. An interesting feature of new groups is that no matter how radical their goals, they tend to have a low level of tolerance for deviance. This can be explained in terms of the individual/community paradox. If a group's existence is new (and particularly if it is controversial in the larger society), its boundaries are fragile. Members must therefore be highly compliant and willing to make sure that others are equally compliant if the group is going to take root and become a significant force in society.

During the mid 1800s, among the many dozens of alternative communities that sprung up in the new west, several espoused very radical philosophies, such as open sexuality, nonmonogamy, and "group marriage." Despite the emphasis on open sexual relations, many persons continued to form bonds as couples and wanted to be sexually exclusive with one another. This pair-bonding did not reflect the philosophies on which these groups were based. Eventually many of these would-be sex radicals drifted off to live more traditional married lives. The sex-radical groups that had any long-term duration were those that realized the philosophy of nonownership of another person by enforcing a policy of nonmonogamy with strict regulations. One such group was the Oneida Community.

John Noyes, the founder of the Oneida Community, based his philosophy of nonmonogamy on an interpretation of biblical passages from the Book of Matthew and the Book of John.

> In the kingdom of heaven, the intimate union, which in the world is limited to pairs, extends to the whole body of believers. (John 17:21)

> In the kingdom of heaven, the institution of marriage, which assigns exclusive possession of one man to one woman, does not exist. (Matthew 22:23-30)

Noyes came up with several regulations designed to make the new community plan work. These included elaborate rituals of courtship designed to ensure that the less attractive or older members of the community were not left out; regulations about when and with whom men could ejaculate (only with postmenopausal women unless given alternative permission); rules regarding which members of the community could give birth; an individual could not be in the company of the same person for more than a limited number of hours; members were required to have a minimum number of sexual partners every week; and so forth. As restrictive as these rules may seem to an outsider, Noyes deemed them necessary to ensure that the community's radical philosophy was actually practiced. The rules worked. The Oneida "Perfectionists," as they were known, lived together and flourished for many decades.

Groups and communities with considerable longevity have long-standing traditions and well-marked boundaries. Religions and well-established organizations such as universities and some political organizations are examples of such groups. Members of such groups often take the regulatory boundaries for granted. A few infractions won't topple the entire community. When members of such communities do become aroused at a violation of the rules, or a proposed change in philosophy, the resulting debates and outrage constitute a sort of boundary skirmish that serves as a reminder of what the group stands for. These boundary skirmishes generally arise in response to two general issues: (1) whether or not to tolerate/exclude certain members whose practices deviate from the group, and (2) debates about whether to change existing rules and philosophies in acquiescence to larger political pressures. These skirmishes are usually very heated and arouse the hearts as well as the heads of members. These moral deliberations pose a paradox for groups because any resulting change in practices and philosophies may alienate members. Yet failure to reconsider boundaries may result in both internal and external forms of social and political pressure on the group. Regardless of the outcomes, these paradoxes are a useful framework through which to make sense of community dynamics and change.

The Paradox of Exclusion

Consider the third vignette at the beginning of this chapter. Seattle Pacific University is a well-respected, long-established institution founded in accordance with the principles of the Free Methodist Church. In order to ensure the university's distinction as a Christian community, students and faculty members are required to take an oath of allegiance that stipulates adherence to specific religious principles. Persons who wish to attend school or work in this community must also write a statement describing their commitment to Christian principles. This practice is followed in many universities with a particular religious or political mission. The practice is a signal to members that they can expect others within the community to share their beliefs and goals. Rather than see it as a restriction, the members of the SPU community consider it a reasonable requirement for inclusion in the group.

One of the tenets of Christianity that the community subscribes to is sexual chastity. As a community, SPU teaches that sexual expression should be contained within marriage and treated with circumspectial reverence and modesty in any public reference. They consider this belief to be a significant group boundary that sets them apart from general society, especially among contemporary college youth. Thus the discovery that a newly hired English professor, Scott Cairn, had published an erotic poem in an international magazine resulted in a very heated boundary debate. Cairn is a renowned Christian poet. He made his application for a faculty position at SPU in full awareness of the religious philosophies by which the University operates. He wrote an eloquent statement describing his commitment to Christianity. He *wanted* to belong to such a community. He also wanted to stretch the boundaries of Christian literature to include considerations of the body and sexuality. In his own words, "I want to reclaim the body for Christianity." In this regard, Cairn can be seen as a boundary maverick. However, many members of the SPU community did not appreciate his attempts to chart a new frontier.

In his decision to rescind the offer to employ Cairn, the SPU President cites the University's fundamental commitment to sexual chastity and reminds the community that its faculty has an obligation to its students to serve as role models regarding tastes in literature and education. By framing the decision this way, the President explicitly marks a community boundary. A large contingent of the SPU community did not agree with the President and his supporting Board of Regents. Some of the faculty, including the Chair of the English Department, were so outraged at Cairn's exclusion that they resigned their administrative posts in protest. This was definitely a community divided.

Regardless of the position taken by various members of the community, the issue highlights various boundaries that give the group its meaning. Those in agreement with the decision felt strongly that it was necessary to remind themselves and society generally of the group's commitment to chastity. If Cairn were allowed into the community and continued his line of writing, a particular distinctive boundary would be eroded; the group might eventually be no different than secular universities. Those who opposed the decision framed their dissent in terms of the ethic of Christian tolerance and acceptance; how can we be practicing Christians, they cried, if we exclude others on such tenuous grounds?

The sting of this battle still reverberates through the campus. It is illustrative of the paradox of exclusion. Cairn's inclusion would definitely have stretched the group's boundary lines. The distinctive characteristics of the group would have changed as a result of his admission to a prestigious faculty position with national attention. The paradox is that boundary lines have changed anyway. Many members of the community are now disillusioned with their group; they feel they have been betrayed in terms of other meaningful ideals that define membership in a Christian community. Groups exclude some people in order to maintain boundaries, but the practice of exclusion may lead to dissension among members who wish to expand the boundaries.

A community's exclusionary practices may become the subject of disapproving scrutiny from outside. All groups are subject to these internal and external dilemmas regarding exclusionary practices and boundary delineation. Little boys establish an "all-boys tree house" founded on the shared attributes of maleness and then deliberate about whether or not to include the sister—who happens to be the one with the cookies and the newest game; radical lesbians establish a separatist commune based on their shared experiences of oppression as women, and then battle over whether to admit a male-to-female transgendered lesbian; ministry programs in universities are established to provide a systematic study of the theological epistemologies that are often missing in contemporary secular studies, the members of these programs then argue about which religions should be represented.

The paradox of exclusion doesn't provide an answer regarding who is right in these dilemmas, but explicit recognition of the paradox is useful in understanding why group members become so aroused about these debates and how the resulting battles either reaffirm or alter group boundaries. It is also a useful starting point from which to make contextually specific assessments about morality and politics. It is not possible to debate the ethics of the SPU case without understanding the relationship between community solidarity and group boundaries; specifically, the connection between the erosion of group boundaries and the possible erosion of community significance as a result.

Many groups do make significant changes as a result of these skirmishes. These groups may actually find their internal membership strengthened and their public relations improved as a result. At the same time, many loyal members may leave the flock if they perceive the changes to be too "radical" for the community identity that they wish to retain. The paradox remains: If the group moves beyond its definitive boundaries, it will no longer remain the same. For better or for worse, its collective identity will be altered, and beliefs and practices will shift accordingly. The result of these changes may appear in a form similar to that of an animal sloughing off an old skin—same basic form in a new skin, or, depending on how integral the altered beliefs and practices are to the group's identity, the changes may bring about a metamorphosis that radically alters the identity and activities of the group.

Exclusion Versus Adaptation:
The Paradox of Changing Collective Rules

The following case illustrates the complexity of this particular group dilemma and some of the additional tensions involved in boundary skirmishes. St. James Cathedral is a Seattle landmark. It sits atop one of the seven hills of the city and has been the site of many weddings and funerals of important local people. The building is also a sacred meeting place for Catholics. Church youth are enticed into the virtues of virginity with the promise of a grand white wedding in the cathedral if they save themselves for marriage. Christmas Eve Mass in the cathedral is a much-touted event. Local dignitaries expect to be given final rites in the cathedral. In accordance with Durkheim, the cathedral is a sacred symbol that stands as an iconographic representation of Catholic values.

In 1994, two gay men, one of whom described himself as a devout Catholic, submitted a request to hold a commitment ceremony celebrating their union in the cathedral. The request caused quite a stir among many religious groups nationwide and in the local secular society. According to the Catholic Catechism, the official documentation of Catholic beliefs, values and regulations, homosexuality is an affliction that cannot be helped, but should be tolerated. The Catechism states: "[Homosexuals] must be accepted with respect, compassion and sensitivity. Every sign of unjust discrimination in their regard should be avoided." Catholics in general are admonished to treat homosexuals with love and respect; Catholics who are homosexual are required to be celibate. It is the *practice* of homosexuality that is ruled to be a sin. This is a distinctive Catholic stance. To allow two gay men to use a sacred cathedral as a site celebrating their union would be a significant breach of this boundary and would profane the sacredness of the cathedral. Some members even questioned whether such an allowance would make a mockery of the sacredness of marriage in general. Church members who had raised their own children on the virtues of heterosexual monogamy spoke out passionately against allowing the gay men to (ab)use their sacred symbol.

The matter was further complicated by the fact that the local parish often rented the cathedral to non-Catholic groups for special occasions. Some of the Catholics, in concert with local non-Catholic observers, argued that denying use to the gay men would constitute preferential discrimination. Such discrimination, they claimed, would be hypocritical of the Catholic tradition of social justice. Those opposed countered that the cathedral was a Catholic space; they had every right to exclude from their sacred spaces persons whose ways of life were in official discord with Catholic doctrine. The issue caused considerable emotional strife; longtime members found themselves locked in irreconcilable differences of opinion with trusted friends and cherished clergy.

Publicly, the issue exploded as a land mine of contradiction in the field of several cherished American values. The United States Constitution upholds the rights of secular and religious groups to engage in collective practice and to protect their distinctive boundaries so long as these practices do not transgress against the basic rights of others. On the one hand, it can be argued that the Catholics are not doing anything to actively limit the practice of homosexuality among non-Catholics, they are simply protecting their right to maintain the boundaries of their private spaces according to the principles of their own beliefs. On the other hand, it can be argued that as a well-established institution that serves as a beacon on matters of social justice, the Church's decision to deny gays access to the cathedral for unions sends a message of intolerance and discrimination—a denial of basic civil rights.

The debate fueled huge rifts among gays and lesbians as well as Catholics. Many gay and lesbian groups criticized the couple's fight to secure the cathedral as a trespass against group rights and a misguided application of the principle of individual civil rights. At the root of the matter is the basic question of whether everyone should be allowed access to spaces and practices that constitute the domain of a specific group. If groups are not allowed to be exclusionary, they will cease to remain distinctive groups. Conversely, if a group is a powerful purveyor of goods and services (including ideologies) beyond group membership, should they be able to practice selective distribution within a free market system? There are numerous additional ways in which to frame this paradox of exclusion.

In this case, the Catholic diocese arrived at a compromise that didn't really suit any of the most invested parties, but that, upon analysis, reflects a savvy comprehension of the boundary paradoxes. The Church decided to let the men hold their ceremony in the cathedral, but refused to allow them to represent it as a Catholic ceremony. They were instructed to conduct it as a secular ceremony only. The Church's reasoning was that it did not want to appear to be practicing selective discrimination in its rental of the cathedral to secular parties, but at the same time it did not want to give the impression that Catholics condoned a gay union.

The Church-Sect Paradox. Two sociologists, Rodney Stark and William Bainbridge, have proposed what they call the "Church-Sect" paradox as an analytical framework for making sense of some forms of organizational politics. Sects, which they define as fringe cults, offer an alternative to members who seek religious affiliations that are less traditional, less reflective of mainstream society. Sects usually have highly charismatic leaders and offer venues for expressions of passionate spirituality. This charisma and promise of something less ordinary is what draws members to the group. Thus, the group's initial success is largely a function of how distinct it is from the mainstream.

The paradox is this: If the group is successful, it will have an expanding membership, increased visibility and a potentially significant impact in the general society. The success may lead to two related dilemmas. As the sect expands and attempts to exercise greater influence, it may find it necessary to mainstream some of its practices in order to attain resources and credibility. Simultaneously, other groups—for instance, well-established organized religions—may perceive the sect's success as a threat to traditional practices and exert pressure on the sect to curb some of its more extreme practices. To the extent that the sect does assimilate, it will cease to retain its distinctiveness as a religious group. Some members may leave the sect if they feel that it no longer represents the initial mission that compelled them to join. These members are often those who are the most zealous and are therefore the most likely to have been very committed to the group.

Currently, there is a contentious battle being waged between a handful of Baptist churches that have "open and affirming" policies for lesbian and gay members and the Baptist Council that oversees individual congregations. The policies of "inclusion" in these individual churches were authored by congregants who believe that their churches should stand, first and foremost, for "brotherly love." The Baptist Council, however, has denounced these policies as a violation of the Baptist teaching that homosexuality is an abomination. The individual congregations are like sects in that they are composed of several members who feel that their congregation is a radical (and good) alternative to traditional congregations. However, because they share the name and theology of a well-established Church, they find themselves engaged in battles over who can enjoy membership in the Church and what sort of policies should be held up to the world as banners of meaning.

The Church-Sect framework, or the Paradox of Change, is useful in understanding the points of friction that drive social change and the way in which group boundaries are continually defined and redefined. The fact that people become so emotionally invested in these border debates is indicative of the extent to which we derive personal meaning from the groups to which we are committed. The actual content of these debates reflects general social values; the debates themselves are an occasion for assessing and redefining these values. Boundary wars and exclusionary practices also reveal ways in which some groups serve as rallying sites for people who are accorded less status in general society.

One of the freedoms that we cherish in the United States is the right to assemble with other like-minded fellows for social and/or political purposes. A cornerstone of pluralist democracy is the right of such groups to exist. The fact that many countries and rulers forbid and punish "special interest groups" is an acknowledgment that an inspired critical mass *can* accomplish change. Well-organized groups of like-minded persons who share a passion and a cause can and have defined the course of history. "United we stand, divided we fall!" is a truism that reflects both the potential of community action and the difficulties of harnessing individual zeal to the collective wheel. Despite, or perhaps because of this cherished freedom, the American public expresses considerable conflict regarding exclusionary practices and group segregation.

Society as a Web of Group Interests

No group exists in a vacuum. As is illustrated by the Paradox of Change, many of the clashes that groups wrestle with involve relations with other groups and the surrounding society, which can be defined as a web of different group interests. Within this web, some group interests may be seen as more or less legitimate or worthwhile. There is a tendency to think of the United States as monolithic, a single entity comprised of a single people who are united under the banner, "One Nation, One God, One People." In fact, we are a country comprised of many peoples who have many gods, many beliefs and many interests. When someone uses the expression "We believe . . . ," to whom or what entity does the *we* refer? Instead of thinking of society as a general entity, or in terms of a general "we," it is useful to ponder which group's, web of groups', practices and ideals are being referred to. Seeing society as a web of group interests is a way of highlighting the debates, conflicts, contradictions and clashes that underlie the appearance of "general values." Whenever there appears to be a shared set of beliefs and practices among a very large, very diverse group of people, it is likely that there are many subgroups that may disagree, but that do not have the power to be heard at the general social level. What may appear as a shared general ideology, may in fact be the ideals of a few groups that have more power than other groups.

In small, isolated communities, group beliefs and practices are the subject of continual dialogue and debate. The smaller the group, the more likely persons are to participate in these conversations. According to some social theorists, it is this debate itself, particularly the emotion that underlies it, that keeps persons bonded in community. To the extent that persons remain engaged in hashing out definitions of "we," they are acting on a passion that reflects an investment in the collective. Durkheim, like other theorists of the modern age, observed the erosion of collective ties as persons moved from small isolated groups to larger, diverse urban settings. I have already discussed one consequence of this historical shift, the shift toward seeing everyone as a stranger rather than as a member of the group with whom you shared your everyday life as well as your ideals. Durkheim wondered what, if anything, would bind people together in this complex urban environment. Was there a single banner under which strangers might become unified as a group? His answer is prophetic and ironic.

The Banner of Individualism

Durkheim observed that group solidarity would not be automatic or "mechanical" in urban industrial centers where domestic, commodity, social and political spheres were increasingly separated. If community is in fact an ongoing achievement accomplished through the routinization of shared rituals—practices that remind us of our connections to something larger than ourselves—then it will be increasingly difficult to attain in the modern age. Durkheim foresaw an age in which practices of ritual significance (religion) were far removed from the necessities of everyday economic activities. In addition, he predicted the rise of myriad collectivities so diverse that it would be difficult to fix one's gaze on any one of these groups for a sustained time. It is difficult to find and practice collective meaning under such circumstances. What, then, would bind us together as a common community in the modern age? According to Durkheim, we would become united in our worship of the individual. Modern-day people, lacking any other bonds of community, would cast their collective eye upon the Individual as the sacred entity of the twentieth century. Our passions would become aroused in defense of the *Rights of the Individual*.

The United States, which intrigued Durkheim, was a newly emerging social entity. The Constitution of the United States was established within a context of diverse group interests. The ideal that those who framed the Constitution held in common was a belief in the *rights* of individuals to pursue association with and to worship with those who shared their interests and beliefs. They wanted to frame a basis for government that ensured that one group could not, for political or religious reasons, thwart the right of other groups to exist. This is the basis of the philosophy of *cultural pluralism.* Persons were free to join whatever groups they chose, and they could not be compelled to belong to any group or to espouse any belief that they did not choose. The only rule that everyone was compelled to uphold was not to trespass against the freedoms of anyone else. This is the philosophy of *political individualism.* Cultural Pluralism and Individualism are the foundational beliefs ascribed to the "American People."

In theory, this is a philosophy around which most people think they can rally. In practice, it is a bit more complicated. Complications arise because of the clashes inherent in a society composed of a web of groups whose interests are not only diverse, but often conflicting. The early history of the United States is a study in these contradictions. Not only did various *recognized* groups have competing economic and religious differences that often resulted in open conflict, there were also several *unrecognized* groups that, under the banner of "equal rights," entered into the fray. The indigenous "Indian" Nations were being overrun in the name of Anglo individualism. Women and slaves were not considered "individuals" and therefore, presumably, were outside the web of individual and group interests, except as property of their husbands and masters. Many battles have been fought and won in the United States as different groups, groups that have been historically disenfranchised, laid claim to the full rights of citizenship under the banner of Pluralism and Individualism. At the same time, there is a prevailing sense that in the web of social groups the interests of some groups carry more weight than others. On occasion, these groups even presume to speak for the country as a whole, they lay claim to be the "legitimate" voice of the "American people."

Many contemporary social debates and issues can be analyzed in terms of group dynamics. The passion and intense discussion that fuels these debates demonstrates (1) that society is a web of different group interests (rather than a monolithic belief system), (2) groups often have contradictory beliefs and goals and (3) groups are the basis of individual meaning and attachment. To conclude this chapter, I describe some of these contemporary conflicts. I hope to provoke further discussion based on these examples and invite you to explore the issues that arise in terms of the "group paradoxes."

The Possibility of Pluralism? Intergroup Conflicts

Two particular realms of contemporary social debate reflect some of the dilemmas that are inherent between the *philosophies* of pluralism and individualism and the *practice* of these philosophies. One realm concerns "group rights versus individual rights." Another realm is the debate about "balkanization" versus "common values." Both instances illustrate the ways in which individuals derive meaning from collective associations, and the potential for the different interests espoused by these groups to clash.

Group Rights Versus Individual Rights

Recently the media have focused on "hate groups." The right of "hate groups" to exist is debated in terms of freedom of expression—individual and cultural pluralism. How much freedom should be given to groups whose raison d'être is organized around hating others? Should we turn a blind eye of "civil indifference" toward groups whose practices include singling out other human beings as the target of their collective wrath and doing what they can to limit the progress of these "targets"? In a book called *Women of the Klan*, sociologist Kathleen Blee describes her interviews with women who were members of the Ku Klux Klan in the 1930s. Blee starts off with this note:

> To understand why people embrace political movements based on hatred and fear we must examine the multiple, even contradictory, levels on which reactionary movements seek to attract ordinary people. . . . Women of the Klan drew on familial and community ties—traditions of church suppers, kin reunions, and social celebrations—to circulate the Klan's message of racial, religious and national bigotry. They spread hatred through neighborhoods, family networks, and illusive webs of private relationships. The Klan's power was devastating precisely because it was so well integrated into the normal everyday life of white Protestants. (1991:3)

One of the startling revelations shared by these women is that for many of them the Klan was merely a way of community life. Many of them saw little or no contradiction between their racist ideologies and support of economic redistribution and feminism. These women are hesitant or unable to recollect the atrocities perpetrated by their husbands. The women, most of whom are now in their seventies and eighties, recollect the primary doctrinal belief that the white man has the true claim to this country. Yet the memories that arouse their interest are centered around the social community they shared with other women of the Klan.

I was pondering Blee's research while walking in the Roslyn cemetery recently. Roslyn, Washington, got its start as a coal mining town and found its fame, nearly a century later, as the filming site of the popular television series, *Northern Exposure*. A striking feature of the old town cemetery, which is now a historical landmark, is that it is divided territorially by fraternal orders. Citizens of the town were buried under the sign of lodges such as Elk, Moose and the International Order of Odd Fellows. Fraternal orders are totemic clubs dating from the nineteenth century. They arose out of a recognition that a secular government set up to protect individuals from the excesses of state authority provided no actual form of community. For settlers, many of them new immigrants who had left kin and nation behind, these orders served as a sort of "extended family." A man's order was charged with taking care of his wife and children should he be injured or meet an untimely death. The lodges also provided a basis of distinguishing oneself in terms of a particular "brotherhood." Members of lodges shared secret knowledge and displayed symbols indicating their distinctive allegiances. On the western frontier, in a time of no insurance, away from extended kin and without well-established communities, these orders served both social and economic functions for their members. The significance of these orders is marked by the fact that even in death, lodge members have chosen to have themselves and their families buried under the sign of their order.

Across the way there is a separate cemetery for black coal miners. These men (and their families?) were put to rest in unmarked graves. They were excluded from the lodges and buried without ceremony or recognition as individuals or as members of a significant group. At the time there were African American fraternal orders, just as there were Irish orders and Chinese orders, but these secret brotherhoods were largely underground, except for their organized existence in some, predominantly black, townships in the South. Thus it appears that the black coal miner making his way to a new beginning in the West was identified only by the color of his skin. He was faceless. In contrast, the lodges were groups wherein one gained face and access to activities and practices that constituted the fabric of community in that historical context.

How is this form of exclusion different (or not) from the Klan's active organization under the banner of white supremacy? What (if any) are the differences between groups that form on the basis of shared circumstances and the cultivation of shared interests, versus those groups wherein the primary interest is to advance themselves and impede those not like themselves? When I define it this way, it might be said that a sports team that seeks to win is no different than the Klan. What conceptual and ethical distinctions can be made between the two groups and their interests? Blee notes that many women of the Klan saw themselves as participating in a sisterhood whereby they assisted one another with the difficulties of economic depression and enlivened one another's lives through the bonds of community. This seems a far cry from the image of the Klan as a group of hate mongers who felt entitled to maim and kill in the pursuit of their own interests. How do we determine the right of such groups to exist in a country that presumably practices cultural and political pluralism?

In a recent book, *White Lies,* sociologist Jessie Daniels chronicles the content of over 300 current publications distributed by self-described white supremacy groups. Acting on slogans such as "The white man built America, America belongs to the white man!" members of these groups preach "racial cleansing" and cite biblical and judicial precedent in favor of racial discrimination. Though such groups claim not to condone outright acts of violence, they admit to looking the other way when members are "moved to violence" by the passion of their invective. Daniels argues that this tacit approval is tantamount to putting a bounty on someone's life. How large a threat are such groups? Where do we draw the line on their right to exist and to practice their beliefs? Daniels assesses it thus:

> [One] percent white supremacists may seem an insignificant, if unfortunate, statistic. If, however, you are a person of color, and you are a *target* of white supremacists and their discourse, then white supremacists may represent a material threat to your life. Thus, the thought of 40,000 avowed white supremacists means that there are that many more threats in the world that you must deal with. (1997:4)

The Klan has used the ethos of individual democracy as a justification for active intolerance of blacks, Catholics, Jews and anyone else not deemed a member of the white Protestant club. Judges who look the other way when "hate" crimes are committed are protecting the rights of one group to perpetuate its ideals at the expense of the rights of specific individuals. A Texas judge recently made this remark when he acquitted a man who had confessed to murdering a gay man: "I put homosexuals on the same level as prostitutes. I would be hard-pressed to give anyone time for killing a prostitute." Is this judge defending individual democracy or is he acting in defense of the values of a taken-for-granted group with which he unreflexively identifies?

Awareness of group paradoxes can help us make sense of these tensions. Seen through Daniels's lens, for instance, the debate regarding white supremacy groups can be evaluated in terms of individual rights versus collective rights. We may need to judge the magnitude of the rights in question in this case: the right to practice racial superiority as a particular creed, versus the individual's right to basic life, liberty and freedom from fear. These paradoxes reveal the dilemma of a "live-and-let-live" philosophy; this represents us as isolated individuals rather than social creatures who invent and practice shared ideals as a means of creating structures and boundaries.

"Balkanization" Versus "Common Values"

A focus on group paradoxes illuminates a struggle not only to forge distinctive group ideals, but to establish these as ideals to which everyone else should aspire. When the political, economic and social resources of a country are used to promote a single set of ideals, these ideals constitute a *hegemony*. In a hegemonic society, one group or a particular constellation of groups acts as if their collective ideals and practices are the best and most desirable for everyone. If these groups have been relatively successful in countering contradictory claims, they may even come to believe that their ideals and practices are shared by everyone. It is common for members of dominant groups to think that *everyone* belongs to their group and sees things as they do. Thus they may be suspicious and dismissive of groups that don't share their interests.

A current example of this form of group conflict is in the responses to the formation and recognition of campus organizations for women, and for racial, ethnic and sexual minorities. The formation of these groups has been the basis of a very heated debate on many college campuses. Many of the same people who are concerned about protecting the rights of "hate groups" to freedom of expression are disgruntled at the idea of "special interest groups" for those who have been historically disenfranchised and underrepresented in many public institutions. Groups that have as a purpose providing a "culturally safe space" for those whose experiences and interests may not be well represented in the general domain are being accused of "balkanization." Balkanization is the fragmenting or splintering of a single entity into different, usually conflicting, units. The concept of balkanization presumes an original entity that was, at some time or another, united with the same political and social goals. Balkanization is considered problematic because it may dilute the meaning, strength and impact of the original entity. Splinter groups drain resources away from the original entity and divert focus to more complex interests.

Those who see minority groups as a "balkanizing threat" tend to believe that there has been a single, unifying creed and set of interests in the United States. Hence, these "splinter groups" are seen as a threat to the continuation of the "common values" represented by the single entity. In fact, there has never been a single set of interests in the United States, rather there has been the *illusion of common systems of belief* as a result of hegemonic practices. In the United States there has been a history of silencing and disenfranchising certain groups by denying them access to the political and economic resources necessary to be heard. Interpreted through this history, the rise of such groups signals a claim for "equal participation and recognition in a pluralist society," not the "balkanization" or breakdown of a single, common entity.

Consider the rise of organized minority groups on college campuses. In addition to recognition and a "safe space," many of these groups have mounted campaigns for curriculum changes. The requested changes would include accredited programs in areas such as Native American studies, African American studies, Women studies, Queer studies and so forth. Some colleges and universities have implemented corresponding curricular changes with very little resistance. Others have become embroiled in intense battles over the issue. Just a few years ago on the UCLA campus, several members of a Chicano student organization barricaded themselves in university administrative offices in protest against the administration's refusal to recognize a Chicano/a studies program. One of the many issues that this battle raises is the need for group recognition. Certainly students are free to pursue Chicano/a studies on their own. However, accreditation through the university marks the pursuit with a general legitimacy. It gives it cultural capital in the public eye. Is this what UCLA wanted to avoid? The public legitimation of the study of one of the groups that constitutes a significant portion of the cultural and political landscape of the United States?

The converse side of this particular issue is the presumed erosion of one form of studies as the cornerstone of higher education, namely, the "classical canon," if students are allowed to pursue various specialized areas of studies instead. The strongest arguments against these "special issue topics" made by the keepers of the canon are that they are "fringe" interests that draw attention and resources away from "central" issues. Underlying this debate is the more general issue of whether some groups, and their histories and traditions, count more than others. Faculty and administrators who oppose the recognition and organization of alternatives to the classical curriculum understand one of the realities of group paradoxes: Failure to promote and defend the "traditional curriculum" will likely lead to dissolution, or at least alteration, as students learn to evaluate it through the lens of cultural pluralism. Once this is understood, however, it becomes possible to ask: *To what end* should this traditional canon be defended so vociferously? If it is so well institutionalized, why does the threat from alternatives seem so great?

I wonder how to make sense of cultural-political debates as diverse as these. On the one hand, how can we be so deeply troubled and confused by whether or not to limit the rights of groups who actively practice hate and violence against others? On the other hand, how do we explain the disgruntled indifference toward groups that are trying to stake claims for recognition and legitimation in what is presumably a pluralist democracy? We forge a sense of self through group attachments. These battles reflect not only the rights of groups to full expression, but our stake in the group as a manifestation of self, and a collective stake in the web of groups as a manifestation of general cultural ideals.

Hegemonies are antithetical to the practice of pluralism and, by extension, to the preservation of individual rights. Within a hegemonic system, certain persons and groups are granted the right to speak and to pursue their goals and interests over and above others in the name of "common values." In this way, the language of "common values" legitimates the goals and interests of certain groups and denies those of others. I cannot say that I believe in the rights of all groups to exist, to forge a collective voice and to pursue group interests, and then turn around and say that some groups are have more rights than others and deserve more attention and resources than others simply because they think their ideals are "better" or more "general" than those of others. The reality is that groups clash over the practices of being heard and the practices of pursuing their goals and passing on their ideas to subsequent generations. How we should collectively deal with these clashes is a moral and ethical question that is pivotal to the practice of political pluralism. According to political pluralism, groups have to come together and duke it out. Ideally, in this process of discussion, they may be able to settle some differences or to establish bases of compromise.

Hegemonic language, the language of "common values," stifles the discussion and debate that is necessary for the practice of pluralism. In theory, when one enters into a discussion with the representatives of another group, or with another who holds different interests, one is obligated to treat the other with respect. Respect is not the same thing as indifference. It implies a willingness to listen to the other and to be open to the possibility of having one's own mind changed. Sometimes the differences between groups seem irreconcilable. In this case, if the intergroup conflict involves a competition for political or cultural resources, a third, presumably neutral, party may be called upon to make an assessment of each group's claims. This judging body is expected to be "fair and impartial"—to make assessments based on the merits of the specific claims within a specific context and web of interests. In any case, the philosophy of pluralism entreats each party to be able to articulate its position relative to the specific context and in terms of consequence to other groups and individuals. For a group to claim, "We are allowed to do this, including to have our way over another group, because we represent 'common values' " is a moral cop-out and a political travesty.

Poet Audre Lorde has said, "The center cannot hold." By "center" I assume that she means a particular group that has had a stranglehold on the conscience and the resources of the American politic for several decades. This group takes its position for granted and exercises privilege in the name of the religion of "common values." Perhaps one of the most intriguing ironies of the late twentieth century is that the proliferation of this ideology has spurred those excluded from the privileges exercised by this "center" group to claim more for themselves. The irony is that those who have been excluded are now using these categories of exclusion (women, sexual/ethnic minorities, disabled) as a basis for challenging a hegemonic center group. In the process of being "othered" we have formed allegiances, shared aroused passions and come together as collectives. We have formed group identities and our own exclusion.

Conclusions: Some Afterthoughts on Pluralism and Conflict

Are Mormons automatons? How are we to understand Rachel's choice or the actions of Seattle Pacific University? These questions take on a different cast when assessed in terms of group paradoxes: the tension between self-definition and achievement, and the desire to belong to and to perpetuate the historical significance of something beyond ourselves. Sociopolitical debates regarding the rights of various groups can also be framed from this perspective. They indicate that community struggles take place within a larger web of social relations. The direction and content of the debates reveal a great deal about the hierarchies and other external factors that shape group activity.

Historian Helen Wheatley refers to a shift in group boundaries and an acceptance of new ideas and practices this way: "the village loses its insularity and gains in its ability to accommodate transience without a loss of identity. The price is a loss of particularity; but the reward is survival and perhaps even prosperity." The question, in accordance with the group paradoxes, is under what circumstances might such shifts occur? A decision by the Council of Churches to extend an embrace to homosexuals, even to allow homosexual clergy, does not necessarily erode the basic identity of these religious communities. Nor is their existence threatened. Similarly, recognition of programs of study focused on the histories and cultures of various minority groups is hardly likely to bring down the overall tradition of higher education as a community of learning. In both cases, what does happen is that more voices are represented at the collective dinner table, so to speak. The inclusion of these voices is likely to affect the beliefs and practices of the group over time, but not likely to threaten its existence. In contrast, a handful of John Books sitting at various family dinner tables among the Amish could very well result in an out-migration of enough younger members to decimate the size of the community within a generation. Viewed through the prism of group paradoxes it is possible to cast these questions in terms of the relative strength of community solidarity: How much can a group stretch its boundaries without losing its particular identity?

Pluralism, by definition, is an acknowledgment of community as a source of meaning and value, and the inevitable clash of communities as they compete for a place at the table. In a meditation on ethics, Zygmunt Bauman, a British sociologist, proffers the reminder that moral collectivity—a sense of responsibility toward the Other—arises from face-to-face communion. We are not islands unto ourselves. We derive our self-meaning through attachments to real and imagined groups. The collective enactment of this meaning is etched onto slate as value and morality. To the extent that we are aware of the connection between our local community and self-interest, we can become responsible for the choices we make in the name of the group. This includes an awareness of the potential clashes between groups and the conflicts that arise through boundary skirmishes.

It strikes me that the conversation at the table, contentious though it may be, will be altogether different when persons acknowledge the particularities of their interests and commitments, when they view them through the lens of group paradoxes, rather than claim transcendent morality based on a presumably "common" standard. In fact, inter-group conflict may be a postmodern truth. This conflict, far from being a harbinger of moral decline due to an erosion of "common standards," may lead us to a new morality, a morality based on a recognition of our collective commitments. Such a morality must also take into account the likelihood of conflict between groups. A loud din of social debate regarding intergroup conflicts and interests may be the a sign of a healthy-heart pluralist democracy beating.

In my assessment, John and Rachel made a wise decision. Their mutual awareness of the collectives through which they each derived their own meaning and sense of self enabled them to approach one another with respect. Neither of them felt pressed to throw off the cloak of who they were, as shaped by particular collective attachments, in order to join the other. Nor was either of them inclined to demand this of the other. Rather, their brief communion reminded them both of their respective web of attachments and of the irreconcilability of these webs. We realize who we are through acknowledgment of the communities that forge us. We practice pluralism when we are able to take our place at the collective table as responsible representatives of these communities—this means acknowledging both the pride and the shame of the group—without feeling the need to achieve consensus or to have our position prevail. We may grow wise in the process of wrestling the contradictions that this implies.

Which Box Do I Check?

Paradoxes of Social Difference

PARADOX

People distinguish themselves from one another in terms of significant social categories. These categories include gender, race, age, social class, sexuality, religion, and body type and ability. There are several myths and paradoxes associated with these ways of marking differences between people. One myth is that these differences are essential, that they are anchored in the very nature of the individual and are unchanging over time. Related myths are perpetuated in beliefs that these differences are associated with other social characteristics, for instance the belief that blacks are less intelligent than whites, or that women are less intelligent than men. A paradox of social differences is that in order to recognize the differences, we teach ourselves to see certain features or characteristics that we associate with these differences. These ways of marking difference become stereotypes. There is a tendency to then see people in terms of the stereotype. This process of stereotyping is a useful shorthand for organizing our perceptions and encounters with others, but it often results in mis-impressions and inaccurate assessments. Stereotypes also reveal prejudices; people are not just considered different, but more or less deserving and valued in the social hierarchies that underlie these ways of marking differences. Individuals face the dilemma of taking on particular identities associated with these differences, but not wanting to be seen only in terms of these categories of distinction.

It is true—
I've always loved
the daring
    ones
Like the black young
man
Who tried
to crash
All barriers
at once,
    wanted to
swim
At a white
beach (in Alabama)
Nude.

—Alice Walker

Part of me rejects the language of borders and boundaries. What is between us and within us is not so easily divided, nor are we so easily defined. I want to reject the social mythology that over here is Black America and over there is white America, yet the different realities experienced by people of the two groups persist.

—Ann Filemyr, 1995, "Loving Across the Boundary"

Sociologist Eviatar Zerubavel opens his book, *The Fine Line: Making Distinctions in Everyday Life,* with this dedication to his son: "To Noam, who taught me that socks can also be mittens" (1991:vii). With these words, Zerubavel celebrates the flexibility of mind that enables us to reconsider categories of distinction—socks cover the feet; mittens cover the hands—in a way that might usefully expand our lines of action. If one has no mittens, socks can also be used to cover the hands. All groups of people construct categories of time, space, which foods are edible, who can have sex with whom, whom one can marry, how property is to be divided, and so forth. These categories are the basis of cultural distinction. As Zerubavel points out, most significant cultural categories are permeable; if we think about them creatively, we can cross or alter them.

In the 1970s in the United States, the cultural category of gender was subjected to considerable scrutiny. Scholars documented the many ways in which men and women were more similar than they were different; cultural entrepreneurs manufactured fashions designed to downplay differences and highlight similarities; parents read books and took courses to learn how to raise children to possess the best of both gender qualities. This was the age of androgyny.

It turns out that the elasticity of this line of distinction could only be stretched so far before it snapped back. In the 1980s, the era of Reagan and Madonna, women in particular began to question whether or not "androgyny" was simply synonymous with "maleness" and, if so, whether this was a good thing. Men and women alike expressed a dissatisfaction with the inability to distinguish gender roles. If women increasingly worked in "traditional" male jobs, who would do "the women's work"? Advice columns reflected the frustration experienced by heterosexual men and women in trying to ascertain appropriate dating behavior. Men were confused about whether or not treating women as "equals" meant they should cease to open doors and perform other acts of chivalry for their dates; women wondered if androgynous equality meant paying for themselves, or even, occasionally, picking up the check for the date. In short, the categorical distinction of boy/girl does not appear to be as flexible as that of mitten/sock. Why not?

One explanation is that some categories are wired into our genetic code in such a way that we are "naturally" divided up according to certain essential categories. Another possibility is that some cultural lines of distinction are more entrenched than others, and therefore less flexible. The distinction between mitten and sock is clearly a human construction, a distinction that serves as a point of convenience in indicating that mittens and socks do have some basic differences that make each slightly more suited to its respective purpose. In Chapter 2 I discussed the propensity to treat gender as if it were a natural distinction—a mutually exclusive, unchanging, biologically based difference that is the basis of an essential distinction for dividing humans into groups—in this case, female or male. I suggested in that chapter that there is considerable evidence that gender is a social grouping rather than a natural one. This does not negate the observation that there are recognizable biological and physiological differences between males and females, but it shifts emphasis to gender as a *socially recognized basis of difference*. Every culture is aware of biological and physiological differences between male and female sex (similar to the acknowledgment that mittens and socks do have some distinct features), but all cultures do not place the same emphasis on gender as a means of distinguishing members of the group.

There are many ways of making social distinctions between people. Some common lines of distinction are level of education, income and geographical region of birth. Depending on your interests and experiences, you may distinguish persons according to affiliations, preferences and allegiances, such as Baptist, Republican, Mariner's fan (did someone just boo?) and so forth. These distinctions may or may not reflect a significant personal identity for someone. My students may think of me as "middle-aged," for instance, while I may be inclined to think of myself as young compared to other college professors. You and your friends may share "insider" ways of making distinctions (recall the notorious one-to-ten scale for discussing with your friends whether or not someone is a potential date?). Social distinctions are a form of communication. They are a shorthand way of conveying information in a crystalline form intended to evoke common understanding. Social distinctions regarding persons are part of a code or script that tells us how to respond to the person. The distinctions may or may not be considered an essential aspect of the person. There is a significant difference between distinctions among sports fans (Jazz vs. Bulls), for example, and distinctions of gender. The latter is presumed to be much more essential and immutable than the former. One significant question regarding such distinctions is: Who is making the distinctions, and for what purpose?

The issue of which distinctions are most significant in a culture (e.g., religious affiliation vs. employment) is another level of difference. The relative significance of employment status as a way of distinguishing someone in this culture is reflected in the question, "What do you do?" Most people understand this to be a reference to employment and recognize it as a common and acceptable question to ask a new acquaintance. The question, "What do you believe?" is much less common. Were you to ask that of a stranger sitting next to you on a plane, the response might be a confused, "What do you mean? Are you asking about religion? Politics? Metaphysics?" In this society, employment is a more central everyday distinction than spiritual beliefs.

My focus in this chapter is on certain ways of making distinctions among people, distinctions such as race, gender, class, age and physical form. In the United States, these socially constructed distinctions have become *solidified as systems of difference*. They are distinctions that are often assumed to reflect something *essential* about the person and about her or his place in the social order. They are also *primary* lines of distinction in the United States. These differences seem to matter more than others in shaping people's lives. I will explore some of the reasons for and the implications of these particular ways of drawing lines of difference.

Making Distinctions

Consider this. All groups must have a shared means of carving up time, space and other significant aspects of everyday life. These shared distinctions about time and space enable people to communicate successfully with one another regarding pragmatic ventures such as what time we will meet and where. You and I may both understand that time is measured differently across cultures. The idea that time categories are ultimately relative and therefore infinitely flexible may be interesting, but is of little use to us if we are trying to arrange a meeting. Imagine that we had to consider an infinite variety of ways to mea-sure time before we could settle on when to meet. Probably none of us would make it out of bed in the morning. Similarly, space can also be carved up differently. I can respect your belief in a fourth dimension, but because this is not an awareness of spatial form that we comprehend culturally, it is not likely that I would be able to meet you there anytime soon.

Our shared understanding of significant categories of distinction enables us to com-municate, plan and act together. Suppose we agree to meet at 7 p.m. at my house. This simple phrase conveys a remarkable amount of cultural information. The concept "my house" denotes a distinction made in this society between "public" and "private" space. Similarly, the time frame implies a probable distinction between "social" and "work" time. If you arrive at my home in the evening and proceed to lay out your work materials as if you are in a public library at midday, it is likely that I will consider you to be "out of line." Likewise, you would think me odd if I served dinner in the "bathroom" and later took the dirty dishes to the neighbors' for washing. Thus, shared categories of distinction are the basis of cultural meaning.

These categories of time and space, which are social constructs, are a basis of shared understanding that allows members of the same group to name the situation and to know how to behave within that situation. Common lines of distinction map a shared land-scape—they tell us where to go and what to do if we wish to be in sync with one another. Basic categories of distinction are marks of convention. In the Western world we have a social form that distinguishes private/public goods and space. This distinction is a human construct (i.e., there is nothing "natural" about it), but this does not mean that it is infinitely "flexible." Transgressions against the convention of "private property" get the transgressor into trouble. They may be punishable by imprisonment. The convention of private property has become a sociopolitical institution through formal legal code. Categories of meaning and social conventions emerge from social relations. The categories of distinction that become embedded in our everyday lives are what we refer to as social "systems" or social "institutions." They are like metaphorical structures with corresponding rooms, hallways and levels. Just as currents of water and wind taking the same course year in and year out etch a pattern into a physical landscape, social categories of distinction shape the way persons move about within society with the result that real patterns begin to form on the social landscape. These patterns of seeing the world and being in it have very real consequences.

To be socialized is to be aware of and capable of organizing behavior according to the lines of distinction that constitute the significant social systems of one's culture. In other words, you can "read" the social landscape. Social patterns fix limits on the possibilities of who we can be and what we can do as members of a social group. I cannot do whatever I please with space that is designated "private"—at least not if I expect to remain a member of the group in good standing. *A paradox of social lines of distinction is that, although they channel and limit the possibilities of individual action, they also provide a basis of shared cultural order and meaning.* If I have a personal definition that something is "private" and you do not, then you are likely to "violate" my space. The concept of civilization is based on the idea that, together, groups of humans construct significant social patterns and voluntarily act in accordance with the boundaries established by these patterns. They do so because the patterns etch out meaning in what would otherwise be an amorphous, undifferentiated social landscape.

Social order arises from a mutual awareness of and agreement to uphold the lines of distinction that give a culture its distinctive meaning. One implication that follows from this is that social order is a fragile, dynamic enterprise, dependent always on the actions of members of the group to reaffirm meaningful boundaries. This means that the potential for change, and for members continuously to (re)shape culture is always present. The dilemma is that, because we need taken-for-granted patterns in order to function personally and collectively, we tend to act as if these patterns were "natural" and unchangeable. When we reify lines of distinction into iron bars that we believe we cannot cross, we contribute to the construction of our own prisons.

Sociologists are interested in the social systems that we use to differentiate self and other and to give structure to interaction. We could not function if we simply treated everyone in every encounter as an undifferentiated entity. We need lines of difference to determine who we are supposed to be relative to others; these differences give us a script for how to act. In other words, they structure interaction by positioning the participants in terms of roles of intent, authority, dominance and so forth. The primary systems of difference in the contemporary United States are class, gender, race, age and sexuality. Together, these lines of distinction constitute a social landscape that channels access to cultural, economic and political resources and shapes everyday journeys and encounters for all individuals.

Social lines of distinction bring certain groups of people together and keep others apart. The metaphor of "fault lines" helps us make sense of these lines of difference and the ways in which they affect us. At times, the fault lines may be largely unnoticed, but they reflect deeply chiseled fissures of history underlying a society. Various outbursts and corresponding movements reflect the earthquakes that can erupt along these fault lines. You and I may think that we are standing on the same ground of agreement and interest until an incident of, say, sexism, creates a tremor that rips the ground beneath us, leaving us standing on opposite sides of a chasm of historically wrought differences in experience and privilege. Sociologists pursue questions about the basis for these differences—how they are established and reinforced. They also study the personal and political implications of these differences.

The Necessity of Difference

Philip Blumstein, a sociologist who studied intimate relationships, observed that initially it is "sameness" that brings persons together to form a couple. Individuals bond around their perceptions of how they are similar to each other—shared tastes in music, entertainment and hobbies, shared goals, beliefs and opinions. Persons with newly formed bonds of intimacy may feel a jolt when they stumble into circumstances and conversations that reveal gaps of difference. Eventually, they may work out the differences by finding more underlying similarities. A sense of enduring coupleness is forged through sameness.

Once this coupleness is formed, Blumstein noted, persons begin to require some differentiation from one another, particularly in their everyday affairs. This difference is necessary to solidify what they mean to each other. Like the teeth in a zipper, couples work out little interlocking differences that form the basis for an extended grip of togetherness. Both may enjoy cooking, for instance, but one may tend to make main courses and the other desserts. Over time, through repeated discussion and comments such as "Alex is the baker in our house," or "Rose has a gift for marinades," these attributions of difference take on a solidity of identity. For individuals in intimate relationships, these differences are the basis of meaningful communication and understanding about who each is in the relationship and what roles they will play with one another.

Although they are not forged in quite the same way as the differences illustrated by Blumstein, socially institutionalized differences are also necessary for extended, meaningful interaction. It is through these differences that we recognize our expected cultural roles vis-à-vis one another. Culturally recognized differences enable us to figure out who to be and how to behave in response to each other. Persons do not interact with one another willy-nilly. When we encounter one another we organize our own actions and responses in terms of particular social roles attributed to the other—is this a momentary greeting among equals, a potential date, a request for employment? There are countless possibilities. In each interaction we draw lines around the possibilities, we frame the moment in, so to speak, by establishing who the other is in accordance with known social roles.

Gender, according to many social theorists, is one of the primary systems of cultural difference by which persons sort out how to behave. This process is so embedded in our culture that it may seem automatic, but consider what happens in the case of gender ambiguity. Recall "Pat," the *Saturday Night Live* character whose appeal is in the fact that he/she/it is indefinable according to traditional gender roles. Each episode of "Pat" turns on the tension of gender ambiguity and the resulting confusion that this elicits among persons who encounter the character. We search in fascination for clues to Pat's "real gender," only to be thwarted at the end of each episode by yet more ambiguous information. Note that Pat's gender ambiguity does not erase traditional gender lines, rather it reinforces them as we collectively assemble the "facts" in our attempt to organize Pat's behavior along lines that make sense to us. An interesting point is that in the presence of this ambiguity, interaction often grinds to a confused halt.

Searching for clues to the "real" gender is an indication that gender is a system of roles and rules for behavior. If someone's gender status is ambiguous, others may find it difficult to know how to act in the presence of this person. In Chapter 2 I discussed the writing of sociologist Judith Lorber. Lorber suggests that gender is a system of entrenched social differences:

> [G]ender] is one of the major ways that humans organize their lives. . . . One way of choosing people for the different tasks of society is on the basis of their talents, motivations, and competence—their demonstrated achievements. The other way is on the basis of [institutions of difference such as] gender, race, ethnicity—ascribed membership in a category of people. (1998:319)

Know Me, Know My Gender

Several scholars have suggested that gender is the primary system of social difference in the United States. What this means is that gender differences are the main way in which we organize our own behavior and figure out how to be with others. Traditionally, men are expected to do certain things, fulfill certain roles and behave in particular ways and women have their own repertoire as well. This order is "useful" in that it provides a basis for organizing social situations.

When the workforce was organized along conventional gender lines, it was easy to tell who the managers were and who the secretaries were. Simple equation: Men were managers and women were secretaries. The advantage of this, if one is interested in easy interaction rules, is that because gender is strongly marked, one can figure out without much effort who should be treated like a boss and who can be asked to get coffee. When women began to transgress these traditional lines and moved increasingly into positions of management, men and women alike complained that they were often confused. What they meant was that they often found themselves behaving inappropriately by treating a woman as if she were a secretary, only to find out that she was the boss. How embarrassing. One of the reasons all of us participate in the perpetuation of institutional differences is that these are the basis of our cultural scripts. We are all conservative, meaning that we engage in behaviors that are likely to reinforce and conserve these systems to the extent that we grow accustomed to certain rules of interaction; we resist the confusion that results when the differences that shape these rules break down.

Interactions in on-line communication provide an intriguing illustration of this process. When persons first began communicating electronically, it was suggested by many users that this would be a utopian site of interaction. Cyberspace was heralded as a new frontier in which lines of distinction such as gender, race, age and physical ability would not influence the way persons treated one another. Why? Because persons can't see one another in on-line communications. Early users claimed that cyberspace would privilege "how people think" instead of how they looked.

The realities of on-line interactions have not matched this hype. It turns out that persons don't know how to behave if they don't know the gender of the person with whom they are interacting. The most frequently asked question among users new to various electronic "rooms" or bulletin boards is, "Are you male or female?" Persons who are coy or evasive in their response to this query are dropped from the conversation. It is assumed by others that if a person doesn't want to state a gender, that person must be hiding something.

Many people use the physical anonymity of electronic communication as an opportunity to experiment with gender bending or switching. Interestingly, this activity has not made gender less significant as a category of difference. Instead persons have become increasingly vigilant about "detecting" gender clues. The systems operators for several "date" or "chat" lines have developed means of checking up on the "real" gender of users. These methods include contacting credit card companies for biographical information and calling users at home unexpectedly to hear their voices. This policing reinforces rather than erodes gender as a primary form of difference. It appears that attempts to stretch this particular line of difference are met with resistance from others and ostracism from communication. What this suggests to me is that gender is an entrenched system of difference: a primary way in which we determine who we are, who others are and how to treat them. Without this line of difference the social landscape is too amorphous for us to accomplish meaningful communication.

There is a considerable amount of discussion among on-line communicants regarding the ethics of gender "crossing." People who use on-line services for communication are usually doing business, in which case they are likely to know the person with whom they are in contact, or seeking personal friendships and romantic encounters, in which case, they often do not know anything about the person with whom they are "chatting" on-line, except what that person tells them. Many users report that when they discover they have been interacting with someone who has been "crossing" that they feel "mind-raped." This response indicates just how entrenched gender is as a cultural system of difference. We consider gender to be an essential marker of who someone is, a feature of identity that we can count on no matter what else shifts. Overtures of friendship and romance are fraught with worry and vulnerability. When we enter such tricky territory, we want to know who we are "really" dealing with. The interesting thing about gender switching in on-line interactions is that the possibility of it suggests that gender is not a fixed feature of self. On the other hand, we want it to be "fixed" because we think it tells us something that we can count on about the other person. We "trust" them to have a "true" gender. If this proves not to be the case, we feel betrayed.

Social differences are necessary in that they enable us to establish an understanding of the role of the other and, following from that, to figure out our own responses and feelings. We expect some lines of difference to be fleeting and to shift with circumstances. Primary differences are assumed to be more fixed and therefore to become a basis for determining a more reliable and stable understanding of who someone is and what that person stands for. If someone plays it a bit fast and loose with these markers of social difference, the basis for solid understanding of the other appears to shift and we become uncertain about how to figure out who or what the person "really" is. This uncertainty makes us uncomfortable.

There are a couple of noteworthy points about this process. One is that we expect persons to have semi-stable "selves"—some basically stable features that are essential to who they are; features that can be relied upon by others as unchanging, regardless of circumstance. Another point is that we use cultural systems of primary difference as a basis for establishing the "essence" of the individual. These markers become anchor points from which we endeavor to make sense of everything else about the person's behavior. If behavior is consistent with the expectations for the category of distinction, then we consider the person "normal" and think little else about it. If behavior is inconsistent, we spend energy trying to make it "fit" our expectations. The paradox, again, is that as a culture, we need lines of distinction in order to trace meaning onto our cultural landscape. Individuals may or may not fall neatly within the lines, however.

The social tendency is to encourage persons to solidify their own positions of difference so that others can know more immediately, and reliably, who they are dealing with. This social tendency is manifest in the notion that these differences are "essential"— an aspect of selfhood that can be counted on to steer our responses toward the other. Blumstein refers to this tendency as "anchors against drift." Once we think we have established something about a person in terms of social categories of distinction, we entreat them not to change or "drift," not because they are incapable of drifting, but because such shifts, when they occur, require similar shifts from us. If a spouse who has shown no previous interest in religion, suddenly takes up churchgoing with enthusiasm, the mate is likely to experience a sort of vertigo. He or she will have to make adjustments in order to accommodate and "relate" to this new aspect of the spouse. These adjustments are likely to be a source of tension. Similarly, social shifts that realign persons in terms of relations of difference, such as race and gender, are likely to cause confusion and tension. If a man is accustomed to carving up the world in terms of men (in charge) and women (submissive), he may find himself cast adrift when the "weaker" sex no longer behaves in accordance with his categorical expectations. His rantings about "putting the woman back in her place" reflect a cultural system that has served as the basis by which he has organized his understanding of himself and others and their respective places in the world.

Marking Differences

Recently, I was walking with a four-year-old when we encountered a young person with a shaved head and pierced nose, wearing black jeans, black T-shirt and a black leather jacket. "Is she a boy or a girl?" the child asked. What was this child seeing that prompted him both to assume a fundamental gender—"she"—and to question the manifestation of gender? How do we recognize differences? If these distinctions are not innate, but are socially constructed systems of difference, how do we figure out who belongs in various categories? Characters in certain types of plays wear masks, or makeup and costumes, that are culturally associated with distinguishing roles, such as "villain" or "hero." These masks convey information about the role the character will play in the unfolding drama. They tell us both who the character is and who he or she is not. Because we recognize the masks and costumes and are able to associate these with various social categories, we know what to expect.

Some systems of difference are so entrenched that we take recognition for granted. In Chapter 2, in the discussion of gender as a form of socially enacted difference, I noted that distinctions are made from birth and continue on throughout almost every aspect of daily life. The conflation of gender as an essential ("natural") aspect of self and as a social performance is apparent in cases where the manifest "costume" reveals a gender that is presumed to be at odds with other features commonly used to mark gender—secondary sex characteristics such as facial hair or breasts. Someone with a beard and chest hair who is seen wearing a dress, pearls, heels and layers of makeup is presumed to be a "man playing at being a woman."

In this section I invite you to consider what it is that we think we "know" when we make attributions of difference, particularly in terms of race and gender. What do the ways for marking difference reveal about the various underlying purposes for sorting people according to social categories? In order for systems of difference to serve the purpose of organizing interaction, persons have to be able to tell who belongs in which category. Ambiguity results in interactional confusion. Cultures mark important social boundaries in ways that signal that the line of difference is significant. The characteristics that constitute a particular category of distinction are called *collective representations*. Collective representations are stereotypes that indicate the basic features of a social category. To the extent that members share an understanding of these features and organize their behavior accordingly, the representation can be said to be "normative." Without these shared representations, we would not have any basis for collective communication and could not organize interaction with one another. Specific features and behaviors are associated with specific distinctions in order to make them reliably visible.

In lesbian cultural histories, the 1950s are commonly known as the "bar era." To socialize with other women like themselves, lesbians frequented bars and pubs that had a reputation for "tolerance." These bars provided an atmosphere in which it was assumed that the women present were interested in romantic and sexual relationships with other women. Once inside the bar, the question was *which* women were potential dates, potential friends, or possibly competitors? Each is a different role in the script of romantic courtship. Many lesbian novelists of the time used this ambiguity as a basis of fictional humor: the would-be heroine standing on the threshold of new adventure, only to discover that she is not certain whether she is supposed to be the "pursuer" or the "pursued." These roles, which are assigned to boys and girls, respectively, in heterosexual culture, break down when the border of heterosexuality is crossed.

Lesbians in the 1950s imposed order on this ambiguity by adopting traditional heterosexual roles toward courtship. They sorted themselves into "butches" and "femmes" and adopted related behaviors. These roles also provide a visible and known means of determining who is to play what role in dating. The distinction of butch/femme sorts the pool of potential partners into meaningful subcategories of difference. By incorporating the shared cultural institution of traditional male/female markers of difference into the subculture, women can signal to one another how they intend to behave and how they expect their potential partner to behave. The script is already written and thus contributes to smooth interaction. One question to ponder is whether or not butch/femme activity reinforces or erodes the traditional dichotomy between male and female as a major system of difference.

Butch/femme culture was a highly nuanced, stylized routine for structuring personal and interactional roles in lesbian mating. Like any subcultural variation of a dominant theme, butch/femme activities are an adaptation of and, in many ways, an inverse denial of traditional gender roles. Butch/femme roles were an artful performance spun from existing cultural stereotypes about men and women. In this way, the behavior is innovative and serves as a cultural critique of taken-for-granted stereotypes. It has the potential to be subversive. At the same time, by relying on traditional ways of marking difference, these markers are reinforced. Lipstick for the role of the woman; ties for the role of the man. The fact that biological women play both roles de-natures them. At the same time, the enactment reinscribes a common *social* significance accorded these roles.

The ways of marking difference are not inherently "natural," but they serve the important cultural function of providing information to members of the group about which positions each might take relative to others and how the interaction is likely to proceed. Without these cultural scripts, we don't know how to position ourselves or the other, and we don't know what to say or do. Thus categories of difference enable us to define ourselves, the others with whom we come into contact, and the parameters of the situation in which we are engaged.

In seventeenth-century France, social class was the most significant social system. One knew how to treat others and what to expect from them based on the behaviors associated with different classes. These classes were called "estates." The First Estate consisted of members of the nobility, the Second Estate was composed of priests, merchants and petty nobles, and the Third Estate was made up of peasants. The historical record carries several impassioned editorials written by members of the First Estate who had observed that it was becoming increasingly difficult to differentiate between members of the various estates. It seems that persons in the lower estates were dressing and affecting behaviors suggestive of a higher estate. Members of the lower estates were apparently snatching up clothing and uniforms cast off by the higher estates. In donning these costumes, which were presumably markers of one's social class, these people were "passing" as members of an estate not commensurate with their assigned lineage and position in society. According to the authors of the complaints, these "poseurs" were scoundrels. To remedy the situation, they called for a "uniform" to be worn by the lower classes. Something that would set them apart at a glance so that all could tell who they were and know how to treat them.

Items of clothing such as the maid's apron or the butler's gloves and tie are markers placed upon the person by those in authority over them, those who do not want to confuse "the help" with those of "higher station." Lorber offers interesting illustrations of the conflation of gender with additional differences in social status. In cultures wherein positions of authority are associated with men, the occasional woman who also occupies a position of authority is treated as an "honorary man." When Queen Elizabeth II visited Saudi Arabia, for example, she was made an "honorary man" so that she could confer with and dine with other heads of state. Throughout history, and still today in countries with rigid gender divisions between public and private spheres, women who work in public spaces in traditionally male jobs also dress as men. For the most part, these women may still consider themselves women, but the clothing signals a more complicated social status.

Fred Davis was a sociologist who wrote about clothing as a marker of status and difference. Americans, noted Davis, use clothing to signal an "ambivalence" about social class as it has been traditionally enacted. American ideals of equality and a distaste for ostentatious displays of wealth are reflected in the "studied casual" look. Davis devotes an entire chapter to blue jeans as an indicator of American cultural ambivalence toward wealth as a mark of status. Blue jeans are the uniform of the working man, but they are a self-selected uniform. They are also a symbol of American durability and work ethic. Blue jeans, when worn with expensive accompanying items, such as a cashmere sweater or wool blazer, signal the intent to be "equal minded" but the ability to "flock with the wealthy"—subtle but effective in marking one as culturally "complicated." Blue jeans enable some line crossings because they invite multiple interpretations.

In the contemporary United States, as in most cultures, we tend to mark differences with physical characteristics and attire. Clothing, hairstyles and jewelry, for example, are used to communicate age, gender and ethnic distinctions. Persons may use a combination of accessories to enhance distinctions that they want to emphasize to others. For instance, many of us want to be treated according to the expectations associated with particular age categories and will "dress the part" in order to communicate this to others. I prefer to wear cutoffs and a baseball cap when I write at home alone, but when I teach I "dress up" so that I will look "grown up" enough to be taken seriously as a college professor. Because I am relatively young, it is necessary for me to highlight or "mark" my status with appropriate props and behaviors. Alternately, I sometimes take advantage of my ambiguous age/professional distinction to see what sort of interactional confusion results when persons initially treat me as someone who can be easily dismissed—"She's some young college punk"—and then discover that I may actually occupy a position of authority over them. The behavioral shift is as palpable as if I had been physically transformed in front of their eyes. Lines of interactional difference can be that powerful.

Race, like gender, is a deeply etched line of difference for North Americans. In this culture we mark race by skin color. At least we tend to think that skin color is a reliable marker of real racial differences. Actually, the recognition of ethnicity is based on complex compositions of phenotypical features, hair and other characteristics that we have learned to associate as markers of distinction among humans. Certain features, behaviors and expectations are associated with the categories black, brown, red, white and yellow. In fact, as I list them, you are likely conjuring the ethnic and national origins associated with each color. These distinctions exist in our individual heads as collective representations. Physically, skin color is as diverse as the color swatches for a home-remodeling kit. Phenotype by itself is actually not a very reliable marker of racial composition. In this society, however, because race is a significant social system, we have taught ourselves how to "see" racial color and to sort what we see into one of the related categories. When we encounter someone whose racial composition appears ambiguous, meaning we can't tell if they are phenotypically African, Anglo, Asian, or Indian, we search for additional clues that will enable us to make a racial distinction.

There are many cultures in which race is significant, but not along the same lines as the United States. In Brazil, for example, race is associated with class. Someone whose skin color is deep chocolate may check the box coded "white" on official documents and will be thought of as white among friends and acquaintances who share the understanding that race = class background. An anthropologist, France Winddance Twine, uses the phrase "the elasticity of whiteness" to explain that "white"/"nonwhite" categories are "stretched" in Brazil and, as a result, race is marked and negotiated in ways that are not so obvious to North Americans. In the case of Brazil, it is not that members of society are "colorblind," but that they highlight and pay attention to different markers. Physical characteristics such as nose and head shape, as well as skin type, and additional features such as clothing, accent and family name comprise the code that Brazilians use to type race. This may seem like a lot of features to pay attention to, but Brazilians can take all this in at a glance because they have learned that these are the institutional features associated with race in their culture (Twine 1991).

In another project, Twine works with a sociologist to demonstrate that racial boundaries are not "fixed" according to biological features (Warren and Twine 1997). Rather, they shift according to the emphasis that a culture places on the socioeconomic characteristics and perceived contributions of particular ethnic and racial groups. Whether members of a society "see" these distinctions depends on the extent to which they are institutionalized in cultural representations of difference. For instance, in England there is a strong cultural difference between the Irish and the British. Historically, the Irish were considered nonwhite. When an American asks a Brit how he or she knows that someone is Irish, the Brit is likely to be surprised at the American's inability to see such an "obvious distinction." It is not at all obvious to Americans because we do not share the same lines of distinction and have therefore not developed institutional markers for "seeing" these differences.

Journalist Amy Pagnozzi writes of her own experience regarding the fluidity of racial markers across different cultures:

> A few years back, on vacation in New Zealand, my husband and I noticed a couple of things: a) there were so many sheep; and b) there were so many white people. The people were very white. Not New York white (i.e., ethnic, blended, beige) but naked, pasty, underdone: white, white.
>
> It didn't surprise me when a local we'd befriended asked what it was like for blacks in New York City. As a journalist, I was flattered, styling myself a miniexpert on race relations. I trotted out theories on assimilation, disenfranchisement, and the growing African-American middle-class—then her eyes glazed over.
>
> "No," she said, shaking her head. "I want to know what it's like for you being black."
>
> I have to tell you, this woman was crushed when she found out that in New York City I am perceived as white. She demanded my ethnic breakdown. When I told her Italian, Syrian, French, Swiss and English she brightened considerably on "Syrian."
>
> "Well, you wouldn't be white here," she said grinning. (1991:130-4).

"Invisible" Differences

Sexuality is an interesting line of difference to consider because one's status is not as visibly marked and as easy to read as are gender and skin color. The significance of sexuality as a social system in this culture is indicated by the various ways in which persons attempt to display and figure out what the status of others might be. In cultures in which codes about who one can have sex with are not determined primarily by gender, homosexuality is relatively unremarkable. In this society we seldom give much attention to trying to figure out the religious status of someone's mother in order to determine their "sexuality," but in some cultures, this is *the* significant basis of distinguishing who can mate with whom.

"Queer culture" involves a wide variety of ways to communicate sexual orientation to others. These ways include styles of dress and the affectation of particular mannerisms and modes of speech as a means to display one's status. The extent to which one can control the display of characteristics that are associated with particular systems of difference determines how much power one has in an interaction. Because my own sexuality is not immediately apparent to members of mainstream society, I can choose to put on different costumes that enable me to "pass" as either straight or gay. Yet to the extent that I *cannot* lapse into conversations or mannerisms that might convey my status as a lesbian, for fear of negative reprisal, I am not completely at ease in many interactional settings. The decision to "come out" is a milestone among gays and lesbians because it is statement that one intends to display behaviors and position oneself in a way that acknowledges the significance of sexuality as an organizing basis of distinction in interaction with others. To do so puts gays and lesbians at risk, but it also frees us from having to be constantly vigilant about "hiding" "undesirable" behavior.

Differences as Markers of Inequality

My main theme to this point is that we have to differentiate ourselves and others in order to engage in meaningful interaction. The lines by which we make these self/other distinctions are social institutions that make smooth interaction possible and organize who and what we can be. I have suggested that in the United States the primary institutions of social difference are gender, race, age and sexuality. This makes us a sexist, racist, ageist and heterosexist culture. These terms can be read as a benign description of the way in which members of U.S. society are sorted into meaningful categories—but we do not experience the terms as benign. Rather, they are culturally volatile and likely to raise impassioned debate and to stir deep emotional biases and prejudices among most Americans. We have to categorize ourselves and our experiences in order to make sense out of life. But why is it, in the words of the esteemed social psychologist Gordon Allport, "that categorization inevitably shades into prejudice?" Why do our differences result in such complicated disharmonies?

Racial Differences as the "Trope" of Prejudice and Inequality

In the contemporary United States, when we speak of "difference" we usually mean "race." Henry Louis Gates, Jr., a Harvard scholar of African American studies and author of several books, states that "Race" has become a sort of stand-in, or shorthand term for "differences of language, belief system, artistic tradition and gene pool." "Racial character" is used as a notation for supposedly natural attributes, such as rhythm, athletic ability, intelligence, business acumen and even sexual fidelity. "Race" is also what comes to mind when we think of prejudice and inequality. The use of one word or idea to stand for many other practices and issues is a "trope." For Gates, "race" is a contemporary trope in U.S. society.

Social Differences as Hierarchy. As is apparent in the case of social class, social differences often reflect social hierarchies. How does one come by one's place in a particular social order? Is relative superiority or inferiority an accomplishment or a legacy of birth? Is one's position of authority or submission earned or assigned? In the chapter on meritocracy I discuss the American ideal that one's social and economic position should reflect one's individual accomplishments. I argue that this ideal is a myth. Many of the opportunities and obstacles that we encounter as we attempt to pursue goals and interests are related to systems of difference. As I noted at the beginning of this chapter, some differences are more significant than others—race, gender, economic class, age and, increasingly, sexuality are some of the primary categories of difference in this culture. Hence, we refer to them as "systems of difference." Within a system of difference, some ways of being different are considered *better* than others. People are not only different from one another, they are better or worse, depending on the cultural story underlying the difference.

The cultural legacy underlying many manifestations of racially marked difference is that there is a sort of color pyramid with "white" at the apex. The concept of "whitening" reflects the cultural bias that to be white is to be superior, not just different. A similar bias is present in the United States but is usually expressed more subtly. For example, persons who identify as ethnic minorities but who have light skin and could pass as white are often asked why they choose to embrace openly a nonwhite ethnicity. The assumption underlying these queries is that being white is more desirable and, given a choice, certainly the identity one would choose for oneself. Such assumptions highlight social systems that not only designate difference, but arrange the attributes of difference hierarchically and associate privilege accordingly. In the collective mind, different racial and ethnic categories are associated with more or less value.

This legacy is known as "white supremacy." The mention of white supremacy may conjure up images of the Ku Klux Klan and other "hate" groups who advocate for segregation from and the destruction of nonwhite groups. In an insightful and harrowing book, *White Lies* (1997), sociologist Jessie Daniels points out that the "white lies" perpetuated by these extreme groups may seem ridiculous to the average person, but that, in fact, they are directly related to several ideals and notions that many of us take for granted. White supremacy is perpetuated in the ideology that "race" is a "natural difference"—something that is innate, essential and immutable. Henry Louis Gates, Jr., has this to say about it:

> Race, as a meaningful criterion within the biological sciences, has long been recognized to be a fiction. When we speak of "the white race" or "the black race," "the Jewish race" or "the Aryan race," we speak in biological misnomers, and, more generally, in meta-

phors . . . all sorts of characteristics have been inscribed through tropes of race, lending the sanction of God, biology or the natural order to even presumably unbiased descriptions of cultural tendencies and differences.

Biology does not recognize "race" as a real natural difference among humans. When we essentialize race as a primary difference, we fall into the trap of assuming innate racial differences, differences that presumably tell us something about a person's character and potential. White supremacy is based on the ideology that the characteristics associated with "whiteness" are more desirable, more highly evolved and more deserving of God's favor than the features associated with being "nonwhite." Qualities that are assumed to be markers of valor, integrity and deserved accomplishment have been historically associated with being white. Thus, as a category of difference, whiteness comes to be associated with cultural and economic success.

White supremacist ideologies are not based in a science that describes any real differences in the abilities and inclinations according to racial categories, but they are buttressed by the belief that race is a natural and essential distinction. The problem with this logic is that racial differences cannot necessarily be reliably ascertained at the physical level. What we think of as "natural markers of difference" are usually culturally based features that we have learned to be attuned to because our culture emphasizes such features. Another example from Gates serves as an illustration of the cultural basis for recognizing racial differences:

> In 1973 I was amazed to hear a member of the House of Lords describe the differences between Irish Protestants and Catholics in terms of their "distinct and clearly definable differences of race." "You mean to say that you can tell them apart?" I asked incredulously. "Of course," responded the lord. "Any Englishman can."

These differences may not be anchored in nature, but as I suggested in the chapter on the nature/nurture binary, using nature as a claim for the realness of the differences is a way to legitimate the presumed hierarchies and subsequent inequalities associated with these differences. For this reason, and despite the misgivings of many natural scientists, researchers continue to look for evidence that differences in social behavior are rooted in "natural differences." Differences that are assumed to be essential provide a justification for those who claim more privileges based on a social hierarchy rooted in categorical differences.

Normative Differences and Privilege

The tension regarding systems of difference is this: These lines of difference are not benign, they are one basis by which persons are sorted into a social order and accorded privileges. Many of us have been raised on the cultural creed that "America is the land of difference" and "difference is to be tolerated." If the differences were simply that, differences, there might be less tension, but the fact is that in a competitive economy there is inequality. All cultures have decision rules for the distribution of resources. In this culture, whether we are aware of it or not, resource distribution is associated with cultural status. Cultural status is associated with certain features and behaviors that are linked to differences, such as race, gender, class background and sexuality. The proposition is that social and economic inequality is connected to a hierarchy of differences. Social privilege and political rights are *systematically* accorded to some people and denied to others based on categorical standing and denied to others.

A useful way to think about this proposition is to consider taken-for-granted rights and privileges presumed to be the birthright of *all* Americans. Franklin Delano Roosevelt referred to these as the "four freedoms": freedom of speech, freedom of religion, freedom from want (meaning economic destitution) and freedom from fear. I would add another one, the freedom to go about your daily business without encountering obstacles based on categorical differences. For instance, when you enter a store to browse are you accustomed to being greeted with courtesy or suspicion by the salesclerks? How often, if ever, have you been followed by a store detective, or pulled over for a "vehicle check" while driving in a neighborhood in which the dominant population is of a different race? These are common, everyday experiences for black, Latino and Native men in the United States. How often is your citizenship or English proficiency the subject of scrutiny? Persons of Asian or Latino heritage are frequently asked for "green cards" and other proof of citizenship, even when it is apparent that they are U.S.-born citizens. What about your freedom to make ideological statements or to claim membership in certain groups without fear of reprisal? If you are lesbian or gay and wish to display any sort of "pride" insignia on your car or your clothing, you are likely to do so with the fear that your windows may be bashed in or you yourself may be the subject of verbal and physical assault. If you "come out" to your employer or landlord, you face the fear of being fired or kicked out, simply because you are an open homosexual.

Persons who are accustomed to basic everyday rights—such as the right to negotiate your way through your day without unprovoked harassment or undue scrutiny—find it difficult to believe and to understand that many others do not enjoy the same rights. In some cases, these "rights" are as basic as being granted respect (or at least, indifference) by those whom you encounter. Persons who find themselves in a position of using food stamps to make purchases are immediately aware of the shame to which they are subjected by those around them. One woman, a student in one of my classes and a single mother who had been unexpectedly let go from a middle-manager job, teared up when she described the rudeness to which she and her children were subjected whenever they bought groceries with food stamps:

> Before [being laid off] people either left me alone, or smiled nicely, or maybe even flirted. All of a sudden, I'm using food stamps and people come out of the woodwork with stares of disapproval and feel like they can say all sorts of things. Every time we stood in the grocery line, someone would say, something like, 'why don't you get a job like the rest of us, lady!' I can't believe they would say these things with my children standing there and knowing nothing about our circumstances.

A complexity of cultural pluralism is that persons have the "right" to be bigots. My neighbor has the right to hate me for what I stand for, but does he have to right to obstruct my freedoms and to threaten my safety? One of the indications that the "four freedoms" are granted differently to persons depending on their categorical standing is in legal settings in which persons attempt to have wrongdoings—violations of their freedoms—addressed. For instance, do police follow up on crimes perpetrated against persons of color and persons in lower-income neighborhoods with the same tenacity as they enforce the law in upper-income, predominantly white neighborhoods? What does it mean when judges refuse to prosecute persons who beat and kill gay men? How should we interpret the actions of courts that fail to find fault with employers who dismiss or deny promotions to workers on the basis of gender or race? What conclusions can be drawn from the fact that Asian and Anglo women continue to make approximately 30 cents less for every dollar that their male counterparts in similar positions make? African and Native women and Latinas make as much as 50 cents less and are concentrated in the lowest-paying jobs with the fewest benefits, despite the fact that the work that they do is usually in domains that require intensive physical labor.

In each of these illustrations it can be argued that the person's "freedoms" are mediated by attributions of race, gender, class and sexuality. *The rights associated with these freedoms—including the right to redress in the case of wrongdoing—are granted differently on the basis of the social statuses of race, gender, class and sexuality. D*espite the ideology that *all* Americans are "born equal," in practice some persons are considered to be less deserving of their birthright. This sense that some persons are less deserving of "equal rights and protection under the law" is based on a taken-for-granted notion that certain people do not *belong* as much as others do. Some theorists refer to this sense of "belonging" in terms of "center" and "marginal" positions. When you join a new group, start a new job, or attend a new school, you are initially on the margins of the group. You may experience this marginality as a sort of discomfort, or hanging back, not really being sure of what your rights are and whether or not you fit in. Initially you may spend a lot of time figuring out how to say and do the right things in order to be accepted by those who comprise the "center." If and when you do gain access to the center, you may come to take for granted your rights of navigation within the group, you may feel "at home" with the people in charge and in the space itself.

Social theorists suggest that race, gender, class and additional differences such as sexuality, family status, religion and political allegiances, are the basis for being treated as if one really belongs or not, without question, in America. Being Anglo, male, middle or upper-middle class, married with children and Protestant is considered the "center" or "normative" position. This does not mean that the majority of Americans have this status. What it means is that in the United States this particular group, and the behaviors and values associated with this group, is portrayed *as if it is the desired and most deserving group.* If one falls within these categories, one is considered to be in the "center" of a web of belonging. One can take one's rights for granted, or at least expect justice to be served if these rights are violated. Everyone else finds themselves in a position of having to make a claim for their basic rights.

One difficulty that my students encounter as they try to grapple with the concepts of "center" and "marginal" positions is the tendency to conflate a social-level phenomenon with individual behaviors and statuses. To say that the heterosexual WASP position is the normative or privileged position in the United States, does not mean that all white men are "privileged" at the expense of everyone else. Rather, it is a statement about historical circumstances and legacies whereby certain groups have held most of the power for determining the politics, economics and culture of the United States. Like a high school clique, persons who represent this group constitute the "popular" group. One consequence is that persons who appear to be a part of this group (i.e., individual white heterosexual middle-class males) pass through life able to take basic rights for granted. Much of what they encounter culturally reinforces their sense of deservedness. Having these rights is not a problem. The problem is that other persons, persons who don't fit the expected or "normative" profile, are often not granted the same rights. What white middle-class heterosexual men have that others do not is the privilege of taking their rights for granted.

Much of the current "race war" and "gender war" is due to the misperception that women and people of color want to strip white men of their rights. Most white men do not abuse their rights. What they may fail to understand is that many other Americans are unable to take their rights for granted. Anyone who has enjoyed a life of unquestioned freedoms (and this can and does include many individual white women and some persons of color) is likely to think that the world is a "fair place." From this vantage point it may be difficult to understand programs such as affirmative action. These programs were conceived with the understanding that in the United States many persons are not given the same opportunities for success because of historical legacies and practices that have *systematically disadvantaged persons on the basis of gender (female) and race (non-Anglo)*.

As much as Americans wish to say that they are "individuals," the historical legacy of sexism and racism is cut deeply into the cultural and economic landscape. These lines of difference mark persons and shape their perceptions, ambitions and sense of belonging accordingly. An understanding that distinctions such as race and gender carry normative implications about who is more or less deserving and likely to "get ahead" is a first step toward a more complicated and insightful discussion of the anger and mistrust underlying the race and gender "wars." Two consequences of the American history of a hierarchy of status based on race and gender are "assimilation" and "internalized hierarchies."

Assimilation. Consider again the idea of the "center" in terms of the high school clique of popular students. Because they are popular and well treated, individual members of this group may feel encouraged in their academic, athletic and extracurricular activities. They may find that many doors of opportunity seem open to them—teachers and friends may tell them about chances for participation in student government, how to get scholarships and how to get special help with their projects. They have "insider" status and, as a result, may excel in a variety of endeavors. Repeated success may make them additionally confident and subsequently more successful. Certain styles of dress, tastes in music and hobbies and particular behaviors may come to be associated with the popular group and, hence, with success. Anyone else who wants to enjoy the benefits automatically conferred on this group may find themselves doing whatever they can to become as much like this group as possible. They may take up similar hobbies, cultivate similar tastes in clothing and music and adopt similar beliefs and mannerisms in order to "fit in." This process is called *assimilation*.

One sociological question about the process of assimilation is whether or not persons who seek certain positions in one domain, say employment, find that they have to cultivate tastes and behaviors shared by those who constitute the "center" of the domain. For instance, if you are interviewing for a corporate job, do you think it will help, hinder, or make no difference in your chances if you dress "ethnic"? Social research reveals that managers who are making hiring decisions, when confronted with a choice between candidates whose job-related skills are similar, will select the person most like themselves in cultural tastes and demeanor. In fact, there is considerable evidence that, in the absence of any criteria for affirmative action, employers search for a potential candidates among friends and associates with similar tastes and ideals. Thus, the pool of candidates ends up looking very much "like us."

There is nothing wrong with wanting to associate with like-minded fellows and wanting to be with people who share your interests and tastes. A problem does arise, however, when these interests and tastes become an implicit condition for being granted employment or full social and political rights in society more generally. In a well-researched book about morals and manners in corporations in the United States and France, sociologist Michele Lamont presents information based on interviews with several upper-level managers. The managers were all white, male and from upper-middle-class family backgrounds. These men indicated that they went out of their way to hire others like themselves. A main reason for doing so was supposedly "trust"—"people like me can be trusted." As Lamont notes, "birds of a feather tend to flock together." In this case, in addition to the requisite employment qualifications of education and experience, the successful candidate is expected to have a similar cultural background to those in charge. In this way, social differences such as gender, ethnic and class background become a form either of cultural capital or cultural liability.

The term *model minority* is a reference to someone who has presumably adopted the cultural mores and ideals of those in charge; instead of appearing too "ethnic," they look and act "like us." The practice of rewarding assimilation has led some observers to call the United States a system of "just-us" justice, where "just-us" in this case is associated with the cultural attributes associated with being white, male and middle class.

When women first began to move into management positions in the workforce they did not do so by altering the characteristics associated with these positions; that is, characteristics associated with being straight white men with upper-middle-class values. They did so by "learning how to be boys." Women who wanted to be successful in their professions did so by crossing the gender line and highlighting features that made them more like their male counterparts. Similarly, men of color who are striving to improve their economic position often must de-emphasize the particulars of their background if they want to "fit in."

One consequence of this behavior is that these individuals may be considered "gender" or "race" traitors by those who share these distinctions with them. Sometimes the price of moving toward the privileges of the center is that one must work to disassociate oneself from those characteristics that are associated with the "margins"; one must downplay the femaleness or minority ethnicity in order to "assimilate successfully." Another consequence is that the general features associated with the center remain the same; the presence of a black woman in a high managerial position does not indicate that the center has shifted. To the contrary, to the extent that this woman has "assimilated" by de-emphasizing her race and gender and highlighting her Ivy League education and suburban upbringing, the features of the center remain intact, as do the behavioral expectations of those who occupy these positions.

Even as I write this I am aware of my own privilege in being able to do so; as a white woman, my discussions of racial differences are likely to be considered "enlightened," possibly "progressive"; at least I am not likely to be considered "shrill" or "demanding." Perhaps most indicative of the centrality of my racial position is the fact that I really don't have to think much at all about whether or not writing about race will affect me negatively. In contrast, my colleague, a black American Indian, from whom I have learned a great deal about the negotiation of racial differences, carries a heavy leather briefcase with her everywhere and always seems to me to be "overdressed" for the weather and my notions of comfort. When I asked her about this seemingly cumbersome set of accoutrements, she reminded me that as a young woman who "looks black" she has to go out of her way to be taken seriously as a college professor. For her, this means constantly toting cumbersome accessories that will increase the likelihood that she looks as if she really "belongs."

Internalizing Hierarchies. The university at which I teach recently sponsored a panel presentation titled "Light Skin/Dark Skin." The panelists were persons of color who spoke about the emphasis on skin color among people of color. My students who attended the panel noted a couple of themes. One theme is the wide spectrum of color that can be used to describe the variation in individual skin tones. Descriptions include dark chocolate, cinnamon, latte, almond and more. Each of the panelists described the ways in which references to shades of black/brown/red/yellow/pink saturated their conversations with other persons of color. "Pink people" or "persons of pallor" may think and talk less about the skin color spectrum because "whiteness" is taken for granted. If one is obviously white, that's all that matters in terms of social privilege. This leads to the second theme. Several of the panelists described situations in which they had been turned down for dates and picked on in a variety of ways because they were "too dark." One young woman, who described herself as "ebony," told of purchasing special pumice stones that the "ivory" clerk promised would lighten her skin. She scrubbed herself daily, rubbing until she bled. The persons of pallor in the audience were aghast at this description of self-mutilation. The theme expressed by panelists was that they had learned that "lighter skin was *better* than darker skin."

Later, in a class conversation about the panel, several white students made statements along the lines of "I had no idea there was so much racism within communities of color." One student proffered the assessment that it seemed strange that "oppressed people would oppress each other." The students were saddened by the idea of a person suffering "within her own community" and being teased and judged by family members on the basis of skin tone. But they seemed unaware of the basis for the cultural practice of prizing light skin. White supremacy is an umbrella legacy that covers us all. Accordingly, whiteness, as the presumably valued position, is taken for granted. This does not negate the existence and consequences of a racial hierarchy. This hierarchy is *internalized* in a self-attitude that can range from "unaware" (i.e., white) to a sense of self-hatred (i.e., I'm too dark). This internalization is reinforced in the way one is treated by others. If your skin color is not something that others remark on, then you are likely to think it a nonissue, something that isn't much of a determining aspect of who you are and where you fit into the social order. If you are repeatedly harassed, called names and made the object of scrutiny based on your skin color, then it will become a major aspect of how you see yourself. Many persons of color have internalized the cultural legacy of white supremacy and, accordingly, the notion that the darker one's skin, the lower one is presumed to be in the social hierarchy. This presumed racism among persons of color is a manifestation of an internalized legacy of white supremacy. The "Black Pride" movement was a concerted attempt to present skin color as a full-range spectrum, a "rainbow" of different hues, rather than a reflection of a white/black hierarchy. The privileges and rights associated with light skin are real consequences of this legacy, however. For this reason, it is a difficult cultural practice to dismantle.

The Paradox of Social Differences

When a map of cultural privilege is laid over a map of socially recognized differences, the resulting picture is very complicated. If one occupies a position of marginality and one desires the resources and privileges associated with the center, then one has two courses of action. One can either attempt to cross existing lines of difference toward the center position or one can try to alter the lines themselves so that the center shifts. The consequences of these two courses can be contradictory and are the source of a great deal of current cultural and political dissent. To be located on the margin is to have less status and therefore less privilege. Thus, many Americans who value "economic equality for all" insist that the lines of difference need to be redrawn in a way that either "broadens the center" or redistributes resources to the margins. This issue is one of the predominant themes in contemporary cultural and economic politics. A thorough understanding of the issue involves a comprehension of the paradox between the necessity of social differences—the source of cultural distinctiveness and intra/interpersonal meaning—and the fact that in this country there is a long history of using social categories of difference as a basis for granting or denying rights, education and employment. In short, the paradox of social differences is that they serve as a basis of self- and cultural identity. Yet, at the same time, they are a basis for the practice and justification of stereotypes and inequalities.

Poet June Jordan provides one way to think about this complicated paradox. She says,

> There is difference and there is power.
> And who holds the power decides the meaning
> of the difference.

It can be useful to discuss social differences in terms of *objective* and *subjective* definitions of difference.

Objective Definitions of Difference

> Americans are experiencing a "crisis of representation," the sense of our own and others place in the world and how to represent these and act them out.
>
> —Edward Said

The other day I heard a student, a young black woman, complaining about the depiction of the "black family" in her sociology textbook. The text describes black families as being "more at risk" and cites the reasons for this "risk" as a higher percentage of absent fathers. "Black children are more likely to become involved in crime," the text goes on to report, "because they have less parental supervision." The student was not complaining about the statistics reported in the text. She was criticizing the manner in which the information was reported. If this is the only information that you read about the "black family," then you may be likely to conclude that black men are bad fathers and black parents supervise their children poorly. The textbook presents the "black family" as an object outside of any social and historical context. The presumption is that the "black family" is a thing that can be picked up and scrutinized on its own. In this case, the object of "black family" is being held up for comparison with another object, the "white family." In making this "objective" comparison, the author perpetuates common stereotypes about the relative worth of each "type" of family and tells us nothing about the dynamics underlying this objectification.

Consider the difference in meaning between the statement regarding the propensity of black children to take up crime, and the presentation of this information: There is a correlation between the number of children who lack supervision and opportunities for community involvement and the number of children who are charged with misdemeanor offenses. Assuming this correlation accurately reflects a social pattern, what is the possible connection to black children? Some researchers suggest that the pattern reflects a difference in economic circumstances—there is a significant number of black children who live in poverty. Poverty is often associated with fewer resources for "supervision." Areas of high poverty also have higher rates of arrest for misdemeanors, in general. Whatever the explanation, it must be carried out within a context that accurately reflects the economic, social, cultural and historical circumstances.

Contemporary news reports and academic writings tend to treat racial and ethnic groups as monolithic structures that can be scrutinized out of context. Comparisons are often made that solidify lines of difference in terms of stereotypical characteristics. For example, it is frequently reported that black men have a higher rate of arrest for violent crimes than white men. What is not usually reported alongside this statistic is that black men are also more likely to be the victims of this violence. It is a significant social problem that a large number of men in this country appear to be at war with one another. The appropriate sociological questions should be about the historical, cultural and economic practices that underlie this anger and conflict. The presentation of comparative statistics between black and white men as objective groups does little more than reinscribe the stereotypical differences that are the basis of continued racism.

Similarly, consider the reports of alcohol abuse among Native Americans. Who is doing the reporting and for what purposes? Do these reports make any sense outside the context of a history that is grounded in the attempted economic and cultural annihilation of entire nations—nations that had flourished prior to the arrival of Anglos? Jordan's admonition is useful advice if one wishes to understand the cultural and economic politics that continue to scorch contemporary discussion of difference. Who has the power to define the Other?

Simone de Beauvoir raised this question in her pivotal essay, "Woman as Other." Writing in 1949, de Beauvoir pointed out that women are always defined in terms of men: in terms of their relations to men—how they should serve men and comport themselves for men's benefit; relative to the tastes and temperaments of men and so forth. Women, she concluded, have no subjectivity of their own. They exist only as an object in the orbit of men. A woman does not know how to define herself except with respect to the men in her life—she is a daughter, a wife, a mistress, but never anything unto herself. Consider that there is no male equivalent in Western languages for "Miss/Mrs." This term marks a woman's marital status, and its common use indicates that marital status is her primary status. She is defined in terms of her legal connection to a man. Whereas men, be they married or not, have a variety of statuses that can rightly be called their own. To the extent that women are Other, they are considered to be parenthetical or auxiliary to the human enterprise. It is not too much of a stretch to understand the denial of full rights and equality to a creature whom history has, for so long, marked as an object, a representative of a category. Woman has only recently become able to achieve subjectivity, the expression of her own voice, the right to define herself on her own terms. Still, the tendency for men to presume that they can exercise control over women is rooted in a long historical legacy whereby She was not a person deserving of respect in and of her own right, but rather an object for man to do unto as he pleased.

In 1903, W. E. B. DuBois wrote a poignant essay on being black and being an American. "How does it feel to be a social problem?" people used to ask him. Reading this for the first time, many of my students remark, "This could be me today." The implication is that many people of color have the experience of being seen first as an Object representative of a particular social category. A problematic category, at that. DuBois, who was raised in a predominantly white, wealthy town in Massachusetts, was first made aware of his status as an object of repulsion when a first-grade classmate refused his offering of a greeting card. "It dawned on me with a certain suddenness that I was different from the others . . . shut out from the world by a vast veil." DuBois describes his life as an attempt to reconcile his being separated by a veil that simultaneously renders him Other and denies him the basis for achieving subjectivity.

Patricia Hill Collins, a contemporary sociologist and self-defined black feminist, states that social studies cannot advance without using race, class and gender as bases for analysis. The challenge is to recognize the distinction between the study of these categories of difference as a historical basis for setting persons apart from one another and understanding these differences as a basis of self-awareness. The first is a matter of comprehending social-level patterns of racism, sexism and other forms of categorical privilege and obstruction of rights. The latter is a matter of subjectivity—persons speaking for themselves regarding how they experience social differences.

Subjectivity

> Since the self, like the work you produce, is not so much a core as a process, one finds oneself always pushing one's questioning of oneself about the limit of what one is and what one is not. When am I Vietnamese? When am I American? When am I Asian and

when am I Asian-American or Asian-European? . . . The question is no longer: Who
am I? but When, where, how am I?

—Trinh T. Minh-ha

Which box do you check when you are filling out forms that request information about
your racial/ethnic identity? The most common forms use a system of categorization
defined by the U.S. Census Bureau. The categories are: American Indian/Alaska Native;
Asian or Pacific Islander; Black; White; Of Hispanic origin. Does this set of choices
present any dilemmas or questions for you? If your family ancestry is Vietnamese, do you
mind checking a box that will also be checked by persons of Chinese, Japanese, Filipino,
or perhaps Laotian descent? Do you care that all Indian Nations are grouped under a
heading that designates them as a single cultural entity? What do you do if your mother
is black and your father is Latino? How often do you have to leave out some part of
yourself whenever you check the boxes? Or do you check Other? What does it feel like
to be Other?

For many people, checking official boxes is an occasion for reflection on the disjuncture between how they experience themselves and how they are treated as an objective
social category. What is the purpose of the boxes? The answer to this question isn't so
easy. The "boxes" represent a historical struggle for recognition of the diverse cultural
groups that form the mosaic of American society. The boxes also signify attempts by
official counting bodies to gather informational statistics about the representation of
different groups of people in terms of education, employment, geographical distribution,
health care and just about anything else that you can think of. In some cases, racial/ethnic
categorization is potentially meaningful for analyzing systematic differences in the
distribution of resources. Sometimes, knowing someone's ethnic background is a useful
source of cultural information in terms of health care history or related services. The
"boxes" represent the underlying significance of categories of difference, particularly race
and gender, in the late twentieth century.

Checking a box is as activity that reminds us that individuals are more than a composite
of their gender/race/class/sexuality profiles. At the same time, the boxes signify that in a
society with a history of economic, political and cultural emphasis on these categorical
distinctions, the differences matter. All of us derive a sense of self-understanding from
the cultural legacy in which we are raised. In the United States this legacy is likely to
include ethnic and racial origins. If your ethnic origin includes a history of antagonism
with the dominant culture, then this cultural legacy will also be etched with political
implications that may shape how you think of yourself.

For instance, most persons of Japanese descent whose grandparents and parents lived
in the United States will recall, as part of their family history, the internment camps during
World War II. Thousands of law-abiding citizens were escorted from their homes and sent
to camps where they were held "under surveillance" until the war ended. Each Japanese
family has its own memories and interpretations of this event. For some it is a continuing
source of shame, for others, a source of anger. But in each case, there is a shared sense of
being singled out as Other, of being marginalized for reasons connected to categorical
distinctions rather than personal behavior. Through this shared history, the social distinction becomes personal. It also becomes political.

Identity politics is a term that acknowledges that social differences in this society are connected with access to resources and privileges. Self-identification in terms of social categories of difference is intended to raise awareness of the multiple groups and cultures that populate this country, and as a statement that these different groups do not all have the same rights of belonging. This self-identity can foster a sense of belonging and historical anchoring for the individual. At the same time, like all group memberships, it can be a source of limitation and frustration. How do you determine whether someone is black enough, or gay enough, or the right kind of feminist? Do you have to have experienced oppression in order to participate in liberation politics? Do you have to be Chicano/a in order to teach courses in Mexican history and politics?

These questions reflect the ongoing struggles and tension that every group experiences in its attempts to establish a significant collective identity. Collective identities are forged within a context of cultural and economic politics. Those who share similar positions, interests and experiences in terms of social categories are sometimes referred to as a "community"—for example, the lesbian and gay community, the Latino/a community, tribal communities and so forth. The people grouped together under the banner of "community" may share a similar objective status in terms of a social difference, but this does not necessarily mean that they have similar ways of expressing themselves in terms of these differences, nor that they want to be part of a "community" based on these differences. One issue that arises in discussions of so-called minority communities is who has the authority to speak for whom? Those who view themselves largely in terms of a marginal minority identity may have very different views on whether others who share their position should press for assimilation or for wider acceptance of their differences.

Every year in every major city in the United States, gays and lesbians fight about whether "drag queens" and other flamboyant "queers" should be allowed to march in Gay Pride Parades. Women and people of color throughout the United States are deeply divided about affirmative action. There is a long history of tension and mistrust between white feminists and women of color who feel sold out by their white sisters. These conflicts and controversies reveal that self-concept, including minority subjectivity, is an ongoing process. Experiences of racism, sexism and homophobia are not objective, unchanging phenomena that can be easily articulated in simple slogans that make for good diversity banners. This tension of "who" to be, of wondering whether you are "authentic enough" or "political enough" or whether the "community really speaks for you" is one of the few experiences that persons in minority positions have in common. As one colleague puts it, "It's like always being under a microscope. All my actions are scrutinized in terms of my race. I want to get myself a T-shirt that says, 'I am not a role model today.' "

This tension of having continually to make determinations about whether your actions will reflect poorly on your minority status and whether you are "authentic" enough is sometimes referred to as the "tyranny of solidarity." In order to participate in collective claims for recognition and equality, one must emphasize membership in marginal groups and be attentive to forms of behavior that have the potential to alter negative stereotypes. At the same time, this continual self-scrutiny can become a tedious and limiting basis for self-expression.

As a personal example, I find that I am often impatient with discussions of "gay marriage." I do not have a strong or compelling interest in embracing what seems to me to be a strongly entrenched patriarchal institution. At the same time, I recognize that the institution of marriage is one of the primary bases for being granted the full privileges of belonging in this culture, including access to basic things like family health care plans and assurance that your relationship will be legally recognized in terms of "next of kin" issues. For this reason, I am politically in favor of gay marriage, but I'm not sure that "gay marrieds" represent my version of a queer community. I'm not even sure that I like to hang around with people whose primary concerns are weddings and children. Yet, because this is a civil rights issue, I find myself spending more and more time engaged in conversations about marriage and parenting.

Subjectivity and difference are an issue of who has the power to define themselves and within what context. If your sense of self and subjectivity is forged largely as a response to false claims and negative stereotypes, there may be less opportunity to develop a self-image that is a reflection of your own unique interests and tastes. The self is not a stable, core thing, and objective labels of difference are sticky and can be difficult to wriggle out of, particularly in a culture that is keen on marking such differences. The challenge is to identify the context in which definitions of difference arise and take shape. This is an issue of "framing."

Framing Difference

In a recently published book called *Freaks Talk Back,* sociologist Josh Gamson chronicles the proliferation of "freaks" as guests on television talk shows. The "freaks" have replaced what are now considered more run-of-the-mill sexual deviants—the garden variety gays and lesbians, married bisexuals, transsexuals, spouse swappers and the like. "Freaks" are two transsexuals married to one another, or parents who have sex with their children's dates, or lesbians who cruise gay men, or anything with a slight twist on the usual "nuts, sluts and perverts" theme. According to Gamson, "freaks" now saturate daytime television. His analysis of the consequences for the American public are mixed. The prevalence of "freaks" on television poses a paradox. On the one hand, the frequent appearance of people who do not fit stereotypical impressions of the "normal person" may stretch the definitions of "normality." A woman who mentions to a friend that her husband likes to wear her underwear may be comforted when the friend replies, "Oh, I saw that on television. It happens all the time."

On the other hand, daytime talk shows strive to be as sensationalist as possible. The person presented is being presented as a "freak." For the show to be a commercial success, the person has to be framed as "wacko" or "really out there" or "a real pervert." The television network is in the position to define the deviant behavior, and in order to attract viewers, it must play up the angle of "freakishness." If the "freak" is portrayed as "too normal," then the show loses the interest of the viewer.

The representation of these differences or deviations as freakish can be compared with the representations of black transgendered prostitutes in a book researched by another sociologist, Leon Pettiway. Pettiway interviewed dozens of gay black men who work as transgendered prostitutes. In considering how to present this information to an audience of scholars, Pettiway decided to let the subjects speak for themselves. The book consists of an author's introduction followed by the stories of five subjects. The stories are literal transcriptions from the interview tapes. In both the television shows and Pettiway's book, the subjects are talking about themselves. But the frame is very different in the second case wherein Pettiway's intent is to "give voice" to persons who are frequently not heard from, and when they are, only through stereotypical presentations that reinforce their objective marginality.

Consider the following statement written by nationally syndicated columnist Russell Baker. Baker, writing from the position of someone "much older," was reflecting on what it was like to turn fifty. "You wake up. You're still here. You realize fifty isn't so bad. You're going to make it after all. The problems begin when you turn fifty-one. You find yourself considering hair transplants (or if you are a woman, liposuction). . . ." How are women rendered in this sentence? What if the sentence had read, "You find yourself considering hair transplants or liposuction . . ."? In the first utterance, the sentence is written as if Baker imagines his audience to be men, and then he thinks to himself, "Oh yeah, perhaps some women are also reading my column," and so adds a parenthetical reference intended to speak to women. As a woman, I get tired of being referred to with asides and parentheticals. The second sentence implies an audience of both men and women; each can read the sentence and pick out which of the issues applies directly to her or him. The second construction is not unwieldy or grammatically problematic. It is inclusive and, dare I suggest, is evidence that the author "gets it."

"How are we supposed to learn all the right PC language?" one of my students asks in frustration when I ask my class about the Baker sentence. It's a reasonable question, but wrongheaded in that it implies that there is a single "right way" to be and to behave. In the Baker sentence, the issue isn't the words that he used, per se, but that the words reveal that in a default or everyday sense, he sees women peripherally. Instead of worrying about specific words or actions taken out of context, I find it useful to consider the audiences that I carry in my head. To whom do I imagine myself to be speaking and for whom do I think I speak when I use words such as *we, us* and *them?* How diverse is the audience in your head? When I start with this question, I quickly recognize which positions I may be taking for granted and what sort of stereotypes might be shaping how I think, speak and respond.

There is no single answer to the question of who or what should constitute the audience in your head. Rather the related question is: To what extent are you capable of "taking the role of the other"? This is a complicated endeavor and one that can never be fully achieved, according to many philosophers. To what extent can we share an understanding of and empathize with the complicated experiences of someone who is very different? A character in Salman Rushdie's novel, *Midnight Children,* answers, "To understand me you will have to swallow a whole world."

"Getting It"

Many a well-intentioned white person has been heard to remark, "I'm not racist, I believe in a 'colorblind' society." The problem with this conception is that "colorblind" is often a euphemism for the practice of systematically ignoring a hierarchy of differences. It's easy to be blind to the injustices connected to difference if you are on the top of the pile and free to see beyond these differences. "Colorblind" is also a euphemism for "white." The fact of the matter is that in this country, in this historical moment, "color" is present in all social encounters and images. People who don't see it are not equal minded. Rather, they don't get it. Entreating someone to be "colorblind" is to ask them to put aside their own cultural and political history. We won't "get it" as a country until we become more literate in the histories of these differences, including the atrocities and injustices that have taken place because of them. The key is to become more aware of how persons experience these differences, and to grant them the power to define the differences for themselves.

Ronald Takaki, in an article on the history of multi-culturalism in the United States, suggests that the trick is not to try to be like me or to comprehend everything about my experience, but to forge connections that enable both of us to make sense of how we experience our differences. This requires listening and asking questions with a spirit of respect. Respectfully listening to someone means that you are open to the possibility that your ideas on a topic will change. This can be a difficult thing to do for persons who are accustomed to privilege. Sometimes it is easier for such people to be told "what the problem is" so that they can "fix it." Listening with the intent to understand the complexities of someone else's life can be especially difficult if the other person's experiences include mistreatments by members of a group with which you are associated. Those who are able to override their defensiveness in such conversations find that they will, eventually, be rewarded with a greater understanding and new ways of forging connections. Mostly this process requires a tolerance for ambiguity and contradiction and a willingness to stay engaged in emotionally charged encounters.

Ultimately, systems of difference are the lines that mark sociocultural reality. They constitute the framework of social order and are the blueprint for meaningful patterns of interaction. These differences are a necessity—without them we would have no basis for determining ourselves, others and behavioral expectations; in short, we would have no shared reality. Systems of difference are also a source of prejudice because they constitute the basis of determining which characteristics are central and valuable and which are less so. This is a contradiction in a society that has individual merit and equality of opportunity as its primary creed of assessment. It may be the case that for the citizenry of the United States to mature in its ideals of pluralistic democracy, we will first have to develop a discourse of difference that acknowledges these complexities and contradictions.

In a moving essay called "Loving Across the Boundary," Ann Filemyr, a white writer whose words open this chapter, describes the pleasures and difficulties involved in having chosen another woman, a black artist, as a life partner. She describes an incident in which their son, the biological product of his black mother, is shot at while walking home from school in a Milwaukee neighborhood. The boy is seven years old:

> What could you say to him about how to live on the mean streets of a bully nation? We did not live on those same streets even though we lived in the same neighborhood. His experience, my experience, his mother's experience—we walked out the front door into three separate worlds, worlds we did not define or control except in how we would respond to them.

Many North Americans are fond of the idea that we are an "open-minded" people. Presumably this means that we are tolerant of others and endeavor to reserve judgment until "the facts are in." A thorough understanding of social forms of difference makes this matter a bit more complicated. Ask yourself these questions: How free are you to pass through society as the opposite of your biological sex? Would you, if you could, assume the position of someone with a different color of skin? Have you ever been denied access to spaces/occasions because of your age? Can you have a sexual interaction with anyone you would like to?

As I noted in Chapter 3, all groups have boundaries that regulate the behavior of members. If anyone could be everyone and do anything all the time, personal identity and interpersonal relationships would have no meaning. Chaos would reign. Thus groups attempt to establish meaningful patterns of behavior that mark personal and collective distinctiveness and make interaction relatively smooth and predictable. Positions of difference provide us with a script for who we're supposed to be, how to behave toward others and what to expect from them. These social institutions generally arise out of practical, economic, political and ceremonial circumstances. They often start out as recipes for collective living. If these recipes endure as a formula for collective behavior, it is generally because a similar combination of sociopolitical circumstances prevails. As the recipes become institutionalized they can be said to calcify, or harden into ideologies. What was once a flexible formula for achieving a particular purpose becomes "the way it must be done." An initial step toward understanding and dealing with these systems of difference is acknowledging that they exist and that they shape and constrain the possibilities of who we can be and how we interact with one another.

How Do We Cut the American Pie?

The Myth of Meritocracy

PARADOX

Many citizens in the United States believe that those who get the most rewards in terms of money and assets are those who have worked the hardest and are the most deserving. Meritocracy is the ideal that anyone who wants to apply herself or himself can get ahead. In reality, this ideal is a myth. There are several structural factors, such as the number of available positions in the best schools or the number of available jobs, that determine whether or not otherwise deserving individuals actually get the education or job that they deserve. There are also several economic and cultural factors that shape one's life advantages. For instance, children in wealthy families are more likely to be educated in the best funded schools and these schools tend to emphasize college preparation and to socialize these youth for high paying jobs. In addition to these factors, a very small number of Americans have a very large piece of the economic pie. This same group makes most of the political and economic decisions in this country. These decisions reflect the particular interests of this group rather than the ideals of democracy and meritocracy. One consequence of this is that the United States has the widest gap between the rich and the poor of any modern industrial country. Why do so many Americans believe in the myth of meritocracy despite the overwhelming evidence that this is not how wealth and resources are distributed in the United States?

I'm looking at the front page of the *Seattle Times,* my local newspaper. One of the headlines announces that a proposed hygiene center for the homeless has angered retailers who are trying to revitalize the neighborhood. The article (Chiu, 1995) quotes a local merchant whose sentiments reflect those of others in the area: "A hygiene center has merit and I'd be willing to contribute to it financially, but to place it in an area you're trying to revitalize as retail is insanity." The paper calls this a case of NIMBY—not in my backyard. The hygiene center would provide area homeless with access to public rest rooms, showers and laundry facilities and would include several low-income housing units. The good citizens of the neighborhood agree that the homeless should have these basic facilities, but they'd prefer to have them located somewhere else, someplace not intended to attract people who have money to spend.

Next to the article about the hygiene center is a story about lab rats. Apparently, the nation's lab rats are plagued with a problem quite the opposite of that faced by the nation's homeless. Lab rats, the headline announces, are too fat. The lab rat's daily routine is to "sit around with bottomless bowls of chow and nothing to do but snack." Presumably this is a problem for Americans because lab rats are the primary means of testing substances as safe or deadly. Fat rats obscure the test results; they may react negatively to a substance because they are fat and out of shape, not necessarily because the substance is toxic. A researcher jokes that the most toxic substance tested in FDA laboratories in the past two decades is an overdose of food.

In an issue on the distribution of jobs and wealth, *Time* reports that the United States has the largest gap between the rich and the poor of any major industrial nation. And the gap is widening even more. The rich are getter richer and the poor are getting poorer. The theme of the *Time* feature article is whether or not tax cuts proposed by the House will continue to perpetuate this ever-widening gap by providing breaks to the rich at the expense of the poor (*Time,* November 6, 1995).

Pondering this reminds me of a study conducted in the early 1970s by sociologists Joan Huber and William Form (1973). They asked both poor people and middle-class people to give their opinions about why the rich are rich and the poor are poor. For the most part, middle-class people commented that the rich earned their rewards through discipline, intelligence and hard work. The poor tended to say that the rich are rich because they are born into wealth and they keep it by stepping on the backs of the rest of us. No surprise in those responses.

Is Equality the American Ideal?

Is America the land of equality? Are wealth and income fairly evenly distributed? Social and economic demographics indicate that income and other forms of wealth, such as property and stocks, are unequally distributed among the population in this country. The article in *Time* estimated that approximately 50% of all pre-tax income goes to about 20% of the population—the upper crust, so to speak. The bottom 20% get approximately 5% of the total income earned annually in the United States. This estimate is consistent with projections made by economists showing that in recent years the upper one fifth of the population has claimed more than 50% of the nation's income. These same projections indicate that the "slice of the pie" claimed by this group is getting bigger and the shares for the other four fifths of the population are shrinking. Think about it this way. Imagine that you had $100 to split among one hundred people. According to these estimates, 20 individuals will each get $2.50 (for a total of $50), the middle 60 will each get 75 cents and the bottom 20 each get 25 cents. The term for this form of economic distribution is *stratification.* The response to the question about the distribution of wealth and income in the United States is most certainly, no—the pie is not divided up into roughly equal shares for all Americans. It strikes me as noteworthy that we don't talk about this much in the United States. Is it because we don't notice the "fat rats" who are apparently eating a lot of pie? What about the "undesirables" who have no pie? How do we make sense of this distribution?

Consider these comparative questions regarding the United States and other countries. Is inequality explicitly acknowledged? How is the inequality in income explained among the members of the society? An interesting feature about the question of equality in the United States is the absence of a social discourse that explicitly acknowledges the inequity among groups of people. This can be compared with the language of social and economic status in other countries. The population in India, for instance, is divided into "castes." Brahmans occupy the top rank and "untouchables" occupy the bottom rank. An Indian person can tell you which caste he or she belongs to. The caste system in India is "closed," which means that one is born into a particular caste, that of the family, and remains in that caste for the duration of this physical life.

England, though less closed than India, has an explicit rank order as well. Persons who are born into the "upper class" expect to have particular privileges and benefits not available to those born into the lower classes. In return for these privileges, the "elite" are expected to educate themselves for service to the country in the form of leadership and politics. Whether or not they actually provide these services is an empirical question that we will not address here. The noteworthy point is that several countries have a *political-economic philosophy of elitism.* Some members of the society are expected to have more than others, and in return, they are expected to provide political, social and moral leadership for the rest of the citizens.

Elitism is a philosophy that dates back to Aristotle, who suggested that those best fit to govern were those who were most "virtuous." The most ostensibly virtuous were those who were born into the upper social strata. Acquiring one's position by right of birth or other features that are not within the individual's control is called *ascribed status.* In cultures in which there are explicit ranks based on ascribed features, individuals know which stratum they belong to and which benefits they can expect to have as a result of this position. Another feature of such cultures that is different from U.S. culture is the presence of stories and images about fate. Persons often use these stories to describe the reasons for their own economic and social positions. It may be said of a person that his low place on the economic totem pole is a matter of "bad karma" or, alternately, that someone's wealth and status are a consequence of "her lucky birth to a rich family." In such cultures, differences in wealth and income are explained in terms of historical and ideological traditions that grant some persons more than others as a birthright.

Other countries have different philosophies regarding how resources should be distributed. In Sweden, for instance, the philosophy of wealth distribution is one of "equality"; all persons may not have an equal share of the pie, but in theory anyone who contributes to society *should* have an equal share. Sweden has the lowest gap between the rich and the poor in industrial nations. It also has the most extensive form of central regulation of wealth distribution. The gap that does exist between people is explained as the result of preceding centuries of inequality when wealth was distributed among noble families. In time, with fine-tuning in the design of government means of distribution, the

Swedish hope that the gap will become almost nonexistent. Thus, among the Swedes, inequality is philosophically unacceptable. To the extent that it exists, it is explained as the outcome of inadequate government design and the spill-over of history into the present day.

The American Philosophy of Individual Merit

What is the American philosophy of resource distribution? The answer to this question is a source of confusion for many Americans. The ideal of "equality" leads some to think that, like Sweden, the U.S. political economy is based on the philosophy that everyone who is a citizen should have an equal share of the resources in this country. This is a false assumption. The political economy in the United States is based on the *philosophy of individual merit*. This philosophy emerged from two lines of thought that form the foundation of the American declaration of independence from the British. One is the belief that neither the government nor fate should control the destiny of any individual. Early Americans embraced the philosophy of *"individualism"* as a response to the arbitrary rule of kings. Every person has the inalienable right to make her or his own destiny based on hard work and merit.

Individualism is matched up with a *philosophy of competition* as a basis for determining who should get which rewards in a society. As in a fair game of sport, individuals compete for the prize to be awarded to the winner. In this sense, rewards are distributed based on individual *merit* demonstrated in a particular setting. Contrary to socialist equality, the American philosophy is to be wary of equal distributions regulated by a central government. The rationale for concern is that if persons can expect to get a reward simply by being a member of a society, they will not be motivated to contribute their best efforts. The philosophy of reward based on achievement presumes that competition will spur individuals to do their best and will result in superior goods and products for everyone. Thus, the philosophy of individual merit holds that not everyone can have an equal share; those who get the most will be those who contribute the most to society.

One implication of this philosophy is that Americans are less likely to attribute individual rewards to birth or fate and more likely to think in terms of "self-determination." According to the philosophy of individual meritocracy, the gap between the rich and the poor is a reflection of which members of this society work hardest and are the most dedicated to achievement. It is assumed that those who are the most talented and dedicated are at the top, those who have the least ability and drive to succeed are at the bottom. Americans are uncomfortable thinking of themselves and others as belonging to a particular social class that has real consequences for their life opportunities. The idea that one's rank is determined by birth or by government design is inconsistent with the ideal of meritocracy, which holds that access to economic ranks is open or fluid. One is not stuck in a particular "class" by accident of birth, nor is one placed in a particular rank by government forces beyond individual control; rather, Americans can move up and down the ladder of success depending on will and effort. Or so the story goes.

This chapter is an exploration of the tensions in the American system of economic distribution. In the remaining pages we will look at how realistic the ideal of meritocracy is. Some questions to keep in mind as you read this material are: What sort of equipment and training does someone need to compete in the American economic game? How do individuals get this equipment and training? By drive alone? If you have the training and drive, what other social factors might complicate whether or not you are taken seriously as a "player"? It turns out that there are many factors that throw a wrench into the gears of the American ideal of individual achievement. To put it succinctly, the equation we will be scrutinizing is:

$$\text{Does achievement} \rightarrow \text{reward?}$$

Structures of Scarcity

Sociologist Mark Abrahamson has written a provocative article in which he uses the metaphor of a deck of playing cards to demonstrate stratification and mobility in a resource structure. Stratification, as I have noted, is a system wherein some persons have more (more money, more power, more social status) than others. *Mobility* refers to whether and how one can move up or down in the stratified structure. A closed system means that there is no mobility.

I used Abrahamson's idea to create an experience for students in one of my sociology courses. It works like this. Imagine you arrive in class and are asked to pick a card from a shuffled deck of playing cards. Everyone picks a card from a master deck. You end up with a Ten of Spades. "Don't lose your card," I announce. "Your final grade will be based on it, or at least on this starting point." Several people look alarmed; presumably they have low cards and assume that this is associated with a low grade. Several others cheer. Apparently they hold face cards. I go on to explain that this is not a closed system but is an opportunity for advancement based on merit. The card simply marks your starting point. "Anyone who gets a ten or above on the next fifteen-point paper can trade in their current card for the next step higher." Those who were alarmed relax and some even express enthusiasm at the idea of a challenge.

I inform the class that although they may not be entirely happy with their initial card rank, this is equivalent to the American system in which we are born into circumstances that predetermine our starting rank. These circumstances, which sociologists call *socio-economic status* (SES), are measured by father's level of education, type of occupation and level of income. In our system of meritocracy, occupations are rank-ordered according to which jobs presumably contribute the most to society and require the most training and preparation. Individuals who are willing to undergo this preparation, to put in the effort and to make the sacrifices necessary to train for the position, should receive rewards commensurate with their efforts. Thus, we would expect to see a link between level of education (training), the importance of the job, and the amount of income. The higher the level of education, the higher the rank of the job and the higher the pay. In short, *effort should be rewarded by high pay*. The ideal of mobility within a meritocracy is that one can move up from the initial starting position by putting forth the effort to train for highly rewarded positions. When someone moves beyond the level of their father's SES, it is called *upward mobility*.

I reiterate to the class that the cards simulate this structure and that everyone simply needs to work hard at writing a good paper in order to have a chance to move up in the game. A hand goes up. "What's your card?" I ask the hand. "King of Clubs." "Speak right up." "Is it possible to move down?" she asks. "Yes, if you get less than ten points on your paper." Several people, those holding face cards, murmur in disappointment. "But don't worry too much about it," I continue. "After all, you *are* the King of Clubs." She brightens visibly and exchanges a high-five sign with the Queen of Hearts.

Another hand goes up. "What's your card?" I demand. "Three of Diamonds," comes the reply. I'm distracted by another hand and so ignore the "Three." "I'm the Ten of Spades," you announce. "State your question," I say. "Are you going to add more cards to the deck after you grade our papers?" you want to know. "No, I don't control the deck," I remind the class. You look perplexed. "Does that mean that in order for me to move up to a Jack, someone above me has to drop down?" you inquire further. "Don't worry about it," I soothe. There are at least three people above you, one of them is bound to drop down so that you can move up. Besides," I add, "you're a Club, we can probably find room for you." You don't look convinced and several others have begun to shift uneasily in their seats.

Many hands go up and people begin to talk at once. To control the din and be able to listen and respond completely to important questions I tell those holding red cards (Hearts and Diamonds) that for the sake of efficiency, only those with black cards (Spades and Clubs) will be allowed to speak in class; red cards should direct their questions and concerns to those with black cards during the break and the black card holders can voice these issues later in class. This seems fair to me, but because it places undue responsibility on the black card holders, I give them the option of trading for a red card of equal rank before proceeding. None of the blacks want to switch to red so we move on.

One of the tensions in the American system, as illustrated by the playing card metaphor, is that the overall supply of those occupations that command the best rewards may be less than the demand for them. In a perfect meritocracy there is no tension *if* the number of positions available is equal to the number of persons who have achieved the right to occupy that rank. For instance, in my courses I generally give A's to all those who have demonstrated a mastery of the material based on their performance on assignments and exams. In theory, this means that I can give out as many A's as there are persons who deserve them. There is no real limit to the number of A's available to me to pass out, so each person can expect to get exactly the reward that he or she deserves. However, if there are fewer positions than there are claimants, a situation of *scarcity* exists. Thus, when I finish grading the papers for this class that is stratified by playing cards there may be many people who *deserve* to exchange their current cards for the next highest card, but there may not be enough cards available for them actually to get what they deserve.

The cards in this game symbolize rank-ordered jobs and/or the actual amount of income for the job based on the level of training and effort required to do the job. *To what extent is there a scarcity of occupations/rewards in this country for willing and qualified individuals?*

What is the relationship between the number of "high-reward" positions that exist and the number of people who aspire to these positions? If there are few positions and many qualified people, several of the qualified will have to be content with a lower position. If you just looked, at a glance, at how people were distributed throughout the structure of positions—that is, who holds which cards/jobs, how could you tell whether some persons were "underrewarded" or "underemployed" for reasons that had to do with a *scarcity* of positions rather than training and effort? Looking at who gets which rewards in terms of how many positions there are in the structure is called a *structural analysis of economic rewards.* The logic is that we cannot tell, just by knowing various individuals' actual positions, whether they are in a low position because they weren't capable or talented enough, or whether they are in a low position because there is a scarcity of high positions. *Structures of scarcity* complicate the equation:

$$\text{Effort} \rightarrow \text{Reward.}$$

Personal Preferences Versus Structural Circumstances

Some sociologists and economists argue that in a system of unrestricted competition there will eventually be a natural equilibrium in which persons will seek an occupation/reward level that is consistent with their own level of talent and ambition. Seen from this point of view, the gap between those at the top and those at the bottom reflects the different talents and ambitions of the persons who occupy these positions. It is useful to consider the feasibility of this explanation in terms of the relationship between the number of positions (the overall employment structure) and those who aspire to hold the positions.

Thomas Schelling, an economist, provides a helpful illustration of structural dynamics and the distribution of different preferences. Schelling invites us to consider the seating in a movie theater. Not everyone desires the same seat. If you arrive reasonably early, say five to 10 minutes prior to the show, you can probably have the seat of your choice, and so can everyone else who attends the movie. This is a situation in which there is no tension between preferences for seats and the number of seats available. Everyone is happy. If the movie is extremely popular, however, you may have to go quite a bit earlier to get your desired seat. The rub, as Schelling points out, is that many others who are also aware that the movie is likely to be crowded may also go early and thus, although you put in the extra effort, you will not necessarily get your desired seat. You may be lucky to get any seat. The likelihood that you will get your desired seat depends as much on the structure of the situation—in this case the ratio of desirable seats to those who want them—as it does on the effort you expend to get what you want. Most of us are generally aware that structure plays a significant role in such outcomes as movie seating and traffic jams, but how aware are we that socioeconomic structure plays a major role in determining our access to occupational positions and rewards?

According to the philosophy of meritocracy, persons will work hard because they can expect to be rewarded for their efforts. If the structure of the rewards is such that persons will not get what they think they deserve, how satisfied will they be with the system of production and distribution? In such a case there might be a tension between cultural ideals of merit and structural circumstances that don't reward merit. The widening gap between those who seem to be getting rewards in our current economy and those who don't might suggest that something is amiss—certainly so many people are not suffering "downward mobility" because they have ceased to put in any effort. The *reality* of the current structure of distribution is in tension with the *ideal* of a perfect meritocracy. How, collectively and individually, do we deal with this tension?

People have different goals and ambitions; some may prefer occupations that are very demanding and require a high level of training, others may want to lead a more leisurely life and will pursue less technical and demanding jobs in return for more free time. If the structure of this situation were a "schelling point"—in other words, if we all had different preferences and there were enough positions to accommodate these preferences—then persons would select the positions they desired, undergo the appropriate training, assume their jobs and everyone would be content. As we have already noted, this works only if there are enough positions for those who desire and train for them. When there are not enough positions, persons have to compete for them.

In reality, there appears to be a great deal of "scarcity" in the American employment structure and in the rewards associated with specific employment positions. Shifts in employment sectors change the number of jobs available in an area. For instance, when an automobile manufacturing firm, such as General Motors, closes down factories in a town and moves the industry to Mexico where labor is cheaper, tens of thousands of jobs are taken out of the "structure." Are the newly unemployed in this situation because of structural circumstances or because of personal preference not to work? Currently, employment is up in some labor sectors, but the real wages for many jobs have actually decreased in recent years. For instance, there are more jobs for primary and secondary school teachers now than there were a decade ago. The training requirements are also higher than a decade ago. Many teachers are likely to have a master's degree rather than a bachelor's degree. These teachers are trained and they have jobs, but they are making less money when standard of living is taken into account (another structural factor). Estimates indicate that these teachers are bringing home about 27 percent less income in real wages than a decade ago. For many of these individuals, this means that they need to find an additional source of employment to make ends meet. What are the consequences of unlivable wages for individuals' quality of life? What does this trend indicate about the values of this country?

Most sociologists study a person's position in terms of the "big picture" of economic and income structures. This picture suggests an increasing gap between effort and reward. The interesting question is how the American public makes sense of the gap between reality and the ideals of meritocracy. How do we explain this gap to ourselves? One way is to focus on the fairness of the game rather than the outcome—a sort of "someone has to lose" philosophy. A related means of reconciling the philosophy of meritocracy with a reality in which there may not be enough positions for everyone who wishes to compete is to redefine the standards about who is deserving. We can also perpetuate a false awareness that meritocracy is working by pretending that some of the population does not exist. In the next few pages I will look at some of the myths that we use to perpetuate the idea that the United States is a meritocracy, despite a reality that suggests otherwise.

Education and Equal Opportunity

One way to make scarcity seem less troubling is to redefine *fairness*. There may not be enough positions for everyone who is qualified to fill them, but in the collective American mind, virtue is bestowed upon those who at least try their hardest. This ideal is captured in expressions such as "effort is its own reward" and "it's not whether you win or lose, but how you play the game." We're relieved if we can convince ourselves that the "competition was fair" and "the better person got the job." If this is the case, then we don't have to feel so bad about the fact that people are getting less than they'd tried for and expected. Fairness resolves the tension by reframing the situation in terms of an honorable battle well fought, rather than as a situation of hopelessness. A fair competition means that all individuals come to the game equally equipped to play—everyone had an *equal opportunity* to compete. The outcome of the encounter is judged according to impartial standards whereby some individuals edge others out because of superior talent and ability.

This raises the question, What is equal opportunity? What do you need to compete? The primary means of access to the American competition for jobs and income is education. A pivotal step in the climb to success in the United States is higher education. Americans who have a college degree earn an average of 75 percent more than those who do not. In theory, every American deserves an equal opportunity to develop the level of skills necessary to compete for various positions. Is education available to anyone who is willing to pursue it? The rationale for a public school system in the United States is that all Americans should have access to the basic training that will enable them to pursue whatever positions they might desire. Assuming that education is *available* (this is a large assumption, but for the sake of ease, one that will be granted for now), is the *quality* of education equal? There are two parts to assessing this question: the quality of the content and the prestige of the certificate of training.

Stratification in Higher Education: Relative Quality and Prestige

Does it matter which institution of higher education you attend? Every morning on my way to work I pass by three different institutions of higher learning; each trains a different segment of the population toward different goals. First I drive through what locals call the "U" District. The heart of this neighborhood is the University of Washington campus. This campus, which is often cited as one of the most beautifully landscaped universities in the country, is a central hub of research, intellectual, and cultural activity in the state of Washington. Undergraduates who attend the "U Dub" are mostly Washington state residents, they pay $3,000 annually (in-state tuition) and take an average of five years to complete their degrees. Most of them go on to jobs in the professional service sector, which in Washington includes engineering, design and executive positions with major employers such as Boeing and Microsoft. Admission to the undergraduate program at the UW requires a 3.2 GPA from high school. In addition to undergraduate education, the primary emphasis at the UW is graduate research training. UW faculty are considered forerunners in their respective fields and are connected to research facilities, advisory councils and other executive industries around the country. One of the main benefits of training at the UW is the opportunity to work with faculty who are well situated to assist their students in gaining desirable jobs.

Leaving the U District I drive south across a channel of water that locals refer to as "the moat." A few miles on I encounter the traffic jam that builds up each morning as students rush to their classes at Seattle Central Community College. *Campus* is a generous term for this cluster of industrial red brick buildings that line one side of the busiest street in Seattle's most densely populated neighborhood, Capitol Hill. Approximately 65 percent of all college students are enrolled in community colleges. Enrollment at Seattle Central Community College reflects the wider economic, ethnic and age differences that typify community colleges in the United States. SCCC offers certificate training for a range of administrative and technical positions. The school also boasts a popular cooking program that has trained many of the well-known area chefs. There are relatively few full-time faculty at SCCC; most of the instructors are local experts in their area or graduate students from the UW who teach two or three courses on a nonsalaried basis. The emphasis at SCCC is professional training with the goal of providing students with certification for mid-level service and skilled labor positions. Students who are enrolled in liberal arts courses at SCCC usually aspire to transfer to UW or similar schools when they can afford to do so and/or have improved their overall ranking for admission.

Once free from the congestion of Capitol Hill, I continue on a few blocks and turn into the gateway of the Seattle University campus. SU is located at the intersection of three of Seattle's most diverse neighborhoods. Along the external perimeter of the campus is a mix of warehouses, multiple-unit housing, fast-food chains and gas stations. Immediately to the south is the Central District, an area known as home to a primarily black and Asian immigrant population. The perimeter itself is a marked line between the noisy chaos outside and the sculpted serenity inside. Inside the small campus, fountains mask the sounds of nearby city traffic. The buildings are aesthetically pleasing and are set among ornamental shrubbery and carefully tended gardens. An herb garden borders the path from the parking garage to my office, which is located in a building that features a five-story atrium. Seattle University is a Jesuit institution in which the goal of "educating the whole person" is paramount. The physical surroundings, as well as the intellectual content, are intended to promote contemplation and reflection toward the goal of "awakening the deeper passions of the soul" and engaging the whole person in acts of service to community. SU education emphasizes mastery of the liberal arts. The university also encourages a spirit of community. It achieves this goal through the allocation of significant resources into cultural and community activities for students, staff and faculty. A high proportion of SU students continue their educational training in top-ranked graduate and professional programs around the country. Many of the city's local officials and high-ranking executives are SU alumni. Tuition at SU is $8,000 annually.

All schools are not created equal. My daily drive to work is a journey through the stratification of American Higher Education. The ideal education, measured by the quality of content and experience during school and the opportunities for employment afterward, would be undergraduate work at SU followed by graduate training in the field of one's choice at the UW. This is obviously the most direct, successful and personally fulfilling route to advantageous life positions.

Stratification in High School: How Persons Are Channeled Into Different Colleges

If merit is the only factor that determines where one goes to college, then every high school graduate in the state of Washington should have an equal chance of gaining admission to the college of her or his choice if he or she has the earned admission based on scholastic achievement to date. Because private and highly ranked state universities cannot admit all students who apply, additional criteria of admission are established to determine who should be admitted. High school GPA and standardized achievement tests are used to determine the winners of the competition for a slot in the best schools. Community colleges are available as a form of "second chance" for those who might not qualify initially. Are these the only criteria of admission? Does everyone have an equal chance to attend the college of their choice if they have achieved the level of mastery required for admission? Do some high schools provide more directed training and credentials for college than others?

Access to Quality Education

Students from low-income backgrounds who do want to go to college may not be able to afford to do so. In theory, higher education is presumably available across economic classes; if one cannot afford to attend Harvard or Yale, there is also the community college. If all high schools provided equal resources for college prep and every student therefore had similar training toward college entrance exams, regardless of SES background and geographical neighborhood, then, all else being equal, we would expect the number of applicants and subsequent admissions to be evenly distributed across SES groups and school districts. This is not the case. There are two possible interpretations for this: Either students in lower-income neighborhoods who attend the public schools are inherently less able or less motivated than their counterparts in high-income neighborhoods, or there is a patterned difference in the content and quality of the education across schools.

A journalist, Jonathan Kozol, has written about the differences in the type of education that children receive in different neighborhoods. According to Kozol, who has spent several years observing differences in schools in cities such as St. Louis, that have very poor and more wealthy neighborhoods, students in higher-income districts have assess to special programs for tracking skills such as reading. Many of these schools employ specialists whose main job is to monitor reading skills and to intervene with assistance as soon as a child appears to fall behind. These schools also have resources for field trips, music and art courses and other "extracurricular" activities intended to introduce young people to various aspects of middle- and upper-middle-class culture. In stark contrast, Kozol describes one school in East St. Louis that can't even afford to keep a back stock of toilet paper, let alone art and music supplies and special programs.

The quality of education is a function of the quality of the teachers and the materials, including the physical environment in which the education takes place. These features are a function of the tax base of the area and the persuasive involvement of parents who have the knowledge and the connections to shape and monitor the content of the education that their children receive. Parents who have the means to do so find ways to send their children to schools that have well-paid teachers and good resources. Do these children have an advantage over other children?

It is noteworthy that there is a disproportionately high rate of young people from upper-income backgrounds who *prefer* to go to college. It is possible that in addition to basic skills, certain schools offer something in the way of content and student-teacher interaction that socializes students to think that they may (or may not) be able to succeed in college. It is also possible that certain schools may have better developed programs for preparing students to take college entrance exams, pursue applications and so forth. In other words, some schools may be "college-tracked" and others may not be.

Some Additional Factors That Determine Success in Higher Education

Clearly, money is a factor in determining who can go to which schools. Students who are admitted sometimes cannot attend the school they would like because they cannot afford the tuition. In addition, success in college depends on the amount of time one has to become absorbed in the educational experience, including both the time to study and the time to participate in associations such as clubs, friendships, and more, that increase the student's exposure to ideas and to key faculty members. Students who have obligations such as family and outside employment may feel excluded from key opportunities not because they do not have the skills, but because they do not have the luxury of extra time. A disproportionate number of these students attend community colleges because the course offerings are often more flexible and more likely to include evening degree programs. In addition, the financial circumstances of many would-be students are such that they cannot afford the option of an education in the liberal arts as a precursor to shaping their decisions regarding career goals. Many students find it necessary to enroll in professional certificate programs that will place them directly into the employment sector as soon as possible.

Is this simply a different choice regarding training and career, or does it reflect a patterned inequity in who can pursue different types of education? Family income is the single best predictor of whether and where a person will go to college. Upper-middle-class families have the income to send their children to college immediately following high school without having to stop over for a period to earn money for college. Even if the preparation for college were equal across high schools, something we have already questioned, a number of those who have earned the *right* to attend college, based on their achievements to date, may not be able to afford to so. This means that, all else being equal, a disproportionate number of those who attend the best colleges will be those whose families have already achieved financial success. In other words, the playing field may be tipped to favor those who already have the resources for which everyone is presumably competing equally.

Balancing the Equation of Unequal Higher Education

A possible strategy for balancing this is need-based scholarships. Individuals who have been able to climb a substantial distance from their family's initial starting point have often gotten a leg-up through financial assistance that gives them access to good colleges and the chance to study without the distraction of part-time jobs. Critics of financial aid and need-based scholarships claim that the government should not intervene in the otherwise unfettered process of individual competition. If an individual does not have the financial means necessary to pursue higher education, then central government should not attempt to "correct" this. Proponents claim that since higher education is the main gate of admission to the competitive playing field for employment, no one should be denied access based on lack of initial funds. This is, they claim, contrary to the ideal of equal opportunity.

Most Americans fall somewhere in between the Social Darwinist position of the extreme critics and the optimistic ideal of equal education for everyone. Americans are ambivalent about who should pay for education. Most agree that everyone should have access to high-quality education, but we are deeply divided as a nation about whether or not funding for this equal access should be provided from our pool of collective resources. Since the mid-1980s, the Reagan years, funds available for financial aid have been cut substantially. Currently, the House is supporting a bill that would further reduce the allotment of these funds. The immediate consequence of this action is that fewer Americans who are in the middle, lower-middle and working classes will be able to pursue higher education, even though they may be intellectually qualified to pursue this goal and may have worked to achieve the right to take this next step toward the American Dream. The disproportionate access to education based on income calls into question whether or not the actual criteria for advancement in this country are based on effort and merit or on existing financial resources. State and community colleges are presumably one remedy to this inequity in access. Is there a significant difference between the educational training that one receives in a community college and, say, Harvard?

Cultural Capital

Obviously each institution has a distinct cultural history, level of prestige and ambiance. But does this really matter in the pursuit of the necessary training and credentials that will enable one to compete for a desired job? One sociologist who has written extensively on this topic is Randall Collins. Collins's research suggests that there are two related ways in which different types of educational institutions provide differential access to pursuit of the American Dream. One way is in the form of *cultural capital*.

Cultural capital consists of a fund of experiences, information and contacts that makes one more or less likely to "fit in." These are "status resources" that operate in subtle but significant ways to determine one's opportunities. For instance, when the number of qualified applicants for college admission is larger than the number of positions available (structural scarcity), other criteria may be used, knowingly or unknowingly, to single out who the "best" candidate really is. When the standard criteria for admission have been met and an admissions board must make finer distinctions among the candidates, they may be inclined to favor candidates whose attitudes and manners most resemble their own. They may also be aided in the decision by factors such as stereotypical assumptions about the applicant's background, the prestige of recommendation letter writers, and so forth. Students from economically privileged backgrounds have a disproportionate amount of cultural capital. Whether they are aware of it or not, they already belong to "the club."

Collins has also written that education and employment in the United States are not simply a rank-ordered stratification systems. There are actually two distinct systems that don't necessarily overlap. One is a system of *productive labor* and the other is *distributive (political) labor.* Most of the population, according to Collins, work to produce our national wealth. A smaller proportion of the population determine how this wealth should be divided up and used among us—these people include high-level lawmakers, politicians and CEOs, what some researchers call *the capitalist class.* This class of people has considerably more prestige, makes more money and enjoys more privileges than the "productive classes." According to Collins, access to the types of colleges and universities that garner admission onto the playing field for the capitalist class is based on cultural capital rather than merit.

The implication is that most Americans may be competing for positions and rewards on the ladder of production while a special few reside in arenas that determine how many positions will be on this ladder and just how much of the resources produced will be shared among these positions. In short, one group makes the wealth and another makes decisions about how it will be distributed. Collins demonstrates that certain colleges and universities, namely those considered to be "Ivy League," are a direct pipeline to the political labor sector. Regardless of one's individual achievements in any college, a degree from the "upper universities" serves as a credential or entrance ticket to the small elite who control production and distribution in the United States.

Americans know that education, not necessarily the training itself, but the *prestige* of the certification, is the principal ticket to highly respected and rewarded positions of employment. There is a direct connection between graduation from a prestigious university and first employment in a highly respected company. The CEOs of Fortune 500 companies, for instance, mostly hold degrees from Ivy League schools. Because of the connection between education and employment, there has been a great deal of debate about the "fairness" of affirmative action programs. The purpose of these programs is to target persons whose background circumstances make it likely that they will slip through the cracks—that they will otherwise never make it to the playing field. Because of presumed scarcity in positions in elite educational institutions, Americans are understandably concerned about the standards that determine who gets slots in these schools.

It is interesting, therefore, that what we don't seem to know about or pay attention to is the number of positions that are granted to persons simply on the basis of the fact that they already occupy elite positions by birth. In a recent analysis of admission policies in Ivy League institutions, sociologist Jerome Karabel estimates that as many as 40 percent of the current admission slots for these schools are *reserved* for the children of former graduates and donors. These reserved positions are called *legacies.* Legacies are a sort of affirmative action program for the rich.

Let's return to my class, who are currently stratified according to a deck of playing cards. I have assured them that they will indeed *deserve* to trade in their cards for the next highest position if they earn a qualifying grade on assignments. We are in the second day of using this system. Someone, the Nine of Clubs, wants to know why I have required that they identify themselves by card type on their papers. She implies that I may be biased in my assessment of their individual work based on the rank and suit of their card. Before I have a chance to respond, the King of Clubs steps in and points out to her that this is a much more efficient means of identifying them than the use of social security numbers or some other feature that is presumably anonymous. Besides, he notes, in his opinion I have not been biased to date. Several others sitting near him nod affirmatively. The face cards are sitting together today I notice. And, he tells her directly, you're a Club, you should want people to know this. She considers this, nods and seems appeased.

During the break some of the face cards gather around to talk with me. They express concern that some of the lower cards are disgruntled and don't seem to understand that this is a fair situation and that they will have their chances for success. I ask them how they know this; none of the lower cards have been voicing any dissent in class. Have some of the reds been asking you to speak for them, I inquire? Well no, they respond, they just have a sense that some people are unhappy. I remind them that this is a democracy and that anyone with a question or complaint need only speak up. The face cards nod approvingly to one another and seem content. The Queen of Clubs, in a particularly grand gesture, tells the Queen of Hearts that maybe she should talk with some of the lower reds and remind them that they have nothing to worry about if they just work hard. He emphasizes that if they have real concerns he would be happy to speak on their behalf. She thanks him and says that they probably are just a little slow at "getting it." The King of Clubs reminds the others in the group that they should all try to set a good example.

Following the break I notice that the face cards are increasingly animated. They have assumed responsibility for the class and are eager to explain how the game works to those who are less certain about the potential benefits. I am glowing with pride at how quickly they have gained an understanding of their positions. I am enjoying our conversations tremendously because they seem so bright and engaged. Fewer and fewer low cards are speaking. I can only assume that this means that they are now satisfied or that they don't care, which is their own fault. Perhaps some of them are wisely sitting back and assessing how they too can learn to become such an engaged participant.

Race and Gender: Systematic Differences in Education and Employment

Consider the fact that for every dollar that men earn, white women earn approximately 70 cents. Black women earn approximately 63 cents for every dollar that men make, and Hispanic women earn approximately 57 cents. These numbers reflect real differences across these groups. In other words, even though each of us can probably name individual African, Asian and Latin American men and women, and Anglo American women, who earn a great deal of money, these individuals are the exception in these categories rather than the rule. There are systematic differences in the distribution of income across these groups. What explains these differences?

One answer is that perhaps members of these groups work in lower-paying jobs (see Table 5.1). It does appear to be the case that while white men are distributed throughout each of the employment categories, persons in the other groups are disproportionately concentrated in occupations that are less prestigious and garner fewer rewards. What might explain this pattern of difference in occupations?

If we follow the logic of preferences and merit, a possible explanation is that members of these groups are less likely to aspire to high-paying occupations. Perhaps they choose to forego the training and sacrifice necessary to become highly paid executives and professionals. Or perhaps these employment paths are not open to certain groups? As we

Table 5.1   Occupations With Highest Concentration by Race/Ethnicity/Sex

Black Women	Social workers; postal clerks; dieticians; child-care workers and teacher's aides; private household cooks and cleaners; nursing aides and orderlies
Black Men	Vehicle washers and equipment cleaners; bus drivers; concrete workers; guards; sheriffs; bailiffs, and other law enforcement
Hispanic Women	Private household cleaners and servants; child-care workers; janitors and cleaners; health service occupations; sewing machine operators
Hispanic Men	Janitors and cleaners; construction trades; machine operators; cooks; drivers; laborers and helpers; roofers; groundskeepers, gardeners, farm and agricultural workers
White Women	Physical therapists; dental hygienists; secretaries; bookkeepers; accounting and auditing clerks
White Men	Marketing, advertising, and public relations managers; engineers, architects, and surveyors; dentists; firefighters; construction supervisors; tool and die makers
Asian Women	Marine-life workers; electrical assemblers; dressmakers; launderers
Asian Men	Physicians; engineers; professors; technicians; cooks; launderers; longshore equipment operators
Native American Women	Welfare aides; child-care workers; teacher's aides; forestry (except logging)
Native American Men	Marine-life workers; hunters; forestry (except logging); fishers

have already discussed, education is a key factor in being able to pursue high-paying jobs. Education is not equal across different neighborhoods, and those who have economic resources to begin with are likely to have an advantage in gaining admission to the top schools and training programs. Black, Cambodian, Latino and Vietnamese Americans are disproportionately concentrated in the lower strata of American society (see Table 5.2) It is difficult to accurately assess the talent and ambition of those who may not have opportunities for education. These parents may be just as eager to school their children but may face considerable disadvantages in the quality of facilities, teachers, time and resources for special programs such as SAT study programs and other college-track preparation.

Still, according to the myth of meritocracy, where there's a ill, there's a way. There are members of each of these groups who have attained high levels of education and employment. A good test of whether or not these observed differences reflect systematic forms of discrimination is to look at different groups in the same occupational and educational categories. Do women and minorities make the same amount of money as their counterparts in similar jobs (see Table 5.3)? It turns out that they do not. *The differences in income hold for women and minority groups who hold similar jobs.* Comparable worth legislation was enacted to assure that individuals in similar jobs received comparable pay, regardless of gender, race or ethnicity. Recent estimates indicate that the gap between men's and women's earning may be getting smaller, but apparently

Table 5.2   Poverty and Welfare Receipt by Race and Ethnicity, 1991

	Non-Hispanic				
	White	African American	Asian[a]	American Indian[b]	Hispanic
Percentage in poverty	9	33	14	32	29
Percentage in deep poverty[c]	13	16	7	14	40
Percentage receiving welfare	13	47	19	51	44
Percentage of poor receiving welfare	61	85	62	87	29
Numbers in 1,000s[d]	188,667	30,758	6,065	1,730	22,039

SOURCE: Author's analysis of the March 1992 Current Population Survey.
a. Including Pacific Islanders.
b. Including Eskimos and Aleuts.
c. Below 50% of the official poverty threshold.
d. Weighted sample.

this is because of a *decrease in men's real wages* in some employment sectors, not because of a rise in women's wages.

The figures indicate that there may be systematic differences in access to education and opportunities for employment in highly competitive fields and salary and promotion. These differences appear to be based on gender, race and class of origin rather than "merit."

If one is dealt a Two of Diamonds, the chances to move up are relatively low—not because one is or is not motivated and capable, but because there may not be enough positions and resources to allow one to move up. The opportunity for upward mobility may be further hindered by ascribed characteristics—Spade/Club, race/gender—that are systematically associated with who has access to the playing field.

In structures of scarcity, stereotypical assumptions often stand in as a shorthand form of information when schools and employers must make fine-grained decisions between seemingly equally qualified candidates. As we have already noted, those with cultural capital are more likely to be perceived as the "best candidates." The fact that they already appear successful stands in as "evidence" for their probable merit and potential. Thus, those who are dealt high cards to begin with may have a disproportionate opportunity to maintain their positions. In this country, Anglo American males hold a disproportionate number of the high cards. All else being equal, regardless of their intentions as individuals, these men hold a disproportionate number of the existing executive and administrative positions. Given that the number of available positions is scarce, it is reasonable to assume that these men will do everything possible to retain or improve their rank and to ensure similar privileges for their children.

In this way intergenerational mobility looks a lot like the passing of the parent's card to the offspring. The parent hands on existing resources that provide the child with an opportunity to push slightly ahead—up one rank, possibly. This has been the trend among most groups of Americans for the past few decades. The figures reported at the beginning

Table 5.3   Average Monthly Income, by Sex and Educational Attainment, 1993

Level of Educational Attainment	Monthly Income	
	Male Workers	*Female Workers*
All workers	$2,230	$1,186
High school dropout	2,211	621
High school graduate	1,812	1,008
Some college, no degree	2,045	1,139
Associate degree	2,561	1,544
Bachelor's degree	3,430	1,809
Master's degree	4,298	2,505
Professional degree	6,312	3,530
Doctorate	4,421	4,020

SOURCE: U.S. Bureau of the Census, 1995a.

of this chapter suggest that currently those born into the upper strata can expect to retain their position and privilege, and perhaps even move up, while those in the middle and lower-middle strata are moving down. According to many observers, the middle and lower-middle-classes are more *pressured* in attempts to maintain their position because they have to scramble more just to remain competitive. The upper-middle and upper classes tend to take for granted the resources that enable them to maintain high positions—resources such as easy access to quality education and the possession of cultural capital that stands in as a signal that they are deserving. Simply put, these classes don't have to try as hard for the larger piece of pie that they have been granted.

Strategies for Maintaining the Myth of Meritocracy

Whether or not Americans perceive the playing field as fair depends on their current position. Those who have achieved financial and social success are likely to feel that the system is fair and that their rewards are justly deserved. Those who occupy the lower ranks generally feel that they have to work harder for less and that the system works against their efforts. A significant number of lower-class citizens feel that those in higher positions achieved their success by exploiting the lower classes.

A noteworthy point is that very few Americans who enjoy economic privilege challenge the general ideals of competitive individualism and the *possibility* of meritocratic advancement. Even when it is obvious that the structure of the situation is such that there are not enough rewards for all those who may deserve them (structural scarcity), and when experience suggests that there are many factors besides talent, training and effort (i.e., cultural capital) that determine who gets what, a majority of Americans persist in the belief that our system of economic distribution is meritocratic and fair.

"Fairness" as an Attribution of Success or Failure

The reasons for the tenacity of this myth are probably different among different economic ranks. Those who experience success wish to maintain the illusion that the system is fair in order to justify their own positions; those who have relatively few rewards may maintain the illusion in order to perpetuate the belief that they have control over their own lives. Social psychologists have demonstrated that Americans who are raised on the ideals of individualism and self-determination would rather attribute their lack of success to their own shortcomings, something that can presumably be remedied if they just "get it right," rather than attribute failure to actual lack of opportunity, a condition that leaves most of us feeling helpless. An interesting feature of the connection between evidence and belief is that people need to have their beliefs confirmed only about 50% of the time in order to adhere to their myths. We tend to dismiss evidence that is inconsistent with our ideals and to heed evidence that supports these ideals. Popular culture and various media portrayals encourage us to forget about the millions who are not making it and embrace instead stories about the one family member who did make it. Horatio Alger tales of a single disadvantaged person's climb from rags to riches stoke our collective faith in the ideal that a Two of Clubs really could rise to the rank of Queen or King. All it takes is "the right stuff."

Success Is a Matter of "Character" Rather Than Structure

Periodically throughout the history of this country, major world and demographic events have dramatically altered the structure of available positions in education and employment. These changes can be likened to adding more cards to the existing master deck. For example, as Abrahamson notes, during the World Wars, many domestic positions of employment were vacated by men who went to war. This opened up an opportunity for a greater number of women to enter the paid labor force and to attain higher-than-usual positions of authority and responsibility. Of course, when the men returned home, positions once again became relatively scarce in certain occupational strata. However, a shift in the type of labor followed World War II. The money that had been spent on war technology was redirected into domestic production. One result of this was the creation of several new forms of employment in research and technology. The new availability of these positions meant that those who were willing to undergo the correspondingly higher level of training had a good chance of actually getting a job that was commensurate with their drive and ability.

Many people were raised on stories told by their grandparents of how they had skipped up two or even three rungs in the ladder of upward mobility. A spate of Horatio Alger, "rags-to-riches" movies appeared during this era as well. What is interesting to note about these stories is that they rarely attribute the individual's climb to success to the fact that new positions were added; rather they focus on the drive, perseverance and high moral integrity of the individual. The notion of the rise from rags to riches was enhanced by the relatively low expectations that preceded this change in the structure of available positions. Immediately prior to this shift in the economy, the Great Depression put many Americans out of work as the country struggled with how to restructure its domestic economy.

Another example of a structural shift is based on fluctuations in the demographics in this country. One consequence of the return of soldiers from World War II battlefields was a significant increase in the number of newborn children. This "baby boom" among members of the middle class, who were themselves rising in affluence due to the new employment positions, prompted parents to push for an increase in services and educational facilities for their children. The result of this is that those who entered the labor force in the early 1960s (themselves the members of a relatively small cohort of babies, due to the absence of men during war years) found a large surplus of jobs available in educational and service sectors. Subsequently, with the arrival of the "babyboomers" on the employment scene, jobs quickly became (over)filled once again.

The current generation faces an increasing shortage of positions based on these demographic trends. The apathy attributed to "Generation X" may in fact be the outcome of a more general awareness of the lack of positions available, despite ambitions or merit. The preceding generation surfed high on a wave of peak opportunities that has broken just as the current generation entered the waters. In the words of Xer author Douglas Coupland (*Generation X*), "it's a bit like being invited to a party where you are made to stand outside the fence watching others eat all the cake and then you're expected to be grateful for the crumbs."

Contemporary observers of popular trends and culture note what they call a more marked gap between "slackers" and "trackers" in this country. Many comment that the "slackers" are evidence of the moral demise of basic American values and institutions such as the family and religion. Another interpretation, one based on the logic of structural inequality, is that a significant number of these young people realize that all that awaits them, regardless of how hard they train, are crumbs. Meanwhile, the intense competition among the "trackers" may reflect desperate attempts to maintain the illusion that the rewards are there for those who are willing to harness themselves to an increasingly fast-paced treadmill. The choices are extreme. They mirror the trend toward an increasing gap between a few who are clawing their way higher and the many who are falling lower. The positions are few, the competition severe. Many young Americans may be questioning whether economic success is the only measure of worth, given the current price and the relatively high chance of failure regardless of merit.

Connections Between Social and Economic "Class": Money = Morality

A lack of understanding about structural scarcity may explain the gap between the reality that there are significant and persistent economic divisions in our society and the myth that everyone has equal access to pursuing the American Dream. This gap between the reality and the myths of our economic structure is supported and perpetuated by another set of American ideals, the equation of economic success with morality. In societies that acknowledge that not everyone can have the same rewards and that some people are simply dealt different cards than others, economic status is less likely to be associated with personal morality. The American tendency to conflate economic standing and morality has two consequences: We continue to ignore real differences in the opportunity structures available to different groups of Americans, and we perpetuate the notion that those who are at the top are there because they deserve to be. In short, we insist that economic class doesn't matter.

Several political and social scientists have noted that people in the United States do not talk about economic class. Instead, our public discourse consists of the language of "superior/inferior" or "moral/immoral." This language stands in for discussions of economic position to steer discourse away from the realities that people face when they have inadequate resources. Someone who is shabbily dressed is not "poor" but rather is "unclean." In the collective mind we associate uncleanliness with poverty. The lack of public discourse about the structure of poverty inclines us to think that people are poor because they are unclean, rather than the other way around, they are dirty because they don't have the means to be clean in the expected middle-class way.

Author Benjamin DeMott articulates the theme that the myth of classlessness in American society enables the perpetuation of what he terms "The Imperial Middle." According to the mythology of the imperial middle, Americans *do get what they deserve.* Therefore, if someone is poor it is because he or she deserves to be. DeMott demonstrates the manner in which this mythology is perpetuated in the news media. According to DeMott's interpretation of these stories, the news media tend to describe the activities of those who occupy lower economic ranks in terms of weak minds and/or shaky morals. Class differences are transformed into other kinds of difference, differences that call into question the intentions and ability of those who are disadvantaged.

DeMott offers an extended example of a Chicago paper's discourse on the concern of parents for their children's safety and schooling. When an abandoned industrial district was transformed into an upscale neighborhood near the city's South Side, the new occupants, mostly young middle-class families, asked the board of education to build a new school for their children. The completed school was located equidistant between upscale condominiums and a public housing project plagued with drugs and crime. Parents in both neighborhoods wanted to send their children to the new school with its excellent and relatively safe facilities. A bitter struggle ensued about whose children could attend the school. DeMott shows how the news coverage of this event vilifies the parents from the housing project as "being obsessed with fairness" while it is assumed that middle-class parents would of course fight for the safety and quality of their children's education. The same action—a claim for the rights of one's children—is judged differently depending on whether one is or is not affluent. This illustration and numerous others documented by DeMott indicate that class distinctions are generally reframed in terms of moral and intellectual virtues or vices: The affluent, it is assumed, have virtuous intentions; the less affluent are represented as greedy, dishonorable and untrustworthy.

As I noted in Chapter 4, Michele Lamont's *Money, Morals and Manners* reports information gathered from interviews with upper-middle-class businessmen in the United

States and France. Lamont was interested in the question of whether or not these men, who are economic and cultural gatekeepers, have particular attitudes about the relationship between money and who is a deserving and worthwhile human being. The French, she notes, are much more ambivalent about money than Americans. French history is much longer than that of the United States and includes a great deal of emphasis on "great and noble" families who lost their wealth and position due to political revolutions and shifts in the economy. These historical stories separate money from morality in that they convey the message that one can be without economic means and still be "great and noble." Furthermore, they suggest that a person's economic standing is not necessarily based on individual ability, assets or effort, but that it can fluctuate drastically for reasons beyond the individual's control. As a result of this cultural legacy, the French, according to Lamont, are disinclined to associate money with goodness and morality. Rather, they tend to focus on intellectual and artistic ability, along with "old manners," as signs of "goodness." One group of respondents actually viewed money as "impure." Many of the French interviewees informed Lamont that they find the American obsession with money to be crass, overly materialistic and a poor substitute for "real manners."

In contrast to the French, the American businessmen were inclined to view money as a good indicator of someone's self-worth. Having money is viewed as a sign of hard work, perseverance and ingenuity—all traits that Americans value. Lamont's information on the relationship between perceptions of honesty and money points to an interesting paradox in the attempt to "class climb." American businessmen reported that they loathed "phonies." The phony is a "social climber" who is "obvious." Overt social climbing is apparently an indication of "low morals." When pressed for details these men related stories of individuals who were "obvious phonies" in the way that they "worked" professional networks, "feigned" interest in the well-being and circumstances of colleagues while actually just "playing the role to get ahead," and so forth. "Social climbers" are immoral because they are pushy and manipulative. Herein lies the paradox: Presumably, in order to "get ahead" on the very competitive American ladder to success, one has to use whatever means one can to sharpen one's advantage. But rather than view these actions as expressions of ingenuity and perseverance, they are dismissed as "immoral" by those who occupy the upper ranks. It appears that these men want to have their proverbial cake and to eat it too. They want their own success to appear as if it were "natural" and "correctly" attained; those who expose some of the means that may be necessary to actually get ahead inadvertently shatter the illusion that there is something special and morally distinct about those in the upper echelons.

Consider this implication. If the opportunity structure is tipped to favor those who already have financial and cultural capital, then those most likely to have to use strategies such as making a strong claim for their rights of admission, resorting to documentation of incidents of fairness, and so forth, are those who are structurally disadvantaged. By equating these activities with "low morals," those in the highest ranks can effectively keep their ranks limited to only those who do not have to engage in such "manipulative" or "pushy" strategies. In other words, they can happily note that the only truly qualified candidates for the top rungs of success are persons such as themselves: persons who already have considerable wealth and influence and who therefore don't need to draw attention to themselves in the attempt to attain mobility.

Suburban Life as an Illustration of the Illusion
That Affluence = Social Character = Merit

There are countless ways in which Americans maintain the ideal of a perfect meritocracy in which the playing field is level and the resulting inequitable distribution of jobs and rewards is attributed to personal flaws rather than structural circumstances. In her book *Belonging in America,* anthropologist Constance Perrin researches some of the ways in which we determine who really belongs and who doesn't; in other words, who is really deserving of their rights as an American? Perrin's reasoning is that the social dissonance manifest in the widening gap between the rich and poor can be alleviated by acting as if many of those who are lowest on the totem pool really don't deserve to be counted. In terms of the card exercise, if we can collectively agree that only those who hold high cards are deserving, we needn't feel so badly about the scarcity of resources for those at the bottom. Perrin's research is consistent with other observations that those who consider themselves to be most deserving are those who are already affluent. How do they maintain this belief, she wants to know?

Perrin's study focuses on the suburbs. The suburbs are the site of everyday processes that reaffirm the values and activities of the affluent. American suburbs are, by definition, geographically removed from the more densely populated areas of cities in which one is likely to encounter a wider representation of economic classes. The physical uniformity of the suburbs is a signal that all is in order; middle-class Americans are inclined to associate order with safety. The price range of single family housing with attached yard and garden is a deterrent to those who have not achieved the right degree of economic security. The attainment of economic security is a sign that neighbors hold similar (correct) values. As further evidence of this, neighbors monitor the outward appearances of one another's lawns and homes. An orderly home is a sign of control over one's circumstances and an indication that one realizes that the maintenance of one's own home improves the resale value of every home on the block. Attention to these details signals that one can be trusted to uphold the basic value of the community—market exclusivity. Zoning laws further protect these sites of exclusivity by disallowing multiple-family dwellings. Multiple units usually mean "renters," and renters cannot be trusted to share the same ideals regarding the ultimate statement of belonging: property ownership. Multiple units also lead to crowding and crowding means difference. The presence of difference shatters the illusion of equality and similarity favored among the "imperial middle."

The suburbs are not utopia, however: Dogs sometimes roam off-leash and soil the yards of others; crabgrass and other lawn weeds that have no understanding of property lines creep from one yard to another if not religiously monitored; enterprising developers may attempt to build multiple-housing units that will sell at a lower cost and thus reduce neighborhood property values as well as encourage infestation by "outsiders." In short, the suburbs are under constant threat, from within and without, of erosion of the core signs of safety and affluence. This puts the suburbanite in a difficult position. To confront these issues directly is to risk becoming engaged in open conflict—a sign of disharmony and a blot against one's character. Fortunately for the suburbanite, there is another means.

The "anonymous complaint" enables suburban home-dwellers to see to it that order is restored without having to dirty their own hands. Perrin reports that one city office in Minneapolis employs a full-time official who does nothing for eight hours every day but take and record calls of neighbors tattling on one-another or complaining about threats to their haven. City officials in every state that Perrin investigated proudly report that they make every attempt to follow up personally on each one of these complaints. The result, Perrin notes, is that suburbanites do not have to deal with any conflict except through third parties. This satisfactory relationship with city officials contributes to the notion that they have a personal relationship with the government. This reinforces the belief in the legitimacy of their positions. The government exists to serve and protect their interests: Life is as ideally imagined—orderly and marketable—for those who claim it.

Suburban folk, according to Perrin, feel completely justified in expressing moral indignation at those who threaten the sanctity of the suburbs. Whether it be the unruly neighbor who neglects to cover the garbage or the hapless intruder who happens mistakenly to drive through the well-patrolled streets, violations are not tolerated. Such violations call into question the association of property ownership with achievement of the American Dream and the equation of this with morality. The equation of affluence with "goodness/rightness/deservedness" is reinforced by laws and law enforcement agencies that provide a wall of protection against outsiders whose presence may shatter the myth. Physical walls, such as those that surround "gated communities," are an additional means of maintaining the illusion of equality by shutting out evidence to the contrary. In Perrin's concluding words:

> The social shame that wealth can inflict and the social envy privilege can provoke leave Americans vulnerable. The strongest domestic tranquilizer is the persisting American belief that there are only two classes, middle class and working class, which makes it possible to deny the existence of the really poor and the really rich and the doubt each casts on the American creed "All men are created equal. . . ." Fences wall in the American Dream and wall out its nightmares of reality. (1988:102)

The presence of homeless individuals in America casts a shadow across the otherwise bright illusion of equality, achievement and the satisfaction of a position well-earned. To maintain this illusion it is necessary to fear those whose huddled presence in doorways marks a rift in the ideal that all is well. Lack of property, dishevelment and begging are used as evidence of a lack of motivation and an expression of inferior morality. This interpretation cements the presumed connection between affluence and achievement. This connection is reinforced by the genuine fear experienced by those who, by virtue of their lives within the walls of class morality, have not encountered evidence of economic disparity. Through increased exposure, fear may give way to a heart-felt indignation that the presence of these individuals signals "idleness"—the worst of all American evils, and frightens away "those who have money to spend."

NIMBY ("not in my backyard") politics about low-income housing and centers for the homeless indicate that Americans who are affluent feel they have the right to be protected from evidence that there is not enough of the pie to go around. Equating money with moral virtue maintains the twin myths that those who have it deserve it and those who don't have it must be "bad." The alternative explanations disturb Americans: Either all people are *not* created equal, or all people *do not* have equal opportunities to play the game of success. Accepting one of these accounts leads to the uneasy implication that those few who are in possession of most of the nation's resources must develop a rationale for their disproportionate advantages and then, more disturbing still, defend what they have against those who have not. Those who lead protected lives walled in by both physical and symbolic attestment to the legitimacy of their position are the least likely to be motivated to consider their wealth as the outcome of factors other than personal achievement. Yet it is this same group that, if Collins (1979) is correct, makes most of the decisions about how wealth should be distributed in this country. Left to themselves, a few fat rats who are kept cozy and well fed are not front page news, but when these rats are used as an indicator of the health of the nation it is likely that we may grossly misperceive just what ails us.

Class Consciousness

We are at the end of the week, my stratified class and I. Several transformations have taken place. Those holding low cards are visibly disengaged from the class activities; I'm surprised that they bother to come to class. Their presence seems to annoy those in the higher ranks, who have become increasingly vocal and jovial as a group. They dominate class discussion and reinforce one another's ideas. There is a lot of high-fiving and back-slapping among them. Some high-ranking reds have attempted to speak for themselves, only to be shouted down by the blacks. In fact, these occasions are the only times that the low-ranked black card holders speak out any more.

For a couple of days a group of middle-range blacks raised the question of "fairness." The high cards engaged them in spirited debate and pointed repeatedly to the fact that they too would soon be in the "top" if they just got a good grade on the next paper. I am not certain whether or not the mid-range blacks were persuaded or simply ran out of steam. Yesterday the face card blacks disengaged themselves from the small group activities that the class was engaged in and came to talk with me. They seem to feel entitled to do whatever they want in the class space. They noted that the small group activities had gotten uncomfortable for many of them because the low cards seemed so apathetic and lazy. They proposed that small group work now be divided by card-rank groups. They also informed me that the high reds were constantly badgering them about the "fairness" issue and wanted them to raise it with me. I asked if they wanted me to do something about it. No, was the quick response. We can talk to them, we just thought we'd tell you they're a bit noisy.

I decide to bring the experiment to a close. I inform them that everyone can talk and then call directly on some of the low cards and ask them to describe how they feel about the situation. The Three of Diamonds, an A student to date, speaks haltingly at first and then states that as soon as she received her card she felt stigmatized, "even though I knew it was just a random draw, I felt like it reflected something about my ability." Several of those holding Fives through Sevens describe an immediate sense of apathy upon recognizing that no matter what they did they wouldn't get ahead unless some of "those loudmouths" dropped down. They also note that it seemed like the high cards were going to retain their positions because they seemed to be controlling all the conversations. A few of the low card holders express the intriguing position that since it appears that the game is rigged against them, they feel a sort of freedom to just drop out and do what they want. This makes some of the high card holders mad. As a group they have become increasingly agitated since we began this conversation. My refusal to acknowledge their interruptions is causing them to murmur loudly to each other. The King of Clubs finally bursts out, "It's people like you that ruin it for the rest of us. It's like being a poor sport just because you didn't get the best card to begin with. Just grow up and make the best of what you've got."

The Two of Diamonds, the lowest of the low, looks pensively at the King of Clubs and says,

> Interesting how as soon as you drew your high card you starting acting like a hot shot and telling everyone how fair the game is, as if you'd had to work for your card. But now when you get called out on this you start whining about how it's no one's fault who gets which card, they should just make the most of it. Make a choice, man. You can't have it both ways. Either you are more deserving than the rest of us, if so, then quit whining, or you're not, in which case, you got lucky. We didn't so you may just have to put up with us being pissed at you. Either way, we're not going to adore you *and* also let you have all the privileges.

Elitism Versus Democracy

Aristotle believed that the "noble" should govern and make decisions for the rest of the populace. This is a very different philosophy of social organization than the philosophy of democracy. According to the former there is a certain class of people who are more virtuous than others and should therefore be in charge; they bear the unique burden of trying to improve the lot of everyone by endeavoring to make examples of themselves and organizing society according to their own high standards and abilities. This is a philosophy of elitism. According to this philosophy, the elite are "special." A society based on their unique ideals, desires and achievements will come closest to achieving general perfection. These nobles are charged with improving life for all. "Noblesse oblige" is the philosophy that the elite should use their talent toward creating better circumstances for everyone; but in order to perform at top capacity these nobles must be "protected" from everyday struggles such as the need to earn a living and to maintain their own food and shelter. Those at the bottom must, in effect, be sacrificed in order to support the tastes, activities and passions of the elite.

Some observers of political economy in the United States remark that the real current of resource distribution in this country is elitism; those who are not in the upper strata are caught in the undertow of this current. Knowingly or unknowingly, the majority of Americans are being pulled under by the same wave that is making the very rich richer.

Democracy, as a political ideology, requires that a substantial majority of the population share relatively similar economic positions; that is, there must be a large middle class. Sharp differences in economic standing require those who have resources to protect them from those who would like them and can't get them. This protection can be accomplished through struggles to control the politics of distribution through various property and tax laws; it can be accomplished by segregating the rich from the poor physically and intellectually, and it can be accomplished through ideologies that represent the rich as morally superior and more deserving than the poor. It can be expected that those with the resources to do so will manipulate the political and ideological arrangements to protect their interests. However, such activity may be antithetical to the democratic philosophy of the greatest good for the greatest number.

One way to explore whether or not the United States works more like an elite society than a democracy is to study various laws that provide "protection" for the rich. In an unfettered competition those who do not have resources are likely to use whatever means they have to try to gain some for themselves. To thwart the possibility of loss to themselves, those with the resources to do so are likely to channel additional resources into the protection of what they have. In other words, they remove themselves from the same playing field as the rest of the members of the society. Some of the ways in which the rich might do this are to isolate themselves geographically—we have already discussed how zoning laws enable the wealthy to remove themselves from some of the realities of the everyday struggle for survival faced by many Americans.

Whether or not competitive individualism in a capitalist economy really works to produce a higher standard of living for a greater number of people is an empirical question. The United States is not an adequate test case of this theory because truly open competition has never been practiced. There have always been protectionist strategies designed and promoted to advantage one group or another. What does seem to be the case is that Americans are less aware of the strategies that protect the very rich, but are suspicious of policies aimed at improving the opportunities for the very poor. A failure to understand structural inequality may perpetuate this mind-set. The *ideal* of meritocracy leads us to believe that those who are at the top have earned their position, and those who are at the bottom are there because of their own shortcomings and lack of effort.

In my class experiment with the cards it was striking that within minutes those who had been dealt high cards assumed an attitude of entitlement to their position. Many of them became angry and felt offended when their right to their positions was challenged by those below them. Similarly, those at the bottom felt stigmatized and, even as they struggled to recall that theirs was a randomly dealt position, they tended to sink into silence. This silence was further perpetuated by the tendency of those with high cards to take advantage of their position and dominate the conversations about how to play the game and the perceived fairness of it.

Conclusions

It's Thanksgiving morning. The "fattest" newspaper of the year has just arrived. Stuffed with spread after spread of glossy ad inserts, this newspaper ushers in another significant

American holiday: the "busiest shopping day of the year." While relaxing at home on Thanksgiving, considering how much we have to be grateful for, we are also invited to contemplate how much more we could have. In order to enable us to have and consume more, stores slash prices and promote bargains and offer special incentives to lure us away from home and hearth and into the malls post our Thanksgiving Day feed. On this special shopping day, even "less-affluent" Americans can afford a few luxury items—if they buy smartly. Some stores offer drastically reduced prices to those who are first to arrive for early openings. "The early bird gets the worm!" announces one colorful insert for a national department store chain.

There it is. Through careful contemplation, planning and effort the American Dream can belong to anyone. Or at least a small slice of it. Read the ads, clip the coupons, plan your shopping strategy and arrive early and you can purchase tokens of American success. Consumption has become the primary means by which middle-class Americans assure themselves that they are doing all right; that the American Dream is alive and well. A vast array of brightly packaged consumer goods sold in pleasant environments by eager salesclerks makes us feel all is in order. We can be grateful. Inside safe, well-lit, cheerful shopping malls middle-Americans practice their freedom and individualism by expressing consumption preferences.

To enhance the shopping experience in the downtown area of my city, citizens recently voted to reopen a street that was closed off several years ago to make a pedestrian square between major department stores. A good idea at the time—shoppers could walk easily from store to store and purchase treats from vendors en route—the area quickly became a corridor for panhandling. Beggars make shoppers feel guilty. Given the opportunity to consume in moderate but consistent ways, middle-America is grateful and content. We would rather not scrutinize just how much of our productive output is being used to build a fortress of protection and exclusivity for the very rich. And for the most part, we fail to see any connection at all between the lives of the rich and famous and those huddled masses of the unemployed and the homeless.

Ultimately however, even the acts of shopping and consuming—pleasantly numbing as they might be—cannot completely eclipse the fact that there is a very real class war taking place in America. The uneasy truth for many Americans is that in a system of extreme structural inequality, the "have-nots" cannot be expected to peacefully affirm the rewards granted to the "haves." Such a system inevitably induces two forms of slavery: those who are prisoners of need and envy and those who are prisoners of the fortresses that protect them from the hungry eyes beyond the wall. In a structure of extreme stratification, the more one acquires, the more one must protect it from others.

What strikes many non-American observers as odd and somewhat naive is that many middle-class Americans are righteously indignant about the hungry and envious stares that confront them when they venture out to perform the ritual of consumption. This indignation is fed by the belief that, as individuals, we are structurally independent from everyone else; that what we have, we have earned through our own efforts. The idea that someone's gains may come at the expense of another's efforts is inconceivable to most middle-Americans. We may feel sorry for those who are "less fortunate" and perhaps relatively grateful for what we do have; but we actively resist the idea that there is a connection between our lives and the misfortune of the Other. This active resistance is expressed in our endeavors to rid our streets of reminders of inequality; to patch up holes in the walls that separate the haves from the have-nots. Such active resistance suggests that in the deeper recesses of the collective mind we suspect that there is a connection between "us" and "them." But acknowledging this means confronting the twin pillars of belonging and success in America: merit and achievement. Whose merit? What counts as achievement? To probe these ideals is to unsettle the very foundation upon which middle-America creates a meaningful and orderly existence.

The poor are not going to go away. If the current economic trends continue, more of us can expect to join the lower ranks and a very few will continue to grow even richer. Opportunity and income in this nation are distributed unequally. Those who were born into positions of affluence are likely to maintain their rank for two reasons: They have a disproportionate amount of the monetary and cultural capital needed to compete for success in the American "meritocracy," and they have a disproportionate amount of control over forms of production and distribution. These are simple conclusions based on a structural analysis of the distribution of education, occupation and income in this country. The complexity is in sorting out the way Americans do or don't acknowledge the realities of stratification. The very rich, those 5 percent who control 35 percent of this nation's wealth, are well hidden from the rest of America. To the extent that a substantial number of Americans can purchase single-family homes, provide their children with higher education, and exercise freedom of choice in purchasing and consumption, it is possible to maintain the illusion that effort leads to reward; within the ranks of the middle classes, this may even be true, to some extent.

Yet the middle-classes are dwindling as a direct result of those few who are getting richer. As the upper classes take larger and larger pieces of pie for themselves, there is less to be divided among middle and lower-middle classes. Because the rich are so well isolated, it is easier for someone in the middle or working classes to blame personal loss of opportunity on others who are competing for similar positions and rewards. Others who are somehow different, say, in terms of race, ethnicity and gender. Americans are currently divided along lines of race, gender, sexuality, religiosity, and various other ways of marking ourselves as different. We battle about the relative merits, opportunities and accomplishments based on these group divisions. However, if education, occupation, income, and related spending power are really the means and indicators of having achieved a piece of the American Dream, *then the real battle is a class war.*

The paradox is this: A sustainable system of meritocracy requires relatively *equal access among a large majority of the population to the means for success.* When this condition is met, then we will be in a position to fight about fairness and justice for all and to make moral judgments about who is or is not deserving. But, to the extent that one very large group of Americans does not have the basic resources to compete at all and another holds a disproportionately large amount of the pie for which it is not held accountable, then we cannot say that the United States is a system of open competition based on individual merit. This means, minimally, that before you can evaluate your own merit, or the merit of anyone else, you must first determine your relative positions on the playing field of social class. There are at least three in this country—the very rich, the middle classes, and the disempowered poor. The circumstances of the competition are largely determined by the class circumstances of your birth. A "fair-minded" American is someone who is able to plot the structural advantages and disadvantages that are associated with these vastly different starting positions. Informed participation in the American political system requires each of us to examine more closely the myth of meritocracy and its consequences.

Americans are schooled on the ideals of democracy—the best form of government is one based on the voice of the largest majority, and meritocracy—the best distribution system is one in which persons are rewarded for their contributions. Many of us believe in these ideals. In reality, however, it appears that while a great majority of Americans produce the national wealth, a very small number possess most of it. This same group may also have a disproportionate say in government policies about how resources should be distributed and protected. The hard question that faces Americans is whether or not we want to perpetuate what may actually be an elite form of political economy. In order to address this question realistically, Americans must better understand the structure of resource distribution in this country and the processes by which one does or does not have access to the opportunities to share in the collective pie. To the extent that we are reluctant to acknowledge that there are extreme differences in wealth—the presence of the very rich and the very poor—we close our eyes to the real issues that confront us as a nation. There are arguments to be made both for and against elitism; perhaps this is the argument that we should be having. As it stands, however, because we do not have an explicit discourse of economic and social class in this country, we tend to justify what are largely inherited positions of wealth and privilege as the result of real effort, talent and drive. This illusion maintains the myth of meritocracy. Can we, as a nation, afford to perpetuate this myth?

6

Family Equations

Whose Family? Whose Values?

PARADOX

When we speak of "family values" do we mean a particular form of family organization or the functions that the family represents? Contemporary "family values" rhetoric conflates a particular family form (heterosexual, two-parent, sexually monogamous, single-dwelling unit) with a particular set of values (unconditional love and support, economic self-subsistence, the transmission of cultural values). Is this the only family type that is capable of perpetuating these values? Why are some families who fulfill the functions but not the ideal type vilified? How realistic is it to expect any family unit to meet these values and expectations on their own? What other forms of social and economic support are necessary for families to fulfill these expectations? Do middle-class, suburban families have some taken-for-granted advantages that make them appear more traditionally ideal than other types of families? To what extent do these appearances perpetuate a myth that is historically inaccurate and misleading?

Dear Abby: I'm going through the most confusing period of my life. I am 18 and working both a full-time and a part-time job to support my children, a daughter who is 2 and a 1-year-old son. My life is crazy. Abby, I'm thinking about giving custody of my son to a couple at church. Raising two children is too difficult at my age. I'm a single mother and cannot support two children financially. I am unable to give my son the love and care he needs, and I want him to be happy. I don't want to give him up, but I want the best for him and I know I can't provide it.

—Confused, Crazy Mother

A couple of news items caught my attention recently. One story was about a fourth grade class in Delaware. Parents were petitioning to have the teacher fired based on what they called "unseemly" activities. According to the story the teacher had asked the students to select a classmate to whom they were willing to commit their friendship for the year. The teacher then had the students write essays about what friendship means and concluded the lesson with a ceremony in which the students pledged to stand by their chosen friends. Why would this activity stir such outrage among the parents? According to the news story, many parents expressed a concern that the ceremony mimicked, and thereby legitimated, marriage between homosexuals. How did they arrive at this conclusion? Well, fourth graders are nine and 10 years old. Children this age tend to prefer the company of their own gender. Thus, when asked to pick a friend for life, most of them picked someone of the same sex. The teacher, who was apparently quite baffled by the parents' response, stated that her intent was to have the children experience the significance of making a commitment to someone and sharing trust. She felt this was an important lesson in an era in which people feel increasingly alienated and alone.

As I read this story I couldn't help but think that the parents were being overly defensive. What are they so worried about that they would balk at an occasion for their children to learn the honorable responsibilities that accompany friendship? Is homosexuality more threatening than the erosion of trust and responsibility for the other that is undermining our communities? In the past five years 42 states have attempted to introduce legislation that would outlaw gay marriages. The rationale: Gay unions undermine "family values." To my knowledge, none of these same states has expressed any interest in the development of programs that promote skills in caring for and acting responsibly in the interests of others. Is it easier to scapegoat homosexuality than to examine the reasons why heterosexuals and homosexuals alike find it harder and harder to maintain bonds of friendship and to engage in lifelong familial commitments?

Another news item reported that a handful of state legislators have written a bill that would outlaw divorce. If they had their way, people would not be allowed to divorce except under extreme circumstances. The example given of an extreme circumstance was if the spouse was imprisoned for life. According to the bill, the state would hold the authority to decide who could divorce. As a rationale for the bill, the legislators cited high divorce rates and suggested that people no longer take marriage seriously. In their view, outlawing divorce would prompt people to be more thoughtful about who they marry and force them to work out their problems instead of just walking away from them. Outlawing divorce would be a step toward "restoring family values."

Similar stories appear daily in the news. The phrase *Family Values* is tossed back and forth as a shorthand statement for everything presumed to be right and wrong with the American people: The country is in crisis due to the erosion of "family values"; we have lost a sense of morality and responsibility because we lack "family values"; individuals are miserable or corrupt because they don't have "family values." The simple remedy proposed for everything from individual depression to high crime rates is to "restore family values."

Have we all gone nuts? I find myself wondering whenever I read or hear the phrase "family values" being offered as a panacea for all that we imagine to be wrong with ourselves and this country. The "Family" is considered to be our fundamental social building block. The family is the social institution that the vast majority of Americans, sometimes despite experience to the contrary, equate with the potential for happiness. Most of us are taught from a very young age to believe that ultimate satisfaction comes through belonging to an "ideal family." Not money. Not fame. Not even knowledge. It is "family" that equals happiness and spells success. And not just any family, but the "right kind of family." Conversely, no matter what their other accomplishments, many Americans feel that they are failures if they do not have the right kind of family.

Given this emphasis on the family, it is surprising and disturbing that we know so little about what the family actually is: as a social organization, as a political concept, and as an economic institution. The family equations that I describe in this chapter are not difficult to comprehend. Yet one of the most intriguing paradoxes in contemporary American discourse is the fact that many of us eschew this understanding in favor of moralisms about the "ideal family." Rather than examine the economic and community bases that are the foundation of the American family ideal, we blame personal character, individual shortcomings and moral erosion for the so-called failure of the family. In truth, we could probably exercise greater control over our individual happiness in terms of the love and support that we share with our families, whomever they might be, if we had a better understanding of the family as a form of economic and social organization. To gain this insight, however, we must be willing to scrutinize some of the contradictions and impossibilities inherent in the ideal of the family and to see that it may be a potentially damaging myth.

In this chapter I critique some of the myths that underlie the rhetoric of "family values." Many of the myths about how families *should be* are rooted in delusions about what families *really are*. It is helpful to separate these delusions from definitions of the *functions* of the family. The functions of the family can be referred to as the *value of the family*. When we put it this way, we can then ask what the value of the family is—for individuals, for communities and for society. We can also ask whether our expectations of families are realistic, and what sorts of resources (economic and social) are necessary for families to thrive according to these expectations.

The Rhetoric of "Family Values"

Stephanie Coontz is a social historian who has become a tireless researcher of the history of the "way families really are." Her first book, *The Way We Never Were*, is a historical critique of the myths and delusions about the *Happy Days* family idealized in the 1950s. Her second book, *The Way We Really Are,* is a presentation of historical facts about how families really have been throughout history. Coontz took up this research in an attempt to provide some "reasoned and factual" response to the rhetoric of family values that has been sweeping the country. According to Coontz, "family values" rhetoric promotes a number of false assumptions.

The main notion held by the proponents of "family values" is that the "traditional family" is an ideal social unit. The traditional family is described as a monogamous, heterosexual married couple who share a household with their children. Ideally there is a division of labor in which the man fills the role of the economic provider and the woman raises children and maintains the private household. The man acts as "head of the household" and his authority is respected as such. According to the proponents of "family values," this "ideal" family has always existed in the history of the United States and is the *cause* of the social and economic success of both individuals and societies. Hence, the current "crisis" in America is the result of a disorganization in the traditional family. In short, if we return to the traditional family structure, society will improve—crime rates will drop, the economy will improve, communities will have a more solid base of moral and emotional commitment. In family values rhetoric, the "traditional family" is cele-brated as being moral. "Alternative" arrangements are denounced as immoral. Accord-ingly, "Family Values" advocates point to those who deviate from the traditional family structure as the *cause* of moral decline and social problems. The most frequent targets of these accusations are low-income single mothers and people who have obvious "alterna-tive" sexual and domestic arrangements, such as lesbians and gays.

The flaw in this rhetoric, according to Coontz, is that historically, the "traditional family" as described above has been more of a myth than a reality. There is a tendency to assume that this structure was one that met the social and economic needs of all family members, Coontz remarks. The reality, however, is that where this structure appears in the early history of the United States, it often resulted in abuse and poverty for women and children. Only the "male head of household" really benefited from the arrangement. It was expected, for instance, that the man would keep most of his earnings for himself. He needed spending money to socialize with friends and expected to eat food and wear clothing that the rest of the members of the household did not have. It was assumed that this was his right because he spent his time in the public sphere. Women and children remained tucked away at home in what, according to Coontz's research, was the equiva-lent of an indentured, second-class servitude. Hardly the picture of the ideal family.

The economic situation improved for the traditional family only with the advent of government subsidies for housing and other economic benefits that came as a result of a boom following World War II. For the first time, individual middle-class families had enough money to feed, clothe and school the entire family, not just the male head of household. In cases where the traditional family did approximate the lifestyle portrayed in the ideal myths, Coontz argues that this was the *result* of economic and social improvements that helped families launch a more stable and civil life together. These improvements enabled family members to achieve economic parity with one another, but they did not necessarily constitute the basis for the blissful and loving relations that are portrayed in the myth of the traditional family.

The Family as a Moral and Emotional Center

Coontz notes that there is a tendency among most Americans to see the family as both the moral center of social life and the emotional center of personal life. Again, she counters, this view is based on myth rather than reality. Historically, many institutions other than the family have been the center of social morality. Churches, schools, even places of employment, have been the sites where persons were expected to learn cultural, moral and ethical values. The primary moral center, traditionally, has been the extended community, not the nuclear family. As I discussed in the chapter on communities, until the rise of industrial capitalism, persons tended to be enmeshed in the daily routines and rituals of a social group that included immediate kin, extended kin and neighbors. The "village" was the primary collective wherein they learned codes of conduct and were held responsible for their actions.

The notion of the isolated family farming and fending for themselves with no near relatives or neighbors is a myth, Coontz contends. This sort of myth has been perpetuated to promote the ideals of the "western maverick." Coontz even suggests that the myth of the "lone family" was a political ploy developed to counter the socialist leanings of the Jackson administration in the early 1800s. Those who are anti-big government play up images of the isolated maverick family as evidence that Americans can "do it for themselves." Coontz provides an interesting side discussion of the revisions of Laura Ingalls's diaries by her daughter, who was responsible for the publication of the materials that became *Little House on the Prairie*. According to Coontz (and the story is corroborated by several scholars), the original diaries describe community relations and a social interdependence that suggest a much different experience than the isolation and independence illustrated in the book. Apparently Laura's daughter was vehemently antigovernment and altered her mother's diaries to fit the idea of a frontier that matched her political intentions.

It is also a myth that the family has been, historically, the main site of emotional attachment and gratification for individuals. This myth is manifest in the current image of the "loving couple" as the basic building block of the family. In contemporary culture, we tend to assess our own success and happiness in terms of whether we are part of a "loving couple." We also expect this love, interest and devotion to extend to the relations between parents and children as a *primary* basis of emotional arousal and support. Another myth, says Coontz. Historically, people married for social and economic reasons. Love had very little to do with it. And even if the couple had a devoted affection for another and for their offspring, these relations were not expected to be the primary emotional and social focus of individual family members' lives.

Coontz has been studying diaries from the 1800s. She notes, laughingly, that when she was young and kept a diary, everything that she and her friends wrote about and talked about centered on the "one"—the man who would become the husband, the emotional center of the young girl's universe. Coontz was therefore surprised to find almost no mention of courtship and dating in the diaries. Where references to finances and spouses do appear, they are perfunctory. There is none of the emotion and romance that we have come to associate with impending marital relations, nor that we see in representations of eighteenth- and nineteenth-century life. It's not that people weren't romantic and emotional, Coontz says. There wasn't a cultural expectation of emotional attachment to one's spouse. Rather, primary emotional attachments were intended for close acquaintances, usually same-sex friends. Siblings were a basis of emotional attachment, particularly for many women, but the basis for this is that the sister has proven worthy of close friendship, rather than an expectation that there should be closeness because of a kin relationship.

Coontz is an excellent read in the social and economic history of the family. Using an impressive array of historical facts, she chisels away at the various myths that form the monumental illusion of the ideal American family. One question that arises from her research is how these myths became so cemented in American culture. If they are not based in historical fact, why are we so keen on sculpting these myths into American ideals? To address these questions it is useful to look at some of the functions or values that we currently expect from the family.

Values of the Family: Definitional Equations

What is the family? People who love together? People who share a residence? People who are bound by blood or the law? To examine the value of the family, I find it useful to start with an assessment of the *functions* commonly associated with the family as an economic, social and personal unity. Imagine that you are an anthropologist from another culture who is trying to figure out the basic structure of the American family. What does it look like? How is it organized? What functions does it serve? When asked what a family is, most Americans (regardless of their own circumstances and beliefs) describe a heterosexual, two-parent household in which the father is the primary breadwinner and the mother runs the home. Children are the biological offspring of the parents. Parents provide economic, emotional and cultural support for the children during their developmental years. The family lives together in the same household. A "good" family, according to most people, is one that provides "unconditional love and support" for its members. When asked, What does family mean to you?, common responses are: "It's the place where I can be myself. Where I can really let my hair down. Where people care about me no matter what." These perceptions of the family are based on ideals of the functions of the family. This functional definition can be expressed like this:

Ideal Family = Biological Reproduction/
Cultural (moral) Reproduction/Economic Unit/
Emotional, Loving Support

where reproduction includes both a biological and cultural function. This form of family organization calls for the parents to pass on cultural ideals, manners and expectations as well as to reproduce themselves physically. The family is supposed to be a moral (cultural) center. The family is also considered the primary economic unit in U.S. society. Families are designated the responsibilities of providing food, shelter, clothing, child care, medical care, education, elder care and so forth. In addition to these functions, the family is expected to be an emotional harbor from the storm of everyday public life, a hearth where its members can shed their daily cares and expect to find loving, supportive companionship.

Who constitutes the ideal family? The presumed basic building block of the ideal family is the heterosexual couple; a man and woman who together perform all of the above functions and whose union is, ideally, recognized by the state through legal marriage. According to common representations, this couple fulfills the following functions for one another:

Ideal Couple = sexual monogamy/
companionship/true love/soul mates/best friends

There are variations on the theme of the ideal couple. What doesn't seem to vary is the perception that true happiness is based on being a part of an ideal couple who are building an ideal family. Many people feel that they are failures if they have not achieved this ideal. Yet these are extensive, potentially conflicting demands to make on two people: Produce children, provide all their economic needs, teach them everything they need to know to eventually make it on their own, and do all this while being best friends, constant companions, unconditionally supportive and forever attracted to another. That's a lot to pack into a single equation.

In practice, as Coontz and many other scholars have observed, many of these functions are shared with other social institutions. For instance, schools carry some of the responsibilities of cultural reproduction; through education children learn the values and expectations of their culture. Churches also provide a venue for cultural reproduction. In addition, they are a source of support and community beyond the nuclear family. Neighborhood groups and extended family members often assist in domestic/economic tasks such as child care, elder care, food production, household construction projects, money lending, entertainment and friendship. Those who meet the legal definition of a "family" (a legally married couple and their legally documented dependents) are also entitled to certain benefits—insurance sharing, inheritance rights, tax rebates and so forth, without having to make a special case for their eligibility. A peculiarity of the myth of the American family is the ways in which we overlook these other forms of support.

By perpetuating the notion that the family is a self-sufficient unit able to meet all the functional expectations listed above, we burden individuals with what may be an impossible set of demands. We also tend to blame the family for social and economic problems that may be rooted elsewhere. Coontz remarks that "family values" rhetoric places the blame on individual families and deflects our attention from very real problems, such as teen pregnancies, drug use, crime and violence. According to Coontz, and I agree, the family is not the *cause* of these social problems. Rather, families who meet the functions described above are able to do so *as a result of economic and social conditions that make this possible.* If we want the family, however we define it, to be a stable and nurturing place for its members, then we need to take related economic and social factors into account. We also need to examine the basis of the myths of the modern family to determine how realistic they really are and how they distract us from seeing underlying social and economic supports.

In the next section I explore some of the cultural stories that are the source of the modern ideal of the traditional family. These images have proliferated largely through popular television and advertising. Many people believe that these images reflect real life because of middle-class practices that give the *appearance* that the images are real. In this sense, the images have become the basis of a cultural delusion whereby we really believe that "most people" have ideal families. Furthermore, "good people" have ideal families.

How Television Created the Ideal Family

I grew up with the Bradys. *The Brady Bunch* is an iconographic representation of what several scholars have called the "model American family." It and other shows such as

Leave It to Beaver, Father Knows Best and *Ozzie and Harriet* have provided generations of Americans from all walks of life with a storybook definition of what the ideal family should be like. These TV families live in neatly landscaped, single-dwelling suburban homes with large sunny kitchens and comfortable furnishings. The father has a stable professional job, usually as a lawyer, doctor or architect. The mother tends house, hearth and children with a never-ending smile. The children are well groomed and above average in school and social achievements. They participate in extracurricular activities such as drama, music lessons and sports. The plot lines, which are always comic, revolve around common mishaps, miscommunications or the small trials of adolescence, all of which are resolved within a half hour's time through the wisdom of the two parents, who confer frequently and respectfully with one another.

Scholars who study the history of the TV family suggest that the early portrayals of domestic bliss were not so much a rendering of existing fact as they were suggestive of what Americans could become. Some researchers go so far as to argue that the ideals presented in shows such as *Father Knows Best* were intended as a form of social engineering; a recipe for how the "good" family should conduct itself. This engineering was necessary, the argument goes, precisely because the traditional family had not been blissful and harmonious, or even middle class. Increasing prosperity and the expansion of the middle class resulted in more families living in relative isolation in single-family homes in the suburbs. People had more leisure time than they had enjoyed previously, and they were in a position to purchase new consumer goods. Some cultural, religious and civic leaders worried about what this new life of wealth and lack of scrutiny from neighbors would bring. Television was a means of broadcasting the moral values of the community into the home.

Other scholars emphasize the role played by advertisers who had new products to market. A focus on the nuclear family as a site of domestic accomplishment and leisurely enjoyment provided a basis for the promotion of new products—products designed to make "every wife's life easier" and to "bring the family together for fun and games." In a compelling and thorough analysis on the history of television families, *Prime Time Families,* Ella Taylor notes it is not likely that the developers of these television programs intended actively to promote a particular family agenda. Rather, as has always been the case with the medium, television programming was driven by marketing, by perceptions of who the audiences were and what could be sold to them. In Taylor's words, "the successful network careerist adopted the motto, 'least objectionable programming.' " At best, the programmer created programs that would serve as lively conduits for delivering images of the large quantities of consumer goods that were pouring off production lines. Television families who lived this consumption happily and without conflict were an ideal venue for marketers. Whether or not a large number of Americans actually achieved the *Happy Days* ideals portrayed in 1950s and '60s programs, these television families gave the impression that such hopeful ideals were a reality. Taylor concludes, "[families such as these] were both advertising and embodying the American Dream" (1989:40).

Whether the emphasis on the family as a moral and emotional center was intentional or a by-product of advertising, one thing seems certain: Television was becoming the source of information for many people about what was possible and desirable. And the messages about the family were very clear.

Good Families Prosper and Prosperous Families Are Good. One message was the equation of "happy families" with "economic prosperity and consumption." A survey of television families reveals that the prime-time families who most embody the image of the ideal family are also the most prosperous. An interesting feature of this prosperity is that it is rarely the subject of the plot. We seldom see situations of economic instability or threat, and if one does arise, it is usually quickly settled through family unity. Instead, the prosperity serves as a backdrop that gives the impression that it somehow happens automatically to "good families." The plots in these shows revolve around family squabbles, miscommunications, and conflicts of interest that are inevitably resolved through caring dialogue intended to reveal the strong moral fiber underlying the surface conflict. The implicit message is that family solidarity somehow sustains or is unproblematically enmeshed in economic stability.

This message was buttressed by early shows that juxtaposed financial woes with shady or goofy characters. The trend continued with the creation of shows such as *One Day at a Time, All in the Family,* and *Roseanne.* Some observers applaud these shows as more realistic portrayals of the typical American family. Taylor counters with a thesis that is a bit more complicated. These shows, she contends, reinforced the cultural stereotype of middle-class families and good families by highlighting what is deviant about those families that are not middle-class. This deviance from the ideal family norm is the basis of plot tension. The mother is divorced in *One Day at a Time.* Archie is a racist and a bigot, not to mention an ill-educated cad, in *All in the Family,* and Roseanne's family is plagued with all sorts of undesirable characters, including a drunken, greedy grandmother and a sassy, disrespectful daughter. The good family = middle-class family stereotype is reinforced by locating deviance in working-class families. In short, Taylor concludes, it is easy to dismiss these families as nonthreatening to the general ideal of family because they are somehow incomplete, poor, or both. They don't really count as much, or at least that's the cultural message.

In contrast, when Murphy Brown found herself pregnant and decided to raise the child by herself, former Vice President Dan Quayle made a display of publicly denouncing her (it's an interesting aside that he denounced the fictional character portrayed by Candace Bergen, a married, real-life mother, rather than the show or its producers). In his debate with this fictional character, Quayle accused Murphy of eroding family values by conceiving a child out of wedlock and choosing to raise it without a father. Why was this single episode of *Murphy Brown* so much more threatening than any single episode of *Roseanne* (excluding the "lesbian kiss")? Perhaps because working-class people are not expected to act in accordance with "family values" whereas Murphy Brown, a highly professional, upper-middle-class character, should know better.

My Family Role Is Who I Am. Another noteworthy message that has had tremendous social psychological impact was the transformation of social roles and duties into desired ways of "being." As portrayed by shows such as *Ozzie and Harriet* and *Leave It to Beaver,* fathers whistled their way to work while wives cheerfully maintained a cozy haven. Husbands earned a living not only because it was their duty to do so, but because they loved their wives and children and wanted the best for them. Wives were expert homemakers by nature, an extension of their presumably natural drive to mother and nurture. The good woman tamed her man and then made it worth his while by providing home and hearth as a haven from the conflicts and struggles of the workplace. The picture renders the role of woman as natural nurturer. If she is good, she will follow her nature and make the warmest possible nest for her family. The good man, according to this portrayal, does all that he can to provide the building materials for this nest. A division of labor that initially separated home and work, women and men, for the sake of industrial growth became encased in a moral arrangement that equates goodness with the ability to internalize and become one's role in this arrangement—the ability to embody "family values."

Shows that depicted ideal family roles were aired concurrently with programs whose characters were a bit more rowdy. Programs such as *I Love Lucy, The Danny Thomas Show,* and *The Honeymooners* displayed the antics of stock characters intended to get a quick laugh. The shows featured a star known for her or his comedy routines. These are not "real people" whom we, the viewers, are expected to emulate. Rather, in juxtaposition with the other shows, they teach the difference between contrived raucous comedy and what are presumed to be real-life scenarios that bring families closer together—something to laugh at in later years.

My choice of programs is obviously selective. My point, however, is that these programs, which were rapidly becoming a major medium of communication in the middle and lower-middle classes, presented a very particular image of the ideal family. This family was economically stable, a site of moral reaffirmation and a source of emotional respite and dependability. How these families achieved this ideal remained a mystery, at least in TV Land. They just were. The implicit message was that as long as they maintained a devotion to their family roles, they would remain as they were.

In a poignant and ironic story about his own childhood, writer Gary Soto describes long afternoons of watching *Leave It to Beaver* and similar television shows in the 1960s. Soto was a kid at the time, living in a barrio neighborhood with his siblings and a single, working mother. He spent his days playing with friends and doing odd jobs for pocket money. The neighbors looked out for him while his mother worked. The family ate dinner together as often as they could, but sometimes it was hard to wait for mother to return when she stayed late to serve dinner to the family for whom she worked as a maid. In his story, Soto describes the plan he hatched as a 10-year-old entrepreneur. Based on his assessment of *Leave It to Beaver,* he determined that if he could convince his family to wear shoes to the dinner table and to eat the same sorts of meals, they too would become "the ideal family."

The Brady Bunch movie was created as a parody of this ideal. The opening shot zooms in on a modest but impeccably landscaped single-family dwelling. Inside the house a cheerful morning bustle unfolds as children ready themselves for school; Alice (the maid) makes cookies while Mike (dad) and Carol (mom) drink their coffee and read the mail and flirt lovingly with one another. Modest tensions arise as the siblings vie for the bathroom and Marsha and Jan fight over socks. The camera lingers for a minute on Marsha's sock drawer, which reveals rows of neatly coiled, brilliantly white knee socks—a symbol that the family has no dirty laundry, literally or metaphorically. The family next door provides the contrast that further delineates the Brady's relative perfection. While the Bradys cheerfully eat breakfast together and benefit from the wise insights of an involved father, the foul-mouthed, punk-clad youngsters next door fend for themselves. The self-absorbed father is running on a treadmill while drinking a Bloody Mary and carrying out shady business dealings on the phone. The mother is nursing a hangover and making lewd comments about her desire to help Mike Brady "wrap his Christmas packages." All the stereotypes are here. Within 10 minutes we see the stark distinction between the morally upstanding family and the "failures" next door.

The plot in the movie revolves around the tension of a misplaced tax notice—the next-door neighbors received the Brady's mail and failed to pass it along, thereby demonstrating yet another shortcoming: messy organization. When the Bradys finally receive the notice it is so overdue that they are required to pay $20,000 in back taxes within a week or lose their house. The plot unfolds as the Bradys work together to construct various plans to save the day—which, of course they do in the end. The moral of the story: Family values lead to economic victory. Put another way, the moral family (as depicted by the Bradys) can overcome any economic adversity.

The Gap Between Television and Reality

Sociological experts on the family, such as Lillian Rubin and Stephanie Coontz, claim that although there was a period during the 1950s and '60s in which Americans achieved greater economic prosperity, had more leisure time and seemed more inclined to participate actively in progressive civic affairs than at other times in the nation's history, these developments must be understood within the context of the economic climate of the times. Post-World War II economies were booming, and veterans received assistance for housing, education and small business loans in amounts that have never since been paralleled. Additional government programs provided training and work for women and youth. It was within this context that the family came to be seen as the "well-oiled building block of a benignly conceived American society founded in affluence and consensus" (Taylor 1989:3). The middle-class pulse of the nation was pumping. The family was its heart. Or so it would seem.

Coontz, Rubin and others agree that economic prosperity was at an all-time high, and divorce and "desertion" rates were low compared with the preceding decades (during which war played out its own havoc as a force of social change). But they caution against interpreting economic and organizational stability as a reflection of domestic bliss and the triumph of monogamous unions. There is no evidence to suggest, based on these factors alone, that middle-class families of the 1950s and '60s were the emotional and moral havens that we have romanticized them to be. In fact, as more scholars and social workers examine this period of our social history, it appears that the middle-class suburban family may have been much more of a prison for some of its members than a haven.

Incidences of physical, sexual and psychological abuse may have been the norm rather than the exception; infidelity was considered a given, but overlooked, practice among married men in this century just as it was in the nineteenth century. One notable difference is that women were now more isolated from one another, particularly in middle-class suburbs. It's not clear that this particular period was any better or worse than other times in our recent history; the separation of work and home, as argued by Christopher Lasch in his renowned book, *Haven in a Heartless World,* created severe stresses in family life. The achievement of both economic success and a sustained high level of loving romance and enthusiastic companionship was likely the exception, rather than the rule. Yet along with the television reruns, the myths persist.

Family Harmony and Family Appearances: Economic Factors

How accurate are representations that equate family harmony with middle-class economic prosperity? To assess this I have my students engage in a simulation called "Life Happens." This is a class activity conceived and written by sociologist Tracy Ore. The students divide into groups and receive family profile cards. A group might select a profile card that describes a two-parent, two-child family in which the father is employed at Microsoft at a salary of $90,000 a year. The family has $500,000 in assets. The mother has chosen to work in the home. An extreme comparison would be a family profile in which the father is employed as a janitor at $21,000 a year and the mother works as a secretary for $18,000 a year for a combined total income of $39,000 a year. This family rents a modest house and has no assets in the form of real estate, stocks or other investments. If you are a struggling college student $39,000 may seem like a lot of money, but imagine trying to extend this to a family of four. The significant question is the relative economic stability of each family.

The object of the game is to create a family budget based on a list of prices for housing, food, clothing, child care, medical care, education, travel, entertainment and so forth. Obviously, the families who make more money will be able to afford nicer homes, better food and more exotic travel and entertainment. In addition, the mock family groups must make allowances in their budgets and family planning for various unexpected events ("life happens") such as health emergencies, pregnancies, home repairs, and one-time costs such as special school trips, weddings, funerals and so forth. Clearly the families with the most money will be able to absorb these costs with relative ease. This means that higher-income families may be able to meet some of the *functions* expected of the family with more ease than lower-income families. What does this have to do with the practice of "family values"? Some functions that seem separate from money, such as loving companionship, may actually be related in indirect ways. For instance, couples who must work opposite schedules and who struggle with finances may find it difficult to make the time and emotional space to enjoy one another's company frequently. Does this mean they lack a commitment to the value of loving companionship?

The Appearance of "Family Values"

Consider: Your elderly mother has injured her hip and no longer feels safe living alone. She wants to move in with you. How will this affect your family? In one scenario, students in the wealthy family used some of their assets to build a separate cottage on their property for the mother. They also hired a physical therapist to come to the home regularly to help the elderly relative regain her strength and resume her hobbies of gardening, traveling and visiting friends. The students in this mock family speculated that such an arrangement was likely to enhance their relationship with their mother/grandmother. The children would have an opportunity to spend more time with her and the family could enjoy her wisdom and experience. In short, a possible upset was transformed into an opportunity for enriching family ties.

The family with a more modest income also welcomes grandma into their home. Unfortunately, however, they have only three small bedrooms and cannot afford to move to a larger house. Rather than have their teenage son and daughter share a room, they ask the son to give up his room for his grandmother. He will sleep on the couch. He does so obligingly, but the increased crowding causes a strain on the family. Grandma brings with her a modest pension but this extra money is eaten away with medical expenses for her hip. The family cannot afford special therapies and so grandmother becomes increasingly bedridden and requires additional home care. The mother cuts back her hours as a secretary in order to care for her own ailing mother. The father picks up some additional shifts of janitorial work. He has always worked swing shift and the mother day shift so their time together as a family has been limited. Now the father sees even less of his family. At least the rent is paid and the car is still running. But the son has begun to spend more time away from home. Who can blame him? He no longer has a room in which to listen to his music or entertain his friends. His parents seem even more tired and irritable. Although his school counselor has indicated that his grades make him a good contender for a college scholarship, the son decides to drop out during his last year of high school so that he can earn enough money to move into a place with his girlfriend. The father, who has worked hard in order to give his children a better life, becomes inconsolably depressed and angry and refuses to talk to his son.

Which family appears to have greater love and compassion? Factor in other events that come to mind—opportunities and emergencies. Which families are more/less likely to be able to vacation together? To enjoy a variety of entertainment and related activities—the stuff that makes for cherished memories and provides a basis of "quality" time? Consider the relative ease with which different families absorb unexpected events that include a financial burden. How might these costs increase strain in some families and not others? What additional resources—such as counseling—are available to families to help them deal with tough times? How are these resources connected to economic circumstances? Imagine, for instance, that both mothers in the above profiles become pregnant. Is it possible that the different economic circumstances of each family will result in a difference in whether they are able to welcome this news, no matter how much both families may desire another child? What about the father who finds himself forced to choose between working extra shifts so that his daughter can pay for college applications or spending "quality time" with her. Or the working mother who has to decide whether to take a sick child to day care or risk losing her job?

Sociologically, the point is that economic stability enables and enhances the sorts of relationships and activities that are commonly associated with traditional family values. This stability is often taken for granted, affording the economically stable family more occasion to focus on other family functions, such as companionship and cultural enrichment. Furthermore, many of the mundane tasks and tensions associated with everyday domestic life are reduced to background features in popular depictions of the ideal family. The creators of the Brady Bunch movie bring this to the foreground and parody it in the role of Alice the maid. How is it that Carol has so much time to stand behind husband Mike (which she literally does throughout the film)? To drink coffee with him in the morning, lavish loving greetings on him when he returns from work and generally play the eager ear and loving supporter to his twin roles as family provider and sage father? Carol has time to be the model mother and spouse because Alice does all the housework. While Carol and Mike trade quips over coffee, Alice makes breakfast. While Carol and Mike counsel errant teenagers and tattle-tale youngsters, Alice folds and distributes the laundry. Doing the "shitwork" is both the basis and the bane of domesticity.

Economic circumstances do not *cause* people to be loving, compassionate and responsible family members. Many working-class people describe their families as strong and idyllic; many people from middle- and upper-income families suggest that they suffered from various forms of neglect and abuse in their families. Money doesn't make the family, but it is a major factor in the extent to which a family is able to practice many of the activities associated with family ties and to avoid the strains caused by economic instability. A provocative and revealing photo essay in David Newman's book *The Architecture of Society* depicts some of these differences. In one frame a middle-class, stay-at-home mom loads bags of groceries into her mini-van. Later the children mill around a well-lit kitchen, laughing over snacks of name brand foods while she puts the food away. In a contrasting shot, a single working mother juggles a couple of bags of groceries, an infant in her arms and a toddler holding her hand as she tries to negotiate a seat on the bus. The caption explains that she is unable to purchase cheaper bulk food items that would save her money because she can't buy more than she can carry home in a single trip. Another photo shows the middle-class mother reading in the background of a well-appointed, tidy living room while her son receives piano lessons. The working-class mother is shown stretched across the bed in her one-room apartment, reading to her two young children. Both mothers are interested in the cultural education of their children, but the ways in which they express this tend to be valued differently in our culture. And these ways are directly related to their income. Middle- and upper-income families simply have more options at their disposable when it comes to the *execution* of "family values." They have more ease in presenting an appearance that is closer to the expected ideal.

Appearances of (Im)propriety

The issue of teen pregnancy provides a useful illustration for pondering the impact of economics on the appearance of family values. What if one of the teenagers in each of the profile families becomes unexpectedly pregnant? Which family has more options for dealing with this unexpected event in a manner that will appear consistent with "family values"? It is a common public perception that only women from poor backgrounds get pregnant unexpectedly and out of wedlock. In assessing the accuracy of such images it is important to keep in mind that families with larger incomes have more options for dealing with teen pregnancies in ways that keep the matter "quiet." The financial ability to send a daughter "away" for a semester or to pay for an abortion is one means of avoiding stigma. Middle- and upper-income families also have access to private counseling services that may help the young woman see her way toward adoption and reintegration within her community with very few traces of the "unfortunate" event. This assumes that the young woman tells her family about the pregnancy. Sensational news stories about teenagers hiding pregnancies from family and friends and then killing the child upon birth tend to focus on the "good" background of these young people. It is likely that this same tragedy occurs across class lines, but the stories are rendered as sensational among middle- and upper-income families precisely because we expect these families to be models of "family values."

In contrast, consider that working-class families, who may be less financially able to keep up the *appearance* of family values, may also be better prepared to make accommodations for raising a child from an unwanted pregnancy within an extended family network. In such a case the child receives love and attention from a group of interested caretakers and the teenage mother is able to pursue her education—an absolute necessity if she is going to provide for her child over time. Because the extended family may not be able to absorb all the financial costs of an unexpected child, the mother may apply for welfare in the form of Aid to Families with Dependent Children. These are the same people that advocates of "welfare reform" seek to vilify. These are the mothers who are repeatedly portrayed in the media as trying to "scam" welfare.

Recall the letter at the beginning of this chapter. What was your initial impression of the young woman who wrote Dear Abby asking for advice about giving up one of her children? To what extent is your opinion of this person based on stereotypical impressions and to what extent did you try to factor in possible scenarios that take economic and community options into account? Were you inclined to think of her as a whore who is incapable of sexual self-determination? How can you be sure she is any more or less sexually permissive than her middle-class suburban counterpart? The only difference may be options for hiding one's circumstances. To what sorts of lengths might a mother who wants the best for her child have to go if she doesn't have many options?

Politicians who employ the language of "eroded family values" to denounce AFDC recipients neglect to note that the average length of time these women receive welfare assistance is 16 months, with an upward range of two years. Mothers may turn to this form of assistance only as a last resort and usually as a means of supplementing an already near-poverty-level income while they engage in attempts to better their own employment options (i.e., complete high school equivalency, technical school, etc.). The rhetoric of "family values" stigmatizes these women because they are "single parents." This rhetoric doesn't take into account other possible scenarios, such as extended family networks and/or giving a child up to another couple. In short, a poor single mother is likely to be stigmatized if she does seek aid, and to be stigmatized if she seeks other options, such as giving the child up. She falls afoul of public approval either way. Meanwhile, we really know very little about what sorts of difficult choices a middle-class woman makes because she is more able to "keep it within the family."

The occurrence and outcome of unexpected pregnancies is directly related to the sorts of resources that a woman has. Reports that harp on the relatively higher rates of teen pregnancy among working-class women rarely take these other factors into account. Given the extent to which the problem is portrayed as a lack of morality among the lower classes, it is possible that researchers don't think to ask additional questions. The rate of teen pregnancy in a small town in Southern Utah provides an indirect comparison and simultaneously underscores the difference between the *practice* and the *appearance* of within-marriage births (a presumed cornerstone of "family values"). I was surprised when I stumbled across a statistic from the U.S. Census that showed that this area has the highest rate of (illegitimate) teen pregnancy per capita in the nation. My surprise stemmed from the fact that I knew this area was populated largely by Mormons—a predominantly middle-class group who zealously emphasize the value of the traditional family unit. Further investigation revealed that this community had consistently voted against the establishment of Planned Parenthood offices in the area.

A picture of the actual scenario that might explain the statistic began to take shape in my mind when I learned that the local high school was across the street from a state university that recruited students from the intermountain region. It is plausible that many high school women (most of them Mormons) dated men from the university (most of them non-Mormons). The religious emphasis on the grave immorality of premarital sex combined with a lack of information about birth control may perpetuate a silent ignorance that explains a relatively high rate of unexpected pregnancy. The noteworthy point here is that the families of these otherwise "upstanding" young women had the means to protect their daughters, and by extension, their community, from the stigma of these unexpected pregnancies.

The tragedy, as I review the case, is that the appearance of sexual inactivity, rather than prevention of pregnancy through education, seemed to be the primary concern among these parents. Cases such as this should at least give us pause regarding the extent to which teen pregnancies are really rooted in the presumably amoral behavior of the underclass. In the case of the Mormon town, the relatively high rate can be explained in terms of attempts to maintain appearances (of sexual inactivity) at the expense of education. Deviations from the path of morality that is defined in terms of "family values" may actually be commonplace among all classes and religious groups. Social groups vary, however, in the means that they have to maintain the appearance of propriety. One question worth further study concerns the emotional and mental costs to individuals who must strive to keep up "appearances" equated with family morality.

Infidelity, another marker of family immorality, is also difficult to assess. Stereotypically, those who are in the working classes are portrayed as morally "loose" and more likely than their middle-class counterparts to engage in extramarital sexual activity. It is possible that if you grow up in a middle-class environment you are less likely to see people "cheating." Does this appearance of middle-class fidelity verify the stereotype? Again, the role of economic differences in who can hide socially unsavory behavior is a significant factor to consider. If you are professionally employed, tend to travel away from home and have credit cards, it can be relatively simple to hide your affairs. You can bring dates to your private offices, check into high-class hotels and generally absorb your infidelity into your relatively private daily routines. Privacy is minimal among people who do not live in single-family dwellings, do not have private offices and/or access to discreet hotels. The same logic can be extended to the analysis of other presumably unsavory actions that are at odds with "family values," such as physical and psychological abuse and drug and alcohol consumption.

Appearances of the Good Provider

I had occasion one afternoon to visit the county courthouse with a friend who was changing her name. My friend, who is a college professor, was changing her name to honor her recently deceased grandmother who was a member of the Muskogee tribe in the region of Oklahoma. My friend was instructed to go to "Counter 4" to pick up the appropriate form. At Counter 4, while I waited for her to fill out the form I noted the difference in the manner that the clerks, all of them young women, dealt with those who approached their windows. Counter 4 consisted of five windows. Three different official transactions were handled at Counter 4"—name changes, petitions for citizenship, and payment of fines for violation of restraining orders. The logic (if there was one) of this juxtaposition of types of transactions escaped me. But I was struck by the fact that there was actually a window for the sole purpose of paying fines for the violation of restraining orders.

When we hear about a restraining order we may tend to think of some sort of deranged stalker. However, restraining orders are more commonly filed against men whose wives have accused them of abuse or the violation of custody arrangements. What captured my attention was the contrast in the way in which the clerks treated those engaged in the different transactions. They were brusque and impatient toward persons filling out petitions for citizenship and name changes (the majority were people of color and many did not speak English as their first language). This could be chalked up to typical bureaucratic boredom. What startled me was the respect and rapt attention that they paid to the men in suits who were peeling off wads of bills to pay fines for having *violated* an order to stay away from their wives. Any casual observer might have taken the transaction to have been a sale of perfume to a gentleman in a posh department store. I was astonished. And disturbed. This is admittedly an impressionistic response based on a fleeting experience, but the image made me reconsider much of what I take for granted about those people who appear to be upstanding representations of "family values." What was particularly striking was the manner in which these men so cavalierly shrugged off their apparently official transgressions as fathers and husbands and were made to feel good about themselves in a brief transaction. Not much penalty against abuse if you can afford the fine.

A slightly different but equally compelling illustration of the connection between economics and the appearance of family success comes from Katherine Newman's book, *Falling From Grace*. The author's intent was to explain another remarkable statistic, the comparatively high rate of suicide among male middle-level managers. Corporate down-sizing has threatened the jobs and subsequent economic stability of many middle-class men in the United States. One consequence of this downturn in economic stability is the erosion of the basis for the appearance of a successful family life in accordance with traditional values. Newman reports that many of the men become violently angry or deeply depressed at the idea of having their wives work to supplement the family income. Many of these men try to hide from their families the fact that they have lost their jobs. Newman concludes, and I am inclined to agree, that it is the stigma of being unable to keep up the appearances associated with traditional family roles that drives many of these men to suicide. This illustrates that economic success, or lack thereof, is seen by many in the middle classes as a basis for assessing both personal and family success.

How to Explain the Lack of an
Ideal Family: It's All My/Your Fault

The ability of the middle class to hide and/or deny the inconsistencies in the practice and expectations of the functions of family may actually be a part of the problem. Middle-class life is notoriously private and, subsequently, potentially isolated. A particularly insidious reality of life in the suburbs during the 1950s and '60s was that families who were less than perfect themselves had only public and television portrayals as role models. In their own minds, it is likely that they believed themselves to be the only abusers/sufferers, the only drunks, the only inadequate families on their block. The perception that yours is the only family that isn't wallowing in domestic bliss may lead to a tendency to internalize the cause as personal failure. Blaming yourself or other individual family members reaffirms the myth of the self-sufficient family. The inability to recognize one's family behavior as a reflection of the social and economic trends in which it is embedded perpetuates the myth that most families approximate the ideal equation. Your family is the only "deviant" one.

One interpretation of the relatively stable divorce rates during the 1950s is that many people, particularly women without skills for the labor market, may have felt they had no choice but to "gut it out" despite the abuses and the stresses. The lack of options and/or worries of being perceived as a personal failure are not motivations that necessarily imply strong family commitment. These conditions may simply foster the appearance of stability. Again, we can ask, at what cost to the individuals involved? A lack of extended support networks combined with increased expectations for marriage as the basis of love and companionship may explain the high rate of middle-class women who were hospitalized for depression and "nervous breakdowns" and subsequently treated with Valium. Addiction to this drug, as well as alcohol abuse, are well-documented problems from this era.

Lillian Rubin contends that many of the tensions experienced by the modern family are rooted in the contradictions between the family's function as an economic unit and the ideals of the family as a primary source of love, companionship and emotional support. Rubin observes that these obligations are often contradictory, especially in an economic context of downsizing, layoffs and increased living costs. As one man notes, "I can either spend quality time with my family, or I can work overtime so that we can make ends meet. I can't do both. But the way it's set up, I'm either a bad provider or a bad father. I can't win."

The lack of a structural perspective—the ability to assess the connection between these functions and the resources necessary to combine them in one family setting—fosters a sense of self-degradation. Family members may be inclined to attribute their failure to achieve the ideal to personal shortcomings. The analytical point worth underscoring is that in most depictions of the ideal family, the economic functions are stable and taken for granted. These depictions focus our attention on the additional family functions: cultural reproduction and unconditional support. In hour upon hour of television time we watch as families grapple with and ultimately resolve these issues. The lesson we carry away is that family problems are rooted in conflicting intergenerational cultural values and strains on unconditional support. These problems are ultimately solved because each family member is a person of good conscience and character, and they really do love one another, and because the American "way" makes it all possible.

The intensity of these expectations is exacerbated by the paradoxical cultural emphasis on sexual activity as an expression of true love. Historically, cultural rules that strictly enforced sexual behavior, usually for women, did so for the political and economic reasons of ensuring paternity. Marital sexuality was a matter of lineage. The laws were necessary precisely because sexual desire was not presumed to be something that could be contained within single relationships. Christianity attempted to curb expressions of sexuality as a form of desire by equating self-mastery with denial of the "inner beast" and inscribing sexual relations within a single relationship for the purpose of fecundity. The romantic association of sexual arousal with a sort of divine madness that portends a transcendent union has continued to the present day and is now heralded as the benchmark of domestic bliss.

This expectation is paradoxical. Most of the functions as portrayed in the ideal family require husbands and wives to regulate their individual passions within the marriage, to sacrifice urges for self-pleasure in pursuit of the larger goals of family security. How, then, is one supposed to stoke the fires of passion? Perhaps one of the most intriguing of the tensions in modern family life is this paradoxical expectation of simultaneous domestic tempering with ongoing smoldering passion. Yet one of the most enduring expectations of a successful marriage is that it be based on "true love," with true love indicated primarily through sustained sexual arousal and unwavering fidelity.

Rubin also points out that we overemphasize "true love" as the pinnacle of family achievement at the expense of domestic accomplishment. The family's domestic accomplishments are generally taken for granted. (Yet, if you've ever struggled with roommates, you know how demanding domesticity can be.) In contrast, the achievement of "true love" between the soon-to-be married couple is the focus of our interest and the rod against which we measure family success. Rubin notes that most people in our culture equate personal happiness with a loving spousal relationship. This is the ultimate meaningful goal; if you have it, you are supposed to be happy. Thus we are saturated with cultural messages about how to attract a mate, but corresponding lessons regarding the challenges of establishing and sustaining domestic life are conspicuously absent. The assumption seems to be that if you find "true love," everything else will take care of itself. And when it doesn't, we blame it on "the wrong mate" and/or our own shortcomings as lovers.

This is a curiously shortsighted and narrow view of the components of family life. Rubin, and many others, suggests that it is this cultural lore and the corresponding inability to make sense of the structural components of family that sets people up for failure in their own relationships. It's a bit like being expected to make a fabulously beautiful, rich-tasting souffle as an indication of cultural success, but being given no recipe or ingredients for doing so. The insidious aspect of "family values" rhetoric, according to Rubin and others, is that it places the blame for this lack of recipe and ingredients on individual morality.

What is clear today is that the economic burdens on middle- and lower-income families are increasing while the means to fulfill these burdens are decreasing. Once-upon-a-time measures of success such as home ownership and the ability to pay for college tuitions and to help offspring get a start of their own are diminishing realities. The United States has higher infant mortality rates, higher health care costs per capita, and less innovative forms of child care and elder care than any other "advanced" nation. Politicians and moral pundits who blame these problems on "deadbeat dads," single mothers and mothers who work outside the home are putting the cart before the horse, or reversing cause and effect. There has never been a time in the history of this country when a large majority of Americans has been able to fulfill *all* the expectations in the functional definition of the ideal family. To the extent that this ideal was approximated in the 1950s and '60s, it was because of generous government incentives, comparatively higher salaries and lower costs of living that made it possible for people to maintain single-income households and to put aside modest savings. Those times are gone. Any analysis of the dissolution of the ideal family form must take into account the simultaneous shrinking middle class and the actions of the multinational capitalist class responsible for this.

The Relationship Between
Family and Community Networks

"But it is possible to achieve this ideal!" insist many of my students from such back-grounds. And of course it would seem so because they are living it, or at least they think they may be. In such cases it is useful to take into account the economic and social factors that contribute to a family's ability to practice the ideal functions. If you are a member of a family that approximates the ideal, it can be instructive to analyze the sort of extended community in which your family is situated. Upon examination it is generally found that people who practice "family values" are part of a larger network through which they obtain (taken-for-granted) guidance and resources that enable this practice.

Many religious communities that emphasize the significance of the family also provide formal and informal training about how to be a good family member. Rather than assume that "good people" automatically know the recipe, these organizations go to great lengths to provide guidance and follow-up support. For instance, couples planning to marry within a particular church may be required to attend a series of counseling sessions and workshops designed to assess their compatibility and to instruct them in ways to deal with potential obstacles and tensions. Many churches also incorporate lessons about "appro-priate" family behavior into their weekly meetings. In some cases, even romance is not taken for granted. Mormon men, for instance, are instructed to treat their wives as their "sweethearts" and to make good on this by taking them on a formal date at least once a week. In Sunday School lessons, children participate in activities and crafts projects that encourage them to reflect on and show appreciation for family members. These are just a few illustrations of ways in which a larger network of relations may contribute to a sense of familial obligation and provide instructions for how to follow through. Such networks also provide rewards for those who do follow through and deterrents against behaviors that are not consistent with family values. For example, if one belongs to a church or extended friendship group that values family, one is likely to spend time discussing family outings, seeking advice regarding child care, and so forth. These conversations can be rewarding reinforcements of one's role as a family member. Similarly, someone who is inclined to engage in an extramarital affair may feel considerable pressure about being caught not just by the spouse, but by the entire community.

Sociological research indicates a strong relationship between extended network support and family stability. Couples who have support from friends and extended family members are more likely to decide to marry and to remain together. This is due in part to the fact that these friends and family members serve as a source of guidance and support. Conversely, couples who do not receive family and community support, usually because of differences in background—religious, ethnic, educational, class—tend not to stay together. In general, families who are embedded in a larger community tend to work harder at solving family problems, tend to experience less stress regarding economic and domestic upsets and tend to enjoy one another's company and find family life fulfilling. Some explanations for this may include the fact that if you are part of a larger community, you may find people with whom to share concerns and tensions regarding family life—stress outlets. You may also be less inclined to divorce if divorce includes the possibility of losing significant ties to the larger group. Extended family and community groups also tend to help one another with domestic tasks, especially child care, and to pitch in when a family experiences hardships. This external support not only provides assistance with the family's function as an economic unit, but may enhance a sense of family enjoyment by helping to balance the demands of work and family life.

In considering the roles of economics and community support as part of the family equation, I am reminded of my own childhood. My father was a corporate engineer during my youth in the 1960s. Like many young men who graduated from high school in the 1950s, my father achieved upward mobility—that is, went to college—on the basis of generous government assistance awarded him through his own father's military career. A scholarship and summer employment generated through a Park Services youth work program, one of many such programs available at the time, enabled my mother to leave the rural poverty that she grew up in and set out for college. Cheap housing and a low cost of living allowed her to finish. Jobs were plentiful and so were housing subsidies for first-time buyers. With this assistance and some money set aside in savings bonds by my father's parents, my own parents were able to buy a modest home. Like so many couples in the late 1950s, they were able to live on my father's salary alone. In addition to expensive insurance coverage, his corporate employer provided a car, which was replaced with a new one every two years. At the time of replacement, the employee was given the option of purchasing the older car at cost. Thus, my family always had two relatively new cars at our disposal.

This enabled my mother to chauffeur us to various music, art and sports lessons. These lessons were offered by other mothers in the neighborhood who taught in their homes as a way of bringing in a little extra cash. When my mother had errands or my parents wanted an evening or a vacation to themselves, they could comfortably send us to the neighbors. They reciprocated this favor whenever they could. As a consequence, I passed my childhood happily wandering among neighbors; my sense of personal prosperity was enhanced by my access to a larger community of playmates (and their toys) and caretakers (especially their invitations to eat a second dinner). I lived a comfortably middle-class life in a relatively ideal family setting in a quiet suburban neighborhood. Only in retrospect have I begun to realize the extent to which this idyllic arrangement was predicated on the particular economic conditions of the time.

The particular community in which I lived buttressed this arrangement. I was raised in a Mormon family. In addition to a strong emphasis on family unity, Mormons are, as a whole, an economically successful group who constitute a solid middle-class community. A couple of incidents stand out in my mind as reminders of the role that community plays in the ability to practice "family values." The corporate culture of the time assumed that working men had wives who would tend to home and hearth while leaving the men free to foster relationships among their co-workers as they inched their way up the corporate ladder. When I was young, my father was offered a lucrative promotion that would include international travel. He consulted with extended family and community members who cautioned him against compromising family time with more work commitments. After some deliberation, he declined the promotion. Following this he was continually harangued by his boss for spending too much time on family affairs at the expense of career advancements. One day my father, who was considered a bit of a rogue, quit his job on the spot. He walked out, drove home and showed up triumphantly in the driveway. Unaccustomed to having him home during the middle of the day, we gathered around, along with several neighbors, to hear him tell his tale of having taken the "high ground" in support of his family values. In our community, this made him a hero. It also made him unemployed, which turned out not to be much of a problem.

Several members of our church arranged contacts for my father with other engineering firms, firms that they insisted would respect his values as a family man rather than hinder them. In a matter of weeks my father was happily reemployed with a firm that he considered to be better suited to his values. Unemployed families can lose their homes and incur all sorts of unmanageable expenses in a matter of weeks, however, especially if they encounter unexpected medical expenses, or household and auto repairs. Many families unravel during such times of stress. Understandably so. I don't recall any hardship whatsoever during my father's unemployment, however. The reasons for this, I later learned, were that my parents had enough savings to cover the mortgage for a month and members of the community helped out with groceries and other expenses.

It's not possible to say, ad hoc, whether the cushion provided by my parent's economic circumstances and community attachments caused my father to engage in his own particular heroics in the name of family values. What is certain, however, is that this cushion of support and the resulting respect granted him by his community contributed significantly to our experience of this as a positive, binding moment in our family. Without the economic cushion and the community support, it is possible that my father would have never considered such an act. And had he persisted without a cushion, the effects may have been disastrous on our home life.

I do not mean to imply that my father was disingenuous in his stance of defense for his family. My intent is to underscore the point that the practice of so-called ideal family values is tightly braided together with economic and community resources. This doesn't make the acts any less real. Rather it is a misconception to assume that such acts are based on character and valor alone, or that those who do not act similarly lack similar values. They may not have the degrees of freedom to act on principle that my father was able to take for granted.

The success of the family as defined by the equation that I set forth in this chapter is a function of economic stability and community support. Even "true love" is something that people are likely to *learn* rather than to start out with. We learn how to be lovingly supportive and come to enjoy being so during the course of a relationship. Economic instability doesn't necessarily undermine this potential, but the strain of persistent economic hardship can make it difficult to practice. In addition to resources that may relieve some of the tensions of domestic life, community networks provide individuals with the emotional support, role models and guidance that are necessary in order to learn how to practice love and support.

Is the Family in Crisis?

Relative to the 1950s and '60s, in recent decades there has been considerable erosion of both economic stability and community connections. At the same time, there is considerable cultural emphasis on the expectation that one must find "true love" in order to be happy. The result is a messy lack of awareness of what actually constitutes "family," what its functions are supposed to be, the social mechanisms that support these functions and the qualities of companionship and character that emerge as a result of these supports, rather than the other way around. Young people tend to blame family failures on a lack of "true love" and "moral commitment." Several political and religious groups blame family disintegration on a lack of commitment to "family values." These opinions do not take into account the fragility of and the contradictions inherent in the definition of the modern family. These expectations are not possible to fulfill without adequate economic and community resources. Why is this seemingly simple equation so difficult to recognize?

A Historical "Crisis" of the Family

It is instructive to look at the history of discussions regarding so-called crises of the family. In 1948 the U.S. government convened a "National Conference on Family Life" with the purpose of assessing "threats and opportunities in family security." Panelists included university presidents, scholars, medical practitioners, religious leaders, economists and directors of influential private and public organizations. World War II had left many Americans with a sense of both social upheaval and new opportunity. Conferees were interested in what the consequences of this social and political turmoil might be for the American family. The discussion was predicated on the collective perception that traditional bonds of community were in transition. It is clear from reading the transcripts of this conference that the participants took for granted the traditional definition of what constitutes a family and what its functions should be. What I find noteworthy is the extent to which, without exception, a dissolution in this form and/or the ability to carry out these functions is attributed to social factors. Nowhere in this entire documentation of conversations from purportedly strong supporters of the family is there any discussion of individual (im)morality as a causal basis for the so-called disintegration of the nuclear family unit.

The cartoon illustration on the cover of the conference report is indicative of the general tone: The drawing depicts a family (father, mother, child) in a hospital bed. The chart at the foot of the bed shows a graph with the heading "American Family in 'Crisis.' " On either side of the bed a doctor rushes to offer the family a spoonful of medicine. On one side the doctor's bag carries the label, "Eliminating Social, Economic, Political Problems." The doctor on the other side of the bed holds a bag emblazoned with "More Counseling, Guidance, Education." The caption under the cartoon reads: Why Not Use Both Medicines? In one keynote address, Julius Schreiber, an M.D. and the director of the National Institute of Social Relations, admonishes, "Young people should be better educated for marriage and family life. There should be a greater emphasis on counseling, including instruction in planning and caring for babies, education in sex relationships, education in the sharing of homemaking duties, and guidance in solving personal problems."

In response to a question from the conference audience, "Are there any eternal values for the family?" Fisk University President Charles Johnson concluded his own speech with a statement regarding the connection between "values" and economics. "We cannot go back to the good old days. But we can do something about factors in our lives which are creating disintegrating forces—[we need] more employment, shorter hours, better pay, more equitable distribution of housing." The impact of socioeconomic disadvantages on the family was a repeated theme throughout the conference. In the opening remarks, one of the conference organizers notes that the planners have gone to great lengths to assemble diverse groups for discussion. Regarding the "complications and confusions attendant upon 'free-wheeling' discussion of such a tremendous and elusive subject by such a heterogenous group," the organizer suggests that this may actually be instructive. Such discussions, he notes, "are no more complicated, confused and difficult than family living itself; in fact, these dynamics might prove revealing of the subject at hand."

This conference emphasized the necessities of economic stability and education in order for families to fulfill the expected role as a haven from the stresses and disintegrating effects of modern industrial society. The underlying themes of the conference dialogue suggest an understanding that family life is "complicated, confused and difficult"—something that must be achieved rather than taken for granted. The basis for successful achievement of harmonious and productive family life is assumed to be adequate employment, income and housing. And the ability of individuals to create a functioning family is assumed to be connected to ongoing education and guidance. These conference discussions suggest that prior to the 1950s "Happy Days," the family was perceived as a unit that was intricately connected to larger community networks and economic resources. These discussions also imply that community networks and economic resources were seen as *antecedents* to the creation and maintenance of stable, healthy families. In short, the attitude of the day seemed to be: If we want healthy families, we have to provide the social and economic resources upon which healthy family life is predicated. A "crisis" of the family was taken to be an indication of a more general economic instability and disintegration of community.

Current Crisis or Rhetoric?

This earlier perception is in striking contrast to contemporary political and social commentary that steadfastly disavows the causal connection among economics, community and family stability. Attempts to outlaw divorce are an example of a presumably "quick fit" measure that will get the family back on track without any change in the social and economic conditions that underlie divorce. Even more ludicrous are the laments that blame individual families for social problems, such as crime rates and the erosion of community. Let's return to the definition of the functions of the family the connection to other social and economic systems. Let's assume that references to a "healthy" family mean a family that meets the functions defined earlier: reproduction, economic-domestic security and loving support. Overall it can be said that the ideal family serves as a sort of "buck stops here" social unit that is responsible for taking care of its members. This is a particularly important function in a society in which persons are expected to leave their domestic setting for a public labor sector that is often seen as emotionally, mentally and physically taxing, even alienating. As the stresses of public life increase and people become more mobile and disconnected from their larger communities, the family is expected to function as an emotional haven, a form of "hard times" security, and a basis of meaningful bonding with others. Given this, what does a "crisis of the family" mean?

The problem, according to the 1948 conferees, who I assume were setting the political and moral tone for the nation at the time, is a general disintegration in social and community ties. This disintegration is reflected at the level of the nuclear family by increased rates in divorce, truancy, and juvenile crime. Some analysts also interpreted a rise in suicides among certain sectors of the population as a failure of the family ties that presumably act as a cushion against low self-esteem and despair during times of hardship. If the family is considered the most basic source of community for individuals—a haven through which members receive unconditional support and a cushion to shield them from the increasingly stressful and alienating consequences of modern industrial life—then a disintegration of this unit means that individuals are more likely to be "left out in the cold." The implication is that such individuals are increasingly unable to behave in accordance with civil expectations and the demands of public life. In other words, inherent in this logic is the assumption that public life is distinct from domestic life, that it requires knowledge of cultural expectations and even a tolerance for harsh, alienating conditions. People can't be presumed to know what's expected of them, let alone to comply with these expectations, unless they have a nurturing hearth at which to learn the rules and, later on, to cast off their cares and renew their sense of self and commitment to society.

As I have noted, this is a lot to expect of single family units as they are typically conceived. Economic resources and the community networks in which the family is embedded can help to distribute the functions attributed to the family in a way that makes the burden more manageable. For instance, educational institutions share the function of "cultural reproduction." Passing on an entire stock of cultural knowledge and related expectations is not left entirely to the parents. Obviously, this means of cultural repro-duction will be most effective if parents and educators share common goals and if parents have the time and ability to reinforce lessons learned in school within the home environ-ment. Such time and ability is directly related to a parent's employment options, particularly the degree of control he or she has over working hours. Extended family networks, churches and other community groups also share the functions of cultural reproduction and economic and emotional support. In addition, these larger social groups may also provide guidance and lessons in the "how to's" of family life. They also expand a family's emotional and economic support by distributing everyday burdens, such as child care, elder care, meal preparation, and companionship, over a larger number of people. These groups may also be a cushion during hard times.

Concerned civic, religious and educational leaders in 1948 seemed well aware of the sheer mass of the weight on the family as an economic unit. This is something that the current pulpit-pounders for family values seem to have forgotten. The United States is one of the only countries in the developed world that places the entire financial burden of housing, health care, child care, elder care, and education on the single family unit. It is worth pondering the amount of "quality time" that families might have at their disposal, and the related decrease in stress that might result, if some of these financial burdens were removed from American families. How much time and energy would individuals have to devote to the other functions of family—cultural reproduction, loving support and companionship—the functions that we commonly associate with the "good family?"

Is the current family in "crisis" and if so, what does that mean? In the years immediately following World War II and just preceding what has become rooted in our collective conscious as the "golden '50s"—an era of economic prosperity and harmonious fami- lies—"crisis" was understood in terms of the link between the family unit and other social institutions. Discussions at the time indicate a general awareness, a more sociological perspective on functions of the family as the basis of cultural reproduction, economic division of labor and a harmonious haven of support. It seems to have been widely understood that in order for the family to fulfill these functions, larger community services in the form of education and counseling, and economic incentives such as housing subsidies would be necessary. It is no historical accident that the post-World War II wealth was channelled in ways that were largely responsible for the general middle-class prosperity of the time; a prosperity that, at least in form, made the nuclear family seem like a working equation.

Where are we today? Sociologically the question can be posed a couple of different ways. When we speak of a "crisis" are we referring to a breakdown in the traditional family form or to the inability of families, however defined, to meet the functions associated with the family unit? Social statistics used to indicate the stability of the form of the nuclear family yield a complex picture. Rates of marriage and childbirth are up since the 1970s, but so are divorce rates. This could mean simply that more people are getting married (and subsequently divorced), which results in an overall stability rate that is about the same as previous decades. There is some evidence that the rate of divorce in second marriages is actually lower than in previous decades. Does this mean that individuals become better at this complicated relationship the second time around? If so, is this a problem?

Developmental psychologists and social workers disagree on the extent to which divorce creates long-term problems and disadvantages for children. They do agree, however, that a fundamental feature in healthy child development (as measured by self-esteem, success in school, general coping skills) is an environment in which the child feels secure and loved. In many cases, particularly those involving abuse, divorce is the better option for the child. What about the increase in the number of women in the labor force? What are the consequences for the children of single-parent and/or dual-income households? These same experts also disagree on whether or not day care is a problem or an opportunity for children. The consequences of day care are part of a web of circumstances that include both the source and quality of the day care and the quality of time at home. There is no direct evidence that children who stay at home during their preschool years are better off than children who are in day care. There is some research that indicates that if the child does not live in a neighborhood with easy access to contact with other children, then day care may actually enable the development of some skills.

A Crisis of Disillusionment: Changes in the Family Form Versus Function

Upon examination, it's not at all clear that the overall stability of the nuclear family has changed much. Why the sense of "crisis" then? Part of this may stem from a heightened emphasis on single parents and working mothers. There have always been single parents and working mothers, but this fact does not mesh with the middle-class myth. It may be that much of the crisis regarding the nuclear family *form* is actually a crisis of disillusionment rather than a reflection of a lack of interest in building and maintaining family units.

One of the most fascinating contemporary debates regarding the perpetuation of the traditional nuclear family form involves gay marriage. The movement among lesbians and gays who seek the right to marry legally and be recognized as joint parents actually reaffirms the traditional marital unit. With the exception of a lack of gendered differences between the would-be spouses/parents, lesbians and gays who seek these rights meet every definitional criterion commonly associated with "family." And the argument that a homosexual couple can't biologically reproduce doesn't negate these similarities in form. Many heterosexual couples do not have the capacity to reproduce biologically and yet they are still considered full-fledged families in a legal and social sense. Obviously the recent spate of hate and antipathy toward the idea of gay marriage is about something other than a defense of the traditional family form. Yet the argument against this commonly made among antigay groups is that gays and lesbian are making a mockery of the traditional form. The irony is that in seeking to participate in the same type of relationship, homosexuals are actually endorsing and bolstering this family form.

In comparison, another group often targeted for moral derision as responsible for the breakdown of the traditional family form is single and working mothers. If the accusation centers solely on a traditional division of household/market labor, then it is true that these women are wreaking havoc with the form. Is this a bad thing? Many observers, most notably feminists, civil rights activists and even several major religious denominations, interpret this shift in the family form as a sign of progress. A movement away from a patriarchal form that has undervalued domestic labor and kept women comparatively disadvantaged in both the home and public life is championed as a good thing. According to this point of view, these shifts in the nuclear family form expose and address some of the irreconcilable tensions in the traditional family functions.

For instance, one of the presumed tenets of "happy family life" is the family as a site where one is encouraged to develop individual awareness and talents. The modern nuclear family, as opposed to traditional extended families, has had the effect of isolating adult women from one another in their domestic roles. The relative lack of contact with opportunities for self-improvement and self-worth can be seen as a cost that the wife/mother paid in this family structure. This equation reflects a tension in our culture regarding the extent to which an individual's worth (and subsequent control over her or his life) is measured in accordance with earning power. A man who is highly educated and capable of securing a well-paying job may be socially ridiculed if he chooses to be a stay-at-home dad, but he still has the choice of working. A woman who has not been able to educate and market herself does not have the same choice. Thus the traditional family form puts her in a relatively more vulnerable position should she lose her husband through death or divorce. This paradox is revealed by those who use "family values" rhetoric to vilify women who seek education and an enhancement of their working options. These women are accused of being "selfish" for cheating on their obligations as mothers. Yet the same rhetoric is used to vilify mothers who require assistance because they are underskilled and single. Such women are accused of "cheating the system." A very peculiar catch-22.

This rhetoric raises questions about the value of the family (vs. "family values"). Ideally, what are the functions of the family in American society? Do we really want the family to be an economic, moral and emotional center? If so, for whom? And in what form? What collective economic and social resources are we willing to devote to this project? These questions require a realistic look at the different forms that family can take and consideration of ways in which these "havens" can be supported more generally.

What Is a Family? Who Is It For?

Some families fulfill the functions but not the form. To get students to critique their own perceptions of the contemporary family, I ask them to consider alternative family arrangements and groups that meet some of the functions but don't necessarily look like the traditional nuclear family. It turns out that we can name a number of groups that meet all of the functions with the exception of biological reproduction. One example is lesbian and gay families. Most of my students know of one or more such family and are quick to note that with the exception of gendered differences in the couple and the ability to reproduce biologically, this arrangement fulfills all the functions and closely approximates the form. I teach in a Jesuit university. Several students point out that the Jesuit community meets all the functions with the exception of biological reproduction. The Jesuit members of the university share a residence together (on most Jesuit campuses this is a separate house built explicitly for this purpose), they share cars and other resources, they eat most of their meals together, they have pledged vows of love and support to one another. In short, they function very much like a family, as we have defined the functions, rather than a group of like-minded fellows who just happen to live together. Nuns are another example.

I ask the students to interview members of these "alternative families." Based on these interviews the students state that the individuals who are in these arrangements do think of themselves as being in a "family." The Jesuits, for instance, share experiences that reflect similar struggles. Sometimes some of the younger Jesuits don't want to share the common residence; the group worries continually about maintaining its numbers (a matter of reproduction). According to the student interviews, persons in these alternative arrangements also articulate the ways in which outside observers think that the different arrangements might be a problem for the individuals involved. One nun noted that people often feel compelled to express concern that she does not have "a husband and children of your own." "What these well-meaning people don't seem to understand," she responds, "is that I have an entire sisterhood with whom to share love, travel, day-to-day chores and a belief and devotion to God's work that unites us. I feel very fortunate." Members of gay and lesbian families report that what is most difficult for them as families is the stigma that they experience and the obstacles that they encounter. One student interviewed a gay man who said,

> I was raised in a loving family, we got together for all the holidays, helped each other out with problems. . . . I'm trying to do the same thing in my family now. My partner has adopted my children. We have college funds for them. We go to grandma's house and to Disneyland. Sheesh, we're as boring as the Cleavers. But it seems like somebody's always out to get us. My advice is for those folks to stop harassing us and go fix whatever is wrong in their own families.

During a discussion in class a young man who had been raised by a lesbian couple recalled his experiences growing up.

> The biggest problem was that people didn't know what to make of us. Me and my sister and my two moms. Some kids thought that my aunt lived with us. When I tried to tell them that they were both my moms some of the kids just thought I was stupid, but others thought it was kind of neat. What they bugged me about was not having a dad. They always wanted to know what happened to my dad and I'd tell them I just didn't have one. Sometimes they'd pick on me for this. They picked on another kid—called him names—for not having a dad. They'd call his mother a whore and make him cry. I'm really proud of my family now and I don't feel like I missed out on anything by not having a dad around. I don't see why people get so bent out of shape about the dad thing. I mean, if you have one, and he's good to you, great. But is it really so necessary?

I once had a student who was a member of a "polyamorous" collective. The group consisted of a web of connections among heterosexual adults who shared vows of commitment, held all their resources in common, and restricted their sexual intimacy to other opposite sex members of the group. Children in the group were raised with the idea of a common parentage—all the adults in the group were their parents. Every six months members rotated tasks such as child care, cleaning, cooking, and even paid labor. According to the student, the group's intent was to redefine the traditional split between paid and household labor, and nuclear patriarchal monogamy. The group had been in existence for 11 years with five of its original members. Other students in the class peppered the young man with questions, particularly about legal parenthood. He explained that legal custody of the children was assigned to their birth mother. No father was designated. This seemed to bother many students who continued to ask, "But who is the dad?" We all are, insisted the young man. Many of his fellow students were not satisfied with this answer.

One of our most lively class discussions always occurs following a videotaped interview with a woman who is the founder of a local group called "The Sisterhood." The Sisterhood is composed of a group of women, most of them women of color, and their children. Several of the women in the group, including the founder, work for an escort service. The intent of the group is to bring together single mothers and their children to share financial resources, child care, household tasks and emotional and professional support. Many Sisterhood women would otherwise require welfare assistance to support themselves and their children. The money from the escort service enables them to live as an extended family with a division of labor that allows some of these women, who would otherwise be employed in low-skill, low-pay jobs, to take care of the household and the children. As the founder puts it, "We aim to take care of our women, to make them strong women and to support them. Ain't nobody else going to do it for us. We're doing it ourselves. And doing a real good job of it."

Many students in the class don't know what to make of this arrangement. The video footage shows children who are well-groomed, polite, healthy and apparently happy. They appear to live in a stable environment, which is a change for many of them, who have spent much of their young lives in shelters or on the streets. Some of the students state flatly that in terms of the family functions, this arrangement is no different than the nuns, with the exception of the fact that some of the money for the household is generated through sex work. Other students object strenuously to the implied connection between childrearing and sex work. It just can't be a good thing, they insist. The discussion often ends at an impasse. Students who take a functional approach argue that these women are not only providing all the functions of family, but they are saving taxpayers money by providing a working alternative to welfare. Students who disagree persist in making the case that The Sisterhood defiles many of the virtues that we associate with the family.

For me, this class discussion reflects a general paradox of the family. This paradox can be stated in terms of what it is we really value as a society: the conservation of a particular family form—the patriarchal nuclear family, or the enhancement of arrangements that fulfill the functions associated with "family." Careful analysis reveals that the traditional family form—the "model" American family—is an unusually narrow form of social organization (compared with many cultures) that serves primarily as a foundation for corporate capitalism. This economic mode of production places considerable economic stress on the individual family unit. Economic analyses of the nuclear family unit indicate that it is increasingly unlikely that most Americans could attain the standard of living dictated by this code. To the extent that this form has existed, it has done so in tension with other cherished American ideals, such as the right to self-determination and advancement for all people (women as well as men). And those who have both the means and the inclination to enact this family form gain considerable support in their choices from extended family and community networks. Erosion of community support makes the nuclear family even less viable. This family form does not stand alone.

Despite these difficulties and a somewhat naive perception of what it takes to fulfill the functions of family, many Americans still seek the dream. There is very little evidence to suggest that the dream itself is waning. So why the fuss? Perhaps it is because many of us, in recent decades, have become more critically mindful about the family as a form of organization. It may also be that, in the process of becoming a more truly pluralistic society, we have exposed the fact that the traditional family, even if it were tweaked to be more equitable for all its members, is just not for some people. It's worth wondering why this is such a disturbing discovery. In all societies there are differences in the roles that individuals fulfill. The nuclear family may be the primary social and economic unit of our culture, but this does not mean that everyone must organize their lives accordingly.

Many functions of society would not be well served if everyone were caught up in the demands of family life as traditionally conceived. Several of the artists, scholars and political and religious leaders whom we celebrate were not part of traditional families. It's not that family and other functions—artistic, religious and civic—are necessarily mutually exclusive; it's a question of commitment. Many of our most renowned artists, for instance, have been members of artistic communities that served some of the functions of family without demanding any commitments of the person that might distract from a devotion to art. Certainly these enclaves and groups pose alternatives, but is it really likely they are a cause, a pull that leads young people to throw off a lifetime of socialization and decide to give up the dream of a traditional family? I suspect not. Rather, these enclaves may be havens for those who, for one reason or another, don't have the intentions and/or the means of pursuing the traditional family dream. Is this dream so fragile that we have to stigmatize and vilify those who seek an alternative?

Conclusion

I have endeavored to make the case that the rhetoric of "family values" is a moral code used to label as immoral those whose lives do not resemble the *appearance* of the traditional family form. Persons who preach "family values" tend to blame these "immorals" for a variety of social and economic problems. The rationale for why everyone should comply with the traditional form is based on a loosely reasoned, ill-conceived perception that if the traditional family form is robust, the rest of society will be robust as well. Even if the outcome were desirable, the equation is an inaccurate representation of how families are embedded in larger social and economic contexts. Extended community networks comprise the trunk of the tree in which the family builds its nest; education, jobs, and available housing are among the economic factors that nourish and water the tree and provide necessary materials for the nest. If the nest is crumbling because the tree is shriveling up and branches are falling off, it doesn't make sense to blame the birds.

"Family values" rhetoric has gathered its steam by directing attention to the presumably undesirable and immoral behavior of those who do not fit the mold. As I have noted, in many cases these "alternative families" meet the functions expected of families. So why the stigma? One consequence of stigmatizing alternative family arrangements and blaming the problems of the whole tree on those who don't have the right sort of nest is that it deters us from recognizing the real causes of these problems. We need to scrutinize the factors that contribute to the healthy functioning of families—any sort of family—and critically assess the problems of the traditional form.

As a society, do we wish to protect the form or to promote the functions (which may mean acceptance of alternative forms)? Do we value families, or do we value a particular family form? Family values rhetoric is an endorsement of a particular form (the traditional patriarchy) with no corresponding sensitivity to its problems—oppression of women/ children, economic infeasibility, the perpetuation of "true love" mythology, inattention to details of caring and sacrifice necessary to maintain long-term commitments. Increasingly, these problems reveal gaps in the traditional family as a viable form for achieving expected functions. Persons who preach "family values" are not necessarily those who are trying hardest to understand and to fulfill the functions of the family.

Syndicated columnist John Leo recently berated a series of sociology texts on the family. His tirade centered on the point that these texts do not promote "family values." He interpreted the intent of these texts, which is to examine critically the form and functions of the family, as a threat to the very fabric of the family itself. He called the texts "immoral and irresponsible." I found myself wondering what it means when a national figure such as Leo instructs us that morality is attained by conserving a traditional ideal, like fine china, up on a shelf where it is out of reach of most people and turned so that its flaws cannot be observed. The suggestion that it is irresponsible to take a look at this cultural ideal, to examine its fragilities and question its utilities, struck me as a particularly narrow-minded attempt to conserve a family heirloom that has long since proven to have sprouted leaks and be missing pieces in its pattern. Families are like everyday dishes. They must be able to bounce off the floor without breaking, to maintain their usefulness despite missing a few chunks, to be mixed and matched as the occasion demands.

In her response to "Confused Crazy Mother," Abby seems to recognize that the functions and the expectations of family don't always come in the traditional form. She is also aware of the extent to which we gauge love and the corresponding worth of ourselves and others in accordance with these ideals. She writes:

Dear Mother: Follow your heart and give your son to parents who can provide what you cannot. It would be a generous act of love. I would urge you, however, to give the custodial parents a letter to your son that they can give to him when he begins to question the love of a mother who would "give him away."

7

The Paradox of Value in
the Age of Certainty

Reflections on Max Weber
and Georg Simmel

PARADOX

Modern practices of science have rendered our lives more predictable and certain. Bureaucratic management has contributed to the rise of standardized, presumably fairer practices of employment. Rationality has become the bedrock of good sense and even-headed judgment. What are the consequences of this modern zeitgeist for the human spirit and for social interaction? Several nineteenth century social philosophers recognized a paradox in the growing emphasis on rationality, certainty, and standardization. They observed that these practices would indeed support the rise of middle-class, democratic values, more predictable lives, greater economic production and prosperity. But they also feared that these practices would render our lives meaningless. They lamented the loss of the mystery and poetry that they deemed necessary challenges for human social development. How do people create and sustain meaning and value in an age in which all things can and have been rendered in terms of the same common denominator, money? How do we assess self-worth in a culture in which everything that we do can be evaluated in terms of standardized scales such as grades or income? Are we the equivalent of these scales? In rendering the world more predictable and manageable, have we rendered ourselves absurd?

What does it mean to say that we live in an age of certainty? I was pondering this while listening to a group of students report on court cases in which people have successfully sued a business for some mishap or unpredictable unpleasantness that has befallen them. You're probably familiar with the case of the woman who received compensation from McDonald's for burns that she sustained when she spilled hot coffee in her lap. She was driving with the cup between her legs at the time. More recently, a man sued a concert hall for the mental distress he suffered when a woman entered the men's bathroom while he was using a urinal. He made his plea on the grounds that he was unduly surprised. He did not expect to encounter a woman in the men's room. He was traumatized as a result. Similar cases are being reported all over the country.

Ann Landers has been chronicling many of these cases in her column under the heading, "What Happened to Judicial Wisdom?" What intrigues me about these cases is that they indicate an expectation of risk-free living. People who plan carefully believe that they should enjoy a certainty of circumstances, but sometimes life doesn't go as planned. What is interesting is the apparent belief that when it doesn't, someone or something should be held accountable. Holding a business or corporation accountable for unexpected mishaps contributes to the collective ideal that life should be certain, that the virtuous deserve to be able to take things for granted.

Another thing that interests me about these cases is the assumption that corporate America should carry the authority of certainty. Having done away with God and Nature as the masters of our fate, we now look to these businesses to be the keepers of predictability. Our contemporary lives are shaped by patterns of standardized production and consumption. We expect these routines to be as predictable as possible. If they are not, we feel we have the right to be upset and to complain. Justice consists of restoring certitude. Or at least the signposts for it.

Fortunately, nearly every cup of coffee you purchase now comes with a warning stating clearly that the beverage is hot. This is an assurance that you are playing with fire, so to speak. The signs say, approach with caution. In some cases, however, forewarnings may not be enough to assure risk-free imbibing of dangerous substances. The authorities at Wendy's, for example, have decided no longer to sell hot chocolate. It seems that mostly children drink hot chocolate and one thing that is certain about children is that they are unpredictable in their movements. Therefore, in order to assure a risk-free dining experience at Wendy's, it's simpler all around not to serve hot chocolate.

Modernity as the Age of Certainty

The history of modernity can be summed up as a story about attempts to reduce uncertainty. In the first chapter I suggested that methods of science emerged as a means to find patterns that appeared to be fixed and unchanging. Scholars were interested in discovering "truths" that were "certain." They sought to establish "universal laws" that applied to everyone, everywhere, all the time. If it can be established that the world works with the precision of a clock, and you know how the clock works, then you can predict what it will do, and you can play with the parts. Certain knowledge is the key to *prediction and control*. When something is predictable, risks can be calculated and precautions can be taken—you can reduce the possibility of being surprised by external forces. If you know how something works and can learn to manipulate the process, then you can *control* the process more readily. You can avert danger and risks through control of forces. This is what modern scientists sought to do.

Science promised certain knowledge if we followed precise rules of deduction and rigorously systematic methods of observation. This works. We have reduced many of the mysteries of nature to known, predictable patterns. Mastery of the methods of science has enabled us to render certain what once seemed to be capricious and daunting forces. Through technology, we have harnessed these forces into the service of human life. Our certain knowledge has been cumulative. We know a lot. We are the information age. Yet at the same time many observers characterize us as a culture short on wisdom, a culture of absurdity, a people who, for all our facts, lack a means of ascertaining the relative value of things. We are a culture in which designer clothing labels and the ability to accessorize signifies individual worth. A culture in which various media represent the emotional tenor of a bad hair day and the death of a loved one on the same scale. We also know this, which makes us a culture of cynics.

What are the implications of an Age of Certainty for questions of value and morality? How do we determine what something is worth, and whether certain ways of being are more or less worthwhile? These questions have always occupied human societies. They have become the basis for much debate and consternation in recent decades as it has become apparent that "certainty" is achieved through "standardization" —a process can be controlled, or made certain, by making the procedures of operation as standard as possible. When the procedures are standardized, the outcome should be the same in every case. A cookie cutter makes cookies that will be the same in size, shape and taste. You can predict what your cookie will look and taste like every time, but is "quality" the equivalent of "sameness" or predictability? How do we figure out the relative worth of something when everything is the same?

The Problem of Determining Value

How do you gauge whether you like something? When presented with a choice, how do you determine the "best" course of action? How do you know when you have done a good job or performed well at some task? How do societies determine which actions are moral and which activities are worthwhile? Why are some things considered "art" and others "trash"? I conceived this chapter when I was asked to give a talk for a series called The Touchstone Lectures. Questions of value seem an especially fitting topic for such a series. A touchstone originally referred to a type of quartz or jasper that could be rubbed against other stones to determine the presence of gold or silver. Does the touchstone then determine worth, or merely indicate the presence of something considered to be valuable? A thermometer will give an accurate reading of the temperature, but does this reveal the quality of the temperature? Is 70 degrees hot or cold; comfortable or uncomfortable? Precious metals and air comfort are a matter of definition and consensus about value. In whom or what do we bestow the authority of defining value?

Herein lies the rub for the age of certainty: we expect science to expose the mysteries of nature, we expect industry to harness and exploit these discoveries, we expect corporate organizations to put the end products within an affordable, predictable reach and we expect legal systems to guarantee that we are indeed in control, but we don't really believe that these agents of production and predictability are the producers of *genuine* truths about what is good and worthwhile. Paradoxically, we have welcomed these agents of control as replacements for God/Nature as the keepers of fate, but we disavow them genuine authority as keepers of value. Wall Street has the authority to set the terms of production and exchange; Madison Avenue dresses our products up for us and induces us to participate in the ritual of consumption. And we do participate. But if the many who have chronicled the "crises of contemporary alienation" are to be believed, we don't, in our hearts, really consider these sources of production to be authentic purveyors of meaning and value.

Is the loss of meaningful value a cost of certainty? Adam Smith was an eighteenth-century Scottish Moral Philosopher who is credited with many of the ideas that came to be known as the capitalist market system. In his book *The Wealth of Nations* (1776), Smith sets forth the "laws" of interdependence, individual self-interest, supply and demand and a division of labor as the elements of a self-regulating system of economics. Such a system requires minimal governmental direction because the laws of supply and demand will act as an "invisible hand" to regulate exchange between persons. Smith envisioned this system as the most expressive of human interests and the least likely to lead to oppressive tyrannies.

Smith addressed the question of value this way. He had an interest in apples. Or at least, he was interested in the worth of apples. How do you know what your apples are worth, he asks? One way is to ask others what they think of the apple. Value determined this way is a function of *reflected appraisal,* something that is assigned by another. Reflected appraisals are unique expressions of interest—someone might exclaim, "Oh, that apple is a lovely shade of crimson. My favorite color." Someone else might remark, "Apples give me gas." These idiosyncratic appraisals reflect *personal* value, but does this information help you figure out the *general* value of the apple? Suppose the person who made the second statement is the king. Does his opinion carry more weight than the other person's? If so, then *general* value is a function of a high-status individual's *personal* system of value. Recall the ire of broccoli growers when former President Bush casually commented that he disliked broccoli. More recently, Oprah was put on trial for commenting that she would not want to eat beef after she had learned about some of the ways in which cattle are raised and slaughtered. Individuals are entitled to their opinions, but when the individual is highly visible and respected, her or his opinion may become the basis upon which others determine the value of something. In such cases, the worth of an object is a function of the *authority* of the individuals assessing the worth.

Adam Smith, like other Moral Philosophers of his day, hoped to establish systems of valuation that were not based on the personal opinions of those in positions of authority. This form of valuation was considered subjective and arbitrary. The Moral Philosophers sought to establish a basis of valuation that would *transcend* arbitrary individual opinion. They wanted a more standard means of determining value. Smith suggested that this could be ascertained by taking your apples to market and seeing what price they fetch. This is a form of reflected appraisal whereby a standard medium, money, is used as a determining basis of *comparative* value. I may like apples, but I may prefer oranges today. Thus, when the vendor barters with me, I may be willing to pay more for an orange than an apple. This form of reflected appraisal involves a process of *external objectification* of that which is being offered. Whatever intrinsic value the apple may have for various individuals remains unknown. The only thing that can be ascertained objectively is what one is willing to offer for the apple and what the other is willing to accept. If the medium of this exchange is assigned standard value, then it becomes possible to compare not only apples, but apples and oranges. The unique qualities of apples and oranges are transcribed into a standard unit that renders them comparable—but only on that dimension. The dimension in this case is price. If people are paying $1.50 a pound for oranges and $1.00 a pound for apples, then we can say *with certainty* that apples cost less than oranges. But what does this tell us about the quality of each?

Adam Smith envisioned a Wonderful World of specialized mass production driven by cheerful competition, a world in which quality would be high, prices would be low and everyone would be able to wear socks. Smith's primary obsession was the possibility of a moral society based on individual self-interest. He proposed that the average human had an enduring awareness of her own tastes and values as well as specific talents and goods to offer society. If others were willing to pay for whatever someone had to offer, then it could be assumed that the tastes reflected a general good, an emergent morality based on common interest. The conjunction of common desires and the ability to realize these desires made the outcome rightfully good. This basis of determining value took shape as the philosophy of libertarian democracy. According to this philosophy, social value is reflected in whether or not there is a market for a good or service. If persons are willing to pay for spices imported from other countries, it can be concluded that the spices have a market worth. If persons are willing to pay for sexual services, the services must be worthwhile. If persons are willing to pay more for the sexual services than for the spices, the services are considered *more* valuable than the spices. Social morality, in accordance with libertarian philosophy, is a function of market worth.

Much ink has been spilled over the morality of the market system as a basis for determining value. This debate takes the form of libertarian versus traditionalist arguments. The former believe that market dynamics should be the sole determinants of value, the latter insist that there are bases, such as tradition, interpretations of God's will, and so forth, for determining value. Libertarians accuse traditionalists of basing claims of value in arbitrary forces. Traditionalists accuse libertarians of being "morally bankrupt."

Regarding the libertarian-traditionalist debate, however, it should be noted that when Adam Smith and other libertarians were initially working out their philosophies, they were doing so within a system that took everyday morality based on Christian ethics for granted. Many scholars are convinced that when Smith and other Moral Philosophers suggested that the market was the "fairest" way to determine value, they meant, more fair than the arbitrary whims of traditional governing bodies, such as the monarch. They did not mean the system to be a replacement for the Christian ethical system of the time. Contemporary libertarians and traditionalists are arguing about what the best basis of value and morality is during an age in which there is no common agreement about what it *should* be. When Smith envisioned how the market would work, he took for granted the fact that all around him there was a relatively common basis of value already in place. My interest is in the consequences of the "market system" as it has displaced any common basis for determining worth. This displacement is referred to by many observers as the "crisis of the modern age."

The Dismal Philosophers. By the nineteenth century, many observers of the early manifestations of market production were critical of Smith's giddy optimism. These *prophets of doom,* as they came to be known, foresaw the market forces as a monster of our own creation; a monster that would overwhelm us, alienate us from our own essential creativity, and imprison us in a cage of our own making. The darkest of these predictions was that we would become unaware of our imprisonment. Or, if we were aware, we wouldn't care—not because we would become entirely uncaring, but because we would no longer know what to care about. We would lose our faith in the manifestations of our own desires, passions and intuitions as a touchstone of meaning and value.

In this chapter I trace some of the implications of these dismal philosophies. I focus on the writings of Max Weber (1864-1920) and Georg Simmel (1858-1918) in particular. Both of these men were German social philosophers living and writing at the end of the nineteenth century. They were well aware of and undoubtedly influenced by images such as Frankenstein's monster and Marx's spectre of capitalism. These images were widely told tales of caution. My main interest here is the visions of Weber and Simmel regarding the implications of these forces of production for the individual human spirit: what they portend about our ability to realize self-worth and to determine what we value.

This is a story about *transcription: the transcription of quality into quantity.* What these social philosophers feared was not this process itself. They viewed this process as an inevitable outcome of formal rationality and market capitalism. Their lament was the increasing inability of future generations to determine quality in any way except with reference to standard scales. Such measures provide only information about comparative worth in a competitive, hierarchical system. The so-called crisis of the modern age, the alienation experienced by the walking wounded, is not a consequence of the market system, per se. It is a reflection of the fact that we are short on ways to assess worth, and to hold onto it, independent of market mechanisms. This lack of anchors of meaning has cast us adrift in a sea of absurdity.

Standardization and Its Costs:
The Erosion of Passion and Subjective Value

In a world of increasing rationality and standardization, what will we rely on as a touchstone of meaning and worth? This is the question that haunted Max Weber. His outlook was grim. Weber characterized the modern age not only in terms of mechanization and a corresponding capitalist mode of production, but with regard to what he called a *mode of orientation,* a way of being and seeing that would shape both organizations and individuals. He called the mode of orientation particular to modernity, *Formal Rationality.* Formal rationality is distinguished from a traditional mode of orientation in its emphasis on rational means and rational ends as a basis for organization and judgment. Bridge building is an example. The decision to build a bridge is presumably a rational goal; the bridge will serve a practical purpose. The means for constructing a bridge are determined in accordance with the principles of efficiency and effectiveness; the most rational approach is the one that will be the most effective for the least cost. An assessment of the quality of the bridge is a simple matter of calculating whether or not the goal was effectively attained with the most cost-efficient means. Architectural style and the artistic quality of the construction are secondary matters in a system of formal rationality, if they matter at all.

Weber contrasts this form of organization with a traditional mode whereby neither means nor ends are necessarily rational. Ceremonial ends and ritualistic means are the hallmarks of tradition. Quality is in the continual reenactment of the traditional form; authority is passed from one generation to the next without regard for purpose or outcome, so long as the ritual meaning is maintained. Prerational artisan guilds were more interested in aesthetics than in the practical production of goods. A craftsmaster was an artist who took as much time as was necessary to create an item that reflected the qualities and traditions of the guild. Following the rituals of traditional production was much more important during the time of the guilds than just turning out a product. Individuals in a traditional mode of orientation organize themselves and their activities in response to what Weber called an "eternal yesterday."

Products made by certain guilds were highly prized as objects of art. Socks, another of Smith's examples, were carefully stitched using only the finest silks and time-honored methods. The result was a beautiful sock. The value of the sock was in the tradition in which it had been made. Because only a few socks could be made in this manner, they were extremely valuable and very expensive. Hence, most people did not wear socks. Deviation from time-honored methods was grounds for punishment. Weber notes a historical reference to a group of button-makers who were fined by their guild for innovating. In a moment of brash rationality, they had responded to a scarcity of mussel shells, the traditional material for buttons, by using cloth. They were successful in producing a new sort of button, but the guild's masters greeted this innovation with stern disapproval. They had violated the laws of tradition that governed the guilds.

For Enlightenment philosophers, traditional modes of authority were arbitrary and often tyrannical. Formal rationality replaces arbitrary rules with purposeful procedures; individual performance is assessed in terms of the ability to master these procedures and produce desired ends. Once an effective means to an end has been ascertained, it is codified into a set of standard operations that can be broken down into specialized tasks—a division of labor that enables mastery at each level of production and simultaneously enables greater output. Efficiency and calculability—the ability to quantify inputs and outputs—are the hallmarks of rational organization. Standardized procedures and easily measured units of operation imbue the process with predictability and control.

The assembly line was the ultimate realization of this combination of a specialized division of labor and rational principles of manufacture. Two noteworthy outcomes of this process were (1) *mass production*—which for people who cannot afford socks from traditional guilds' crafters is a good thing, and (2) *standard evaluation*. Standard evaluation was considered a progressive administrative form—in theory, individuals are rewarded according to their ability to perform specialized tasks effectively as dictated by standard, codified procedures. This mode of orientation was considered progressive because it invested control and fate in the inclinations and performance of the individual. Standard rules and procedures are impervious to individual traits and qualities. Together, these two outcomes were considered beneficial in that they were largely responsible for the rise and proliferation of the middle class. Mass production of goods and services drives prices down and makes more goods available to a larger segment of the population, thus raising the standard of living for many people. Standard rules of evaluation reward individual skill rather than traditional birth status. By mastering standard rules, anyone has a chance at being promoted.

The Iron Cage of Rationality

Despite this presumably progressive advance in both legal and administrative procedures, Weber brooded about two problematic outcomes that he considered endemic to rational bureaucracy. One is goal displacement, the other is dehumanization.

Goal Displacement. People are not rational by nature, Weber cautions. Rules and procedures, once written down, performed repeatedly and used as a basis of evaluation and advancement, take on a life of their own. They become routines, traditions. People tend to forget the original goal and become attached instead to the means. Ellen Langer, a psychologist who studies routinized habits of mind that result in mindlessness, provides an entertaining example of goal displacement through routinization:

> One day a woman was about to cook a roast. Before putting it in the pot she cut off a small slice. When asked why she did this she paused, became a little embarrassed, and said that she did it because her mother had always done the same thing when she cooked a roast. Her own curiosity aroused, she telephoned her mother to ask why she always cut off a slice before cooking her roast. The mother's answer was the same: "Because that's the way my mother did it." Finally, in need of a more helpful answer, she asked her grandmother why she always cut off a little slice before cooking the roast. Without hesitating, her grandmother replied, "Because that's the only way it would fit in my pot." (Langer 1989:43-4)

This is a somewhat innocuous illustration, but this process of routinization can have grave consequences for groups and organizations that displace their original goals. Many such organizations direct energy into supporting and defending the means, whether or not the original goal has been attained or even needs to be attained. One particularly troubling aspect of this process is that persons may be evaluated in terms of their consistent enactment of the routine. The routine itself displaces the original goal as the act of significance. Anyone who works in a food service industry where people are required to tell every customer the special of the day or to offer them fries and pies even when it is obvious that the customer is not interested, knows how tedious required routinization can be.

This process can be especially frustrating when one is required to sacrifice personal judgment to the routine. While I was writing this chapter, the residents of one of the small islands that dot the region around Seattle became incensed when ferry dock workers refused to grant "priority loading" to a woman who was returning from the hospital to die following unsuccessful brain surgery. Car lines for the ferries that are the only means of transportation through the islands are sometimes several hours long during tourist season. The State Ferry system enforces a strict policy of "first come, first served." The husband of the dying woman presented a doctor's letter to the employee at the ferry gate. The employee refused to grant a priority loading. The husband pleaded and asked to speak with a supervisor, who also denied the request. Other persons volunteered to trade their places in line for the woman, but ferry workers insisted that this would disrupt the flow of traffic and create additional problems. The bottom line was that standard procedures had to be followed. "We can't make judgments about priority loading on an individual basis or else everyone would have some excuse," a ferry worker was quoted as saying. As a result, the woman, who had only a few hours left to live, spent three hours lying in the back of a van on a crowded ferry dock.

In response to public outrage at this apparent excess of bureaucracy, Washington State Ferry officials have apologized and suggested that sometimes employees need to exercise compassion rather than enforce the rules. The problem, one that the ferry system workers seem aware of, is that the employees have a difficult time determining which is more important, compassion for a single individual, or rules that are supposed to serve everyone more fairly? In response, the ferry system is going to conduct classes for employees on being "compassionate." This is the intellectual alienation that Weber was concerned with. Individual workers are encouraged to enforce the rules, regardless of context. They are supposed to follow the routine. In doing so, they may lose the ability to use creativity, insight, experience and compassion to assess specific circumstances.

Dehumanization. How do you become the best that you can be in a rational-bureaucratic system? By becoming a master of standard procedures and never deviating from the form. The best worker, leader or judge in a rational-bureaucratic system is the one whose behavior is the most consistent with rules, the one least likely to be influenced by parochial interests and irrational urges, someone who is not subject to idiosyncratic ticks. The ferry worker who is able to follow procedure unprovoked by specific circumstances. Creativity has no place on an assembly line; innovation throws a wrench in the gears and stops the machine from humming efficiently. Emotion, superstition and preconceived ideas cloud rational assessment by causing one, if only for a flicker of a moment, to focus on particulars rather than general standards.

The most effective workers in the rational-bureaucratic machine are those whose behavior most resembles a cog. The heroes in this system are those who have pushed back passion, driven emotion aside and replaced the wonder of speculation with an ability to calculate certainties. Recall Spock from the original *Star Trek*. He was the embodiment of the fully rational, disempassioned being. Unencumbered by emotion, his evaluations were considered superior to the urges and instincts of his less advanced colleagues. In such a system, Weber warned, persons become intellectually and emotionally alienated. Required as they are to put aside individual consideration in favor of carrying out the routines, they find themselves increasingly without a sense of involvement or investment in the process. This, he states, is dehumanizing.

Some may be frustrated with the potential irrationality of rational systems, particularly if they feel that they are required to engage in meaningless codified routines in order to satisfy employers—another group just doing their job. Ultimately, such processes crush the human spirit. More worrisome still for Weber was the possibility that over time we would begin to take the routines for granted, to cease to question the purpose at all. In effect, we would lose our wit, living out our lives spiritless and purposeless in a cage of our own construction.

The tendency to routinize patterns of activity, especially in bureaucratic production, is antithetical to mindful, purposeful reason. For Weber, the bureaucratic machine becomes an unwieldy dinosaur that sucks up resources with no particular purpose except to keep on in its routine. In this regard, he cautions, rational procedures have the potential to become irrational routines. These routines could be likened to previous traditions with the ironic exception that in the case of routinization of standard procedures, even the original meaning is lost. The nightmare, for Weber, was that in the absence of traditional meaning, and having forgotten the intended goals of rational procedures, we might blindly turn to worship the routines. Various recipes intended as a means to achieving a rational end might become calcified as ideologies in themselves.

If you think that Weber may be exaggerating in his concerns, ask your teachers why they give exams and see how many of them answer in a way that is a defense of exam giving (e.g., "It's part of the process" or "This is how it's done") rather than a statement of mindful purpose. You might also consider some of your own practices that you seek to perpetuate and defend without really knowing why or what alternatives might exist. The question is not just, "Are we in a rut," but, "To what extent have we come to worship and defend the ruts just because they are familiar?" *Value* becomes the equivalent of *familiar* and *predictable*. Standard rules and procedures are "good" because they yield certain results. Regardless of what the actual results are, as long as they are familiar, then they are not too demanding, emotionally or intellectually. In this way, we become increasingly disengaged from the process and from one another. Did the ferry worker see a dying woman or just another car that needed to be loaded efficiently and without further hassle?

I think about the tendency toward goal displacement whenever I am interacting with a clerk in a bank or a business. It is often the case that if I ask the clerk why he is following a certain procedure, he cannot tell me. Or at least he cannot tell me what the presumed outcome of the procedure is supposed to be. Instead, he'll reply: It's just the rules. I don't really think of this as the fault of the clerk. It's likely that he was initially instructed to follow a particular routine and never told the intended reasons for the rule. This same reaction comes up when I'm working with graduate students in sociology who are learning to teach. I ask the would-be instructors: What is the purpose of exams? Initially there is a sort of stunned silence as they ponder what is a seemingly obvious question—there are always exams in college. Eventually, however, we end up in a lively debate as they begin to reconstruct the reasons for giving an exam—providing a study incentive, giving the students an opportunity to demonstrate knowledge, and providing feedback for the instructor on whether students are learning or not, to name a few possibilities. Each of these reasons is a distinct goal that implies a different type of means—a different exam in each case. In some cases, depending on the instructor's goal, an exam may not be the best means. The point, from the perspective of useful rationality, is to remain mindful of one's purpose and to construct means accordingly. In Weber's words, this state of being requires both "passion and perspective."

Discussion of the value of a line of action is meaningless if no particular purpose or motivation for the action can be identified. The attempt to chart standards and certain rules of operation and assessment are not bad in and of themselves. Compared with the injustices of arbitrary rule or the wasted energies of reinventing the wheel, such standards support democratic meritocracies and progressive creation. What Weber brooded about was the possibility that we would forget the ends, cease to question our purposes, discontinue our journeys into the unknown in favor of settling in to maintain the means. Safeguarding the rules and conserving certainty would take precedent over exploration and creativity. Not only would the original thrill be gone, but this standardized routinization would result in an emotional and intellectual alienation that would, according to Weber's view, become entirely dehumanizing. The main motivation for preserving the rules would become familiarity and freedom from hassle—an avoidance of any sort of intellectual and emotional engagement.

For Weber, the costs of standardized reason are a sense of mystery and faith, a loss of enchantment and wonderment, and the erosion of the passion and drive that he considered the touchstones of humanity. Disenchantment is the companion of certainty. Certainty crushes the exploratory nature that is a hallmark of the human spirit. Is this the path to *advanced* civilization, Weber mused? At the end of his famous work, *The Protestant Ethic and the Spirit of Capitalism,* he writes, "for this stage of cultural development it might truly be said: specialists without spirit, sensualists without heart; this nullity imagines that it has attained a level of civilization never before achieved." For Weber, the so-called Age of Enlightenment had actually led us into a "polar night of icy darkness." Formal rationality was an *iron cage* from which there could be no escape. A cage of our own making.

Weber's biographers tell us that he was the son of a fervently religious mother and a father who was a proud, strict man with political aspirations in bourgeois Berlin. The story is told that early in his training as a scholar, Weber was instructed to abandon his passion for fencing. Like other young gentleman of Berlin, Weber enjoyed bouts with the sword. It is said that he loved the thrill of the challenge and the unpredictability of the encounter. He was inclined to spend long hours practicing. It might be said that he was spending much energy pursuing an irrational goal. Weber eventually bowed to the instructions of the elder, eminent scholars whom he wished to emulate. He put aside his sword and turned to a life of highly disciplined scholarship. His productivity was rewarded with prestigious academic appointments and civic respect. A contemporary of romantics such as Rilke, Wagner and Nietzsche, Weber suffered acute bouts of depression while wrestling the contradictions inherent in his own visions of modernity. He suffered his inability to reconcile the potential of the democratic machine with its costs, routine and discipline at the price of passion and creativity. His words were prophetic. Weber's very existence is the harbinger of the modern crisis of alienation, a crisis reflected in the tensions that prompted Nietzsche's quip: "People need play and danger. Civilization gives them work and safety." Weber eventually succumbed to a debilitating depression. He died in 1920 at the age of 56. According to his wife, Marianne Weber, he died in the grip of madness. I wonder now and then if this was the only way he knew to fly out of his cage.

Certain Measures of Worth: Time and Money

A contemporary sociologist, George Ritzer, has written a book in which he describes some of the current manifestations of formal rationality. The title, *The McDonaldization of Society,* is evocative of his thesis. Beginning with the time-motion studies of organizational consultants such as Frederick Taylor, businesses moved increasingly to rationalize production through assembly-line procedures. The best businesses were those that garnered the most profit. Profit is ascertained by subtracting the cost of inputs (time and materials) from outputs (finished products). In order to compare them, inputs and outputs must all be reduced to the same scale—money. The most efficient businesses are those that can reduce every part of the production process to a countable form and then speed it along—maximum output with minimum input. The auto assembly line became the ultimate model of this process.

Ritzer's book is packed with observations of contemporary assembly-line life. According to Ritzer, we have come to expect this routinized predictability in all aspects of our lives. We go to McDonald's because the experience is absolutely predictable no matter where we are. We can expect the same food in a clean, sterile, mildly stimulating environment. In other words, we expect risk-free eating. The "McDonald's standard" has become a sort of touchstone for all features of contemporary life, according to Ritzer's observations. We now have "McDonaldized" forms of health care, education, child care and so forth. When our experience with a service provider is not quick, efficient and relatively predictable, we feel we have the right to complain. It is a paradox that we demand certain, risk-free routines but simultaneously consider unique, personalized service as a basis for quality. We may long for the "old-fashioned" experience of the ma-and-pa grocery, the country doctor, or the old burger and malt stand. There is a tendency to imbue these enterprises with a sort of nostalgia that we equate with quality. When we happen upon such a place, we may congratulate ourselves on having stepped out of the routine and cherish the experience because it was extraordinary. Yet we may be simultaneously disinclined to pay the relatively higher prices and spend the extra time and energy that are the costs of patronizing such businesses.

Rationalized systems emphasize time and cost as measures of effective production. All production systems must be organized primarily in terms of a minimum inputs/maximum outputs model if they are to remain competitive. Following the logic of Weber, Ritzer concludes that in a McDonaldized society, time and cost will become the ultimate appraisals of quality. Consider whether you measure the value of an exchange in terms of the time spent and the costs incurred, or in reference to the experience itself. Can you tell the difference? Consider expressions such as "Time wasted is money spent" or "It was worth the time." You realize that it is impossible to give a standardized rating of the experience of eating at your favorite "greasy spoon" with a trip to McDonald's unless you convert the specific qualities of each to statements of time and money. The more insidious dilemma occurs when you come to believe that you cannot assess the quality of either unless you do so with reference to time and money. These standards do indeed yield certain comparative rates, and they even reveal something about your preferences—for example, if you continue to eat at the greasy spoon diner despite the slow, unpredictable service, this indicates that you prefer the place, but why? What do standardized referents such as time and money reveal about the characteristics, the qualitative features of your preferences?

Is It Art or Is It Money? Standardized Exchanges

Let's return to the question of worth. Imagine that a friend has invited you to join him for dinner in a fine restaurant. Together you enjoy a scrumptious meal, attentive service and the delight of expressing shared interests. While you are lingering over coffee, your companion, whom we'll call Boggs, pulls from his knapsack a project that he has been working on. You lean closer and see that he has been sketching a likeness of a hundred dollar bill. Slightly larger than a regular bill, the drawing is exquisitely detailed. Boggs reaches into his pack and this time pulls out a crumpled hundred dollar bill. He smooths it out and props it against his water glass where he scrutinizes it as he makes the final touches on his drawing. Passersby note Boggs at work and stop to comment on his remarkable talent. "Looks just like the real thing," many of them gasp in awe.

The waiter, who has just arrived with the check, remarks in wonder, "What a splendid talent." "I'm glad you think so," Boggs replies. "I intend to use this drawing to pay for my dinner." At this announcement that waiter might begin to fidget and appear distressed. He may be temporarily reassured when Boggs picks up the crumpled hundred dollar bill and continues, "unless you'd rather accept this in exchange for our dinner." At which point, Boggs reads the dinner tab and notes that the cost of the meal, including tip, is eighty-five dollars. "It's your choice," he informs the waiter. You can either have my drawing in exchange for the meal, in which case, I expect you to give me fifteen dollars in change. Or you can have this model that I used to make the drawing." At this last comment he gestures with the hundred dollar bill.

What should the waiter do? What is the basis for evaluation here? How do we determine the relative worth of a drawing of a hundred dollar bill compared with the model used to make the drawing? What sort of touchstone might the waiter rub against each piece of paper in the hope of determining which acquisition will enrich his life more? What will he have if he accepts the drawing?

Perhaps you are wondering if Boggs is famous? Does this information make a difference in your deliberations if you are the waiter? How? Imagine the scenario played out this way. The waiter decides to take the drawing in exchange for Boggs's meal. This means that he will have to put $100 in the till to cover the $85 dinner tab and the $15 in change. A few days later he is contacted by an art dealer. This dealer asks the waiter if he is willing to part with the drawing. The dealer offers him $1,000 for it. "A thousand dollars for a drawing of a hundred dollar bill? How did you know about this drawing?" the waiter asks. "Boggs sold me a clue: his dinner receipt and the change you gave him. I paid him twenty-five hundred dollars for those items," the dealer responds. "You gave him twenty-five hundred dollars in exchange for fifteen dollars and a dinner receipt?" the waiter exclaims in disbelief. "Actually, it was a five and a ten, and he signed each bill," the dealer replies. At this point the waiter might feel a bit out of touch with the hard stone of reality. "I don't get it," he persists. "You gave him twenty-five hundred dollars for a couple of ordinary bills and a restaurant receipt and you're offering me a thousand dollars for a drawing of a hundred dollar bill. Is this some twisted fetish or what?" "He also gave me the hundred dollar bill that he modeled the drawing on" the dealer retorts, matter-of-factly. "Do you want the thousand dollars or not?"

What does the waiter get if he accepts the terms of exchange? He gets one thousand dollars minus the hundred dollars that he put into the restaurant's till to cover Boggs's dinner and change. What does this art dealer get? A couple of months later you could wander into a gallery in New York and find a sold sticker on a framed collage consisting of these items: the original drawing of the hundred dollar bill, the model—which is an ordinary looking hundred dollar bill with Boggs's initials scrawled onto it, a 10- and a five-dollar bill each with Boggs's signature, and a receipt from the restaurant where Boggs and his companion had dinner. The price for this art compilation is listed at $10,000. So what does the dealer get? Ten thousand minus the $2,500 he gave to Boggs and the $1,000 to the waiter. He gets a total of $6,500 and a bill of sale. Who would pay $10,000 for a drawing, a receipt and some ordinary bills? And if they command such a high price, why doesn't Boggs just sell his drawings outright?

The drawings aren't the art, according to Boggs, whose collages of drawings and related items of exchanges are highly prized among collectors. *For Boggs the transaction is art.* I only "spend" my drawings, he says. In addition to dinner, he's exchanged his drawings for household supplies, airline tickets, clothes. Even beer at 7-Eleven. It's a matter of putting people in a situation in which the standard touchstone of exchange is momentarily out of reach. When Boggs offers a drawing of a bill in exchange for a good or service, he pulls the rug of standard exchange out from under us, leaving us spinning in the temporary vertigo. Given a choice between a drawing of money that *may be* worth something, and money that *is* value, we're not sure what to do. There are no guarantees in this instance; no preset standards of worth. It's a leap of faith.

This is the moment that counts for Boggs; the brief vertigo that we experience when we let go of standard forms of assessment and take a leap into the abyss of uncertainty. Compared with the dealers who traffic in his work, he makes relatively little money from his art. "But I get to experience this *vertigo of value,* this moment when someone really has to stop and decide whether something about my drawings is worth suspending the standard transaction where money, more or less of it, makes the value call for you. Plus," he smiles enigmatically, "I got dinner."

Money as the Ultimate Form of Standardization

How do we determine worth? What is the basis of value of a Boggs drawing? Is its worth a function of the monetary sums that it fetches among dealers? Does it represent a sort of savoir faire among collectors—a sign of taste and urbane sensibilities? A fellow artist might scrutinize the strokes, the craft behind the artistic execution. Perhaps some who encounter one of Boggs's drawings just have a feeling about it. Can a Boggs be compared to a Rembrandt or a Basquiat or a Kahlo? What renders these ostensibly distinct achievements comparable? Georg Simmel would say that in the modern age money renders these items, and indeed all things, comparable. *Money is the ultimate achievement in standardization.* In his words: "Money is concerned only with what is common to all: it asks for the exchange value, it reduces all quality and individuality to the question: How much? In a money economy man [sic] is reckoned with a number. . . . Money is the most frightful of levelers."

Simmel's philosophy of money is a complicated meditation on the implications of a money culture for our ability to know what matters to us. Simmel was interested in what he called the "invisible world of cultural laws which mold generations and shape forms of interaction." In his treatise titled *The Philosophy of Money,* he sets forth a description of modern culture as a money culture. He describes forms of interaction that emerge from a money culture and traces the implications of these forms of interaction for our sense of who we are and how we determine what matters. Money, he noted, is the embodiment of the modern spirit of rationality, calculability and impersonality. A money culture fosters an *emphasis on quantity rather than quality;* the worth of anything can be rendered comparable by transcribing it into dollars and cents. Monetary transactions are a sort of alchemy in which the priceless is transformed into a standard unit of worth. In this regard, money has the potential to level the evaluation of all things to a single question, "How much?" For Simmel, money is the absolute enemy of aesthetics. Simmel suggested that money as form of abstract calculation would come to invade all areas of social life, including areas that were previously the domain of qualitative appraisal. Everything and everyone would come to have its price.

Money as an Expression of Cultural Worth. Simmel conceived of social life as an ongoing tension between our experience of ourselves as both creators and products of cultural forms: Cultural forms mold and shape who we are, but also operate as something alien and external to us. The drama of human life, for Simmel, is in the struggle between individual expressions of subjective value and cultural forms of evaluation. Money is a particularly insidious basis of cultural evaluation because it creates a distance between people and the objects of their creation—by assigning independent/objective value—but then also acts as the means to overcome this distance. For Simmel, this is a sort of double form of alienation. We create objects of quality, the worth of which is evaluated by leveling the quality into a quantitative scale based on monetary units; then we must use money as a means to be reunited with these expressions of quality.

The double dilemma of trying to figure out what your own subjective expressions are worth by casting them into an objective venue for appraisal, and having them no longer belong to you, as they become popular, is illustrated in the poet Rainer Maria Rilke's letters to a young poet who wrote him asking advice. Rilke responds:

> You ask me whether your verses are any good. You ask me. You have asked others before this. You send them to magazines. You compare them with other poems, and you are upset when certain editors reject your work. . . . You are looking outside. And this is what you should avoid most right now. (1986:5)

Then, in response to another request from the young poet, Rilke writes:

> [A]s to my own books, I wish I could send you any of them that might give you pleasure. But, I am very poor, and my books, as soon as they are published, no longer belong to me. I can't even afford them myself. (1986:28)

Rilke is saying that the subjective process of creating poetry cannot be judged by anyone other than the person whose experiences give rise to the expression. Giving the poetry over to the public may garner the artist some esteem, as it certainly did for Rilke, but the artist no longer has control over the life of the creation. Including whether it comes back to him.

Simmel predicted that eventually objects-as-quantity would take on a life of their own and we would begin to see ourselves primarily as a reflection of the monetary worth of these objects. Eventually our selfhood will be split into separate domains of production and consumption. Self-worth in the domain of production will be assessed in terms of the price attached to our products; self-worth in consumption is determined by the monetary value of the selections we make. Who you are—your self-worth in the public eye—is determined more or less in terms of your employment status, the monetary worth of your job. Your status is not in what you do in your job, per se, but in the income associated with the job. People around you can assess your worth at a glance by taking notice of your clothing, car and so forth. Brand names signify expensive items and serve as a testament to your "good taste" and cultural status. In short, an arbitrary means of assigning standard worth has become an end in itself. The slogan "money matters" will be a guiding principle of interaction and cultural organization. In such a culture, individual creativity and productivity will be assessed in accordance with market value, and the quality of self-expression will be symbolized in what you buy. Money becomes both the medium and the aspiration. We become our net worth and our ability to accessorize. I recently saw some graffiti scrawled on a sidewalk that sums this up. It read: "You are what you buy. Spend wisely." In this money culture, Simmel warned, we will eventually come to view the relative pricing of apples and oranges as a statement of ultimate worth. The unique differences of apples and oranges won't mean anything.

This is a frighteningly accurate vision. Simmel's personal circumstances reflect the paradoxes that were his muse. Although he was a popular public lecturer who was sought out by patrons of Berlin's fashionable salons, he was unable to inspire interest among his fellow scholars. These men of learning considered Simmel's ideas unnecessarily complex (which is a bit ironic given that German scholarship was not known for its directness or brevity) and his presentations base. He was undervalued as an academician precisely because of his appeal among the middle classes. He was repeatedly passed over for formal appointments—a mark of distinction that he yearned for but simultaneously critiqued in written parodies. It is a fun footnote to history that Simmel has been posthumously moved from the dusty stacks of obscurity to the front shelves of contemporary scholarship. Scholars representing a wide array of disciplines now refer to Simmel as a highly relevant visionary of the postmodern age. By the new standards of the day, he is a master.

Scrambling to Keep Ahead of the Objective Leveling Machine

The heart and chill of Simmel's vision are revealed in a lecture that he delivered to a ladies' club. In this talk he invokes the subject of fashion as an illustration of his thesis of the paradox of cultural objectification. One indication of value in a culture of mass production is that which is novel and unique, Simmel begins. Imagine that you create for yourself a magnificent new hat. Its intrinsic value is known only to you and is a function of your creativity and engagement in the process. This is a subjective expression. Cultural validation of your subjective expression comes in the response of others to your new hat. The highest praise comes in the forms of requests to copy your hat so that others may adorn themselves similarly. It is at this point that your subjective expression of creativity is snatched up into the jaws of mass cultural objectification. Once the hat becomes a cultural object, not only is it no longer yours, but if you wish to distinguish yourself among this crowd who are all wearing the same hat (your hat!) you will have to make yourself a new hat.

This tension between subjective expression and cultural objectification is never ending, according to Simmel. Unique and novel expressions of subjective interest are recognized and rewarded by transforming them into a mass product. In order to share some of this uniqueness, to acquire it as a symbol of savvy that temporarily elevates the consumer above the sea of standardized products, hordes rush in and create a market for the product. The market machinery gobbles up the novel expression, digests it in the gears of assembly-line production and spits it back out in a cookie-cutter form that renders it available for mass consumption.

"Grunge" as a form of fashion is a contemporary example. Several years ago young people in Seattle who considered themselves to be "antiestablishment" wished to express their disinterest in market-driven consumption routines. One of the ways in which these innovative people expressed themselves and their discontent was to refuse brand-name clothing in favor of secondhand merchandise. The fact that their particular style of dress is now nationally known is illustrative of Simmel's paradox of cultural objectification. Famous fashion designers, always on the lookout for novel marketing opportunities, picked up the "grunge" theme—thereby increasing its general cultural value. The look has become mainstream; spin-offs of the secondhand, oversized, sloppy look are now routinely manufactured by companies as diverse as Diesel, Calvin Klein and JC Penney. Urban Outfitters, a chain with stores in major cities across the United States, specializes in the "grunge" look. Business is booming in secondhand stores. The demand for "grunge" has driven up prices so that those who are poor by circumstance rather than disheveled as a fashion statement can no longer afford to shop in these stores. As for the original grungers, what are they going to do to render themselves unique now that their form of expression has become a national trend?

When culture is objectified, Simmel notes, personal taste as a reflection of subjective worth is an illusion; we confuse conspicuous consumption with expression of choice and assume that the choices reveal something about our self-worth. This is particularly ironic in an age in which the selection of the items that we have to choose from is stamped out on the press of efficient production. As Henry Ford was reportedly fond of saying about the production of Model T and Model A cars, "You can have your car any color that you want, as long as it's black." The market system of commodities is driven by standardizing processes that level all subjective expressions to a single common denominator, the value of which is expressed in monetary form. The individual in the modern crowd must race constantly to stay ahead of this leveling machine. In Simmel's words, we will reach a point where we find ourselves screaming just to hear any expressions of subjectivity above the din of the leveling machinery of mass production. For Simmel, the modern age is a system of competitive acquisition and expression driven by comparative evaluations that are based in the most leveling form of assessment—monetary worth.

Simmel's vision may hold a seed of optimism that is missing in Weber. The notion that we are continually struggling to achieve subjective expression and clamoring to stay ahead of the leveling effects of mass production and monetary evaluations of worth suggests a certain liveliness of spirit that is lacking in Weber's morose images of routinization. However, the reward for this sustained struggle against the machine may be the sort of exhaustion to which some attribute the deaths of contemporary figures of distinction such as Kurt Cobain. This "star-making machinery" as Joni Mitchell refers to it, seems to result in either an eventual implosion or in oblivion. The masses will lift you up for your 15 minutes of fame only to trample you in the 16th-minute dash to cash in on your star.

Cashing In on Fame. During a class discussion of Simmel, a student asked if anyone was familiar with the Internet site, Roguemarket.com. Several students chimed in at once to describe the site and reveal their own dealings in this "personality stock market." Roguemarket.com is a stock market of famous personalities. There are several subcategories of fame: sports, pop singers, movie stars, and more. Persons who sign on are given a specified number of playing chips that signify money. Using these chips, they purchase "stock" in a personality. They then monitor the rise and fall of their selected personalities. This rise and fall is determined by the amount of stock purchased by everyone participating in the market. A famous person's worth in this market is a function of how many people buy stock in her or him. I asked the students whom they were investing in. Several mentioned pop figures such as Madonna, or popular pro athletes. Do you invest in these people because you like their performances and what they stand for, culturally, or because you think they are a good market investment? One student mentioned a pro basketball player whom he confessed to loathe, but said he bought stock in the guy because everyone else was doing so, so this made they guy a valuable investment. All in all, students were mixed about whether they were playing to "win" or to "support" someone that they liked.

We considered the juncture between the two gestures. An act of support was a sort of "charity" purchase. For instance, several students indicated that they were buying stock in a local news reporter whose ideas and opinions they valued. "But he's a big loss, stockwise," they admitted. "No one else really knows who he is so you can't say that he's a 'smart' investment." Other students suggested that there was a big difference between who they "liked" in terms of talent, and whom they invested in in terms of predicted pay-offs. Would Simmel have been surprised? I wondered. A couple of points struck me as noteworthy in the description of Roguemarket.com. First, this is sort of a democratization of popularity. In this market, individuals determine the worth of a star based on their individual investments. In the strict sense of the word, this is a more democratic basis for determining popularity than the opinions of those who work as sportscasters and critics of popular culture—usually an elite bunch. The fame of a person is usually determined by a complicated process that includes how much exposure they get in the media, the type of exposure, connections to advertisers and other corporations, and the reputation of the firms that book that person's talent. The relative talents of any given performer are obscured by the complexities of a profit-oriented "star-making machine." In the case of Roguemarket.com, average janes and joes are able to cast their votes.

Which leads to the second point. In this market, any given star's worth is determined by a single common factor—the amount invested in that person by the people playing the stock market. People make their stock choices based on different reasons. Some of these reasons include the estimation that a particular star is simply a good investment. Given this, it's not possible to say that someone's high stock value is an indicator that she or he is considered to be highly talented. As individuals continue to play the market, it is likely that they will increasingly purchase stock in "winning" personalities—those in whom others have already invested a large amount. In this way, worth becomes a sort of self-fulfilling process determined solely by the amount of "stock chips" awarded to various personalities. Listening to the class discussion, I found myself pondering the consequences of a similar way of assessing the worth of college teachers.

Standardized Measures as the Ultimate Authority of Worth

Theologians tell us that certainty leads to idolatry. In the absence of any other criterion of worth, persons idolize that which is familiar. In the quest to render all things known, and having crushed the spirit of exploration, we turn our sights to a worship of that which is known and the means by which all is rendered certain. Money and other standardized forms of evaluation become not only the ultimate leveler, but, ironically, the ultimate idol. I was reminded of this recently when I was asked to assist the chairman of an anthropology department in determining a fair measure to use for evaluating his faculty's teaching performance. I was taken aback when the anthropology professor asked me to help him determine a quantifiable standard for evaluating the teaching of his nontenured faculty. "How many faculty members do you have who will be eligible for tenure in the next five years?" I asked. Three, was the response. I pondered this in amazement. If I understood correctly, he was telling me that over the course of the next five years, he could not gather specific information about how each of these people taught. Or rather, he could conceivably gather such information—he and other senior faculty could attend the junior colleagues' lectures, talk with students, read responses to the open-ended questions on teacher-rating forms, and engage in an ongoing discussion about teaching methods—but he was not confident that this information would give him an accurate picture of someone's teaching ability.

As I listened to him I realized that he really believed that there might be a magic scale, a sort of measuring stick for teachers, that would give an indisputable answer to the query: Is this person a good teacher or not? Sitting in this meeting with the anthropology professor I found myself ruminating on Weber's misery. Here I was in the presence of a man who was a highly trained professional in the craft of human observation: Someone who should know better than any of us that there are no ultimate measuring sticks, someone who should understand that over the course of five years it should be possible for an accomplished observer to determine the teaching quality of three individuals. What has happened to us, I found myself wondering? Do we no longer trust our own judgments, even in areas in which we have great experience and skill? Or do we no longer have any judgments about what quality is in a specific domain? Are we no longer able to tell the difference between an apple and an orange or do we distrust our own judgment about the differences in the absence of an independent scale?

It may be that the anthropology professor was concerned with standards of fairness. As diversity among the faculty increases in many liberal arts colleges, which are traditionally known for an emphasis on teaching, there are more questions about the fairness of promotion standards. Universities have been fairly traditional systems in that colleagues often evaluate one another in terms of whether one follows a traditional form of scholarship. Many colleges and universities pride themselves on their success in conserving traditional standards. Such "gentleman's agreements" are not necessarily reflective of contemporary faculty and the conditions under which they teach. Whether or not your colleagues "like" the way you teach seems to be a somewhat arbitrary form of evaluation, not unlike the systems that Enlightenment philosophers hoped to overcome. In response to this concern, many of these schools are looking for ways to develop standard methods of assessing teaching. Standard methods presumably promise a less biased basis of evaluation. In such a system, expectations can be made explicit and faculty then held accountable. Overall this would seem like a good thing. The dilemma that I see coming around this particular bend in the road of assessment is that the road itself has come to be mapped out only in terms of quantifiable forms. Often, we no longer accept valid nonquantified expressions of achievement. The means have indeed become an end.

Weber and Simmel feared that in the midst of increasing standardization and quantification, numbers would not only be a form for making comparative statements about otherwise incomparable things, but become symbolized as the *ultimate authority*. In place of the opinions of high-status persons (arbitrary or traditional authority), we would claim to know that something was valuable based on "the numbers." People pay more for mangoes than apples, so mangoes must ultimately be better. Dennis Rodman has more stock chips than Michael Jordan, so he is more valuable. Sometimes the numbers are a useful stand-in for real assessments of value, but in these cases the numbers are connected to concrete, specific settings. They do not mean anything outside of these contexts. Student ratings of teachers, for instance, do reveal something about the overall quality of the course, but these numbers and what they reveal don't mean anything unless you understand the context in which the evaluation surveys were administered and have some additional information about the context and content of the class.

For some reason, this hasn't slowed state legislators from insisting that colleges provide them with "single number measures" of the quality of education. Currently, in the state of Washington, the legislature evaluates the "quality" of all classes in any given department or university using the combined average of responses to the question on teaching rating forms: "Overall, how would you rate this course (on a scale of 1-5)?" These numbers are then used to make highly significant decisions such as whether to fund certain department projects, give them additional faculty members, or perhaps even cut a program.

For Weber and Simmel, as well as many other critics of this form of assessing worth, the problem is twofold. First, the numbers don't mean anything outside the context for which they were intended. They don't provide any real information about quality, they merely suggest possible trends worth further examination. Second, an overreliance on numerical systems of assessing worth erodes our ability to articulate alternative criteria of assessment. The consequence is an abdication of responsibility. When the anthropology professor makes an assessment about whether someone is a good teacher or not, he is making a statement of value and can be called upon to provide the underlying reasons for making his assessment. It can be tempting to rely on the numbers as a reason in themselves, because judgment then seems unambiguous and certain. The fact of the matter is, whether we are aware of it or not, all judgments reveal something about our knowledge of the subject being evaluated. In order to determine what we value about something, we have to immerse ourselves in it, come to know it and to experience what we find worthwhile about it. Statements of worth require some guesswork and a willingness to embrace uncertainties and, ultimately, to take responsibility for them. Rationalized standardization is antithetical to this process. It is a process that lulls us into thinking that the authority is in the numbers and that our personal values are not reflected in the process.

Standardization and Self-Worth. I think about this a lot these days when I'm locked in difficult conversations with students who want me to give them assurance that if they do a particular task they will get a certain grade. I can't really blame them for their attempts to reduce the uncertainty of the quest for knowledge to a predictable act of product consumption—in exchange for this block of time spent they will get this grade—they are in fact only emulating me and my colleagues in our attempts to reduce the uncertainty of our own enterprise to specifiable standards that can be used for tenure and promotion. What concerns me is the extent to which many students seem to feel that they *are* their grade; or at least that this is the only measure of their intellectual worth. They seem grateful for any assessment of qualitative worth that I might offer; they strike me as hungry for words and descriptions that might provide a clue as to who they are. Yet when I ask them to evaluate themselves, when I remind them that they know better than anyone else what the process of learning has been like for them, they balk. They don't *trust* their own experience as a basis for determining value. We are cynical about numerical forms of evaluation; we are well aware of their leveling effects. Yet we still organize ourselves and respond to others as if these numbers were the only authoritative determination of worth. Is this because we are not aware of our part in this paradoxical process, or because we don't know how else to reliably assess worth?

Using standard scales—money, grades—we can make certain comparative statements about items, events, even people. This need not be a problem in itself, but it becomes a paradox when we insist on *certain* appraisals. We lose our faith in the validity of nonstandardized assessments. In the process of transcribing quality into the standard formulas that allow for statements of certitude, we may lose our comprehension of the unique features that imbue people and things with meaning. After a while, we may no longer be able to recognize these features—to see beyond the designer clothing, the prestige of job and degree, or the GPA. Subjectivity fades away to be replaced by standard objectivity. The object becomes the standard. Have you seen people who have a bar code tattooed on their forearms? I take this form of self-expression to be a wry acknowledgment of a misplaced emphasis on efficiency and generic standards of objectivity.

I like to think that I have avoided this leveling process myself, that I am capable of assessing my own self-worth in terms of particular goals and ideals that reflect talents and passions that I have nurtured merely for the sake of expression. But I live in the land of Microsoft millionaires. Occasionally these days I catch myself making evaluations in which I assess my worth relative to the gaggle of 30-something millionaires that has sprung up around me. I go to new restaurants and wonder if the lack of dollar signs tattooed on my forehead (or evidenced in a lack of casually elegant clothing and accessories) will relegate me to a table in the corner by the kitchen door. I find myself entertaining doubts about whether I'm putting my time and talent to good use. These doubts spring up when I look around me and notice that many people my age and younger have far outpaced me in economic worth. When I try to shake these doubts, I find my thoughts reaching to grasp for other comparisons—"They make more money (a lot more!), but I have more control over what I do and create." Do I really buy that line? I teeter back and forth, wondering if I should quit my low-paying academic job and "make something of myself" in the corporate world. Eventually, I remind myself that I have fallen into the trap of trying to make objective comparisons of worth between myself and others. I keep these words written by Martha Graham in a letter to Agnes DeMille taped by my computer as a reminder of this trap:

> There is vitality, a life force, a quickening that is translated through you into action and because there is only one of you in all time, this expression is unique. . . . It is not your business to determine how good it is; nor how valuable it is; Nor how it compares with other expressions. It is your business to keep it yours, clearly and directly. To keep the channel open. No artist is pleased. There is no satisfaction whatever at any time. There is only a queer, divine dissatisfaction; A blessed unrest that keeps us marching and makes us more alive than others.

This quote is a useful reminder that creativity is worthwhile for its own sake. It also glosses a couple of important points. One is the fact that the freedom to engage in "creativity for its own sake" is a function of circumstances. The independently wealthy artist can work at home and shirk public opinion and rave about art for its own sake because he doesn't have to use his talent to pay the bills. A more complicated point, which I will explore in the Epilogue, is the fact that self-expression is meaningless in the absence of social context; we want others to hear us and to engage with us in consideration of our own expressions. The problem that I have been describing here is the tendency to equate self-worth with monetary or other standardized forms of worth. All too often, creative, subjective expression is transcribed into standard evaluatory forms that eclipse the original meaning, intent and process.

The Objective Worth of Self-Expression

My thoughts turned to Simmel's thesis recently while I was attending a rock concert. The *Lilith* tour of 1997 was the brainchild of singer Sarah McLachlan. McLachlan wanted to do something about the underrepresentation of women musicians. She conceived a grand tour that would bring many of these women together. As a Grammy winner and top recording artist, she had clout. The media touted the tour. Huge concert venues across the United States booked performances. Tickets sold out immediately. The concert was an innovative, welcome idea. It had mass appeal. I was lucky to get a free pass from a friend who manages a T-shirt booth at the concerts. When I arrived at the outdoor performance I was let in through a back entrance that led to a large cluster of tents, trailers and other temporary structures that served as storefronts for merchandise. I counted more than three dozen merchandise venues alongside a vast array of fast food eateries. Apparently, in addition to ongoing consumption of pizza, burgers and soft drinks, the complete concert experience includes the purchase of logo coffee cups, Frisbees, T-shirts and other memorabilia that signal one's attendance. I asked my friend if this was a lucrative business. She replied that most of the vendors make enough money to live comfortably and to pay good wages to the college students whom they employ to staff the booths. "It's a huge business," she remarked.

Looking around at this extensive market set up on a remote grassy desert plateau high on a bluff above the Columbia River I was reminded of the bands of gypsies and merchants who trailed after armies in the Middle Ages. These folk made a living by providing traveling soldiers with goods such as cloth and metals for uniforms and arms, and services like blacksmithing and medical cures. Entertainers and storytellers also camped with the troops in hopes of earning some food and pocket change. I realized that a large number of people were now making a living from the willingness of others to purchase markers of their taste in music and their attendance at a "big event." These caravans of merchandisers follow the rock singers all over the country, selling evidence intended to enable one to distinguish oneself as "having been there and done that." You can now buy Lilith products at Starbucks. I can't help but think of this as a sort of "Happy Meal" product for adults. And it's not just rock concerts: I have noticed similar items for sale at the ballet and the opera. Presumably, the purchase and display of these items not only signals support for these enterprises, but marks the distinctive preferences of the individual. Instead of describing an experience with cultural arts to a few friends who might inquire what we have done of note recently, we can advertise our tastes and experiences to all whom we encounter. Through wearable, displayable items we signal our worth in a cultural web of status.

The dilemma is that there are hundreds of thousands of others who are wearing the same T-shirts and thereby rendering our particular tastes an object of mass consumption. Wandering the concert grounds at the Lilith fair I was overwhelmed and dismayed at the huge piles of individual pizza boxes and empty beverage containers that were accumulating into mountains of trash; I was irritated with the assembly-line manner in which the crowd was being managed in a way that maximized opportunities for more consumption. Long breaks between sets seemed calculated to maximize the sales of food and merchandise. The hordes moved between burger stands, beer gardens and ice cream vendors showing off their Lilith fair gear and asking one another where they had purchased this or that item. After a while it began to seem that the music was incidental to the experience, a sort of background din.

The strongest emotion I experienced at the concert was the desire to distinguish myself from this teeming mass. Are we having a good time, I wondered? What will we say on Monday when our friends and co-workers express envy that we were able to go to the

Lilith fair? Will we tell them that we spent too much money on cheap beer and pizza; that we couldn't really see the performers on the stage far below from our hillside perch among ten thousand other fans; will we mention that the grass was damp and that we had to wait two hours in traffic mayhem before being able to exit the parking lot? Or will we wear our T-shirts proudly and reaffirm the envy of our peers with exclamations of what a great time we had?

Tangled up in this trash-heap of an experience is the image of a spectacular sunset painting the cliffs and illuminating the water behind the stage; there is the memory of the collective shiver that moved through the crowd after darkness had set in when Tracy Chapman offered up the first notes of her deeply resonating alto voice. People standing in long lines waiting for Port-a-Potties found occasion to make contact and laugh together for a brief moment. For some groups, the experience of simply spending time together away from their daily routines may have made the occasion worthwhile. Yet I can't help but reflect on the fact that these moments of what might be experienced as genuine, heartfelt worth take place in the midst of largely unnoticed patterns of overconsumption and unconscious abuse of resources and a blind acquiescence to "crowd control" agents whose actions are calculated to line the pockets of merchandising vendors. Sifting the value of the experience from this sludge is, for me, a matter of being able to recognize the "invisible routines" that shape what we think of as the choice set for our tastes, interests and politics. What does it mean, for instance, that for me the real subjective value of the experience is in my ability to distance myself from it and write about it—a subjective expression that takes the form of critique.

Recently, the very act of subjective expression has become a basis for creating a cultural object. Burger King has a commercial in which a man who has brought a Whopper onto a plane is being accosted by fellow passengers and flight staff. What do you want for your Whopper? they all clamor. One by one, stereotypical representatives in the form of a banker, a voluptuous woman and a service rep offer him money, sex and first-class treatment, respectively. He doesn't budge. His Whopper is worth more than any of these enticements. The pilot offers him the opportunity to fly the plane. For this, he gives up his Whopper. What will you give up your Whopper for? the slogan reads. A pilot who will trade the safety of passengers for a hamburger is absurd; the gag line in the commercial pivots on the absurdity of self-expression through consumer choices. Burger King is simultaneously making fun of Whopper lovers for the absurdity of their preference and transforming the absurdity of the expression into a cultural product—a clever commercial that makes us laugh at our own cynicism. This is a remarkable alchemy. In this case, the worth of the Whopper is revealed in the ability to transform individual expressions of value into an objective joke.

The Paradox of Transcendence

By way of conclusion I'd like to remark briefly on what I see as a related paradox, the paradox of transcendence. This paradox hinges on an idea that is frequently unexamined in questions of meaning and value: This is the idea that any valid form of evaluation must be transcendent. We are reluctant to acknowledge local, particular expressions of meaning and worth. This suspicion of parochial value reflects a couple of nested paradoxes: a distrust in our own ability to create systems of meaning and the disjuncture between local impressions and the universal, anonymous standards that are purportedly the pillars of democratic process. The curious outcome is that *we do not trust ourselves as value-makers, nor, for that matter, as value-critics.*

Grappling With Uncertainties: Valuation as a Process

I have a colleague who studies the markets for rice and rubber. A noteworthy fact about rice is that the quality is relatively easy to assess. Most people can learn the techniques for judging rice quality very easily. It's a matter of rubbing rice between the fingers and noting texture and residue. Rubber is another story. The quality of rubber cannot be known until the plant has been made into a product. Buying rubber is, quite literally, an act of faith. Buyers and sellers of rice rarely develop long-term relationships. The market is shaped in terms of accessibility. No one cares who is doing the buying or the selling because the quality of the product itself is immediately ascertainable. Rubber markets, on the other hand, are long-term moral communities. In the absence of certain knowledge, lively and meaningful relationships have developed that, while they do not offer any guarantee about the product, bind the buyers and sellers together in a cooperative effort to grapple with uncertainty. Their aim is not to make rubber production more certain, but rather to support one another in a risky venture. Their coexistence is an expression of faith. Systems of valuation are emergent properties of the means through which they grapple with shared uncertainties. Clifford Geertz, a contemporary anthropologist, believed that cultural value systems are grounded in wonder and awe: Meaning is reflected in a culture's relationship with mystery. Weber's nightmare was that in the process of replacing mystery with certainty we would render ourselves meaningless.

Value isn't a means-end calculation. Value determination is a process. An ongoing process. It is useful to explore *how* people come together to articulate and deliberate about value. Does the process engage persons with one another? Does it entice them to examine the bases of their tastes, desires and beliefs about what is good and valuable? A culture of certainty is based in processes of valuation that push down individual experience and attachments and ignore local circumstances in favor of transcendent, standardized procedures. These procedures are less risky, less emotionally demanding and more predictable because they require that persons be *disengaged.* The process works best when it is *faceless.* The crisis of value in the age of certainty is not so much the lack of an ultimate authority on which to confer the right to determine value. Rather it is our collective inability to engage one another in realistic, possibly conflicting discussions about value within specific contexts. The upshot of such conversations is that we would have to take responsibility for the decisions we make, including the risks and uncertainties.

In what I consider to be his most profound statement about the consequences of routinized standards and dehumanization, Weber ponders war. He is writing during the time that will become known as World War I. The use of chemical gasses to drive troops from the battlefield is a controversial issue of the day. Perhaps recalling his fencing days, Weber muses on the physical act of killing another human being. He compares hand-to-hand combat with the more removed sorts of battles that have been made possible through the manufacture of chemical weapons and large guns. In one-on-one combat, he notes, the soldier is forced to look the enemy in the eye. You feel the bayonet twist in his body; you see the blood gush from his mouth and the fear in his face. You know when the life leaves the body. In this moment, Weber continues, you are locked together in mutual acknowledgment. The enemy has a face. He has a soul, he is marked with the graces of those who love him. It is this face that you are killing. This moment will become a touchstone for the rest of your life. In contrast, the modern war machine will eventually make it possible to annihilate entire civilizations from a distance so far away that the killers will not hear a single cry of pain. We will be able to kill without experiencing any emotion.

One of the noteworthy features of our time is that we are able to comment on the conditions of our own enslavement. We engage in lively and creative critique of our circumstances even as we are simultaneously building new prison bars. It was this awareness that prompted Roland Barthes to remark, "What I claim to live is the full contradiction of my time. This contradiction may make sarcasm a condition of existence" (1957:12). His first clause resonates for me. I'm not convinced of his conclusion, however. Kafka wrote about experiencing an endless sense of astonishment at simply seeing a group of people cheerfully assembled—laughing and crying at the same things. Perhaps the most certain thing about us is that we need each other to figure out what it all means. Value may be intrinsic to the collective process of wrestling the contradictions of our time, a quality reflected in the stories we tell ourselves about how to make meaning and the ways we have of telling them.

It is my observation that we are in the midst of a major paradigm shift; epistemologies and methodologies that favor certainty and univocality are giving way to complexity and multivocality. The page of history is being turned. The only thing that is likely to be certain is our mutual questioning of universal standards and values. What could be a very exciting time to be in the vanguard is simultaneously a time in which, as a nation, we are becoming increasingly mean-spirited and ungenerous. People are mean-spirited and ungenerous when they are afraid. We are afraid not necessarily of uncertainty, but because of a lack of stories for dealing with uncertainty, particularly uncertainties about what matters. Perhaps at this point in our history there can be no touchstone. Our particular challenge may be to throw off the cloak of certainty, including the certainties of being able to say something is more than or less than; better than or worse than; easier or harder than. We may need to reimmerse ourselves in the muck of uncertainty in order to reacquaint ourselves simply with what is.

Epilogue

Paradoxes of Subjectivity

PARADOX

If the self is a social creation, then how do we achieve distinctive character? To what extent are we "free" to determine who and what we are? The myth of the lone individual perpetuates the misleading notion that the ideal person forges herself or himself independent of social experiences. In fact, who we are is largely a process of conversation between our developing consciousness and social experience. We become our "selves" through the process of making sense of where we fit socially. We take on character and definition as we wrestle with the boundaries and contradictions of these social expectations. A particular social force that shapes us involves which social boxes we are put into by others. Some social boxes are more confining than others. One useful question is whether individuals are more or less free to define their own subjectivity. In the United States, due to cultural legacies such as racism and sexism, some people are seen as objects who represent particular social categories rather than as self-determining subjects. For many people, the processes of objectification require a constant struggle to manifest an impression that counters these externally imposed definitions of self. At the same time, these cultural legacies do shape who and what we are. The paradox is in the search for individual identity beyond objectification, while simultaneously acknowledging the ways in which the forces of social objectification shape us.

Why is it, exactly at the moment when so many of us who have been silenced begin to demand the right to name ourselves, to act as subjects rather than objects of history, that just then the concept of subjecthood becomes "problematic"?

—Nancy Hartsock, 1990

In this epilogue, I present some food for thought in response to the question, Who am I? I cannot answer this question in any definitive way, but I wish to draw your attention to yet another binary opposition between individual and society that gets in the way of our understanding of who we are and what our responsibilities to one another are. We are, I assert, both individual and social creatures. We take on our individuality through processes of social interaction. We need to understand this in order to assess the consequences, socially, psychologically, politically and morally.

"People need play and danger. Civilization gives them work and safety." This quote, cited also in Chapter 7 and attributed to the nineteenth-century philosopher Friedrich Nietzsche, is indicative of a suspicion of "society" that was articulated in the 1800s and became a common thread of critique in the 1900s. Nietzsche, like other moral and social philosophers of his day, including Karl Marx, Max Weber and Georg Simmel, was concerned with the ways in which social forces squashed the human spirit. "Civilization" had long been heralded as a form of social progress that tempered the beast within and enabled higher pursuits of mind and spirit. Christianity, for example, was a form of civilization that was supposed to bring order to the disorderly urges and impulses of the untamed body. The resulting order was equated with a peace of mind and a harmony of spirit. In the writings of the nineteenth-century critics, "civilization" was exposed as a contrivance of those in power to control the rest of humankind, to bend the human will to the wishes of the "master." From this perspective, the forces of society (religion, education, occupational standards, scholarship, law and government) were considered the means by which humankind was enslaved.

Nietzsche was one of the most vociferous, emotionally charged and poetic of the critics of civilization. He proposed that the human is driven by "the will to power." He does not mean by this necessarily the will to exercise power over another, rather the will to be a powerful force, an agent of action and change, in our respective universes. Unfettered by civilizing forces, humans are, according to Nietzsche, compelled to be a "presence." Nietzsche was impatient with social groups, institutions and cultural affiliations. These social engagements exert a pressure on the individual demanding of her or him conformity to the rules and codes of "polite" society. Such conformity stifles the spirit and constrains the will to create.

Sigmund Freud's theories are a similar critique of society as a force that causes individuals to repress their desires in order to conform to social expectations. In *Civilization and Its Discontents,* Freud writes of "socialization" as a force that wrestles the urges and impulses of the individual into submission. The "healthy" adult is the one whose inclinations have been tamed to make her or him into "fit company" for the rest of society. In each stage of development we learn to channel our "natural" urges and drives into ways of being that are nonthreatening to others and conform to social convention. To this end, many of our impulses are "sublimated"—pushed "underground" where they percolate with or without a form of acceptable expression. The artist or creative individual is the one who channels these impulses into culturally accepted forms of expression, such as painting or poetry. The criminal or pathological being is the one who is unable to sublimate these urges or to find an acceptable means to channel them. The unconscious, which Freud is credited with having "discovered," is a terrain that yields glimpses of our attempts to wrestle with individual impulses that are not easily channeled into acceptable cultural forms. It is the playground of repressed urges and desires.

Freud and Nietzsche lived and wrote during the Victorian cultural era, a time that is most often described as vapid, sterile, narrow and repressive. The basic theme of all the critics is that the proliferation of bourgeois (middle-class) society demanded a certain conformity that rendered persons roughly equal in manner and habit. In attempts to adjust to their new station in life as keepers of the status quo, the middle classes were very concerned with appearances of propriety and behavior. They wanted to behave in ways that signified that their wealth and prosperity were, indeed, a sign of God's favor. The manners of the nineteenth-century "drawing room" have been the subject of considerable study as a basis of social restraint. They are also the basis of many humorous "comedies of manners." It is within this context that Nietzsche and his fellows are rebelling against the so-called evils of society.

The theme was carried across the Atlantic Ocean and made its way into the manners and lore of the frontier. The mythical hero is the isolated individual who stands alone outside of, and unrepressed by, "society." This thesis resulted in the idea of the individual and society as distinct entities—that society is beyond and apart from the individual, that it is alien and potentially imprisoning. Psychological studies and popular culture since the time of the pioneers and mavericks focus on the "struggle" between the individual and society. "Man" is represented as continually at odds with and pitted against culture. Our legal system reflects these same philosophies of Individualism—the only laws of society that are good are those that constrain individuals the least. Hence, the legal system in the United States is based, in theory, on protecting individuals from actions that thwart their freedoms, either by another individual or by a corporate body.

Certainly there is an element of truth in the representation of "society" as a controlling force over individual impulses. From infancy we are subjected to social designs intended to get us to control our bodily functions, movements and impulses. Part of the exhaustion that is associated with raising toddlers comes from the necessity of constantly trying to enforce habits of body—like sitting still, toilet training, not hitting, and so forth—these demands are attempts to impose the social will over the child's immediate physical impulses. It is also true that cultural forms shape how we can act on impulses such as desire, curiosity and worship. It is true that as individuals we are born into preexisting social circumstances and that most of our lives will be shaped by these social forces. These social circumstances, which include institutions of courtship, knowledge and religion, shape how we express ourselves in each of these arenas. As presented by Nietzsche, Freud and other modern theorists who were critical of social influence, these social forces are alien and serve to imprison the "true" or "natural" human spirit. This conception of *society versus the individual* begs the question, *What* is the individual, independent of social forces? Apart from social influence, who are you?

Nietzsche rebelled against being "controlled by society." In his conception, "society" was a particular group of people (the bourgeoisie) who hold a particular set of beliefs and subscribe to a particular set of customs and behaviors that Nietzsche worried would have a leveling or dampening effect on human creativity. In this regard, he is saying much the same thing as Weber and Simmel. The social customs that accompanied mass production and democratic rule were designed to "pound down any protruding stake of individuality," so to speak. "Society" thus conceived represents the ideals and practices of a particular group that, by virtue of representing the status quo, has the power to enforce its views among those whose inclinations may be different. This is a very different view of "society" than the abstract notion referenced by those who speak of "society" as a general thing that "makes" people do something, as in, "society forces people to conform."

I don't think this is what Nietzsche and his like-minded fellows had in mind. When they cautioned against the "numbing effects of society," they meant a very particular type of society in which they lived and worked and worried about increasing banality among the keepers of the status quo. This does not necessarily mean that all forms of society are equally oppressive, numbing and banal. Rather, as I suggested in the chapter on groups, "society" is a web of various group interests, customs and practices. This web reflects different lines of power and influence. You may feel oppressed in relationship to some of these group dynamics and encouraged by others, but to say that you stand alone, outside the web, would make you a fundamentally isolated creature with no referents for self-awareness, and therefore no subjectivity.

The Contemporary Problem of Subjectivity

Modern conceptions of the individual being trampled by society give the impression that the individual achieves consciousness and holds distinct, organized desires, tastes and goals *independent* of any social influence. According to this portrayal, the individual is a fully formed entity who is engaged in constant battle with alien social forces. *Where did this fully formed individual, complete with desires, tastes, goals and beliefs, come from?* This question is often posed as a fundamental contemporary paradox. In the chapter on Communities and Group Paradoxes, I suggested that who we are—our beliefs and our inclinations and how we think of ourselves—is based on our association with the significant people and groups that form the web of our social life. We take on identities, become self-aware and achieve character through *social interaction with significant groups.* The paradox, which has been succinctly described by sociologist Joel Charon, is that society does shape us, including in ways that we may find confining, but without society we would not have any self-awareness. Society is the basis for the consciousness that enables us to even wonder whether or not we are "free" or "constrained."

The Paradox of Self-Control and Social Control

The dilemma, as Charon describes it, is in the connection between *self-control* and *social control.* When a child learns self-control over bodily functions, she is indeed learning to organize her physical behavior in a way that is consistent with social expectations (i.e., with expectations that are rooted in the will of a transcendent corporate body—society). At the same time, however, she is learning to be *aware* of her own bodily functions. She becomes conscious that she has a body over which she can exercise control. Paradoxically, one is not aware that one has a "will" to exercise unless one is made aware of this will through attempts to control the actions of the body. "Will" is based in self-awareness. Self-awareness is triggered by social awareness, the awareness of others who are trying to get you (the child) to make your body behave in certain ways.

The misperception conveyed in notions of the uncontrolled individual is that this person is still somehow controlling her own behavior. The problem, as Charon points out, is that without self-awareness, you cannot exercise *any* control over your own actions. The *decision to act,* whether in accordance with social expectations or in rebellion against them, is predicated on awareness and the ability to control one's own behavior. Through the process of internalizing social expectations we also gain the self-awareness that enables us to choose to conform or rebel. Freedom of choice is a moot point unless we are socialized.

A child who grows to adulthood without having been toilet trained is not "free" to do whatever he pleases with his body, he is a passive slave to his bodily functions unless he gains an awareness of how to exert control over them. An individual may decide that he is not going to "conform" to social norms about using rest rooms and instead pee any old place that he wants, but this is not the same thing as not being able to control when and where you go. Charon summarizes this paradox by pointing out that before you can "decide" whether to conform or rebel, you have to be able to exercise control over your own drives and impulses. This control comes initially through processes of *socialization.* In short, without some form of socialization we would not be self-aware; without self-awareness we cannot exercise any kind of conscious social action, we would be at the mercy of our own electrical, biological, physiological and psychological impulses.

How we gain and develop "self" is a topic that has occupied scholars endlessly. I don't propose to address this huge topic definitively. I do hope to suggest that there is an alternative to understanding yourself as either a repressed object of civilization or an individual island who stands alone. I do believe that who and what we are consists of elements of nature, spirit and psyche that are beyond scientific comprehension. However, the shape that these elements take as we develop our "selves" is, I propose, largely a function of social relations. This is not a simple cause-effect relationship. "Society" doesn't *cause* individuals to be certain things. We gain subjectivity as we become aware of and respond to the forces that constitute the web of our social environment. The direction our subjectivity (our sense of self) takes depends on how we see and articulate these social circumstances—which include significant people, groups and social customs and practices.

I have written about this paradox of self-control and social control in another book. Joel Charon has also written about this paradox and the connection to individual freedom. His essay on the topic is particularly compelling (see the bibliography at the end of this book). In this chapter, I want to shift tracks and take up the theme of personal subjectivity. The self-/social control paradox is an interesting basis for discussing the *potential* for freedom in human actions, but this paradox is compelling only insofar as we are unable to see that we are social creatures. The more pressing dilemma, as I see it currently taking shape, concerns *who* has the freedoms of subjecthood; the freedom to establish and express their own subjectivity as they experience it within the groups and social affiliations that comprise their everyday lives. This is an issue of social and political expression.

Under what circumstances do persons have the freedom and the authority to consider their histories and to make themselves heard?

The Will to Expression

I want to amend Nietzsche's proposition that we are motivated by the "will to power" and propose instead that we are motivated by the "will to expression." There is more than a grain of truth in the old adage that we wish to "see and be seen." This proposition is not inconsistent with Nietzsche. In the writings of many scholars, poets and novelists who were fascinated with human expression, suppression of will is seen as the equivalent of the oppression of forms of expression. The "dismal" or "critical" philosophers such as Marx, Weber and Simmel were concerned with the ways in which the forces of economic production would discourage the enthusiasm, spontaneity and creativity of expression. Early modern novelists explored themes of death through the erosion of self-expression brought about by the leveling forces of mass industrialization. Characters such as "Everyman" in Rychard Pynson's 1526 classic morality play and Willy Lohman in Arthur Miller's *Death of a Salesman* continue to resonate with many individuals who feel that the demands of a bureaucratic work environment have rendered them faceless, expressionless.

The frequency throughout history of acts of political suppression intended to silence certain groups and individuals is a testament to the power of expression. The First Amendment to the U.S. Constitution guarantees "freedom of expression" as a certain, inalienable right that is deemed fundamental for every human being. Marx saw our labor as a form of creative expression that was basic to who and what we are. When he says that we distinguish ourselves according to the process by which we "wrest our livelihood from nature," he is echoing a theme common among many philosophers; human labor is both an expressive and a practical act. Marx's emphasis on *control* of the labor process reflects an assumption that our subjectivity is forged through the process of labor. Depending on the conditions of production, we are more or less free to engage in acts of expression through production. Simmel elaborated this thesis in his discussion of the paradox between subjective and objective expressions—that which we produce as an expression of our subjective tastes and talents, when mass produced, becomes an object that takes on a life of its own so that we no longer have control over our own subjective expression. This paradox is central to the creation and production of art. It is also central to the creation and production of self-awareness.

The modern lament is that everywhere there are forces larger than ourselves that hamper self-expression and brainwash us into expressing ideas that are "not our own." The implication is that, left to our own devices, we would sing out unfettered. Here again is the false binary that posits self and society as distinct entities in constant opposition. Self-expression is always a social act. Expression is born of the desire to give substance and shape to otherwise amorphous, semiconscious feelings and experiences. Whether you have a particular audience in your head when you express yourself, or whether you are simply trying to "figure something out for yourself," the very act of transcribing feelings, thoughts and experiences into a form of expression is an act of social engagement. It is the desire to share feelings and experiences, to be seen and heard, that prompts us to try to give some recognizable shape to them. This "shape" is usually in the form of commonly understood language and related forms of expression, such as music, painting and dance. These shape-making devices that we use to communicate personal experiences to others are social forms that pre-date us as individuals.

One paradox of subjectivity is that in order to communicate with one another, we must "package" our feelings, thoughts and inspirations into a form that is commonly understood, such as language. In so doing, expression becomes objectified. We give our subjective experiences shape and then cast them onto the social winds, so to speak, and hope that they will be picked up as we intend. At the same time, in giving shape to our subjective experiences, we also "discover" more about ourselves. We name ourselves and talk to ourselves, we listen to others name us and talk to us, in order to figure out who we are. *Thus the self is not a core thing, it is an ongoing process that takes shape as we strive to express ourselves. The self is social in that the forms of expression that we use are socially derived.*

When we are engaged in communication with one another, we are also watching ourselves communicate. We are simultaneously an actor (subject) and an object to ourselves according to social psychologist George Herbert Mead, who was a contemporary of Freud's. Mead was curious about how we take "society" into us (through language and social expectations) and transform it into subjectivity. According to Mead, our sense of self develops as we *watch and reflect* on our interactions with others. Consciousness, in this regard, is the ability to stand outside yourself—to observe yourself as an object. Your sense of "self" is an ongoing conversation that you have in your head in which you sort out, make sense of and react to the actions that you observe about yourself-as-object.

For instance, I might be compelled to smile at a stranger on the street who smiles back. Watching myself do this, I might think, "I'm a kind person" and subsequently file the brief instance away as an affirmation of who I think I am—kind. Later in the day, I might be gruff with a student who comes to my office late for an appointment. Watching the student slink away, head down, and replaying my gruff tone in my head, I might wonder, "Was I too harsh?" This thought might trigger a string of deliberations in which I try to reconcile my tone of expression with the student and my more general notion of myself as being "kind." In reality, I am neither kind nor gruff as an enduring personality trait. How I think of myself is a process of conversation about my own behavior. My subsequent actions will be shaped by these self-conversations.

Mead's theory of the self is much more complex and, in many ways, a more satisfying basis for figuring out the relationship between individuals and society. Once you are willing to wrap your head around the idea that we are social creatures, Mead's theory points the way to a useful set of related questions. For instance, I might ask myself why I want to be "kind"? In thinking about it and talking about it with others, I might come to realize that like many people in this culture, particularly women, I am often praised when I do something "kind." In fact, the people with whom I interact probably expect me to be kind, and when I am, they respond approvingly. When I'm not, they respond in ways that can make me squirm and worry about whether or not what I did was "appropriate." Being kind may not always be the best course of action, particularly when this translates into "letting someone off the hook" who really needs to be prodded or confronted. As I think about this more, I may decide that there is a difference between being kind and being a "pushover." I may begin to experiment with ways not to be a pushover. In doing so, I may forge a new self-image—I'm kind, but tough.

In this regard, my self-awareness emerges, develops and takes on depth, complexity and texture as I interact with others and try to make sense of these interactions—which includes evaluating myself—in terms of existing social customs and expectations. There may be a general social expectation that "women like me" should be "kind," but I don't have simply to absorb this expectation. I forge my character by reflecting on this expectation and determining my own unique basis of expression—which now includes being critical of the expectation that women should always be kind.

This theory opens up a useful line of questioning regarding the possibilities of self-expression and subsequent self-development. What forms of expression are available to people? Which forms are more or less acceptable and for whom? What are the consequences of various forms of expression for different people? As a college professor responsible for my own classes, I have quite a bit of autonomy in terms of how "kind" I want to be. If I want to cultivate gruff forms of expression because I think it keeps students on their toes, or because I don't want to kowtow to senior men who have outdated expectations about how young women should behave, I am relatively free to do so on a day-to-day basis. A flight attendant, on the other hand, is likely to loose his job if he doesn't act kind and friendly while at work. This doesn't mean that he necessarily thinks of himself as "kind and friendly"; his self-concept will include reflections on the fact that he is not in a position to experiment with this particular form of expression in the same way that I might be. The social self is aware of social expectations but is not necessarily "brainwashed" by them, as the individual/society binary suggests. Rather, self-development is a complicated dance between the will to express ourselves and the social circumstances that enable some forms of expression and suppress other forms of expression.

We are not, therefore, merely passive vessels taking in social expectations unquestionably and acting them out robotically. We *engage* the expectations in a process of reflection and expression. Who we are, how we see ourselves, is forged in this engagement. Thus we are both a reflection of our social circumstances and of our unique responses to these circumstances. In this way, our self-expressions have the potential both to reinscribe and to change existing social customs and forms of expression.

Self-Multiplicity

Every individual has a multitude of identities—personas that we enact depending on what the situation calls for and our position in the situation. This observation led William James to comment that "we have as many [identities] as the sum total of everyone whom we have ever encountered." We put on different faces for different people in different settings. How attached we are to a particular "face," whether we think that it reflects something deeper and more meaningful about how we see our "self," is a matter of self-reflection, a matter of engaged consciousness. To be self-aware, you must be aware of the significant attachments and groups that form the fields of interaction in which you express yourself.

Here again, the notion of "society" as a distinct entity is misleading. Most persons are affiliated with a network of different social groups. We pass through many different social spaces in any given day. There is no single society in which we have a single self. Rather, each person, group and setting that we encounter engages us differently. How we make sense of the sum total of these social engagements forms the basis of what we think of as our "core" self.

These everyday engagements can be more or less smooth or fraught with contradiction depending on (1) the various positions that you occupy in certain groups, (2) how smoothly these positions overlap, and (3) how much freedom you have to express yourself as you wish. Social position is a determinant of forms of expression and, therefore, influences self-image. The ways in which social position influences self-image are not the same for everyone in similar positions, but depend, to a large extent on the repertoire of responses that the person has. The source of these responses is also a function of social interaction. We learn various ways to enact social positions from role models and other social sources.

Multiple Experiences: Conflicting or Complementary?

The social positions that we engage on any given day are multiple and shifting. Some people are more aware of this multiplicity of experience than others. For some people the multiplicity goes unnoticed because in most situations they are able to express themselves in ways that are consistent with the self-images that they want to maintain. For others, the multiplicity is a constant source of contradiction that requires a more engaged internal dialogue about what each situation means for the self.

Consider for instance a senior business executive who is also a deacon in his church, a father, a member of the local Rotary club, a member of an exclusive athletic club and a participant in the alumni association of the college that he attended. To what extent do these situations seem to overlap such that he can be mostly the same person across all of them? Perhaps he sees himself as an effective leader, a good citizen, and a reliable, likable fellow who is fairly easygoing. In which of these situations, if any, might he have to express himself in a way that is at odds with this self-image? Consider the other sorts of spaces that he might pass through each day. Perhaps he picks up some groceries, some dry cleaning, attends a concert or a ball game. Do you suppose these encounters reaffirm his general sense of self or challenge it?

Compare this person with another senior business executive, also college educated, a member of her church choir, a member of several local civic organizations including the Association for the Advancement of Colored People. In what ways might her days be the same or different from his? She may also think of herself as likable and easygoing, but find that her authority is often challenged by junior colleagues. She may have to act gruff in order to command the respect to which she is entitled. As a result, her co-workers may consider her "bitchy." Her involvement in civic organizations might be a cause for raised eyebrows as well. She may have to respond to statements that she is "too political" for the company's reputation. How free is she to just be "herself" in the various settings that she encounters?

Try this one. Take the first scenario, but make the man single and gay. If he is not openly gay, to what extent will he have to monitor his self-expressions throughout the day so as not to tip anyone off? If he is openly gay, do you suppose that others will respond to him as they do to the first man? How might the differences in responses shape how he expresses himself and his subsequent self-image? For instance, which of the two men is more likely to be able to speak in favor of gay rights without being accused of "special interests?

Subjectivity is a function of self-expression. Self-expression is shaped to a large extent by the positions you occupy—are you allowed to "be yourself" or do you have to express yourself in a particular way in order to fit the situation? Persons who occupy positions of power in many of the settings in their lives have the *privilege* of expressing themselves as they please. In this regard, their social expressions are likely to be fairly consistent with their sense of self. Many people have multiple and contradictory positions. They often find that they need to tuck away or rein in some aspect of "self" in order to fit the expectations of the situation at hand. Juggling the multiplicities of self can stretch you and add texture to your character. It can also be wearisome and confusing.

Objective Versus Subjective Expressions

In considering the gap between social expressions of self and internal understanding of self, it is useful to keep in mind that the expressed face is most likely to match the underlying sense of face when the individual holds a great deal of power in many overlapping settings. Freedom of self-expression is mediated by social statuses that stigmatize or *objectify* the individual (e.g., the marked differences that I described in Chapter 4). All persons do not have equal privileges in cultivating and expressing their unique subjectivity. For those who have been socially marked as Other, subjectivity is a process of continually forging self-expressions that both acknowledge the "mark of difference" as an integral aspect of self-experience, and that transcend the *objective stereotypes* imposed on the individual through this marking. Alice Walker conveys both the frustration of being historically marked as a social Object and the challenge of transcending imposed objectivity in this comment, which she made in response to an artist's collection of Stereotypes and Caricatures of Afro-Americans:

> These caricatures were really intended as . . . prisons of image. If you look hard [at each grinning sambo] you will begin to really see the eyes and then the hearts of these despised relatives of ours, who have been forced to lock their spirits away from us. . . . I see brothers and sisters, mothers and fathers, captured and forced into images they did not devise, doing hard time for all of us. We can liberate them by understanding this. And free ourselves.

Through her own writing, Walker has been tremendously successful in establishing her own subjectivity and reclaiming the subjectivity of those objectified through black stereotypes. Her choice to write fiction about black subjects in American history is, of course, a reflection of these inherited circumstances of objectification. In this regard, it can be said that her subjectivity is being shaped by preexisting social conditions, but this does not mean that she is "controlled" by society. Her creativity is in the way in which she has transformed a history of objectification—a history that portrays blacks as shifty, grinning Sambos, Aunt Jeminas and Uncle Toms—into a subject in its own right. She is forging forms of expression where they have been long denied.

Objectification Both Denies and Shapes Expression

For many of us subjectivity is complicated by the fact that self-expression is forged in response to cultural practices that blatantly portray us as incapable or unworthy of expression. The following outrageous comment was made by a white painter, Steve Gianokos, in response to a discussion about the lack of venues that present art by people of color and women:

> I don't think people won't show blacks because they're black, but because they don't do interesting work. It has nothing to do with color. It's like women. Women happen to be inferior artists to men, and it's the same with blacks. They happen to be better at peddling dope. Maybe that's their talent. I mean, why should blacks be good at art?

Gianokos's statement denies the power of expression to certain individuals by lumping them into categories that he associates with a lack of talent. Unfortunately, his statement reflects a common sentiment among Euro American and European gallery owners and art dealers. If you are an artist who is also a woman, a person of color, or both, the expression of your art will be influenced by this culture of objectification. Whether you choose to "talk back" directly or to sidestep this portrayal, it is likely to be an element of consideration in your choices of expression.

The conundrum regarding objectivity and subjectivity is not that society directly impels persons to behave in certain ways and to become specific sorts of people. The question is: To what extent are we free to author our own subjectivity, to express ourselves and be seen and heard as we would like to be? Some persons are born into this culture with less likelihood of being cloaked in preexisting objective roles that deny them subjectivity. Recall Simone de Beauvoir's discussion of Women as Other (see Chapter 4). To speak of woman as object and man as subject is to assume that the male child will take on a personality and develop character according to his own doings and experiences. Woman, on the other hand, has historically been Object or Other. Who or what she is was determined from birth and defined relative to the man. She is someone's daughter, and then someone's wife and someone's mother. Any subjectivity that she might achieve and wish to express is left on the sidelines and considered unimportant. Woman as Object was a nonperson. Likewise, persons marked by racial stereotypes are seen as objects first. If and when subjective recognition is achieved, it is usually considered and evaluated in terms of the objective role. Thus, we hear that someone is a female athlete or a Mexican poet, or a black painter.

This challenging pronouncement made by James Baldwin is an expression of this dilemma of self and subjectivity:

So where we are now is that a whole country of people believe that I am a "nigger," and I *don't*, and the battle's on! Because if I am not what I've been told I am, then it means that *you're* not what you thought *you* were either! And that is the crisis.

Baldwin's comment raises the concept of *intersubjectivity*—who I can be is a function of how you respond to me. If we engage one another as subjects in the moment, then we are engaged in an intersubjective dialogue in which we both have the possibility of exercising and expanding self-expression—hearing and being heard. This is what is often meant by "genuine" communication. You allow another to see and touch bits of you and the other responds accordingly. This form of engagement and expression is the basis and source of intimacy and understanding. On the other hand, if you see me only as an objectification of some social category in which you have placed me, the interaction will require me either to refute or affirm whether who I am is accurately represented by the objective stereotypes through which you view me. In any case, how I can express myself will be a function of the limits of the objective form.

Imagine for instance an employer who "compliments" a worker by saying, "You haven't turned out to be nearly as lazy as I expected an Indian to be. You don't even drink." This remark doesn't reflect an awareness of an individual's subjective performance. It is an evaluation made in terms of an existing stereotype. The employer thinks of the employee as an object and is comparing him with preconceived notions of how this "object" is likely to behave. Baldwin is saying that if I refuse to be the object that you want me to be, then you will have to reconsider your relationship to me. When Baldwin says I'm not going to play nigger to you, he is also saying, I am going to tell my own story. And in telling it, you may lose some of the freedom that you have had to define yourself as you wished vis-à-vis the object that you consider me to be.

In recent years, variously disenfranchised people who have been treated primarily in terms of their positions as social objects (women; people of color; disabled persons; lesbian, gay and transgender persons; sex workers; persons who are poor) have begun to claim the right to speak for themselves. Many of the resulting expressions of subjectivity include accounts of suppression, discrimination and abuse by those who have perpetuated the objectifications. These expressions affect how others have seen themselves as well. They change what we have been told about who we are and our histories. One particular sea change that currently confronts Americans as a result of the proliferation of expressions of subjectivity from previously disenfranchised groups is a major realignment in what many people have been told about the legitimacy of Euro American hegemonies. The response among many white Americans and others who have benefited from this particular historical narrative is that the new expressions of subjectivity among diverse peoples are "reverse objectification."

Peer Intersubjectivity Versus Subject/Object Relations

Self-expression is always mediated by social interaction. What this means is that whenever we interact with someone else, how we express ourselves and how we are understood will be influenced by what the other is willing and able to hear. There is a significant difference between whether expression takes place between peers who are battling about how they want the other to see and hear them, or whether one can dismiss or deny the other by treating the other as an Object. One friend might call another a cheat and the other may disagree with this assessment. They may fight about whether he is really a cheat. The conversation may be a source of conflict and consternation for both of them, but they are peers arguing together about the self-images that they are willing to grant one another.

This is very different than showing up for a job interview and being asked to defend yourself against the possibility that you might turn out to be a cheat "because all Mexican housekeepers are cheats." A genuine peer encounter holds the possibility that your subjectivity will be influenced by the other. You may change your mind and your self-understanding as a result of the encounter. This is both the risk and the thrilling potential of social engagement. How the other responds to you will affect you. The moral question, and the question that underlies subjectivity, is, to what extent are you willing to *engage* the person in discussion about who each of you are relative to the other?

The subjective being who treats the other as Object is denying the possibility that the other has any potential to affect the interaction, except as defined by the expectations of the subject. Persons long accustomed to treating others as objects may therefore react with surprise and displeasure if confronted with an Object who claims the rights of a Subject—the right to engage the other. Currently, in the United States, as more and more people claim their rights of subjecthood, there is considerable backlash from those who are not accustomed to granting these people subjectivity, especially if that subjectivity includes the expression of a history that includes decades of suppression and denial. It is curious, noteworthy and in some cases ridiculous to witness attempts to reinforce this denial of subjectivity. Presumably benign expressions, such as "I don't care about racial differences, I'm colorblind," reflect a subjective position of not having to care about the differences. By entreating others to not care either, the person who is "colorblind" denies others the rights to expressions of their own histories and experiences.

Then there are the feeble responses intended to silence expressions of discrimination that take the form of "she doesn't want us to objectify her, but look at how she objectifies me by calling me oppressive." This remark is often made by men who feel excluded from women's activities. When the traditionally disenfranchised person expresses a reluctance to engage someone who has traditionally held a position of objective power, she is not objectifying him. She is making a subjective statement. The statement is: Who and what you represent makes me nervous or suspicious. With good reason. The man who "gets this" will recognize that he too, like most of the rest of us at some time or another, will have to engage the woman by acknowledging where she's coming from.

Similarly, when a person of color expresses a frustration with "whites," she is not engaging in "reverse objectification" so much as she is saying, "Engage us as subjects," subjects whose histories include tremendous injustices and silences. Expression of these long silences is not necessarily finger-pointing at the "white man." It is curious and troublesome that so many white Americans who have always had subjectivity are reluctant to grant freedom of expression and subjectivity to others on the grounds that their stories affect what we have been told about ourselves. Why are we so quick to assume that the desire and need to express these subjective histories is the same thing as blaming us?

Multivocality: Freedom of Expression and the Authority of Subjectivity

I opened this chapter with a quote from a political scientist and eloquent feminist, Nancy Hartsock. Hartsock is questioning why, now that so many of us are realizing that our personal and political futures lie in the ability to be seen and heard on our own terms, many academicians and politicians are questioning whether there is any such thing as "subjectivity." Her statement is aimed at certain postmodern theorists, or rather, at those who have interpreted postmodern theories in ways that continue to deny and suppress the subjectivity of all people.

Conceptions of Postmodern Subjectivity as "Problematic"

In this brief space I cannot do justice to the numerous theories and statements on the "postmodern" self that have been written in recent years. I hope this rather concise summary will suffice. The topic is worth reading about in detail; see the end of the chapter for suggestions. In brief, postmodern theories of the self take literally the idea that we are a composite of innumerable social interactions and social influences. These influences are so many that who we are is in a constant state of flux and adjustment. We have no self, just lingering memory traces and habits of conduct that give us the impression that our behavior is consistent. This impression of consistency gives us the *illusion* that we have a core self. In reality, we are stable only insofar as we strive to maintain stable conditions around us, conditions that don't require us to shift much in experience and perspective. We *conserve* social traditions, beliefs and codes of conduct so that we can *preserve* a sense of stable identity. Yet even our sense of what our history has been changes constantly, depending on the current perspective that we hold. We only think that we have a stable history because we don't recognize that we are always creating our sense of history through hindsight. Theoretically, there is no such thing as a stable self with a single, stable history. We consist of multiple voices.

For the most political of the postmodern theorists, meaning those whose work extends from the critical theories of Marx and others, the implication is that individual subjectivity in any given moment is a function of social circumstances—who has the authority to speak and be heard? Collective subjectivity (culture) is shaped through the web of intersubjective relations among various groups that are clamoring to be heard. The upshot is that we have no "true history," only variations on stories as told by different people and different groups. The political and moral implication is that there is no single voice, no universal basis of truth and no ultimate authority. Justice, then, consists in having as many voices as possible at the collective table and granting them all the authority and respect to be heard.

For many, this theoretical premise holds the promise of turning the tide toward more equitable human relations. For many others, the notions of shifting, multiple, contradictory selves and the subsequent ambiguities of governance and morality that these imply are very threatening. The response, which is a conservative response arising from surprisingly diverse political and academic corners, has been to try to shore up the existing hegemonies against the turning tides of change. The logic underlying this conservative response is a rather odd twist based on the premises of postmodernism. One prong in the attack against multiple subjects and voices goes like this: If we don't really have a core self or a core history, if we are all just momentary social constructs, then there is really no such thing as the subjectivity of women, or of Chicanos/as, or Native Americans and so forth. All of these are fleeting "special interest groups" whose presence is a momentary construction. The second prong, which is loosely forged but seems to have found its mark anyway, is that since Euro American traditions have withstood the test of time and are so well entrenched, they deserve to retain the status of the one truly uniform basis through which to understand ourselves, our cultural history and our political and cultural future.

Suppressing Subjectivity: The Tyranny of Silence

With this neat feat of twisted logic, the "keepers of the status quo" seek to continue the silences about the multiple histories that comprise our collective cultural "subjectivity." The most recent attempts at silencing the subjectivity of multiple groups come in the form of "concerns" regarding campus programs, such as African American Studies, Asian Studies, Latino Studies, Women Studies, and Gay and Lesbian Studies. The opponents of these programs worry about the "balkanizing" consequences. They view such programs as separatist and a distraction from "our shared cultural heritage."

Ward Connerly, a conservative African American who lobbied successfully in California for the repeal of Affirmative Action laws, has now set his sights on a "new enemy of the united people." Clarence Page, a journalist critical of Connerly's views, interviewed Connerly by phone. In the interview, Connerly admits that he doesn't really know much about the programs that he is attacking. He was also surprised when Page informed him that the courses are taken by a variety of students, not just those "represented" by the topic. Still, Connerly expressed doubts about whether the programs are "truly academic or merely exercises in academic cheerleading. This is probably something that people can learn from their parents, at home, without the taxpayers paying for it." In his commentary on Connerly, which he titles "Would Critic of Ethnic Studies Prefer Good Old Days of Exclusion?" Page poses a parallel question:

> Do we really need all those classes in Socrates, Milton, Shakespeare, Mozart and Chopin? Are they going to get you a job in today's global economy? Or are they merely exercises in ethnic cheerleading? Are they something "people can learn from their parents at home, without the taxpayers paying for it?" Hey, didn't your mom always keep a copy of Plato's "The Republic" within easy reach, right next to Dr. Spock and Betty Crocker? (1998:17)

Page continues with a reminder that the so-called unified days that people such as Connerly pine for came at the expense of silence and exclusion:

Ah, yes, whatever happened to those halcyon days of old, those days of unity, those days before those Balkanizing ethnic studies came along? Whatever happened to those jolly days of housing covenants, legal job discrimination, segregated lunch counters and other aspects of American togetherness? How united we were when the only people who really counted in history and literature classes were white and, for that matter, male. How light-hearted our students could be, unburdened by any obligation to learn about anybody else. . . . Wouldn't it be nice to return to the days when we were equal. Equally ignorant.

These discussions raise the question of the legitimacy of subjectivity. Power is the ability to define who can be heard and what they can say. In the chapter on group paradoxes I raised this issue of college curricula, specifically the resistance by some to certain programs of study. The basis for this resistance is loosely reasoned and ill conceived. The fear of "balkanization" is predicated on two assumptions: (1) that there is a central body of knowledge representative of the histories and experiences of all people, and (2) that learning other histories will undermine or dilute the impact of this body of knowledge. Even if the first assumption were true (and I don't believe that it is), the second assumption does not necessarily follow, unless the "traditional" body of knowledge consists of lies that would be challenged by alternative histories. If this is the case, then the real argument against area studies is that by giving voice to the subjects whose histories have long been denied, there is a risk of challenging the assumptions put forth by "traditional" knowledge.

It is quite possible to have a solid education in traditional Western civilization and also be critical of many of the ideas and practices contained within these ideas and practices, just as it is possible to be both learned and critical of Native American history (it's not all about spirit healing and longhouse gatherings), or Chicano/a studies. No culture or people that I am aware of is above critical scrutiny. Scholarship and learning entail looking at many aspects of the subject within specific contexts. The issue is one of subjectivity—who or what is authoring the history or representing the voice? Euro American education has been presented as a single voice and a single truth for decades. All other histories have been conflated within this perspective and treated as objects that are significant only in relation to Euro American interests and practices. Being included parenthetically is not the same thing as having a voice at the table.

When I listen to people such as Connerly question the "usefulness" of area studies, I think of this as a skirmish intended to keep certain people and certain voices away from the table. Consider the difference between engaging someone about their perspective, versus questioning their right to express their own perspective. By what authority do Connerly and others like him think they can question the *right* of others to be at the table? As a scholar and a subject with my own views and history, I may not agree with what some of the other voices at the collective table say, I may not even like it, in which case, I can engage with the other in dialogue and debate. But on what grounds can I question someone's *right* to be at the table?

Some would say, well, there's the issue of the tax payers. Should "the taxpayers" be footing the bill for these areas of studies? This argument is groundless, economically. College courses and programs of study are self-supporting through enrollments. Economic considerations about the validity of any college program of study have to be addressed within the current climate of underfunding for higher education in general.

Then there is the question, "Which" group of tax payers is Connerly referring to? As a tax payer myself, who supports funding for public education, I might be inclined to raise my eyebrows about certain other area studies, such as Military Science or various specialty courses in engineering. These courses have very low enrollments relative to the number of students that I teach in my courses in the liberal arts, but receive sometimes as much as double or triple the amount of funding.

Some people point to the fact that some of those most opposed to area studies are themselves African American, Asian, Latino/a or Native American. Connerly is black and is opposed to affirmative action and suspicious of African American studies. Therefore it must be bad for blacks? This sort of logic is a second-order form of objectification. Connerly has his own subjectivity. It is not the case that everyone who has been objectified as being similar, that is, "black," has the same subjective experiences, opinions and perspectives. Angela Davis and Cornel West, to name a couple of scholars who are also black, differ widely and loudly on many issues. These differences in perspective do not negate the fact that, until recently, African American history was not treated as a subject in its own right, but only as a historical footnote in the Euro American studies of the "settlement" of the United States, especially the "war between the states." One of the rights of subjectivity, of having a voice, is to be able to disagree with others who may share your objective position but not your subjective opinions. The fact that there are so many different African American voices is an indication that some strides have been made toward ensuring rights of expression to all people. When these historical forms of expression are granted a wider audience, the tone and content are likely to reflect the oppression and opposition in which they were forged. This may make some segments of white America squirm, but is it grounds for renewed attempts at suppression? We cannot claim to be in favor of plural democracy and at the same time say that certain people and their stories are not worth telling and teaching simply because they have been squelched or kept out of mainstream forums of expression, such as education, until recently. We cannot preach "freedom of expression" and at the same time systematically deny subjectivity to large segments of the population.

Chiseling Subjectivity Out of Objectification: Dilemmas of Solidarity

Let's return to the question of how one achieves subjectivity. I have proposed that our sense of self is forged through interactions with significant groups and in terms of significant experiences. One of the paradoxes of subjective/objective self-development is that the very process of being treated as an object, of being denied subjectivity and expression, is itself a significant experience. All of us long to distinguish ourselves as individuals. The paradox is that our individuality is a reflection of significant experiences that may include the pain, suffering and imposed silence associated with being treated as an object. The "caged bird sings" to affirm its existence despite being enslaved. An interesting question is, How do you know what to sing? If you have always been treated as an object, where do you find *forms* of expression that enable you to achieve self-awareness as a subject?

In an essay called the "Transformation of Silence Into Language and Action," Audre Lorde asks:

What words do you not yet have? What do you need to say? What are the tyrannies you swallow day by day and attempt to make your own, until you will sicken and die of them, still in silence?

These words suggest that not only does freedom of expression matter, but that in order to cultivate forms of expression that are reflective of our feelings, experiences and histories, we need certain vehicles of expression—language and culture that resonate with how we feel and live. We also need role models who serve as reminders that we are more than the limits suggested by objective boxes. We cannot develop a multifaceted subjectivity in the absence of a language and examples for doing so. To this end, we need others who share our subjectivity and can provide us with the forms of expression that enable us to give shape and substance to our feelings and desires and enable us to name ourselves accordingly.

Solidarity and accompanying forms of expression are often chiseled out by those whose subjectivity is actively denied them by powerful groups. Anglo American colonists attempted to assimilate indigenous peoples by requiring that the children attend "training schools." In addition to being made to wear the "white man's" clothing and to adopt the "white man's" customs, Native children were given new names, Anglo names. It became a source of collective pride and solidarity to remember one's "true" name and to use it only with other members of the tribe. In this way, the name served as a beacon of collective subjective belonging maintained under circumstances engineered to erode or strip away one's subjective face.

The dilemma for many individuals is that at the same time that identification with collective histories, particularly histories of shared oppression, may provide a sense of self, these attachments may also be constraining. Consider this statement from a young artist:

> Sometimes I want to forget it all
> this curse called identity
> I want to be far out
> paint dreams in strange colors
> write crazy poetry
> only the chosen can understand
>
> But it's not so simple
> I still drink tea
> with both hands.
> —Nancy Hom, "Sometimes"

Hom articulates a sentiment shared by many who feel the burden to maintain a collective subjectivity that is in danger of being lost to processes of assimilation and hegemonic backlash. But she also wants the freedom to express her inclinations as an artist in ways that are uniquely her. At the same time, she recognizes that much of what she experiences as uniquely her is shaped by a collective history. She forges herself in response to, in dialogue with, this history.

A 1998 issue of *Time* magazine featured a story on young feminists that is indicative of this same dilemma. The caption for the story blared, "What's the message of the new feminism? It's all about 'me'!" The article described in detail the dissatisfaction of young feminists toward the restrictive and outmoded ideologies preached by feminists in earlier decades. The articulation was accurate insofar as it depicted many "third wave" feminists as being impatient, but I found it very inaccurate and unfair in the implication that this impatience is with the feminist legacy that they have inherited. Many young women are impatient with *stereotypes* of older feminists as male-bashing, frigid, flannel-shirt-wearing women on a rampage against sex and beauty. This is not the same thing as accusing younger feminists of turning their backs on the feminist legacy.

Despite the tremendous strides made by feminist groups in establishing women as subjects with the power to define their own lives, there has been a persistent stereotyping of feminists in the mainstream media that detracts from this potential subjectivity. The fair question might be: Are women holding one another to these collective demands (flannel shirts, no heels and makeup, anti-male ideologies), or are these stereotypes that are yet another form of objectifying women and rendering our expressions insignificant? One explanation of the so-called self-obsession of young women that presumably marks the third-wave feminists (I'll dress as I please, have sex as I please, shave my legs if I please, and so forth) is that they are asserting their right to their own subjectivity. To say that this is an expression of antifeminism and selfishness is to demand that these women return to yet another box and stay there.

The texture, variety and, yes, disputes in expressions of contemporary feminism can be read as a sign of increasing freedom of expression for women as individual subjects—as human beings who have different opinions and perspectives. As I noted in the discussion of group paradoxes, an increasing multivocality among feminists may result in an erosion of any sort of perceived univocal feminist perspective. But the reality is that there has never been a single feminist perspective that accurately represented the experiences of all women. Feminism, in its initial conception, was an expression of the right of subjecthood for women independent of men. The roots of the feminist movement go back long before the days of Gloria Steinem, lesbian separatists, black feminists and others whose views have contributed to the current mosaic. The cultural legacy of feminism in this country rests largely with Iroquois women and men who tried to impress upon the European colonists the idea that there is no natural or political justification for women to "belong" to men. The idea is simple: Each women, being a person, is a subject unto herself. Representations of feminism as a strictly defined, single position are antithetical to the multivocality that the movement seeks to achieve. As Rebecca Walker puts it, writing about "third-wave feminism,"

> The concept of a strictly defined and all encompassing feminist identity is so prevalent that when I [give public lectures and mention] all the different things that you can do and still be a feminist, like shave your legs every day, get married, be a man, be in the army, whatever, audience members clap spontaneously. (1995:xxxii).

The issue, as I interpret it, is not so much what the expression is, but the awareness and freedom that prompt various expressions. Gloria Steinem sums up this point in her Foreword to Walker's book, which is an anthology of contemporary feminist voices:

> If I were to choose one common lesson taught by these many feminisms, it would be this: The greatest gift we can give one another is the power to make choices. . . . In our long journey toward freedom we must cherish another's choices. (Walker, 1995:xxvi)

Which means that we must cherish one another's voices.

Engaged Subjectivity

When there are many voices at the table, all clamoring for expression, there is likely to be a loud and noisy din. There is also likely to be conflict. Some of the questions that accompany multivocality and multisubjectivity include the standards of common expression (should there be a single set of guidelines or form of expression?), assessments of the relative worth of various expressions (how should the NEA decide which forms of art to fund, how do schools determine what to include in the curricula?) and what to do about conflicts. As I noted in the preceding chapter on "Value," the modern tradition has been to attempt to establish a transcendent authority—some sort of independent set of guidelines for determining worth and settling conflicts. The crisis of value and authority described by many postmodern theorists is that history has shown that there is no such transcendent, universal, univocal set of guidelines. Claims that I am "more right than you" become oppressive when they are elevated to a hegemonic position that claims ultimate authority without the possibility of debate. The "safety" that Nietzsche refers to in the opening quote is safety for some from questions regarding the legitimacy of their position and claims to moral authority. Furthermore, if it can be established that there is a transcendent, unquestionable basis for determining worth and legitimacy, then we are "safe" from contradiction and ambiguity.

Many people recognize that most historical claims of universal or ultimate authority are actually based in hegemonic, oppressive practices designed to silence challenges. This silencing has often been achieved by identifying the would-be challengers as objects who have no right to a voice. Therefore, it would seem like a good thing and a progressive thing for humanity that we expose and cease practices of suppression. Accordingly, multivocality is a good thing, especially practices of multivocality predicated on respect, a willingness to hear, even to cherish, the voice of the other. In this way the conversation at the general table should resemble what Chicanos call an *ajiaco,* a colorful, flavorful stew in which each of the ingredients maintains its own distinct flavor and form while adding something to the pot. This is a very different metaphor than the "melting pot."

The problem that some people fear as a result of practices of respectful multivocality and cultural pluralism, is moral relativism: the fear is that we will slip into an abyss where "anything goes" because that's the way "I want it to be." This fear is understandable, given the long cultural illusion that there are univocal expressions of authority that are grounded in noncontradictory, nonshifting universal ideals. The fact of the matter is that to the extent that we achieve and acknowledge the legitimacy of plural subjectivity, we are confronted with hard questions about morality and politics. In the words of Zygmunt Bauman:

> Whenever one descends from the relatively secure realm of concepts to the concrete basis that these concepts are supposed to stand for, one finds merely a fluid collection of men and women acting at cross-purposes, fraught with inner controversy and conspicuously short of means to arbitrate between conflicting positions. (1993:44)

When I began thinking about this chapter, I intended to conclude with a discussion of "respectful engagement" as a remedy, or at least a platform, for discussing the dilemma of moral relativism. Following the teachings of the philosopher Emmanuel Levinas and his interpreters, such as Zygmunt Bauman, I intended to suggest that in the midst of such "cross-purposes" and controversy, a willingness to hear the other, to truly respect and cherish the other's right to expression, is the basis of a common ground upon which we can endeavor to construct additional commonalities, commonalities that will help us to see beyond our differences.

However, as I review what I have written here, I'm not sure that I can make this claim with confidence and honesty. Rereading the blatantly racist, sexist words of artist Steven Gianokos, I can't say, in truth, that I am fully willing to engage him respectfully. I would prefer to sidestep him and his prejudices. I prefer to ignore him. Also, as I write these words, I am aware of the emotionally charged debate taking place in the Pacific Northwest regarding the Makah Indian Nation's intent to resume whale hunting in accordance with cultural legacy. Native tribal members who petitioned for the right to resume whaling made the claim that this form of hunting is an integral aspect of their cultural histories. Who they are as a people is intimately tied to hunting whales. Animal conservationists, who mostly like to think of themselves as tolerant and respectful of the rights of others, find themselves wrestling a deep conflict about the possibility that these tribal groups intend to hunt and kill the whales that they, the conservationists, have devoted themselves to saving. Contemplating this issue, I realize that it is not much different from the huge divide that separates antiabortionists from freedom of choice advocates. Rights of individual subjectivity become muddy when it becomes apparent that the subjectivity of some is tied up so completely in limiting the subjectivity of another. I would like to hope that through respectful engagement we might at least be willing to come to a collective table and debate our differences with the understanding that our individual will may not prevail. In reality, such a process is likely to be frustrating, heart-rending and gut wrenching. It is a process wherein, if I am truly willing to hear you, I am may find myself transformed. This possibility is both exciting and terrifying to contemplate. Personally, as fraught with contradiction, conflict and ambiguity as this path might be I find it less frightening than the prospect of renewed attempts to establish a universal basis of authority.

In a book titled *After Virtue,* Alasdair MacIntyre discusses the difference between the "situated self" and the "unencumbered self." The situated self is the self that I have been discussing, the self that is always and everywhere a product of circumstance and particular interests and experiences. One of the paradoxes of subjectivity is that, as an individual, this self has the right of expression, but this expression will always reflect the interests of the significant groups through which the self achieves subjectivity. The unencumbered self is the self who, while undoubtedly affected by commitments to significant communities, is capable of cutting loose from these ties, at least in perspective; the self capable of attaining a "higher plane and taking from there a long, detached and critical view of community demands and pressures." The idea of the "unencumbered self" resonates for me because it is a self-concept that acknowledges that we are fundamentally shaped by communal attachments and simultaneously capable of achieving other planes from which to scrutinize these attachments—including the moral and political implications that they hold. The question that lingers for me is, what is it that motivates me to seek this "higher plane" of what I would call a critical awareness of my own position vis-à-vis others? Paradoxically, the answer that comes is a desire to *know* the other, to engage respectfully with the intent of understanding rather than persuading. This desire gives me hope. The hope carries me into a new day of questioning. Hope entices me to continue to wrestle the contradictions and ambiguities that appear to be the only thing certain about human existence.

> Human beings suffer,
> They torture one another,
> They get hurt and get hard,
> No poem or play or song
> Can fully right a wrong
> Inflicted and endured.
>
> History says, *Don't hope*
> On this side of the grave.
> But then, once in a lifetime
> The longed-for tidal wave
> Of justice can rise up,
> And hope and history rhyme.
>
> So hope for a great sea-change
> On the far side of revenge.
> Believe that a further shore
> Is reachable from here.
> Believe in miracles
> And cures and healing wells.
>
> > —Seamus Heaney, from
> > *The Cure at Troy*

Used with permission of Faber and Faber.

Bibliography

This list includes references to the work of writers cited in each chapter. It also includes additional sources for recommended reading. References for citations excerpted from various writers, artists and poets are listed in the "Credits" that follow.

Chapter 1

Babbie, Earl. 1998. *Observing Ourselves: Essays in Social Research.* Prospect Heights, IL: Waveland.

Berger, Peter L., and Hansfried Kellner. 1981. *Sociology Reinterpreted: An Essay on Method and Vocation.* Garden City, NY: Anchor Books.

Epstein, Julia, and Kristina Straub (Eds.). 1991. *Body Guards.* New York: Routledge.

Fraser, Stephen (Ed.). 1995. *The Bell Curve Wars.* New York: Basic Books.

Gordon, Avery. 1997. *Ghostly Matters: Haunting and the Sociological Imagination.* Minneapolis: University of Minnesota Press.

Gould, Stephen Jay. 1981. *The Mismeasure of Man.* New York: Norton.

Hayek, F. A. 1979 [1952]. *The Counter-Revolution of Science: Studies in the Abuse of Reason.* Indianapolis: Liberty Press.

Herrnstein, Richard, and Charles Murray. 1994. *The Bell Curve.* New York: Free Press.

Kuhn, Thomas. 1970. *The Structure of Scientific Revolutions.* 2nd Edition. Chicago: University of Chicago Press.

Levine, Donald. 1985. *The Flight From Ambiguity.* Chicago: University of Chicago Press.

Ritzer, George. 1992. *Classical Sociological Theory.* New York: McGraw-Hill.

Rosaldo, Renato. 1993. *Culture and Truth: The Remaking of Cultural Analysis.* Boston: Beacon.

Chapter 2

Blum, Deborah. 1998. "The Gender Blur." *Utne Reader,* September-October:45-48.

Bornstein, Kate. 1998. *The Gender Workbook.* New York: Routledge.

Burke, Phyllis. 1996. *Gender Shock.* Garden City, NY: Anchor Books.

Fausto-Sterling, Anne. 1993. "The Five Sexes: Why Male and Female Are Not Enough." *The Sciences* 22:2.

Gould, Stephen Jay. 1981. *The Mismeasure of Man.* New York: Norton.

Howard, Judith A., and Jocelyn A. Hollander. 1997. *Gendered Situations, Gendered Selves: A Gendered Lens on Social Psychology.* Thousand Oaks, CA: Sage.

Kessler, Suzanne, and Wendy McKenna. 1978. *Gender: An Ethnomethodological Approach.* New York: John Wiley.

Lorber, Judith. 1994. *Paradoxes of Gender.* New Haven, CT: Yale University Press.

Sedgewick, Eve Kosofsky. 1993. *Tendencies.* Durham, NC: Duke University Press.

Tavris, Carol. 1992. *The Mismeasure of Woman.* New York: Simon and Schuster.

Chapter 3

Bauman, Zygmunt. 1993. *Postmodern Ethics.* Oxford, UK: Basil Blackwell.

Bellah, Robert N., Richard Madsen, William M. Sullivan, Ann Swidler, and Steven M. Tipton. 1985. *Habits of the Heart: Individualism and Commitment in American Life.* Berkeley: University of California Press.

Bender, Thomas. 1978. *Community and Social Change in America.* New Brunswick, NJ: Rutgers University Press.

Blee, Kathleen. 1991. *Women of the Klan.* Berkeley: University of California Press.

Collins, Randall (Ed.). 1995. *Four Sociological Traditions—Selected Readings.* New York: Oxford University Press. (See especially, Durkheim, Emile, "Precontractual Solidarity" [1893] and "Social Rituals and Sacred Objects" [1912]).

———. 1995. *Four Sociological Traditions.* New York: Oxford University Press.

Daniels, Jessie. 1997. *White Lies.* New York: Routledge.

Durkheim, Emile. 1915. *The Elementary Forms of Social Life.* London: Allen and Unwin.

Farganis, James. 1996. "Emile Durkheim: Anomie and Social Integration." Pp. 74-100 in *Readings in Social Theory.* New York: McGraw-Hill.

Kanter, Rosabeth Moss. 1972. *Commitment and Community.* Cambridge, MA: Harvard University Press.

Kephart, William M. 1976. *Extraordinary Groups: The Sociology of Unconventional Life-Styles.* New York: St. Martin's.

Leach, Edmund. 1964. "Anthropological Aspects of Language." In *New Directions in the Study of Language,* edited by Eric H. Lennenberg. Chicago: University of Chicago Press.

Stark, Rodney, and William Bainbridge. 1987. *A Theory of Religion.* New York: Peter Lang.

Wheatley, Helen. 1996. "Reflections on the Cosmopolitan Universe and the Role of the Liberal Arts Professor." Pp. 19-23 in *The Forum.* Seattle: Seattle University Press.

Chapter 4

Anzaldua, Gloria. 1987. *Borderland = La Frontera: The New Mestiza.* San Francisco: Aunt Lute Books.

Bornstein, Kate. 1994. *Gender Outlaw.* New York: Vintage.

Daniels, Jessie. 1997. *White Lies.* New York: Routledge.

Davis, Angela. 1981. *Women, Race and Class.* New York: Random House.

Davis, Fred. 1992. *Fashion, Culture and Identity.* Chicago: University of Chicago Press.

DuBois, W. E. B. 1903. "Double-Consciousness and the Veil" from *The Souls of Black Folk.* New York: Bantam.

Feagin, Joe R., and Melvin P. Sikes. 1995. *Living With Racism: The Black Middle-Class Experience.* Boston: Beacon.

Filemyr, Ann. 1995. "Loving Across the Boundary." In *Skin Deep: Black Women and White Women Write About Race,* edited by Marita Golden and Susan Richards Shreve. New York: Doubleday.

Frankenberg, Ruth. 1993. *White Women, Race Matters: The Social Construction of Whiteness.* Minneapolis: University of Minnesota Press.

Frye, Marilyn. 1983. *The Politics of Reality.* Trumansburg, NY: Crossing Press.

Gamson, Joshua. 1998. *Freaks Talk Back: Tabloid Talk Shows and Sexual Nonconformity.* Chicago: University of Chicago Press.

Gates, Henry Louis, Jr. 1986. *Race, Writing and Difference.* Chicago: University of Chicago Press.

Hofstadter, Douglas. 1985. "Changes in Default Words and Images Engendered by Rising Consciousness." In *Metamagical Themas.* New York: Basic Books.

Lippard, Lucy R. 1990. *Mixed Blessings.* New York: Pantheon.

Lorber, Judith (Ed.). 1998. *Gender Inequality.* Los Angeles: Roxbury.

Minh-ha, Trinh T. 1989. *Woman, Native, Other: Postcoloniality and Feminism.* Bloomington: Indian University Press.

O'Brien, Jodi, and Judith A. Howard. 1998. *Everyday Inequalities: Critical Inquiries.* London: Basil Blackwell.

Ridgeway, Cecilia. 1997. "Interaction and the Conservation of Gender Inequity." *American Journal of Sociology* 62:218-35.

Root, Maria P. P. (Ed.). 1996. *The Multiracial Experience: Racial Borders as the New Frontier.* Thousand Oaks, CA: Sage.

Takaki, Ronald. 1993. *A Different Mirror.* Boston: Little, Brown.

Twine, France W. 1998. *Racism in a Racial Democracy.* New Brunswick, NJ: Rutgers University Press.

Twine, France Winddance, Jonathan W. Warren, and F. Ferrandiz. 1991. *Just Black? Multiracial Identity.* New York: Filmmakers Library.

Walker, Rebecca (Ed.). 1995. *To Be Real.* Garden City, NY: Anchor Books.

Warren, Jonathan H., and France Winddance Twine. 1997. "White Americans, the New Minority." *Journal of Black Studies* 28(2):200-18.

Williams, Patricia. 1991. *Alchemy of Race and Rights.* Cambridge, MA: Harvard University Press.

Zerubavel, Eviatar. 1991. *The Fine Line: Making Distinctions in Everyday Life.* Chicago: University of Chicago Press.

Chapter 5

Abrahamson, Mark. 1994. "Stratification, Mobility, and a Playing Card Metaphor." *Teaching Sociology* 22:183-88.

Collins, Randall. 1979. *The Credential Society.* New York: Academic Press.

Coupland, Douglas. 1991. *Generation X: Tales for an Accelerated Culture.* New York: St. Martin's.

DeMott, Benjamin. 1992. *The Imperial Middle: Why Americans Can't Think Straight About Class.* New Haven, CT: Yale University Press.

Domhoff, G. William. 1998. *Who Rules America? Power and Politics in the Year 2000.* Mountain View, CA: Mayfield.

Gilbert, Dennis, and Joseph Kahl. 1987. *The American Class Structure.* Belmont, CA: Wadsworth.

Huber, Joan, and William Form. 1973. *Income and Ideology.* New York: Free Press.

Karabel, Jerome, and Steven Brint. 1991. *The Diverted Dream: Community Colleges and the Promise of Educational Opportunity in America.* New York: Oxford University Press.

Kozol, Jonathan. 1991. *Savage Inequalities.* New York: Crown.

Lamont, Michele. 1992. *Money, Morals and Manners.* Chicago: University of Chicago Press.

Perrin, Constance. 1988. *Belonging in America.* Madison: University of Wisconsin Press.

Rose, Stephen J. 1992. *Social Stratification in the United States.* New York: New Press.

Reskin, Barbara, and Irene Padavic. 1994. *Women and Men at Work.* Thousand Oaks, CA: Pine Forge Press.

Schelling, Thomas. 1978. *Micromotive and Macrobehavior.* New York: Norton.

Wilson, William Julius. 1987. *The Truly Disadvantaged: The Inner City and Public Policy.* Chicago: University of Chicago Press.

Chapter 6

Coontz, Stephanie. 1992. *The Way We Never Were.* New York: Basic Books.

———. 1997. *The Way We Really Are: Coming to Terms With America's Changing Families.* New York: Basic Books.

Lasch, Christopher. 1981. *Haven in a Heartless World: The Family Besieged.* New York: Basic Books.

Newman, David. 1998. *Families: Social Issues and Everyday Experiences.* Thousand Oaks, CA: Pine Forge Press.

Newman, Katherine. 1988. *Falling From Grace*. New York: Vintage.

Rubin, Lillian. 1976. *Worlds of Pain: Life in the Working Class Family*. New York: Basic Books.

Taylor, Ella. 1989. *Prime Time Families: Television Culture in Postwar America*. Berkeley: University of California Press.

Chapter 7

Babbie, Earl. 1994. *What Is Society? Reflections on Freedom, Order and Change*. Thousand Oaks, CA: Pine Forge Press.

Barthes, Roland. 1957. *Mythologies*. Paris: Editions du Seuil.

Bauman, Zygmunt. 1993. *Postmodern Ethics*. Oxford, UK: Basil Blackwell.

Heilbroner, Robert. 1992. "The Wonderful World of Adam Smith" Pp. 18-42 in *The Worldly Philosophers*. 6th Edition. New York: Simon and Schuster.

Geertz, Clifford. 1983. *Local Knowledge*. New York: Basic Books.

Langer, Ellen. 1989. *Mindfulness*. Reading, MA: Addison-Wesley.

Ritzer, George. 1995. *Expressing America*. Thousand Oaks, CA: Pine Forge Press.

Ritzer, George. 1996. *The McDonaldization of Society*. Thousand Oaks, CA: Pine Forge Press.

Weber, Max. 1958 [1905]. *The Protestant Ethic and the Spirit of Capitalism*. New York: Scribner.

Weschler, Lawrence. 1988. "Value: A Fool's Question." Pp. 33-98 in *The New Yorker* (January 18).

Wolff, Kurt (Ed.). 1950. *The Sociology of Georg Simmel*. London: Glencoe.

Epilogue

Bauman, Zygmunt. 1993. *Postmodern Ethics*. Oxford, UK: Basil Blackwell.

Charon, Joel. 1998. "Are Human Beings Free?" Pp. 120-46 in *Ten Questions: A Sociological Perspective*. Belmont, CA: Wadsworth.

Freud, Sigmund. 1953 [1930]. *Civilization and Its Discontents*. London: Hogarth.

James, William. 1981 [1890]. "The Self and Its Selves." Pp. 279-88 in *Principles of Psychology*, Vol. 1, edited by Frederick Burkhardt and Fredson Bowers. Cambridge, MA: Harvard University Press.

MacIntyre, Alasdair. 1984. *After Virtue: A Study in Moral Theory*. Notre Dame, IN: Notre Dame University Press.

Nietzsche, Friedrich. 1967 [1888]. *The Will to Power*. Edited by Walter Kaufmann. New York: Random House.

Rich, Adrienne. 1986. "Split at the Root: An Essay on Jewish Identity." In *Blood, Bread and Poetry: Selected Prose 1979-1985*. New York: Norton.

Terkel, Studs. 1980. "Stephen Cruz." In *American Dreams: Lost and Found*. New York: Pantheon.

Mead, George Herbert. 1962 [1934]. *Mind, Self and Society*. Chicago: University of Chicago Press.

Walker, Alice. 1989. *Prisoners of Image: Ethnic and Gender Stereotypes*. New York: Alternative Museum.

Walker, Rebecca (Ed.). 1995. *To Be Real*. Garden City, NY: Anchor Books.

Credits

Baker, Russell. 1998. *Seattle Post Intelligencer*, May 17, Focus Section, p. 2.

Baldwin, James. 1990. Quoted in Lucy R. Lippard, *Mixed Blessings*. New York: Pantheon, p. 19.

Chui, Glennda. 1995. "Lab Rats Pose Hefty Problem . . . " *Seattle Times*, November 4, p. A1.

de Beauvoir, Simone. 1980 [1949, 1953]. "Woman as Other." *The Second Sex*, translated by H. M. Parshley. New York: Knopf.

Dear Abby. 1998. *Seattle Times*, February 19, p. C5.

Ellison, Ralph. 1994 [1952]. *The Invisible Man*. New York: Modern Library.

Filemyr, Ann. 1995. "Loving Across the Boundary." In *Skin Deep: Black Women and White Women Write About Race*, edited by Marita Golden and Susan Richards Shreve. New York: Doubleday.

Gianokos, Steve. 1980. Quoted by Richard Goldstein, "Art Beat, Darkly Chic." *Village Voice*, March 31, p. 34.

Gordon, Avery. 1997. "Keeping Good Time." *Perspectives: The ASA Theory Section Newsletter*, Winter, pp. 5-6.

Haraway, Donna, and LeVay, Simon. 1997. Quoted in "My Clone, My Self." *Out*, May, p. 32.

Hartsock, Nancy. 1990. "Rethinking Modernism: Minority vs. Majority Theories." In *The Nature and Context of Minority Discourse*, edited by A. Jan Mohammed and D. Lloyd. New York: Oxford University Press, p. 26

Heaney, Seamus. 1998. Excerpted from "The Cure at Troy," published in *DoubleTake*, Summer, p. 3.

Hom, Nancy. 1980. "Sometimes," *Conditions*, No. 6, Summer, p. 208.

Keene, Linda. 1995. "Hygiene Center for Homeless Has Retailers Hot . . ." *Seattle Times*, November 4, p. A1.

Jordan, June. 1994. *Technical Difficulties*. Boston: Beacon, p. 197.

Langer, Ellen. 1989. *Mindfulness*. Reading, MA: Addison-Wesley, pp. 43-44.

LeBon, Gustave. 1981. *The Mismeasure of Man*, translated from the original French and quoted by Stephen Jay Gould. New York: Norton, pp. 104-105.

Lorde, Audre. 1993. *Sister Outsider: Essays and Speeches*. Trumansburg, NY: Crossing Press.

Page, Clarence. 1998. "*Eliminating 'Balkanized' College Programs.*" Chicago Tribune, Commentary Section, June 21, p. 17.

Pagnozzi, Amy. 1991. *Mirabella*, September, pp. 130-134.

Rilke, Rainer Maria. 1986 [1903-1908]. *Letters to a Young Poet*. New York: Vintage, pp. 5, 28.

Security in Family Life: Threats and Opportunities. 1948. (A Report on the National Conference of Family Life. The Survey.) Washington, DC, May 5-8.

Soto, Gary. 1985. "Looking for Work." *Living up the Street: Narrative Recollections*. Portland, OR: Strawberry Hill.

Steinem, Gloria. 1995. "Foreword." *To Be Real*, edited by Rebecca Walker. Garden City, NY: Anchor Books, p. xvi.

Time, 1995, November 6.

Walker, Alice. 1989. *Prisoners of Image: Ethnic and Gender Stereotypes*. New York: Alternative Museum.

Walker, Alice. 1991. "v." *Her Body Blue: Everything We Know*. New York: Harcourt Brace Jovanovich, p. 79.

Wertenbaker, Timberlake. 1985. *The Grace of Mary Traverse*. New York: Dramatists Play Service, Inc., p. 7.

Wray, Herbert. 1997. "How the Nature vs. Nurture Debate Shapes Public Policy." *U.S. News and World Report*, April 12, pp. 72-80.

Index